# Lecture Notes in Artificial Intelligence 4788

Edited by J. G. Carbonell and J. Siekmann

Subseries of Lecture Notes in Computer Science

Daniel Borrajo   Luis Castillo
Juan Manuel Corchado (Eds.)

# Current Topics in Artificial Intelligence

12th Conference of the Spanish Association
for Artificial Intelligence, CAEPIA 2007
Salamanca, Spain, November 12-16, 2007
Selected Papers

 Springer

Series Editors

Jaime G. Carbonell, Carnegie Mellon University, Pittsburgh, PA, USA
Jörg Siekmann, University of Saarland, Saarbrücken, Germany

Volume Editors

Daniel Borrajo
Universidad Carlos III de Madrid, Spain
E-mail: dborrajo@ia.uc3m.es

Luis Castillo
Universidad de Granada, Spain
E-mail: L.Castillo@decsai.ugr.es

Juan Manuel Corchado
Universidad de Salamanca, Spain
E-mail: corchado@usal.es

Library of Congress Control Number: 2007938154

CR Subject Classification (1998): I.2, F.4.1, F.1

LNCS Sublibrary: SL 7 – Artificial Intelligence

ISSN        0302-9743
ISBN-10     3-540-75270-6 Springer Berlin Heidelberg New York
ISBN-13     978-3-540-75270-7 Springer Berlin Heidelberg New York

Springer is a part of Springer Science+Business Media

springer.com

© Springer-Verlag Berlin Heidelberg 2007
Printed in Germany

Typesetting: Camera-ready by author, data conversion by Scientific Publishing Services, Chennai, India
Printed on acid-free paper      SPIN: 12166305      06/3180      5 4 3 2 1 0

# Preface

This volume presents a selection of papers accepted for presentation at the 12th Conference of the Spanish Association for Artificial Intelligence and its associated Conference on Technology Transfer on Artificial Intelligence (CAEPIA/TTIA 2007) held in Salamanca in November 2007. Since its foundation in 1983, the goal of the Spanish Association for Artificial Intelligence (AEPIA) has been to promote AI in Spain within both academia and industry. As from 1985, AEPIA has organized a biennial conference, which has so far been held in Madrid, Alicante, Málaga, Murcia, Gijón, Donostia and Santiago de Compostela.

Two other main objectives of AEPIA have been to establish and keep relationships with other national and international organizations in the AI field and to promote the exchange of information and/or experiences among AI researchers. The first objective was accomplished when AEPIA became a member of ECCAI (European Coordinating Committee for Artificial Intelligence) and a founder member of IBERAMIA (Iberoamerican Conference on Artificial Intelligence). With the second objective in mind, the quality of the CAEPIA/TTIA conference was raised to meet the usual international standards by focusing on international committees, participants and invited speakers. In 2003, an important step in this direction was taken with the publication of a volume of selected papers from the conference written in English, with the aim of boosting a more fruitful exchange of ideas within the international AI scientific community.

In this edition of CAEPIA/TTIA we wanted to focus on improving the international character of the Program Committee (PC), rewarding the most mature papers through their publication in this volume, and fostering the interaction of researchers by accepting more papers to be presented as short presentations. CAEPIA/TTIA 2007 received 134 submissions from 10 different countries. The PC consisted of 120 members from 18 different countries (66% from Spain and 34% from other countries). Papers were accepted either for long presentation (28 papers, 21% of submissions) or short presentation (51 papers). The first ones are the ones that have been selected to be published in this volume.

The editors would like to acknowledge the work of the members of the PC in reviewing and discussing the papers. Also, we would like to thank the invited speakers and all the researchers, who contributed with their valuable work to the high scientific level of the conference. Special thanks to the members of the Organization Committee at the University of Salamanca, and to AEPIA and Springer for making the conference a success.

July 2007

Daniel Borrajo
Luis Castillo
Juan Manuel Corchado

# Organization

CAEPIA/TTIA 2007 was organized by the Biomedicine, Intelligent Systems and Educational Technology (BISITE) Group, Universidad de Salamanca, in cooperation with AEPIA, and the Universidad de Salamanca.

## Executive Committee

| | |
|---|---|
| Conference Chair | Daniel Borrajo, Universidad Carlos III de Madrid |
| Conference Co-chair | Luis Castillo, Universidad de Granada |
| Organization Chair | Juan Manuel Corchado, Universidad de Salamanca |
| Tutorials | José Manuel Molina, Universidad Carlos III de Madrid |
| | Rafael Corchuelo, Universidad de Sevilla |
| Workshops | Emilio Corchado, Universidad de Burgos |
| | Juan Pavón, Universidad Complutense |

## Program Committee

Alvaro Barreiro García, Spain
Adriana Giret, Spain
Agostino Poggi, Italy
Ajith Abraham, Korea
Alicia Pérez, Argentina
Amedeo Cesta, Italy
Amílcar Cardoso, Portugal
Amparo Alonso Betanzos, Spain
Angel García-Olaya, Spain
Antonio Bahamonde, Spain
Antonio F. Gómez Skarmeta, Spain
Antonio Garrido, Spain
Asunción Gómez-Pérez, Spain
Basilio Sierra, Spain
Beatriz Barros, Spain
Beatriz López, Spain
Beatriz Pontes, Spain
Blai Bonet, Venezuela
Bogdan Gabrys, UK
Camino Rodríguez Vela, Spain
Carlos Carrascosa, Spain
Carlos Linares López, Spain
Carolina Chang, Venezuela
Changjiu Zhou, Singapore

Chris Brooks, USA
Colin Fyfe, UK
Cristiano Pitangui, Brazil
Daniel Borrajo, Spain
David Manzano, Spain
Ed Durfee, USA
Edwin Costello, Ireland
Elena Lazkano, Spain
Emilio S. Corchado Rodríguez, Spain
Enrique Alba, Spain
Erica Melis, Germany
Eva Onaindía de la Rivaherrera, Spain
Faraón Llorens Largo, Spain
Federico Barber, Spain
Fernando Díaz, Spain
Fernando Fernández Rebollo, Spain
Fernando Jiménez Barrionuevo, Spain
Fidel Aznar Gregori, Spain
Florentino Fernández Riverola, Spain
Francisco A. Pujol López, Spain
Francisco Guil Reyes, Spain
Francisco Martínez, Spain
Gerson Zaverucha, Brazil
Héctor Geffner, Spain

Helder Coelho, Portugal
Hujun Yin, UK
Inés González Rodríguez, Spain
Javier Larrosa, Spain
Jesús González-Boticario, Spain
John Doody, Ireland
Jorge Baier, Canada
José Angel Bañares, Spain
José Cristóbal Riquelme, Spain
José Hernández-Orallo, Spain
José Luis Ambite, USA
José M. Molina, Spain
Jose Neves, Portugal
José Palma Méndez, Spain
José Santos Reyes, Spain
Josep Puyol Gruart, Spain
Juan A. Nepomuceno, Spain
Juan Fernández Olivares, Spain
Juan J. del Coz Velasco, Spain
Juan J. Moreno Navarro, Spain
Juan Julian Merelo, Spain
Juan M. Corchado Rodríguez, Spain
Juan Pavón, Spain
Kate Revoredo, Brazil
Laura Sebastiá Tarín, Spain
Lawrence Mandow, Spain
Lluis Godo, Spain
Lorraine McGinty, Ireland
Luigi Portinale, Italy
Luis Castillo, Spain
Luis de Campos, Spain
Luis M. Fariñas del Cerro, France
Lynne Parker, USA
M. Carmen Pegalajar, Spain
Manuela Veloso, USA
Mar Pujol, Spain

Marcelo Finger, Brazil
María Cristina Riff, Chile
María Jesús Taboada, Spain
Maria Luisa Bonet, Spain
María Teresa Escrig, Spain
Mark T. Maybury, USA
Matthew Taylor, USA
Miguel A. Salido, Spain
Miguel Angel Alonso Pardo, Spain
Nuria Castell, Spain
Nuria Oliver, USA
Oscar Cordón, Spain
Pablo Noriega, Spain
Pedro González Calero, Spain
Pedro Larrañaga, Spain
Pedro Meseguer, Spain
Rafael Corchuelo, Spain
Rafael González, Spain
Ramón López de Mántaras, Spain
Ramón Rizo Aldeguer, Spain
Ricardo Conejo, Spain
Richard Benjamins, Spain
Riichiro Mizoguchi, Japan
Rodolfo Zunino, Italy
Roman Bartak, Czech Republic
Roque Marín Morales, Spain
Sascha Ossowski, Spain
Serafín Moral, Spain
Sheila R. Murgel Veloso, Brazil
Stefano Cerri, France
Susana Fernández, Spain
Toby Walsh, Australia
Vicent Botti, Spain
Vicente Julián, Spain
Wolfgang Faber, Italy
Yves Demazeau, France

## Sponsoring Institutions

Junta de Castilla y León
Telefónica
Matchmind
Máster en Comercio electrónico
Empleo Inteligente
Colegio Profesional de Ingenieros en Informática de Castilla León

# Table of Contents

# Fast and Informed Action Selection
# for Planning with Sensing

Alexandre Albore[1], Héctor Palacios[1], and Hector Geffner[2]

[1] Universitat Pompeu Fabra
Passeig de Circumvalació 8
08003 Barcelona Spain
[2] ICREA & Universitat Pompeu Fabra
Passeig de Circumvalació 8
08003 Barcelona Spain

**Abstract.** Consider a robot whose task is to pick up some colored balls from a grid, taking the red balls to a red spot, the blue balls to a blue spot and so on, one by one, without knowing either the location or color of the balls but having a sensor that can find out both when a ball is near. This problem is simple and can be solved by a domain-independent contingent planner in principle, but in practice this is not possible: the size of any valid plan constructed by a contingent planner is exponential in the number of observations which in these problems is very large. This doesn't mean that planning techniques are of no use for these problems but that building or verifying complete contingent plans is not feasible in general. In this work, we develop a domain-independent action selection mechanism that does not build full contingent plans but just chooses the action to do next in a closed-loop fashion. For this to work, however, the mechanism must be both fast and informed. We take advantage of recent ideas that allow delete and precondition-free contingent problems to be converted into conformant problems, and conformant problems into classical ones, for mapping the action selection problem in contingent planning into an action selection problem in classical planning that takes sensing actions into account. The formulation is tested over standard contingent planning benchmarks and problems that require plans of exponential size.

## 1 Introduction

Contingent planning is concerned with the problem of achieving goals in the presence of incomplete information and sensing actions [1,2]. This is one of the most general problems considered in the area of planning and one of the hardest [3,4]. In the last few years, significant progress has been achieved resulting in a variety of contingent planners that can solve large and non-trivial problems, usually by casting the contingent planning problem as an AND/OR search over belief space [5] guided by effective heuristics and belief representations [6,7,8].

In spite of this progress, however, a large obstacle remains: there are many problems involving incomplete information and sensing actions whose solutions

D. Borrajo, L. Castillo, and J.M. Corchado (Eds.): CAEPIA 2007, LNAI 4788, pp. 1–10, 2007.

have exponential size. Thus constructing or even verifying plans for such problems would take exponential time. This situation is different than in classical or conformant planning where exponential length solutions are the exception. Contingent plans of exponential size follow naturally from situations where the number of observations that needs to be done is linear in the size of the problem.[1]

The goal of this work is to use domain-independent planning techniques for dealing with such problems. However, rather than aiming at constructing full contingent plans, we aim at an effective *action selection mechanism* that chooses the action to do next in a closed-loop fashion. For this, we will move to the 'knowledge-level' [9], represent sensing actions as normal deterministic actions and map the *action selection problem in planning with sensing* into an *action selection problem in classical planning*, a problem that has good and well known solutions.

We take advantage of two recent ideas: the reduction of contingent planning into conformant planning that is obtained when deletes are relaxed and preconditions are moved in as conditions [6], and the reduction of conformant into classical planning obtained by the addition of conditionals and simple epistemic formulas represented as literals [10]. The two reductions in a row, however, do not suffice as sensing actions are ignored. We will thus extend the resulting classical encoding of a contingent problem $P$ with a a suitable representation of the sensing actions. On the one hand we define an *execution model* $X(P)$ where sensing actions are represented as actions with non-deterministic effects $Kx|K\neg x$, where $x$ is the boolean variable being observed and $KL$ represents that $L$ is *known*; on the other, we define an *heuristic model* $H(P)$ where these effects are relaxed into deterministic effects of the form $Mx \wedge M\neg x$, where $ML$ represents that $L$ *may be known*. In addition, while preconditions $L$ of $P$ must be known with certainty in $X(P)$ and are thus modeled as $KL$, in the heuristic model $H(P)$ they must be contingently known only and are modeled as $ML$.

The proposed *Closed-Loop Greedy planner (CLG)* then works as follows. In current state of the execution model $X(P)$, which is always fully known, an action in $X(P)$ is selected by using the heuristic model $H(P)$ which is a classical planning problem. The selected action is then applied in $X(P)$, its effect is observed, and the new state of the execution model is computed, from which the loop resumes until reaching a state that is a goal in $X(P)$. In CLG, the execution models keeps track of the belief state in the form of a set of literals at the knowledge level (details below), while the heuristic model selects the action to do next. CLG can be used and we will use it also for computing full contingent plans. For this, all the effects of the non-deterministic (sensing) actions applied need to be considered, and their responses cached.

---

[1] It must be said though that problems such as the one above, where balls in a grid are to be located and placed in their corresponding destination, admit compact solutions in languages, closer to the ones used in programming, that accommodate loops and subroutines. Current languages for contingent planning, however, do not accommodate such constructs. Dealing with such constructs in domain-independent planning is a hard open challenge, as hard indeed as automatic programming.

The rest of the paper is organized as follows: we start with the contingent problem $P$, define the translation $K(P)$ of the conformant fragment of $P$ (no sensing actions) into classical planning, consider the execution and heuristic models $X(P)$ and $H(P)$ that result from adding to $K(P)$ an encoding of the sensing actions, make the working of the CLG planner precise, and test it over a number of problems.

## 2   The Contingent Planning Problem $P$

We consider a planning language that extends Strips with conditional effects, a possibly uncertain initial situation, and sensing actions. More precisely, a contingent planning problem is a tuple $P = \langle F, O, I, G \rangle$ where $F$ stands for the fluent symbols in the problem, $O$ stands for the set of actions or operators $a$, $I$ is a set of *clauses* over $F$ defining the initial situation, and $G$ is a set of literals over $F$ defining the goal.

A normal action $a$ has a precondition given by a set of fluent literals, and a set of conditional effects $C \rightarrow L$ where $C$ is a set of fluent literals and $L$ is a literal. The sensing actions $a$, on the other hand, have a single unconditional effect $obs(x)$ where $x$ is a fluent symbol, meaning that after doing action $a$ the truth value of $x$ will be known. Sensing actions can have preconditions as any other actions but for simplicity we assume that they have no other effects.

We refer to the conditional effects $C \rightarrow L$ of an action $a$ as the *rules* associated with $a$, and sometimes write them as $a : C \rightarrow L$. Also, we use the expression $C \wedge X \rightarrow L$ to refer to rules with literal $X$ in their bodies. In both cases, $C$ may be empty. Last, when $L$ is a literal, we take $\neg L$ to denote the complement of $L$. The 'conformant fragment' of $P$ will mean the contingent problem $P$ with the sensing actions removed.

## 3   The Conformant Translation $K(P)$

We have recently shown elsewhere that it is possible to convert conformant problems $P$ into classical problems $K(P)$ so that solutions from $P$ can be extracted from the solutions computed by a classical planner over $K(P)$ [10]. This translation is not complete but has been shown to be quite effective [11]. More recently, this translation has been simplified and generalized into a translation scheme $K_{T,M}(P)$ where $T$ is a set of *tags* and $M$ is a set of *merges* [12]. A tag $t$ is set of literals in $P$ whose status in the initial situation $I$ of $P$ is not known. A merge $m$ is a collection of tags $t$ such that one of them must be true in $I$. The translation that maps the conformant problem $P$ into a classical problem $K_{T,M}(P)$ replaces the literals $L$ in $P$ by literals $KL/t$ for each $t \in T$, whose intuitive meaning is that 'if $t$ is true *in the initial situation*, $L$ is true'. In addition, extra actions, called merge actions, allow the derivation of the literal $KL$, i.e. $KL/t$ with the empty tag $t$, when $KL/t'$ has been obtained for each tag $t'$ in a merge.

If $P = \langle F, O, I, G \rangle$ is the conformant problem, then the classical problem $K_{T,M}(P) = \langle F', I', O', G' \rangle$ is given as:

$$F' = \{KL/t, K\neg L/t \mid L \in F \text{ and } t \in T\}$$
$$I' = \{KL/t \mid \text{if } I \models t \supset L\}$$
$$G' = \{KL \mid L \in G\}$$
$$O' = \{a : KC/t \to KL/t,\ a : \neg K\neg C/t \to \neg K\neg L/t \mid a : C \to L \text{ in } P\} \cup$$
$$\{\bigwedge_{t \in m} KL/t \to KL \mid L \in F \text{ and } m \in M\}$$

with $KL$ a precondition of action $a$ in $K_{T,M}(P)$ if $L$ is a precondition of $a$ in $P$.

The intuition behind the translation is simple: first, $KL/t$ is true in $I'$ iff $t \supset L$ follows from $I$. This removes all uncertainty from $I'$. Then $KL$ is a goal in $G'$ iff $L$ is a goal in $G$. Also, to ensure soundness, each conditional effect $a : C \to L$ in $P$ maps, not only into the **supporting rule** $a : KC/t \to KL/t$ but also into the **cancellation rule** $a : \neg K\neg C/t \to \neg K\neg L/t$ that guarantees that $K\neg L/t$ is deleted (prevented to persist) when action $a$ is applied and $C/t$ is not known to be false. The expressions $KC$ and $\neg K\neg C$ for $C = L_1 \wedge \ldots \wedge L_n$ are used as abbreviation of the formulas $KL_1 \wedge \ldots \wedge KL_n$, and $\neg K\neg L_1 \wedge \ldots \wedge \neg K\neg L_n$. Last, the **merge actions** yield $KL$ when $KL/t$ is true for each $t$ in a merge $m \in M$.

The translation scheme $K_{T,M}(P)$ is always sound, meaning that the classical plans that solve $K_{T,M}(P)$ yield valid conformant plans for $P$ (by just dropping the merge actions). On the other hand, the complexity and the completeness of the translation depend on the choice of tags and merges $T$ and $M$. The $K_i(P)$ translation, where $i$ is a non-negative integer, is an special case of the $K_{T,M}$ translation where the tags $t$ are restricted to contain at most $i$ literals. By a suitable choice of the merges $M$, we show in [12] that the $K_i(P)$ translation for $i = 1$ is *complete* for almost all of the conformant benchmarks. In this translation, $t \in T$ iff $t$ is the empty tag or a singleton $\{L\}$ for an uncertain literal $L$ in $I$, and $M$ is the set of non-unit clauses in $M$. We assume this translation below and we refer to it as $K_1(P)$ or simply as $K(P)$. This is the translation that underlies the conformant planner $T_0$, winner of the Conformant Track of the recent International Planning Competition [11].

For the sake of simplicity, from now on and when $t$ is the empty tag $t = \{\}$ and the singleton tag $t' = \{L'\}$, we write $KL/t$ and $KL/t'$ as $KL$ and $KL/L'$ respectively. $KL$ represents that '$L$ is known to be true with certainty', while $KL/L'$, that 'it is known with certainty that if $L'$ is true initially, $L$ is true'.

## 4 The Execution Model $X(P)$

The execution model $X(P)$ for the CLG planner is the union of a translation of the 'conformant fragment' of $P$ into classical problem, and a suitable encoding of the sensing actions. Both parts are expressed in the language of the epistemic conditionals $K/t$ of the translation above.

## 4.1   The Classical Part $K^c(P)$

The classical part $K^c(P)$ in $X(P)$ is the translation above applied to the 'conformant fragment' of $P$ extended with a set of deductive rules, encoded as actions with no preconditions and unique conditional effects of the form:

1. $KL/t \land K\neg L \rightarrow K\neg t$
2. $\bigwedge_{t \in m}(KL/t \lor K\neg t) \rightarrow KL$

This extension is needed because, while in conformant planning one reasons only 'forward' in time, in a contingent setting one must reason both 'forward' and 'backward'. In particular, if a tag $t$ cannot be shown to be false in $I$, no conformant plan will ever make it false. On the other hand, a tag $t$ may be inferred to be false or true in contingent planning by simply doing actions and gathering observations. Many 'identification' tasks have this form: one needs to act and observe in order to identify a static but hidden state.

In the head $K\neg t$ of the first deductive rule, $t$ refers to the value of the tag $t$ in the *initial situation* only. That is, if the rule is applied in a plan after several actions and $t = L$, then the inference that $L$ is false refers to the initial situation and not to the situation that follows the action sequence. This distinction is irrelevant if $L$ is a *static* literal whose value in the initial situation cannot change, but is relevant otherwise. With this in mind, we combine the use of these deductive rules implemented as actions, with a simple transformation that makes all literals in tags *static*. If $L$ is not a static literal, then we create a *static copy* $L_0$ of $L$ by adding the equivalence $L_0 \equiv L$ in $I$, so that $L_0$ has the same value as $L$ in the initial situation but does not change as it is not affected by action action. The tags are then limited to such static literals.

## 4.2   The Sensing Part $K^o(P)$

The sensing actions $a : obs(x)$ in the contingent problem $P$ are translated into a set $K^o(P)$ of non-deterministic actions

$$a : \neg Kx \land \neg K\neg x \rightarrow Kx \mid K\neg x$$

that capture their effects directly at the 'knowledge level' [9] making one of the fluents $Kx$ or $K\neg x$ true. We make such effects conditional on not knowing the value of $x$, as we do not want these rules to set a true $KL$ literal into a false one. In addition, for each precondition $L$ of $a$ in $P$, we set the literal $KL$ as $^o a$ precondition of $a$ in $K^o(P)$.

Like $P$, the execution model $X(P) = K^c(P) + K^o(P)$ is a contingent planning problem, and due to the soundness of the translation, solutions to $X(P)$ encode solutions to $P$ (although not the other way around, as the translation is not complete). Yet, while $P$ involves incomplete information and sensing actions, $X(P)$ being at the 'knowledge-level' features full information (all literals are known) and no sensing actions. The model $X(P)$, on the other hand, features actions that are non-deterministic. In order to solve $X(P)$, and hence $P$, we consider a relaxation of $X(P)$ that removes this non-determinism and results in a classical problem that is used for selecting the actions in the planner.

## 5   Heuristic Model $H(P)$

The basic change in the transition from the execution model $X(P)$ to the heuristic model $H(P)$ is the transformation of the *non-deterministic actions*

$$a : \neg Kx \wedge \neg K\neg x \ \rightarrow \ Kx \,|\, K\neg x$$

that arise from sensing actions into *deterministic actions:*

$$a : \neg Kx \wedge \neg K\neg x \ \rightarrow \ Mx \wedge M\neg x$$

where $ML$ is an 'epistemic' literal aimed at expressing *contingent knowledge*: knowledge that may be obtained along some but not necessarily all execution branches, and hence which is weaker that $KL$.

By *relaxing* the actions with non-deterministic effects $Kx|K\neg x$ in $X(P)$ into actions with deterministic effects $Mx \wedge M\neg x$ in $H(P)$, a *classical problem* is obtained. The rest of heuristic model $H(P)$ includes *deductive rules* for the $ML$ literals similar to the rules above for the $KL$ literals, and the use of such literals in the *action preconditions* in place of the $KL$ literals.

Deductive rules, similar to the ones for $K$, allow us also to expand the literals $L$ that are assumed to be 'contingently known':

1. $KL \rightarrow ML$
2. $KL/t \wedge M\neg L \rightarrow M\neg t$
3. $KL/t \wedge Mt \rightarrow ML$
4. $\bigwedge_{t' \in m/t} M\neg t' \rightarrow Mt$

In addition, rules $a : MC \rightarrow ML$ are added to $H(P)$ for rules $a : C \rightarrow L$ in $P$.

Likewise, every precondition $L$ of an action $a$ in $P$ is *copied* as a condition in the body of $C$ of every rule $a : C \rightarrow L'$ before the translation (a change that does not affect the semantics), and while the precondition $L$ is replaced by $KL$ in the execution model $X(P)$, it is replaced by the weaker condition $ML$ in the heuristic model $H(P)$.

The introduction of the literals $ML$ ensures that the 'wishful thinking' done over the *action preconditions* does not translate into 'wishful thinking' about their *effects*. A different situation would arise if the non-deterministic effects $Kx|K\neg x$ would be relaxed into the deterministic effects $Kx \wedge K\neg x$, instead of the weaker $Mx \wedge M\neg x$. In the first, a plan for observing $x$ will be a plan for making $x$ true (or false), something that does not result from the latter encoding as the $M$-literals are used only in action preconditions but not in conditions or goals.

Two reasons explain why the resulting heuristic model $H(P)$, which is a classical planning problem, provides a useful heuristic criterion for selecting actions in the contingent planning problem $P$. If action preconditions in $P$ are ignored (after copying them as conditions), the resulting delete-relaxation is a conformant problem [6] whose classical translation is the precondition and delete-free version of $H(P)$. The problem with this choice is that sensing actions are ignored. The model $H(P)$, on the other hand, does not ignore the action preconditions in $P$ but relaxes them in terms of the $M$-literals and uses the sensing actions along with the rules that propagate the $M$-literals for achieving them.

# 6   Action Selection and the CLG Planner

The action selection cycle in the Closed-Loop Greedy planner is based on the execution model $X(P)$ and the heuristic model $H(P)$, relies on the classical FF planner [13], and proceeds as follows:

1. given the current state $s_x$ in $X(P)$ (initially $I'$), $X(P)$ deductively closes it by applying all its deductive rules, passing the resulting state $s'_x$ to $H(P)$,
2. a modified version of the classical FF planner is called upon $H(P)$ with $s'_x$ as the starting state, returning an *improving action sequence* $\pi$,
3. the actions in $\pi$ are then applied *in the execution model* $X(P)$, starting in the state $s'_x$ and *finishing right after the first non-deterministic action* in a state $s_y$ with a true condition applied, letting the environment, a simulator, or a 'coin' choose the effect. If a *full contingent plan* is desired, all possibilities must be tried, recording the action sequences leading to the goal along each possible observation sequence,
4. if the resulting state $s_y$ is a goal state in $X(P)$, then the execution (along this branch in the full contingent plan setting) is successfully terminated, else the cycle repeats at 1 with $s_x := s_y$.

The 'improving action sequence' in Step 3 refers to the action sequence found by FF after performing a *single enforced hill climbing step*, which –if successful– maps the current state $s$ into another state $s'$ that improves the value of the FF heuristic in $H(P)$. If this enforced hill climbing fails, the execution (along this branch) is terminated with failure.

It is possible to prove that if FF returns an action sequence that is a classical plan for $H(P)$ with no actions corresponding to sensing actions, such a plan is a *conformant* plan that solves $X(P)$ and hence $P$. This is due to the soundness of the conformant translation and to the equivalence of the executions of the models $X(P)$ and $H(P)$ when no sensing actions are applied, which implies the invariant $ML = KL$.

# 7   Preliminary Experimental Results

We tested the Closed-Loop Greedy Planner (CLG) over two sets of problems: a set of existing benchmarks, and a new set of problems of our own. We compare CLG with Contingent-FF, run both with and without the helpful actions pruning mechanism [6]. The experiments are obtained on a Linux machine running at 2.33 Ghz with 8Gb of RAM, with a cutoff of 30mn of time or 1.8Gb of memory. For the implementation, we modified the FF planner [13] so that it accepts one PDDL file where the two models $X(P)$ and $H(P)$ are combined, using flags for fixing the right set of actions and fluents, for doing the progression and calculating the heuristic respectively. The actual numbers reported are preliminary as there are a number of aspects in the current implementation that need to be improved. See the discussion below.

Table 1 shows data concerning the first set of problems: *ebtcs-x* stands for *enforced Bomb-in-the-toiled* with $x$ bombs and a single toilet, *elog-x* for *enforced*

**Table 1.** Solution times for Contingent-FF and CLG over the first set of domains. 'nacts' stands for the total number of actions on the solution, 't0 time' is translation time to get $X(P)$ and $H(P)$ from the original problem, 'pddl size' is their size, and . 'time' is total time minus translation time.

| | Contingent FF | | CLG | | | |
|---|---|---|---|---|---|---|
| problem | time (s) | nacts | t0 time (s) | pddl size (Mb) | time (s) | nacts |
| ebtcs-30 | 0,95 | 59 | 0,56 | 3,19 | 3,26 | 89 |
| ebtcs-50 | 11,9 | 99 | 2,04 | 11,27 | 22,83 | 149 |
| ebtcs-70 | 68,01 | 139 | 5,17 | 26,94 | 91,06 | 209 |
| elog-5 | 0,04 | 156 | 0,05 | 0,29 | 0,26 | 130 |
| elog-7 | 0,07 | 223 | 0,05 | 0,32 | 0,36 | 193 |
| elog-huge | > 1.8Gb | | 0,95 | 2,39 | 523,1 | 43835 |
| medpks-30 | 11,72 | 60 | 1,06 | 5,35 | 10,09 | 61 |
| medpks-50 | 164,14 | 100 | 3,94 | 19,17 | 79,17 | 101 |
| medpks-70 | 1114,21 | 140 | 20,92 | 109,31 | > 1.8Gb | |
| unix-3 | 4,02 | 111 | 2,41 | 26,00 | 52,59 | 111 |
| unix-4 | 221,23 | 238 | 24,08 | 226,59 | > 1.8Gb | |

*Logistics, medpks-x* is a diagnose-and-treat domain, and *unix-x* is the problem of moving one file to the root node of tree directory with the *ls* action showing the contents of a directory. All these examples are taken from the Contingent-FF distribution.

Table 2 shows the solution times for some new problems. *colorballs-n-x* is the problem of collecting $x$ colored balls from an $n \times n$ grid whose location and color are not known but can be observed when agent and ball are in the same cell. *doors-n* is the problem of traversing a square room $n \times n$, with walls covering every odd column of the square, except for an open door at an unknown position in every column. The open door can be detected by a sensing action from an adjacent cell.

On the first set of problems, Contingent-FF and CLG are comparable in terms of coverage with the former taking less time. The 'helpful actions' option was not used in order to solve medpks. The number of actions in the table do not measure actually the quality of the contingent plans but the total number of actions along all the branches. For CLG, the size of the domain-pddl file produced by the translation constitutes the bottleneck for solving the instances medpks-70 and unix-4.

On the second set of problems, Contingent-FF solves only the smallest *colorballs* instances, and it fails in the *doors* instances due to a bug in Contingent-FF, confirmed by the authors. In these domains, CLG exhibits a more robust behavior.

In all the cases above, CLG is used for and successfully generates full contingent plans by considering all possible 'contingencies'. An inefficiency in our current implementation for this task consists in that contingent plans are represented as trees rather than graphs, meaning that (belief) states that are reached through different execution paths are explored multiple times. This should be easy to fix and should lead to faster run times and more compact plans (with an smaller total number of actions).

**Table 2.** Solution times for Contingent-FF and CLG over second set of problems. 'nacts' stands for the total number of actions in solution. 't0 time' is translation time to get $X(P)$ and $H(P)$ from the original problem, 'pddl size' is their size, and 'time' is total time minus the translation time. 'fail' means that Contingent-FF (incorrectly) reported a problem as unsolvable.

| problem | Contingent FF | | CLG | | | |
|---|---|---|---|---|---|---|
| | time (s) | nacts | t0 time (s) | pddl size (Mb) | time (s) | nacts |
| colorballs-4-1 | 0,27 | 277 | 0,14 | 0,70 | 0,58 | 281 |
| colorballs-4-2 | 36,33 | 18739 | 0,27 | 1,35 | 39,72 | 18232 |
| colorballs-4-3 | > 30mn | | 0,41 | 2,0 | > 30mn | |
| colorballs-5-1 | 1,83 | 611 | 0,44 | 1,98 | 2,43 | 584 |
| colorballs-5-2 | 867,28 | 71157 | 0,82 | 3,89 | 307,4 | 67945 |
| colorballs-5-3 | > 30mn | | 1,28 | 5,79 | > 30mn | |
| colorballs-6-1 | 7,43 | 1091 | 1,17 | 5,01 | 9,48 | 1021 |
| colorballs-6-2 | > 30mn | | 2,19 | 9,91 | > 30mn | |
| colorballs-7-1 | 42,03 | 1826 | 2,83 | 11,38 | 30,88 | 1614 |
| colorballs-7-2 | > 30mn | | 5,21 | 22,60 | > 30mn | |
| colorballs-8-1 | > 30mn | | 6,02 | 23,62 | 95,73 | 2397 |
| colorballs-9-1 | > 30mn | | 12,78 | 45,53 | 256,59 | 3384 |
| colorballs-9-2 | > 30mn | | 23,58 | 90,79 | > 1.8Gb | |
| doors-7 | fail | | 1,53 | 4,58 | 61,89 | 2357 |
| doors-9 | fail | | 7,22 | 15,00 | > 30mn | |

A main motivation for this work has been to have a fast but informed Closed-Loop planner that can scale up to problems in which the contingent solutions have exponential size and thus cannot be constructed. For testing this, we generated 25 random executions in instances of *colorballs* and *doors*, finding all executions leading to the goal, even in cases like *colorballs*-9-2 and 7-4, and *doors*-9 for which no full contingent plans could be computed due to time or memory limitations.

## 8    Discussion

We have developed a domain-independent action selection mechanism for planning with sensing that can be used as a greedy but informed closed-loop planner or as a contingent planner able to generate full plans. The approach builds on two recent ideas that explain also why the approach works: the first by Hoffmann and Brafman, that states that the delete-relaxation of a precondition-free contingent problem is a conformant problem; the second by Palacios and Geffner, that shows how conformant problems can be translated into classical problem at the 'knowledge level'. Rather than applying the two transformations in a row resulting in a formulation that ignores sensing actions, we have shown however how preconditions and sensing actions can be brought in the formulation by introducing new literals for modeling 'contingent knowledge'. We have also tested the action selection mechanism empirically over a number of problems, showing that it compares well with state-of-the-art planners for computing full contingent plans, while being able to scale up better when used in closed-loop fashion.

As future work, we plan to improve the implementation, clean up the formulation by incorporating axioms or ramifications in the target language of the translation, and redefine the 'enforced hill climbing' (EHC) step that selects the action sequence to apply next so that the deterministic heuristic model $H(P)$ is used for computing the heuristic only, while the non-deterministic execution model $X(P)$ is used in the progression within the EHC. This is needed for ruling out the possibility of loops during the execution.

## Acknowledgments

We thank the anonymous reviewers for useful comments and J. Hoffmann for help with Contingent-FF. H. Geffner is partially supported by Grant TIN2006-15387-C03-03, and H. Palacios by an FPI fellowship, both from MEC/Spain.

## References

1. Peot, M., Smith, D.E.: Conditional nonlinear planning. In: Hendler, J. (ed.) Proc. 1st Int. Conf. on AI Planning Systems, pp. 189–197 (1992)
2. Pryor, L., Collins, G.: Planning for contingencies: A decision-based approach. Journal of AI Research 4, 287–339 (1996)
3. Haslum, P., Jonsson, P.: Some results on the complexity of planning with incomplete information. In: Biundo, S., Fox, M. (eds.) ECP 1999. LNCS, vol. 1809, Springer, Heidelberg (1999)
4. Rintanen, J.: Complexity of planning with partial observability. In: Proc. ICAPS-2004, pp. 345–354 (2004)
5. Bonet, B., Geffner, H.: Planning with incomplete information as heuristic search in belief space. In: Proc. of AIPS-2000, pp. 52–61. AAAI Press, Stanford, California, USA (2000)
6. Hoffmann, J., Brafman, R.: Contingent planning via heuristic forward search with implicit belief states. In: Proc. ICAPS 2005 (2005)
7. Bertoli, P., Cimatti, A., Roveri, M., Traverso, P.: Strong planning under partial observability. Artif. Intell. 170(4-5), 337–384 (2006)
8. Bryce, D., Kambhampati, S., Smith, D.E.: Planning graph heuristics for belief space search. Journal of AI Research 26, 35–99 (2006)
9. Petrick, R., Bacchus, F.: A knowledge-based approach to planning with incomplete information and sensing. In: Proc. AIPS 2002, pp. 212–221 (2002)
10. Palacios, H., Geffner, H.: Compiling uncertainty away: Solving conformant planning problems using a classical planner (sometimes). In: Proc. AAAI 2006 (2006)
11. Bonet, B., Givan, B.: Results of the conformant track of the 5th int. planning competition (2006) At
    http://www.ldc.usb.ve/~bonet/ipc5/docs/results-conformant.pdf
12. Palacios, H., Geffner, H.: From conformant into classical planning: Efficient translations that may be complete too. In: Proc. ICAPS 2007 (2007)
13. Hoffmann, J., Nebel, B.: The FF planning system: Fast plan generation through heuristic search. Journal of Artificial Intelligence Research 14, 253–302 (2001)

# Stacking Dynamic Time Warping for the Diagnosis of Dynamic Systems

Carlos J. Alonso[1], Oscar J. Prieto[1], Juan J. Rodríguez[2], Aníbal Bregón[1], and Belarmino Pulido[1]

[1] Intelligent Systems Group (GSI), Department of Computer Science, E.T.S.I Informática, University of Valladolid, Valladolid, Spain
[2] Department of Civil Engineering, University of Burgos, Burgos, Spain

**Abstract.** This paper explores an integrated approach to diagnosis of complex dynamic systems. Consistency-based diagnosis is capable of performing automatic fault detection and localization using just correct behaviour models. Nevertheless, it may exhibit low discriminative power among fault candidates. Hence, we combined the consistency based approach with machine learning techniques specially developed for fault identification of dynamic systems. In this work, we apply Stacking to generate time series classifiers from classifiers of its univariate time series components. The Stacking scheme proposed uses K-NN with Dynamic Time Warping as a dissimilarity measure for the level 0 learners and Naïve Bayes at level 1. The method has been tested in a fault identification problem for a laboratory scale continuous process plant. Experimental results show that, for the available data set, the former Stacking configuration is quite competitive, compare to other methods like tree induction, Support Vector Machines or even K-NN and Naïve Bayes as stand alone methods.

## 1 Introduction

Diagnosis of complex dynamic systems is still an open research problem. It has been approached using a wide variety of techniques, [2], being the four main approaches: Knowledge Based —including expert systems—, Case Based Reasoning, Machine Learning and Model Based Systems. Currently, it seems clear that no single technique is capable to claim its success in every field. Therefore, an increasing number of diagnosis systems have opted for hybrid solutions. In this work, we propose a combination of Model Based and Machine Learning methods. Our approach relies primarily upon model-based diagnosis, but it has been enhanced via machine-learning techniques to overcome some drawbacks.

In the Artificial Intelligence field, the DX community has developed Consistency Based Diagnosis, CBD, as the major paradigm for model based diagnosis [5]. CBD can be summarized as an iterative cycle of behavior prediction, discrepancy or conflict detection, fault localization or candidate generation, and candidate refinement by means of new measurements. In this cycle, diagnosis candidates can be automatically obtained from conflicts using a minimal hitting set algorithm.

D. Borrajo, L. Castillo, and J.M. Corchado (Eds.): CAEPIA 2007, LNAI 4788, pp. 11–20, 2007.

Although CBD is able to perform both fault detection and localization with just models for correct behavior, the absence of fault models knowledge is partly responsible of the low discriminative power that CBD may exhibit [8]. Particularly in dynamic systems, with low observability, [3], it is not uncommon to localize a set that involves a large number of components, without been able to discriminate between them. Usually, to solve this drawback, knowledge about fault modes is introduced. We have opted for the predictive approach, which use models of fault modes to estimate faulty behavior, as in Sherlock [6] or GDE+ [17]. Based on such estimation, non-consistent fault modes are rejected. Nevertheless, the increase in the discriminative power has a price. For a system with $N$ components and only two behaviors —ok and faulty—, diagnosis must discriminate between $2^N$ behavioral mode assignments. When $M$ behavioral models are considered —one correct, $M - 1$ faulty—, diagnosis must discriminate among $M^N$ mode assignments. This is the problem faced by any model-based diagnosis proposal which attempts fault identification [8].

For practical reasons, this theoretical approach is infeasible in real systems and many approaches have been proposed in recent years to deal with the complexity issue. However, to the best of our knowledge, there is no general architecture suitable for any kind of system. In fact, many approaches just perform fault detection and localization, or rely upon a combination of some kind of heuristic, which helps focusing the diagnosis task. This will be also our approach.

In the recent past, [13] it has been proposed a diagnosis architecture which combined consistency-based diagnosis with machine learning techniques, maintaining the soundness of the CDB approach. CDB was in charge of fault detection and localization, while machine learning was use for fault identification. The identification problem was approached as a multivariate time series classification task and time series classifiers were induce off line from simulated data.

In this work, this approach is explored further, studying the possibilities of Dynamic Time Warping, DTW, [10] as the basis of induced classifiers. K-Nearest Neighbours, K-NN, using DTW as a dissimilarity measure behaves reasonably well for some univariate problems but degrades in the multivariate case. Although DTW can be easily extended for the multivariate case, these extensions are far from optimal. Instead, we have opted for using univariate classification methods to handle each multivariate time series component —itself a univariate time series— introducing an additional classifier to obtain the final class.

The univariate classification method is K-NN with DTW dissimilarity measure; the outputs of each univariate classifier are combined by another classifier to obtain the multivariate time series classifier. This approach is an special case of Stacking [20], a method designed for the combination of classifiers. The classifiers are organized in levels, being the outputs of one level the inputs for the next level. Normally, Stacking is used for combining classifiers obtained with different methods. In the present work, the same method (DTW) is used for all the classifiers in the first level. Nevertheless, each classifier uses a different subset of the input features, the series formed by the values of one of the variables.

The rest of the paper is organized as follows. Next section will introduce the compilation technique used to perform consistency-based diagnosis, which is the basis for our model-based diagnosis system. Section 3 will describe how to induce multivariate time series classifiers based on Stacking and DTW. Section 4 shows how to integrate these classifiers with the consistency based approach to diagnosis. Afterwards, we present some results on a case study plant. Finally, we discuss the results and draw some conclusions.

## 2   Consistency-Based Diagnosis Using Possible Conflict

CBD generate minimal candidates —i.e., minimal set of faulty components— computing the hitting set of minimal conflicts [14]. Hence the central issue in CBD is computing minimal conflicts from symptoms in an efficient way. Reiter [14] gives a precise definition of the concept of conflict. Intuitively, a conflict is a set of components such that at least one of its elements is faulty: other way, there will be a logical inconsistency between current observations, the system description —i.e., the models of the system— and the assumption that all the components of the conflict work properly.

Although Reiter introduced the theoretical framework of CBD, the computational paradigm is the General Diagnostic Engine [6] proposed by de Kleer and Williams. GDE computes conflicts coupling the simulation process with a dependency recording device, an Assumption based True Maintenance Systems, ATMS. Although this approach is quite efficient in static domains with qualitative variables, it does not scale up to dynamic systems described with quantitative equations. Nevertheless, GDE like conflicts computation may be tackled through compilation techniques, avoiding the need of on line dependency recording.

The computation of possible conflicts is a compilation technique which, under certain assumptions, is equivalent to on-line conflict calculation in GDE. A detailed description of consistency based diagnosis with possible conflicts can be found in [11,12]. For the sake of brevity, we just resume how to perform CBD with possible conflicts.

The main idea behind the *possible conflict* concept is that the set of subsystems capable to generate a conflict can be identified off-line. More over, possible conflicts approach provides a computational technique to automatically obtain, from a graphical representation of the system, the symbolic expression of the models associated to each *possible conflict*.

Those models can be used to perform fault detection. If there is a discrepancy between predictions from those models and current observations, the possible conflict would be responsible for such a discrepancy and should be confirmed as a real conflict. Afterwards, diagnosis candidates are obtained from conflicts following Reiter's theory.

## 3   Machine Learning Techniques for Fault Identification

There are several works that use machine learning techniques for diagnosis. Those works use methods as Inductive Logic Programming [9], Neural

*output*

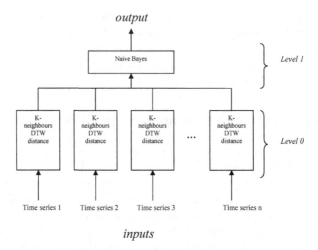

**Fig. 1.** Schema of the Stacking variant used in this work

Networks [19], KDD techniques [16], decision trees [18], and combination of techniques like recurrent neural networks, Wavelet On-Line Pre-processing (WOLP) and Autonomous Recursive Task Decomposition (ARTD) [15].

To take into account the dynamic nature of the problem, we have approached diagnosis as the task of classifying the recent evolution of the variables involved in the system. Each historic episode of a variable may be considered as a time series. Hence, the evolution of the variables of the systems may be registered as a multivariate time series. In this way, the diagnosis of a dynamic system may be managed as a particular case of multivariate time series classification.

In this work we propose to use Stacking for combining several univariate time series classifiers to obtain the classification of multivariate time series. Each of these classifiers is K-NN using DTW distance. The outputs of these classifiers are combined using Naïve Bayes. The schema is showed in the figure 1.

When we use stacking, classification is achieved using a multilevel architecture. Stacking uses a first layer called level 0 that is composed of the *base classifiers*, in our case, the k-neighbors with DTW distance classifier. The inputs of this level are the time series we classify and we have one classifier for each univariate time series. The output of this layer is the input of the second layer called level 1. This layer is composed of the meta-learner that learns how to combine the decisions of the base classifiers. The output of the level 1 layer is the target class.

Naïve Bayes has been selected for the level 1 classifier because it is a global and continuous classifier; these are desirable properties for the level 1 classifier. Against it, it is the fact that the univariate series are not independent. For the domain problem that we are interested in, it seems that some subset of components is adequate to predict some classes and other subsets to predict another. Hence, it is reasonable to expect some independence between different subsets of the multivariate time series components. On the contrary, some dependence must exits among the components of each subset. Nevertheless, the fact of training the level 0 classifiers with different and disjoint data gives a chance to increase independence. Although usually Stacking applies different level 0 classifiers to the same learning set, in this work we propose to use different learning sets with the same level 0 classifier. We can do this because of the nature of the process we are classifying. This approach tries to offer an alternative of multivariate DTW.

## 4   Integration Proposal

Consistency-based diagnosis automatically provides fault isolation based on fault detection results. Using possible conflicts, consistency-based diagnosis can be easily done without on-line dependency recording. The proposed diagnosis process will incrementally generate the set of candidates consistent with observations. In the off-line stage, we initially analyze the system and find out every possible conflict, $pc_i$. Then, we build an executable model, $SD_{pc_i}$, for each $pc_i$.

In the on-line stage, we perform a semi-closed loop simulation with each executable model $SD_{pc_i}$:

1. *repeat*
   (a) *$simulate(SD_{pc_i}; OBS_{pc_i}) \rightarrow PRED_{pc_i}$.*
   (b) *if $|PRED_{pc_i} - OBS_{Opc_i}| > \delta_{pc_i}$ confirm $pc_i$ as a real conflict.*
   (c) *update(set of candidates, set of activated pcs)*
2. *until every $pc_i$ is activated or time elapsed.*

Where $OBS_{pc_i}$ denotes the set of input observations available for $SD_{pc_i}$; $PRED_{pc_i}$ represents the set of predictions obtained from $SD_{pc_i}$; $OBS_{Opc_i}$ denotes the set of output observations for $SD_{pc_i}$; and $\delta_{pc_i}$ is the maximum value allowed as the dissimilarity value between $OBS_{Opc_i}$ and $PRED_{pc_i}$.

Without further information about fault modes, consistency-based diagnosis will just provide a list of feasible faulty candidates. In recent works, [1,13,3] it has been proposed a diagnosis architecture which combines consistency based diagnosis with possible conflicts with induced multivariate time series classifiers. These classifiers provide a ranking of fault modes compatible with consistency based diagnosis candidates. In this way, the logical soundness of consistency based diagnosis is preserved, because fault models are not used to propose non consistent behaviors. Nonetheless, the ranking information may improve fault isolation accuracy and may provide some clue towards fault identification.

Let's *CLASSIFIER_ StackDTW(t; c)* denote an invocation of the classifier induced using stacking univariate DTWs, with a fragment of series from $t$ to the min(current time, $t$+maximum series length), and with the set of candidates $c$.

With this notation, the integration of the fault mode knowledge in the consistency based diagnosis cycle may be simply stated. Just add:

   (d) *CLASSIFIER_ StackDTW ($t_0$, set of candidates)*

to the on-line simulation loop, with $t_0$ the starting time of the series, prior to the first conflict confirmation. In this way, the diagnostician may provide fault isolation a la consistency based, ordering fault candidates according to the confidence assigned to them by the classifiers and providing fault identification information.

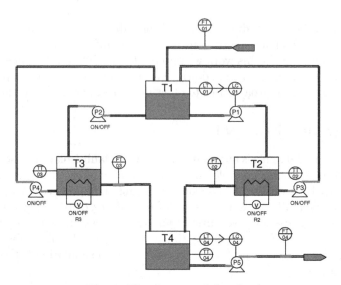

**Fig. 2.** The diagram of the plant

## 5   Case Study

### 5.1   The System to Be Diagnosed

For this work, we have used the laboratory scale plant shown in figure 2. Although a laboratory plant, its complexity is comparable to the one encountered in several subsystems of real processes. It is made up of four tanks $\{T_1, \ldots, T_4\}$, five pumps $\{P_1, \ldots, P_5\}$, and two PID controllers acting on pumps $P_1$, $P_5$ to keep the level of $\{T_1, T_4\}$ close to the specified set point. To control temperature on tanks $\{T_2, T_3\}$ we use two resistors $\{R_2, R_3\}$, respectively.

In this plant we have eleven different measurements: levels of tanks $T_1$ and $T_4$ –$\{LT01, LT04\}$–, the value of the PID controllers on pumps $\{P_1, P_5\}$ – $\{LC01, LC04\}$–, in-flow on tank $T_1$ –$\{FT01\}$–, outflow on tanks $\{T_2, T_3, T_4\}$ –$\{FT02, FT03, FT04\}$–, and temperatures on tanks $\{T_2, T_3, T_4\}$ –$\{TT02, TT03, TT04\}$–. Action on pumps $\{P_2, P_3, P_4\}$, and resistors –$\{R_2, R_3\}$– are also known.

The plant may work with different configurations and a simple setting without recirculation —pumps $\{P_3, P_4\}$ and resistor $R_2$ are switch off— has been chosen.

### 5.2   Possible Conflicts for the System

We have used common equations in simulation for this kind of process.

1. $t_{dm}$: mass balance in tank $t$.
2. $t_{dE}$: energy balance in tank $t$.
3. $t_{fb}$: flow from tank $t$ to pump.
4. $t_f$: flow from tank $t$ through a pipe.
5. $r_p$: resistor failure.

Based on these equations we have found the set of possible conflicts shown in table 1. In the table, second column shows the set of constraints used in

**Table 1.** Possible conflicts found for the laboratory plant; constraints, components, and the estimated variable for each possible conflict

|          | Constraints | Components | Estimate |
|----------|-------------|------------|----------|
| $PC_1$ | $t1_{dm}, t1_{fb1}, t1_{fb2}$ | $T_1, P_1, P_2$ | $LT01$ |
| $PC_2$ | $t1_{fb1}, t2_{dm}, t2_f$ | $T_1, T_2, P_1$ | $FT02$ |
| $PC_3$ | $t1_{fb1}, t2_{dm}, r2_p$ | $T_1, P_1, T_2, R_2$ | $TT02$ |
| $PC_4$ | $t1_{fb2}, t3_{dm}, t3_f$ | $T_1, P_2, T_3$ | $FT03$ |
| $PC_5$ | $t1_{fb2}, t3_{dm}$ | $T_1, P_2, T_3$ | $TT03$ |
| $PC_6$ | $t4_{dm}$ | $T_4$ | $LT04$ |
| $PC_7$ | $t4_{fb}$ | $T_4, P_5$ | $FT04$ |

**Table 2.** Fault modes considered

| Class | Component | Description |
|-------|-----------|-------------|
| $f_1$ | $T_1$ | Small leakage in tank $T_1$ |
| $f_2$ | $T_1$ | Big leakage in tank $T_1$ |
| $f_3$ | $T_1$ | Pipe blockage $T_1$ (left outflow) |
| $f_4$ | $T_1$ | Pipe blockage $T_1$ (right outflow) |
| $f_5$ | $T_3$ | Leakage in tank $T_3$ |
| $f_6$ | $T_3$ | Pipe blockage $T_3$ (right outflow) |
| $f_7$ | $T_2$ | Leakage in tank $T_2$ |
| $f_8$ | $T_2$ | Pipe blockage $T_2$ (left outflow) |
| $f_9$ | $T_4$ | Leakage in tank $T_4$ |
| $f_{10}$ | $T_4$ | Pipe blockage $T_4$ (right outflow) |
| $f_{11}$ | $P_1$ | Pump failure |
| $f_{12}$ | $P_2$ | Pump failure |
| $f_{13}$ | $P_5$ | Pump failure |
| $f_{14}$ | $R_2$ | Resistor failure in tank $T_2$ |

each possible conflict, which are minimal with respect to the set of constraints. Third column shows those components involved. Fourth column indicates the estimated variable for each possible conflict.

## 5.3   Experimental Design

We have considered the fourteen fault modes shown in table 2.

Possible conflicts related to fault modes are shown in the following theoretical fault signature matrix shown in table 3.

It should be noticed that these are the fault modes classes which can be distinguished for fault identification. In the fault localization stage, the following pair of faults $\{f_1, f_2\}$, $\{f_4, f_{11}\}$, and $\{f_3, f_{12}\}$, and $\{f_{10}, f_{13}\}$ can not be separately isolated.

Due to the cost of obtaining enough data for a fourteen classes classification problem from the laboratory plant, we have resorted to a detail, non linear quantitative simulation of the plant. We have run twenty simulations for each class, adding noise in the sensors readings. We have modeled each fault class with a parameter in the $[0, 1]$ range. We have made twenty simulations for each

**Table 3.** PCs and their related fault modes

|        | $f_1$ | $f_2$ | $f_3$ | $f_4$ | $f_5$ | $f_6$ | $f_7$ | $f_8$ | $f_9$ | $f_{10}$ | $f_{11}$ | $f_{12}$ | $f_{13}$ | $f_{14}$ |
|--------|----|----|----|----|----|----|----|----|----|-----|-----|-----|-----|-----|
| $PC_1$ | 1  | 1  | 1  | 1  |    |    |    |    |    |     | 1   | 1   |     |     |
| $PC_2$ |    |    |    | 1  |    |    | 1  | 1  |    |     | 1   |     |     |     |
| $PC_3$ |    |    |    | 1  |    |    | 1  |    |    |     | 1   |     |     | 1   |
| $PC_4$ |    |    | 1  |    | 1  | 1  |    |    |    |     | 1   |     |     |     |
| $PC_5$ |    |    | 1  |    | 1  |    |    |    |    |     | 1   |     |     |     |
| $PC_6$ |    |    |    |    |    |    |    |    | 1  |     |     |     |     |     |
| $PC_7$ |    |    |    |    |    |    |    |    |    | 1   |     | 1   |     |     |

class of fault. Each simulation lasted 900 seconds. We randomly generate the fault magnitude, and its origin, in the interval $[180, 300]$. We also have assumed that the system is in stationary state before the fault appears.

The data sampling was one data per second. However, due to the slow dynamics in the plant, we can select one data every three seconds without losing discrimination capacity. Since we just have eleven measures, then each simulation will provide eleven series of three hundred numeric elements.

### 5.4   Results

In this section, the results from the proposed method are compared to some standard machine learning methods: Decision Trees, Naïve Bayes Classifiers and Support Vector Machines (with the linear kernel).

Moreover, the results for Nearest Neighbor method, for different values of the number of neighbors, are included. They are from [4]. For this method, DTW is used considering that the distance between two multivariate series is the sum of the distances for each variable.

The methods are used with series of different lengths, because the classifiers are going to be used for early classification. We consider some significative length values: 30, 40, 50 and 100% of the series. The length of the full series is 15 minutes.

The results were obtained using 10-fold stratified cross-validation. Moreover, the Stacking method uses another internal cross-validation, also with 10 folds.

Table 4 shows the results obtained using different methods for different percentages of the series length. Stacking DTW classifiers has better results than any of the other considered methods, for all the considered lengths.

Table 4 also shows the average rank of each method. For each method, the average rank is calculated from its ranks in the different folds. For each fold, the methods are ranked. The best method in the fold is assigned the number 1, the second the number 2, and so on. The average rank of the proposed method is always smaller than 2.0. According to Friedman test [7] these average ranks are, for all the considered lengths, significantly different from the mean rank.

The second best method is decision trees. If we compare the results of the two best methods for the different folds, using a paired t-test the differences are significant when using half-length and full series.

**Table 4.** Results of the different methods for different lengths of the series

| | Series Length | Decision Tree | Naïve Bayes | SVM | DTW 1-NN | DTW 3-NN | DTW 5-NN | Stacking DTW+NBC |
|---|---|---|---|---|---|---|---|---|
| Accuracy | 30% | 68.57 | 59.64 | 44.64 | 56.07 | 57.86 | 53.21 | 73.93 |
| (percentage) | 40% | 94.29 | 87.50 | 80.71 | 87.86 | 84.29 | 83.21 | 95.36 |
| | 50% | 91.79 | 91.79 | 84.64 | 91.07 | 87.14 | 83.57 | 96.79 |
| | 100% | 93.93 | 83.57 | 92.14 | 91.43 | 88.57 | 85.00 | 98.57 |
| Average | 30% | 2.35 | 3.60 | 6.45 | 4.60 | 3.75 | 5.30 | 1.95 |
| ranks | 40% | 2.05 | 3.70 | 6.05 | 3.60 | 5.35 | 5.75 | 1.50 |
| | 50% | 3.25 | 3.25 | 6.00 | 3.00 | 4.90 | 6.00 | 1.60 |
| | 100% | 3.05 | 5.75 | 3.50 | 3.30 | 4.95 | 6.10 | 1.35 |

# 6   Conclusions

This work further explores an integrated approach to diagnosis that pretends to be effective in complex dynamic systems, combing Consistency Based Diagnosis with machine learning techniques.

The main contribution of this work is the proposal of Stacking to address multivariate time series classification from univariate time series classifiers induced for each component of the original time series. This new proposal improves previous results because of the better performance of the induced classifier. With 40% of the series, long before the system reaches another stationary state, the new method provides a 95% success rate. The only drawback is the need to train the meta level learner with different lengths of the time series.

The results using Stacking with DTW and Naive Bayes are much better than the results from DTW and Naive Bayes. Hence, the success of the method is not a consequence of combining classifiers that work well isolated. The proposed method has also better results than other standard machine learning methods, such as decision trees and support vector machines.

Although the proposed method was designed for the diagnosis of dynamic systems, it can be used for other multivariate time series classification tasks. The method will be tested with data sets from other domains.

Normally, Stacking is using for combining several methods, while in the presented variant it is used with the same method with different inputs. The two approaches can be used in conjunction, so we plan to test the method using several methods for the first level.

*Acknowledgments.* This work has been partially funded by Spanish Ministry of Education and Culture, through grant DPI2005–08498, and Junta Castilla y León VA088A05.

# References

1. Alonso, C., Rodríguez, J.J., Pulido, B.: Enhancing consistency based diagnosis with machine learning techniques. In: Conejo, R., Urretavizcaya, M., Pérez-de-la-Cruz, J.-L. (eds.) Current Topics in Artificial Intelligence. LNCS (LNAI), vol. 3040, pp. 312–321. Springer, Heidelberg (2004)

2. Balakrishnan, K., Honavar, V.: Intelligent diagnosis systems. Journal of Intelligent Systems 8 (1998)
3. Bregón, A., Pulido, B., Simón, M.A., Moro, I., Prieto, O., Rodríguez, J., González, C.A.: Focusing fault localization in model-based diagnosis with case-based reasoning. In: 17th International Workshop on Principles of Diagnosis (2006)
4. Bregón, A., Simón, M.A., Rodríguez, J.J., Alonso, C., Pulido, B., Moro, I.: Early fault classification in dynamic systems using case-based reasoning. In: Marín, R., Onaindía, E., Bugarín, A., Santos, J. (eds.) CAEPIA 2005. LNCS (LNAI), vol. 4177, Springer, Heidelberg (2006)
5. de Kleer, J., Mackworth, A.K., Reiter, R.: Characterising diagnosis and systems. In: Readings in Model Based Diagnosis, pp. 54–65. Morgan-Kauffman, San Francisco (1992)
6. de Kleer, J., Williams, B.C.: Diagnosing with behavioral modes. In: Eleventh International Joint Conference on Artificial Intelligence (IJCAI 1989) (1989)
7. Demšar, J.: Statistical comparisons of classifiers over multiple data sets. Journal of Machine Learning Research 7, 1–30 (2006)
8. Dressler, O., Struss, P.: The consistency-based approach to automated diagnosis of devices. In: Brewka, G. (ed.) Principles of Knowledge Representation, pp. 269–314. CSLI Publications, Stanford (1996)
9. Feng, C.: Inducting temporal fault diagnostic rules from a qualitative model. In: Muggleton, S. (ed.) Inductive Logic Programming, Academic Press, London (1992)
10. Keogh, E., Ratanamahatana, C.A.: Exact indexing of dynamic time warping. Knowledge and Information Systems 7(3), 358–386 (2005)
11. Pulido, B., Alonso, C.: An alternative approach to dependency-recording engines in consistency-based diagnosis. In: Cerri, S.A., Dochev, D. (eds.) AIMSA 2000. LNCS (LNAI), vol. 1904, pp. 111–120. Springer, Heidelberg (2000)
12. Pulido, B., Alonso, C., Acebes, F.: Lessons learned from diagnosing dynamic systems using possible conflicts and quantitative models. In: Monostori, L., Váncza, J., Ali, M. (eds.) IEA/AIE 2001. LNCS (LNAI), vol. 2070, pp. 135–144. Springer, Heidelberg (2001)
13. Pulido, B., Rodríguez, J.J., Alonso, C., Prieto, O.J., Gelso, E.R.: Diagnosis of continuous dynamic systems: Integrating consistency based diagnosis with machine learning techniques. In: 16th IFAC World Congress, Prague, Czech Republic (2005)
14. Reiter, R.: A theory of diagnosis from first principles. Artificial Intelligence 32, 57–95 (1987)
15. Roverso, D.: Fault diagnosis with the aladdin transient classifier. In: System Diagnosis and Prognosis: Security and Condition Monitoring Issues III, AeroSense2003, Aerospace and Defense Sensing and Control Technologies Symposium (2003)
16. Sleeman, D., Mitchell, F., Milne, R.: Applying KDD techniques to produce diagnostic rules for dynamic systems. Technical Report AUCS/TR9604, Department of Computing Science. University of Aberdeen (1996)
17. Struss, P., Dressler, O.: Physical negation: Introducing fault models into the general diagnostic engine. In: Eleventh International Joint Conference on Artificial Intelligence (IJCAI 1989), Detroit, Michigan, USA (1989)
18. Suárez, A.J., Abad, P.J., Ortega, J.A., Gasca, R.M.: Diagnosis progresiva en el tiempo de sistemas dinámicos. In: IV Jornadas de ARCA, Sistemas Cualitativos y Diagnosis, JARCA'02 (2002)
19. Venkatasubramanian, V., Chan, K.: A neural network methodology for process fault diagnosis. AIChE J. 35(12), 1993–2001 (1989)
20. Wolpert, D.H.: Stacked generalization. Neural Networks 5(2), 241–260 (1992)

# Retrieval of Relevant Concepts
# from a Text Collection

Henry Anaya-Sánchez[1], Rafael Berlanga-Llavori[2], and Aurora Pons-Porrata[1]

[1] Center of Pattern Recognition and Data Mining
Universidad de Oriente, Santiago de Cuba, Cuba
{henry,aurora}@csd.uo.edu.cu
[2] Departament de Llenguatges i Sistemes Informàtics
Universitat Jaume I, Castelló, Spain
berlanga@uji.es

**Abstract.** This paper addresses the characterization of a large text collection by introducing a method for retrieving sets of relevant WordNet concepts as descriptors of the collection contents. The method combines models for identifying interesting word co-occurrences with an extension of a word sense disambiguation algorithm in order to retrieve the concepts that better fit in with the collection topics. Multi-word nominal concepts that do not explicitly appear in the texts, can be found among the retrieved concepts. We evaluate our proposal using extensions of recall and precision that are also introduced in this paper.

## 1 Introduction

Currently, most human knowledge is described in Natural Language, and it is implicitly stored into hugh collections of texts. In order to help users to effectively access to such a knowledge, many text processing tasks have been proposed. For example, Text Indexing and Retrieval, Multi-document Summarization, Text Categorization, Information Extraction, Question Answering, etc. All of them rely on content elements (usually terms or words) to represent the textual contents. The selection of proper content elements is crucial for the success of these tasks.

In this paper, we address the characterization of a large text collection by introducing a knowledge-driven method for retrieving sets of relevant WordNet concepts as descriptors of the collection contents. Our approach considers concepts as content elements instead of terms or words because concepts unambiguously represent real-world objects, events, activities, etc. The method consists of identifying interesting word co-occurrences from the texts, and then of retrieving relevant concepts for each co-occurrence using an extension of a word sense disambiguation algorithm.

There exists many applications for a concept retrieval system. The most direct one is the semantic annotation of texts with respect to an existing knowledge resource like WordNet, UMLS[1] in Medicine or Wikipedia. More specifically, a

---

[1] http://www.nlm.nih.gov/

D. Borrajo, L. Castillo, and J.M. Corchado (Eds.): CAEPIA 2007, LNAI 4788, pp. 21–30, 2007.

crucial task for the development of the Semantic Web consists of annotating web pages with concepts from domain ontologies. To the best of our knowledge, there not exists any general and domain-independent approach for concept retrieval. Instead, several specific annotation tools have been developed for specific domains. For example, METAMAP[2] permits the retrieval of concepts from UMLS. Other approaches can be found for other application domains [3]. Most of these annotation methods use to rely on Information Extraction techniques which require either a large and specific set of hand-made rules or a large training set to induce the appropriate extraction rules. As a consequence, the main limitations of these tools are that they are domain dependent and require much human intervention. In this paper we face the problem of concept retrieval as a domain-independent and completely unsupervised task.

Apart from the direct application of concept retrieval to text annotation, we also propose new uses for it. More specifically, retrieved sets of relevant concepts can be directly used to address both Text Categorization and Multi-document Summarization tasks. Clearly, given the document collection $\mathcal{D}$, the set of relevant concepts $\mathcal{C}^*$ of $\mathcal{D}$, and the relation $\mathcal{R} \subseteq \mathcal{P}(\mathcal{C}^*) \times \mathcal{D}$ that links each set of relevant concepts with each document of the collection it has associated ($\mathcal{P}(\mathcal{C}^*)$ denotes the power set of $\mathcal{C}^*$), it is easy to see that:

i.  $\mathcal{R}$ allows the categorization of each document into categories that can be represented by the sets of concepts or that can be inferred from them, and
ii. each set of relevant concepts $c \in \mathcal{P}(\mathcal{C}^*)$ represents an abstract summary for the set of documents it has associated, i.e., for the set $\{d|d \in \mathcal{D} \wedge (c,d) \in \mathcal{R}\}$.

Comparing with other works in the Information Retrieval area, our approach allows both the unsupervised detection of the topics described by a document collection and the creation of a conceptual summary for each detected topic. As far as we know, there is just one approach in the literature tackling both problems with the same system [7]. However, summaries there obtained are directly extracted from the document sentences, and therefore they are not associated to concepts. As shown in the experimental section, our approach achieves good results in topic detection and acceptable results in their abstract summarization.

This paper is organized as follows. Section 2 describes the proposed method. Specifically, it firstly exposes the identification of interesting word co-occurrences (subsection 2.1), and then explains how concepts are retrieved (subsection 2.2). Section 3 is devoted to the evaluation of the approach. Finally, Section 4 presents some conclusions.

## 2   Methodology

We address the problem of characterizing a large text collection $\mathcal{D}$ in terms of relevant concepts that are retrievable from an external lexical resource. In particular, in this paper we consider the lexical resource WordNet [5], but other

---

[2] http://mmtx.nlm.nih.gov/index.shtml

thesauri (e.g. UMLS), domain ontologies or public dictionaries (e.g. Wikipedia) can be also directly used. Let us denote the set of available concepts by $\mathcal{C}$.

In this paper we propose to retrieve relevant concepts for each possible topic of $\mathcal{D}$, assuming that no prior information about the collection topics is available. Our method proceeds in two phases.

Firstly, topics are detected through the identification of interesting word co-occurrences describing them. For example, we can find the interesting co-occurrence $\{pope, visit\}$ in a collection, which is related to the topic "official visits of the Catholic Pope". As an intermediate result, we obtain a mapping $\mathcal{P}(\mathcal{W}_{\mathcal{D}}) \rightarrow \mathcal{P}(\mathcal{D})$ that associates each word co-occurrence with the documents where it occurs (i.e. its support). Here, $\mathcal{W}_{\mathcal{D}}$ represents the vocabulary of $\mathcal{D}$.

Then, a set of relevant concepts is retrieved for each interesting word co-occurrence. Both, simple and composite concepts are regarded in order to obtain those that better fit in with the co-occurrence meaning. For example, the co-occurrence $\{pope, visit\}$ will be mapped to the WordNet concepts $\{pope\#1, visit\#5\}$.

As final result, we obtain a mapping $\mathcal{P}(\mathcal{C}) \rightarrow \mathcal{P}(\mathcal{D})$ (through the composition $\mathcal{P}(\mathcal{C}) \leftrightarrow \mathcal{P}(\mathcal{W}_{\mathcal{D}}) \rightarrow \mathcal{P}(\mathcal{D})$) such that it associates to each possible topic of $\mathcal{D}$ its descriptor (i.e., the set of relevant concepts) along whith its documents. Next subsections describe both phases.

## 2.1   Identification of Interesting Co-occurrences

Instead of computing a comprehensive set of word co-occurrences from $\mathcal{D}$, which is a hard task even for medium-size collections, we only identify some interesting co-occurrences.

Our strategy firstly consists of finding all word pairs (two-term co-occurrences) occuring with a predetermined minimum support. Thus, we avoid the *quasi exhaustive* search of all word co-occurrences of different sizes that is performed by traditional mining algorithms like Apriori [1]. Then, a set of interesting pairs is built by selecting those pairs that maximize at least one measure from a given set of association measures. Especifically, we use 4 documents as minimum support and the following association measures: *mutual information*, *likelihood ratio*, *support*, F1 and *Yule's Q coefficient* [10]. Finally, each interesting pair is extended with those words jointly appearing in all documents that contain the pair.

## 2.2   Obtaining Relevant Concepts for Each Interesting Co-occurrence

As we use WordNet, we propose to retrieve the relevant concepts for each co-occurrence from both the set of all its possible word senses (simple concepts), and the set of its possibly related multi-word nominal concepts (composite concepts). We consider that a multi-word nominal concept (i.e. a nominal concept that has been lexicalized through a multi-word phrase) is *possibly related* to a co-occurrence if its phrase is composed by at least two words of the co-occurrence.

For example, the WordNet concept *weapon of mass destruction* is regarded as possibly related to the co-occurrence {*baghdad*, *destruction*, *mass*, *inspection*, *site*, *iraqi*}.

To retrieve concepts, we use an extension of the knowledge-driven Word Sense Disambiguation algorithm presented in [2]. Briefly, given a set of words $W$, the original disambiguation algorithm clusters all senses of words in $W$ into cohesive groups, and then selects those senses that compose the clusters that better fit in with $W$ via a filtering process. If the selected senses disambiguate all words, the process is stopped and the selected senses are interpreted as the disambiguating ones. Otherwise, the clustering and filtering steps are performed again (regarding the remaining senses) until the disambiguation is achieved.

In our case, we consider that the set of words to be disambiguated is the co-occurrence (i.e., $W$ is the co-occurrence under consideration), but in addition to all the senses of words in $W$, we include the possibly related multi-word nominal concepts into the clustering scheme. The obtained senses are regarded as the relevant concepts.

Note that the inclusion of possibly related multi-word nominal concepts into the clustering, allows the retrieval of concepts that do not explicitly appear in the texts.

Finally, for accuracy reasons, when a possibly related multi-word concept is retrieved, all the retrieved senses corresponding to its constituent words are ignored.

Algorithm 1 shows the general steps of our proposal for the retrieval of relevant concepts for a word co-occurrence $W$. In the algorithm, *clustering* represents the basic clustering method, and *filter* is the function that selects the clusters. The rest of the section describes in detail each component of the whole process.

---

**Algorithm 1.** Clustering-based approach for retrieving relevant concepts for the word co-occurrence $W$

---

**Require:** A word co-occurrence $W$.
**Ensure:** The set of retrieved concepts $S$.
    Let $S_W$ be the set of all senses of words in $W$, and $P_W$ be the set of all WordNet multi-word concepts possibly related to $W$.
    $S = S_W \cup P_W$
    $i = 0$
    **repeat**
        $i = i + 1$
        $G = clustering(S, \beta_0(i))$
        $G' = filter(G, W)$
        $S = \bigcup_{g \in G'} \{s | s \in g\}$
    **until** $|S|_W = |W|$ or $\beta_0(i+1) = 1$
    Remove from $S$ those senses corresponding to words that compose multi-word concepts appearing in $S$.
    **return** $S$

---

*Sense Representation.* For clustering purposes, word senses are represented as topic signatures [6]. Thus, for each word sense $s$ we define a vector $(t_1 : \sigma_1, \ldots, t_m : \sigma_m)$, where each $t_i$ is a WordNet term highly correlated to $s$ with an association weight $\sigma_i$. The set of signature terms for a word sense includes all its WordNet hyponyms, its directly related terms (including coordinated terms) and their filtered and lemmatized glosses. To weight signature terms, the *tf-idf* statistics is used. In this case, the *tf* part represents the frequency of the term in the word sense, whereas the *idf* represents the inverse frequency of the term in all the senses associated to that word. In this way, we award those terms that are frequent in the word sense and infrequent in the other ones. Topic signatures of senses form a vector space model similar to those defined in Information Retrieval (IR) systems. Thus, they can be compared through the usual IR measures such as cosine, Dice and Jaccard [8].

*Clustering Algorithm.* Sense clustering is carried out by the Extended Star Clustering Algorithm [4], which builds star-shaped and overlapped clusters. Each cluster consists of a star and its satellites, where the star is the sense with the highest connectivity of the cluster, and the satellites are those senses connected with the star. The connectivity is defined in terms of the $\beta_0$-similarity graph, which is obtained using the cosine similarity measure between topic signatures and the minimum similarity threshold $\beta_0$. The way this clustering algorithm relates word senses resembles the manner in which syntactic and discourse relation links textual elements.

*Filtering Process.* As some clusters can be more appropriate to describe the semantics of $W$ than others, they are ranked according to the lexicographic order imposed by the following three-component measure:

$$\left( |words(g)|, \frac{\sum_i \begin{cases} \bar{g}_i & \text{if } i \in W \\ 0 & \text{otherwise} \end{cases}}{\sum_i \bar{g}_i}, -\sum_{s \in g} number(s) \right)$$

where $words(g)$ denotes the set of words having senses in $g$, $\bar{g}$ is the centroid of $g$ (computed as the barycenter of the cluster), and $number(s)$ is the WordNet ordinal number of the sense $s$ according to its corresponding word. Note that the first and second components measure the overlapping between the cluster and $W$, whereas the third one considers the usage frequency of the cluster senses.

Once the clusters have been ranked, they are orderly processed to select clusters for covering the words in $W$. In this phase, all possibly related multi-word nominal concepts are disregarded in the decision making.

A cluster $g$ is selected if both it contains at least one sense of an uncovered word of $W$, and other senses corresponding to covered words of $W$ are included in the current selected clusters. If $g$ does not contain any sense of uncovered words of $W$ it is discarded. Otherwise, $g$ is inserted into a queue $Q$. Finally, if the selected clusters do not cover $W$, clusters in $Q$ adding senses of uncovered words of $W$ are chosen until the cover is obtained.

$\beta_0$ *Threshold and the Stopping Criterion.* Like in the original disambiguation algorithm, we continue the refinement of senses until either all words in $W$ are disambiguated (i.e., there exists a unique sense in $S$ for each word in $W$), or when it is impossible to raise $\beta_0$ again. At $i$-th iteration $\beta_0$ is defined as:

$$\beta_0(i) = \begin{cases} percentile(90, sim(S)) & \text{if } i = 1, \\ \min_{p \in \{90, 95, 100\}} \{\beta = percentile(p, sim(S)) | \beta > \beta_0(i-1)\} & \text{otherwise.} \end{cases}$$

In this definition, $S$ is the set of current senses, and $percentile(p, sim(S))$ represents the $p$-th percentile value of the pairwise similarities between senses (i.e. $sim(S) = \{cos(s_i, s_j) | s_i, s_j \in S, i \neq j\} \cup \{1\}$).

*An example.* For illustrating the concept retrieval process we regard the co-occurrence of nouns {*baghdad, destruction, mass, inspection, site, iraqi*} and WordNet version 2.0. In this example, the set of concepts under consideration is composed by the 18 senses corresponding to the words of the co-occurrence[3] and the multi-word nominal concept *weapon of mass destruction.*.

Figure 1 graphically summarize the retrieval process. The boxes in the figure represent obtained clusters, which are sorted regarding the ranking function (scores are under the boxes).

Initially, all senses are clustered using $\beta_0$=0.082 (the 90th-percentile of the pairwise similarities between the senses). It can be seen in the figure that the first cluster covers 4/6 of the words in the co-occurrence. This cluster comprises the sense *destruction*#3, which is related to death, the multi-word concept *weapon_of_mass_destruction*#1, senses *inspection*#1 and *site*#1, and the 3rd and 6th senses of *mass*, that refer to an ill-structured collection of similar things, and to a multitude of people, respectively.

As it can be appreciated 2nd, 3rd and 5th clusters include senses of words that have not been covered by the first cluster (*iraqi*#1 and *baghdad*#1 in the 2nd and 5th, and *iraqi*#1 in the 3rd), while 4th cluster does not. In the case of 2nd and 3rd clusters, there are "contradictory" senses (e.g. *mass*#5) for the current meaning imposed to the noun *mass* by the first cluster (i.e., *mass*#3 and *mass*#6). Hence, the filtering process selects 1st and 5th clusters, and all other clusters are discarded. After this step, $S$ is updated with the set {*mass*#3, *mass*#6, *destruction*#3, *inspection*#1, *site*#1, *weapon_of_mass_destruction*#1, *baghdad*#1, *iraqi*#1}.[4]

At this point of the process, the stopping criterion does not hold because neither $|S|_W = |W|$ nor $\beta_0(2) = 1$. Consequently, a new cluster distribution must be obtained using the current set $S$.

The boxes in the bottom of Figure 1 represent the new clusters. Obviously, the cluster containing the sense *mass*#6 is discarded because the cluster that includes the sense *mass*#3 is more frequently used, and therefore precedes it in the order.

---

[3] The single senses of *baghdad, inspection* and *iraqi*, the 3 senses of *destruction*, the 9 senses of *mass*, and the 3 senses of *site*.

[4] In the figure, doubly-boxed clusters depict those selected by the filter.

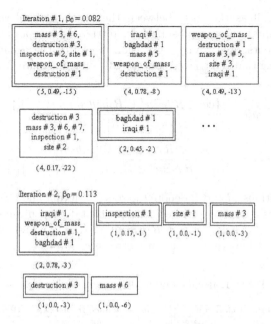

**Fig. 1.** Concept retrieval process for co-occurrence {*baghdad, destruction, mass, inspection, site, iraqi*}

Then, the final set of selected senses is $S$ = {*mass#3, destruction#3, inspection#1, site#1, weapon_of_mass_destruction#1, baghdad#1, iraqi#1*}, but only the senses *inspection#1, site#1, weapon_of_mass_destruction#1, baghdad#1*, and *iraqi#1* are retrieved as relevant because *mass* and *destruction* are included in the multi-word concept *weapon_of_mass_destruction#1*.

## 3   Evaluation

Assuming that there is not a corpus comprising concept-based descriptions of topics for evaluating the Concept Retrieval task, we use a subset of TDT2 collection[5] consisting of 22 topics for which a human annotator identified sets of WordNet relevant concepts by summarizing each topic at a high compression ratio. We compare the sets of relevant concepts that were manually-identified by the human annotator with the sets of retrieved concepts.

We consider that traditional measures of Information Retrieval are not appropriate for this comparison, because they are unable to deal with the subsumption relation between concepts, which is essential when abstractions are tackled. For the same reason, we do not regard other measures of DUC [6] summary evaluation like ROUGE and BLEU either. Consequently, we propose the following extensions of recall and precision.

---

[5] http://www.nist.gov/speech/tests/tdt
[6] http://duc.nist.gov

We define recall as the ratio between the number of relevant (manually-identified) concepts that are subsumed by retrieved concepts and the number of relevant concepts. Accordingly, precision measures the accuracy of the retrieval considering that a retrieved concept can subsume more than one relevant concept. That is,

$$recall = \frac{|\{c|c \in R \land \exists(c' \in \bar{R})[subsumes(c',c)]\}|}{|R|}$$

$$precision = \frac{|\{c|c \in R \land \exists(c' \in \bar{R})[subsumes(c',c)]\}|}{|\{c|c \in R \land \exists(c' \in \bar{R})[subsumes(c',c)]\}| + |\bar{R}_*|}$$

In these definitions, $R$ and $\bar{R}$ denote the sets of relevant and retrieved concepts respectively, $\bar{R}_*$ is the set of retrieved concepts that do not subsume relevant concepts (i.e. $\bar{R}_* = \{c'|c' \in \bar{R} \land \neg\exists(c \in R)[subsumes(c',c)]\}$), and *subsumes* represents the WordNet hypernymy relation between concepts.

**Table 1.** Results obtained for three TDT2 topics

| TDT2 Topic | Manual Concepts | Retrieved Concepts | Recall | Precision | F1 |
|---|---|---|---|---|---|
| Current conflict with Iraq | iraq#1, disagreement#1, united nations#1, inspection#1, weapon of mass destruction#1 | baghdad#1, inspection#1, site.noun#1, iraqi.noun#1, weapon of mass destruction#1 | 0.40 | 0.40 | 0.40 |
| Oprah Lauwsuit | industry#1, law-suit#1, mad cow disease#1, beef cattle#1, texas#1 | disease#1, price.noun#7, beef cattle#1, texas#1 | 0.50 | 0.75 | 0.60 |
| Asian Financial Crisis | asian.adj#1, financial#1, economic crisis#1, international monetary fund#1 | financial#1, international monetary fund#1 | 0.50 | 1.00 | 0.66 |

As in most Information Retrieval systems high values of recall entail low values of precision and vice versa, we decided to evaluate the effectivenes of our method using the macro-averaged F1. This measure was computed in terms of the proposed *recall* and *precision* by using the best matches between manually-identified sets of relevant concepts and the sets of retrieved concepts.

In this experiment, the obtained value was 0.47, which is acceptable regarding the hardness of the task. We recall that the Concept Retrieval task can be seen as an aggressive Multi-document summarization task.

It is worth mentioning that the retrieval of relevant concepts is performed from scratch, without using prior information about the current topics of the collection. Besides, in this experiment we only focus the evaluation on concepts belonging to WordNet, ignoring those proper names like *Monica Lewinsky, Bill Clinton*, or *Oprah Winfrey*, that appear in the word co-occurrences and are also relevant for describing the collection contents.

Table 1 shows the alignment obtained for three of the 22 TDT2 topics. In the case of the topic about Iraq, it is important to mention that even though the phrase *weapon of mass destruction* does not explicitly appear in the text collection, it is a retrieved concept. Also, it can be noticed that the retrieved concepts *baghdad*#1 and *iraqi.noun*#1 are strongly related to the relevant concept *iraq*#1. However, in the current evaluation this has not been taken into account.

As a second experiment, we evaluate the accuracy of the retrieved multi-word concepts in this subset of the collection by measuring its precision. That is, the ratio between the number of retrieved multi-word concepts that are relevant for a topic of the collection, and the number of retrieved multi-word concepts. The obtained value was 88%, which is similar to the precision value obtained by the original disambiguation algorithm when it was applied to the nouns of the co-occurrences (85%).

Finally, regarding the relationship between Concept Retrieval and Text Categorization tasks, we evaluate the impact of our approach in the latter. In this case we consider the whole TDT2 collection, that is, the 192 topics that cover 9824 documents. Each topic can be considered as a category.

We compare the TDT2 topics with the sets of documents associated to the sets of retrieved concepts by using the traditional macro-averaged F1 measure of Text Categorization [9]. The obtained F1 value was 0.77, which shows that our proposal has a good behaviour on Text Categorization. With the use of our simple method, instead of traditional supervised classification algorithms, document categories can be effectively identified and described.

## 4    Conclusions

In this paper, a knowledge-driven approach for characterizing a large text collection with sets of relevant concepts has been presented. The proposal combines a method for identifying interesting word co-occurrences with a modification of a word sense disambiguation algorithm. A major novelty of the method consists of the retrieval of concepts that are not explicitly mentioned in the texts. For this reason, the retrieved concepts can be also used as an abstract representation of the source collection (i.e. a short abstract summary).

For evaluating our approach we propose extensions of recall and precision that consider the subsumption relation between concepts. In addition, we evaluate the impact of the retrieved concepts in the Text Categorization task. In both cases, we measured the effectiveness of our method using appropriate versions of the macro-averaged F1 measure. The obtained values were 47 % in the Concept Retrieval task and 77 % in Text Categorization.

Related tasks such as the generation of very short multi-document summaries at DUC, or gene product annotation at BioCreAtIvE[7] report lower values of F1 (below 40 %), however we cannot directly compare the results as the evaluated collections are very different.

Despite the fact that we only consider WordNet as the repository of concepts, the approach can be extended to deal with other ontology-like resources right

---

[7] http://biocreative.sourceforge.net

away. As future work, we plan to consider broad lexical resources as concept repositories, and to address the retrieval of entity names. Also, we consider to improve recall by combining correlated word co-occurrences.

# References

1. Agrawal, R., Srikant, R.: Fast Algorithms for Mining Association Rules in Large Databases. In: Proceedings of the 20th International Conference on Very Large Databases, pp. 478–499 (1994)
2. Anaya-Sánchez, H., Pons-Porrata, A., Berlanga-Llavori, R.: Word Sense Disambiguation based on Word Sense Clustering. In: Sichman, J.S., Coelho, H., Rezende, S.O. (eds.) IBERAMIA 2006 and SBIA 2006. LNCS (LNAI), vol. 4140, pp. 472–481. Springer, Heidelberg (2006)
3. Corcho, O.: Ontology based document annotation: trends and open research problems. IJMSO 1(1), 47–57 (2006)
4. Gil-García, R., Badía-Contelles, J.M., Pons-Porrata, A.: Extended Star Clustering Algorithm. In: Sanfeliu, A., Ruiz-Shulcloper, J. (eds.) CIARP 2003. LNCS, vol. 2905, pp. 480–487. Springer, Heidelberg (2003)
5. Miller, G.: WordNet: A Lexical Database for English. Communications of the ACM 38(11), 39–41 (1995)
6. Lin, C.-Y., Hovy, E.: The Automated Acquisition of Topic Signatures for Text Summarization. In: Proceedings of the COLING Conference, France, pp. 495–501 (2000)
7. Pons-Porrata, A., Berlanga, R., Ruiz-Shulcloper, J.: Topic discovery based on text mining techniques. Information Processing & Management 43(3), 752–768 (2007)
8. Salton, G., Wong, A., Yang, C.S.: A Vector Space Model for Information Retrieval. Journal of the American Society for Information Science 18(11), 613–620 (1975)
9. Sebastiani, F.: Machine Learning in Automated Text Categorization. ACM Computing Surveys 34(1), 1–47 (2002)
10. Tan, P.-N., Kumar, V., Srivastava, J.: Selecting the right interestingness measure for association patterns. In: Proceedings of the 8th ACM SIGKDD, Canada, pp. 32–41. ACM Press, New York (2002)

# Interoperable Bayesian Agents for Collaborative Learning Environments

Elisa Boff[1,2], Elder Rizzon Santos[2], Moser S. Fagundes[2], and Rosa Maria Vicari[2]

[1] Computer Science Department, Caxias do Sul University (UCS), CEP 95.001-970 – Caxias do Sul – RS – Brazil
Phone/Fax: +55 54 2182159
eboff@ucs.br
[2] Computer Science Institute – Federal University of Rio Grande do Sul (UFRGS)
P.O. Box 15.064 – 91.501-970 – Porto Alegre – RS – Brazil
Phone/Fax: +55 51 33166161
{ersantos,msfagundes,rosa}@inf.ufrgs.br

**Abstract.** Collaborative work can be supported by many tools and it has been included in a large number of learning environments design. This paper presents issues related to an educational portal design and collaboration in Intelligent Tutoring Systems (ITS). In order to achieve the collaboration it was necessary to provide a way to interoperate knowledge among the heterogeneous systems. We have been developing ITS as resources to improve the individual and personalized learning. We believe that individual experiences can be more successful when the student has more autonomy and he is less dependent of the professor. In this research direction, this paper details the Social Agent reasoning, an agent to improve student's learning stimulating his interaction with other students, and how this agent exchange bayesian knowledge among AMPLIA agents. The AMPLIA environment is an Intelligent Probabilistic Multi-agent Environment to support the diagnostic reasoning development and the diagnostic hypotheses modeling of domains with complex and uncertain knowledge, like medical area.

## 1 Introduction

In a cognitive multiagent system, composed by a relative small number of intense knowledge-based agents, it is desirable to enable these agents to exchange knowledge with each other, especially when this agents lives in different applications. Our motivation relies on limitations detected on PortEdu [1], a multiagent portal that hosts educational systems like Intelligent Tutoring Systems (ITS), and provides infrastructure and services for the systems through an agent society. Interoperability is crucial to PortEdu, since its purpose is to provide services to the hosted educational systems, in example, the AMPLIA system. AMPLIA is an Intelligent Multiagent Learning Environment, designed to support training of diagnostic reasoning and modeling of domains with complex and uncertain knowledge [2].

D. Borrajo, L. Castillo, and J.M. Corchado (Eds.): CAEPIA 2007, LNAI 4788, pp. 31–39, 2007.

This paper presents the problem and a solution that we developed for the integration among the Social Agent, an agent from PortEdu system, and some agents of AMPLIA system, an ITS.

AMPLIA is used for collaborative learning in the Web. In order to support collaboration, we add workgroup features in the AMPLIA environment. AMPLIA does not have an agent with such ability. But, one of the agents that composed PortEdu, the Social Agent, can offer this service to AMPLIA.

The problem to be solved is fact of agents involved in this process are modeled using Bayesian Networks (BN), and the communication between PortEdu and AMPLIA is operating via FIPA [3]. Furthermore, there are innumerous BN representations, it is necessary a way to express such knowledge in an interoperable fashion.

FIPA-ACL (Agent Communication Language) does not provide a speech act to communicate probability knowledge. As mentioned before, it is the main problem addressed by this paper: *how the Social Agent can offer its services to the AMPLIA system?*

Our solution relies on the integration of different technologies. The knowledge interoperability is achieved by this work through an ontology-based approach.

The remaining of this paper is organized as follows: section 2 presents related researches; section 3 presents some aspects of the AMPLIA system, PortEdu and specifies the Social Agent model and an interoperability example, and, finally, section 4 presents our conclusions.

## 2 Background

The current Intelligent Tutoring Systems (ITS) research have produced learning environments endowed of social and affective skills. Social issues are focused in works related to coordination in multiagent societies, such as Castelfranchi [4] and Prada [5] research. Student's affective states are discussed and applied in learning environments in the work of Jaques [6], while Conati [7] has developed a Bayesian network-based appraisal model to deduce a student's emotional state based on their actions in educational games. Cheng [8] uses reward mechanisms from social psychology to motivate collaboration in virtual learning communities.

The Vassileva's research is about strategies and techniques of groups. In [8] was proposed a motivation strategy for user participation based on persuasion theories of social psychology.

The Social Agent, described in section 3, is based on social psychology ideas (to support social aspects) and affective states. The design of the agent permits that it changes messages with agents of heterogeneous systems, such as PortEdu (the portal that the Social Agent belongs) and AMPLIA.

BayesOWL [9] was developed to handle the issue of automatic ontology mapping. This approach defines additional markups that can add probabilities to concepts, individuals, properties and its relationships. It also defines a set of translation rules to convert the probabilistic annotated ontology into a Bayesian network. The focus on ontology mapping limits the BayesOWL markups since it was not necessary to represent variables with states different than true or false. The reason for this is that the probabilistic knowledge associated with each ontology concept was used only for telling if two concepts from different ontologies were the same. Since the Social Agent reasoning was modeled with Bayesian Networks, we chose this approach to develop agent's interoperability.

Agent communication issues regarding probabilities are addressed in [10], where is presented PACL (Probabilistic Agent Communication Language). It is an extension of the FIPA-ACL designed to deal with the communication of probabilistic knowledge. PACL specifies new communication axioms that are necessary to model the probabilistic communication. Besides the axioms, the language also designs assertive and directive probabilistic speech acts, which extends FIPA-ACL. The PACL language provides a way to communicate probabilistic knowledge extending FIPA-ACL and allowing more expressiveness to this language. It does not deal with the communication of uncertainty at the message content level, concerning how different Bayesian agents might exchange knowledge regarding their networks and evidences.

The following section presents the Social Agent model, some aspects of the PortEdu and AMPLIA system, and also a necessary explanation to clarify the interoperability problem.

## 3   Social Agent

The Social Agent, described in this section, is based on social psychology ideas (to support social aspects) and affective states. The social agent main goal is create students workgroups to solve tasks collaboratively [11] in the AMPLIA system. The interaction is stimulated by recommending the students to join workgroups in order to provide and receive help from other students. The Social Agent's knowledge is implemented with Bayesian Networks, as presented in the next subsection.

AMPLIA focuses on the medical area. It is a system where learner-modeling tasks consist of creating a Bayesian Networks for a problem that the system presents. The pedagogical design of AMPLIA was based on Piaget´s and Vygostky´s theories [12] [13] in order to support constructivism knowledge construction.

AMPLIA is composed by a set of agents modeled using BN and Influence Diagrams. The ones that hold relevant information for the Social Agent are the Learner Agent and the Mediator Agent. The former represents the student cognitive knowledge on the current subject. The last mediates conflicts that may occur during the construction of the students' solution for a particular problem. The purpose of the interaction among these agents is to suggest which classmate is recommended to work with analised student. More details about the information exchanged among the agents are presented in the section 3.2.

The groups of students intend to generate an appropriate BN for the problem under study. The students that composed each group are working in different places. So, the collaborative work takes place via AMPLIA Net Editor. The Net Editor was designed as a collaborative graphical editor including a chat tool to allow collaborative learning.

In order to improve the collaboration process among students we are using a chat tool integrated in the AMPLIA editor.

The collaborative editor is monitored by the Social Agent. At AMPLIA, each user builds his Bayesian Net for a specific pathology. The Bayesian Net corresponds to the student model (AMPLIA LearnerAgent) for a particular problem solution in the health context. During this task, the Social Agent will recommend students to help other students.

PortEdu, a multiagent portal that hosts educational systems like Intelligent Tutoring Systems, provides infrastructure and services for the systems through an agent society. One of these agents is the Social Agent, responsible for organizing the users in groups considering cognitive and emotional aspects. Figure 1 illustrates a view of PortEdu in relation to its supporting platform. The agents of PortEdu, inside the doted circle, the AMPLIA agents and also agents from other ITS are part of the same platform, allowing direct interaction among the agents of the society. The communication among agents is operating via FIPA platform.

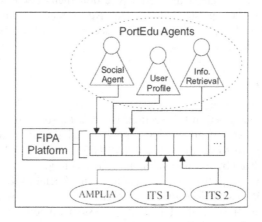

**Fig. 1.** PortEdu Plataform

However, to communicate with PortEdu and AMPLIA agents, it is necessary to express the probabilistic knowledge in a way that these agents may process it (see section 3.2).

### 3.1 Reasoning Model

The individual model has the student features. The information collected that is important to define the suitable student to recommend is: Social Profile, Acceptance Degree, Affective State (Emotion for Self and Emotion for Outcome), Learning Style, Personality Traits, Credibility and Student Action Outcome (Performance). The Social Profile and the Acceptance Degree were detailed in [11].

The socio-affective agent selects the action that maximizes this value when deciding how to act. The influence between nodes is shown in Figure 2.

In order to infer emotion we are using the model proposed in [7], based on OCC Model [14]. The affective states can be considered as emotion manifestation in a specific time. Conati modeled a Bayesian network to infer emotions and consider the students personality, goals, and interaction patterns to reach emotions.

The states of Credibility node are informed by Learner Agent (an AMPLIA agent), as well as the states of Student Action Outcome node that comes from Mediator Agent (another AMPLIA agent modeled using an Influence Diagram). The states values that are exchanged among Social, Learner and Mediator agent are two practical examples of the interoperability necessity, since these agents belongs to different societies of agents.

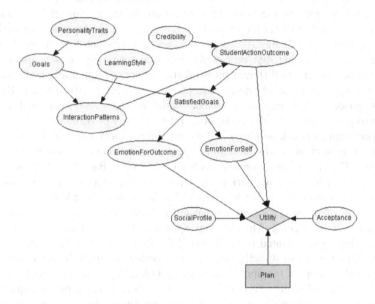

**Fig. 2.** Decision network of student model

The AMPLIA's LearnerAgent represents the student beliefs in that domain, the confidence degree this learner has on the network model he/she had built. It also includes a steady part with basic information about the learner. A High Credibility state indicates an autonomous student or a reflexive one, while a Low Credibility state indicates an undecided or insecure student, because the student often do, undo and redo the net's nodes or arcs.

The Student Action Outcome node represents a possible classification for the student's BN model, according to major problems. The BN model is classified as Unfeasible (Network that does not satisfy the definition of a Bayesian network, such as cyclic graph, disconnected network, etc.); Incorrect (The network whose model is conceptually incorrect, such as presence of an excluder node that should be in the model to refute the diagnosis, while its presence confirms it); Incomplete (Network that presents the lack of some nodes or relations considered important, whether they are diagnosis or findings); Feasible (It is a network different from the built-in model but it satisfies the case study proposed to the learner) and Complete (It is identical to the model the expert built).

The Student Action Outcome node's states are received from AMPLIA's Mediator Agent.

Finally, the decision node Plan is responsible for recommendation, which is the suitable group for a student. Such plans are selected from a function of utility (node Utility).

### 3.2 Interoperable Knowledge Representation

Our approach to allow the social agent to effectively interact with agents from learning environments inside PortEdu is based on the integration of Semantic Web technologies, namely OWL (Web Ontology Language) [15], Bayesian Networks and Agent Communication Languages. We specified an OWL ontology to formalize the Bayesian Network knowledge representation. In the ontology it was modeled the common concepts among different probabilistic networks (graph, arc, node, variable, etc.) and a specialization of these concepts in order to specify discrete Bayesian Network concepts (chance node, chance variable, state and associated prior or conditional probability). A full description of the ontology is available at [16].

The Bayesian Network ontology and its individuals form a knowledge base which stores the Bayesian networks situations, the transitions between situations and the evidences. The base can contain multiple different Bayesian networks. Any modification in a Bayesian network characterizes a new situation, and the sequence of situations represents a history of a network. The knowledge base keeps an up-to-date representation of the social agent's Bayesian networks in a way that can be easily interpreted by other agents. The ontology specification and initial population of the knowledge base were created in OWL using the Protégé tool [17]. In order to allow the knowledge base to be directly updated and queried, we used the Jena [18] toolkit, which provides support for applications using OWL. Specifically, the Jena API is applied to create and insert new individuals on the KB and also to perform queries.

Following, we present an example of Bayesian knowledge exchange among the Social Agent and the Student Model Agent. The interaction of the Social Agent with other agents is done following the FIPA specifications, which are adopted by PortEdu for the platform specification and agent communication. The Social Agent was developed using the JADE [19] framework, which provides a FIPA-compliant middleware for multiagent system development. Developing an agent with this kind of abstraction allows more reutilization and directs the programming towards the agent-oriented paradigm.

Figure 3 illustrates the *Learner Agent* (from AMPLIA) sending a FIPA-ACL message to *Social Agent* (from PortEdu). This message contains state's values of node *Credibility*. This node appears in the Learner Agent's BN and also in the Social Agent's BN. But the *a priori* probabilities are defined in the Learner Agent and informed to Social Agent. The message performative is an *inform*, the content language is OWL and the agreed ontology specifies the Bayesian network domain. This particular interaction describes the interoperation of Bayesian evidence from the *Learner Agent* to the *Social Agent*.

The message content is the OWL code of an individual Evidence that indicates the observation of the state *High*, with probability of *0.33*, in the node *Credibility*. The reception of this evidence by the Social Agent will trigger the Bayesian inference process, generating a new situation in the Bayesian network illustrated in the Figure 2.

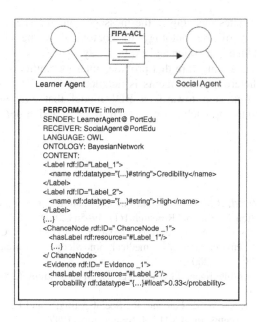

```
                    ┌─────────┐
                    │ FIPA-ACL│
                    │  ═══    │
   ⬤               │  ═══    │              ⬤
   △               └─────────┘──────▶       △
Learner Agent          │            Social Agent
                       │

  PERFORMATIVE: inform
  SENDER: LearnerAgent@PortEdu
  RECEIVER: SocialAgent@PortEdu
  LANGUAGE: OWL
  ONTOLOGY: BayesianNetwork
  CONTENT:
  <Label rdf:ID="Label_1">
     <name rdf:datatype="{...}#string">Credibility</name>
  </Label>
  <Label rdf:ID="Label_2">
     <name rdf:datatype="{...}#string">High</name>
  </Label>
  {...}
  <ChanceNode rdf:ID=" ChanceNode _1">
     <hasLabel rdf:resource="#Label_1"/>
     {...}
  </ ChanceNode>
  <Evidence rdf:ID=" Evidence _1">
     <hasLabel rdf:resource="#Label_2"/>
     <probability rdf:datatype="{...}#float">0.33</probability>
```

**Fig. 3.** Interoperability among Social Agent and Learner Agent

# 4 Conclusions

In this paper, we present a cognitive agent model capable of deals with social and affective skills of students in order to improve collaboration. When students are involved in the same task and with the same goal, they are committed ones with the others. Suggesting students to help others, based on social and affective skill of students, we can motivate collaboration. We aim to reduce the professors' involvement and give more autonomy to students.

The model presented in this paper deals with uncertainties, such as affective state, acceptance, and credibility, in an interoperable way. In order to achieve Bayesian knowledge exchange, we defined an ontology that models the Bayesian networks domain [16].

Our approach does not propose any modification in standards, such as OWL or FIPA, in order to represent uncertain knowledge, differently from PR-OWL and PACL. We apply the current standards to provide a Bayesian knowledge representation through OWL. This approach allows our Bayesian agents to interoperate their knowledge and also contributes to researches on the expression of uncertain knowledge on the Semantic Web.

Interoperability was the key to solve the information exchange among heterogeneous systems. Integrating existing ITS, we are sharing and improving the functionalities of these systems to support individual and personalized learning.

In our case study we concluded that our proposal can be integrated with the FIPA standards, more specifically with the FIPA-ACL. The adoption of OWL as a content language for ACL messages handles the issue of a common knowledge language. Our

OWL ontology aggregates meaning to the message content. The utilization of OWL and the specification of the ontology to contextualize the content, allow the expression of knowledge in an open and explicit way.

The ontology-based architecture that provides interoperability of bayesian network knowledge among heterogeneous agents is detailed in [16]. This agent architecture can be used as a first step towards a BDI model that aggregates probabilistic knowledge. A bayesian approach allows a BDI agent to assign degrees of trust to its mental states.

# References

1. Nakayama, L., Vicari, R.M., Coelho, H.: An information retrieving service for distance learning. Transactions on Internet Research 1(1), 49–56 (2005)
2. Vicari, R.M., Flores, C.D., Silvestre, A.M., Seixas, L.J., Ladeira, M., Coelho, H.: A multi-agent intelligent environment for medical knowledge. Artificial Intelligence in Medicine 27(3), 335–366 (2003)
3. The Foundation for Intelligent Physical Agents: Specifications (2006), Available from http://www.fipa.org
4. Castelfranchi, C., Rosis, F., de Falcone, R.: Social Attitudes and Personalities in Agents, Socially Intelligent Agents. In: AAAI Fall Symposium (1997)
5. Prada, R., Paiva, A.: Believable Groups of Synthetic Characters. In: AAMAS 2005 (July 25-29, 2005)
6. Jaques, P.A., Viccari, R.M.: A BDI Approach to Infer Student's Emotions in an Intelligent Learning Environment, Computers and Education, England (2005)
7. Conati, C.: Probabilistic assessment of user's emotions in educational games. Journal of Applied Artificial Intelligence 16(7-8), 555–575 (2002)
8. Cheng, R., Vassileva, J.: Adaptive Reward Mechanism for Sustainable Online Learning Community. In: AI in Education (AIED) 2005, July 18-22, pp. 152–159. IOS Press, Amsterdam (2005)
9. Ding, Z., Peng, Y.: A probabilistic extension to ontology language OWL. In: Hawaii International Conference On System Sciences (2004)
10. Gluz, J.C., Flores, C.D., Seixas, L., Vicari, R.M.: Formal analysis of a probabilistic knowledge communication framework. In: IBERAMIA/SBIA Joint Conference (2006)
11. Boff, E., Santos, E.R., Vicari, R.M.: Social agents to improve collaboration on an educational portal. In: IEEE International Conference on Advanced Learning Technologies, pp. 896–900. IEEE Computer Society Press, Los Alamitos (2006)
12. Piaget, J.: Explanation in sociology, Sociological studies, New York: Routledge (1995)
13. Vygotsky, L.S.: The collected works of L.S. Vygotsky, vol. 1–6, pp. c1987–c1999. Plenum Press, New York.
14. Ortony, A., Clore, G.L., Collins, A.: The cognitive structure of emotions. Cambridge University Press, Cambridge (1988)
15. Dean, M., Schreiber, G.: OWL Web Ontology Language Reference, Technical report, W3C (February 2004)
16. Santos, E.R., Fagundes, M., Vicari, R.M.: An Ontology-Based Approach to Interoperability for Bayesian Agents. In: International Conference on Autonomous Agents and Multiagent Systems, 2007, Honolulu. Proceedings of AAMAS (2007)
17. Stanford University, The Protégé Ontology Editor and Knowledge Acquisition System, Available from http://protege.stanford.edu

18. Carroll, J.J., Dickinson, I., Dollin, C., Reynolds, D., Seaborne, A., Wilkinson, K.: Jena: Implementing the semantic web recommendations, Technical Report, Hewlett Packard Laboratories (2003)
19. Bellifemine, F., Poggi, A., Rimassa, G.: JADE – A FIPA-compliant agent framework. In: 4th International Conference and Exhibition on The Practical Application of Intelligent Agents and Multi-Agent Technology, pp. 97–108 (1999)

# Knowledge Engineering and Planning for the Automated Synthesis of Customized Learning Designs

Luis Castillo[1], Lluvia Morales[1], Arturo González-Ferrer[2],
Juan Fdez-Olivares[1], and Óscar García-Pérez[3]

[1]Dpto. Ciencias de la Computación e I.A.University of Granada
[2]Centro de Enseñanzas Virtuales. University of Granada
[3]IActive Intelligent Solutions

**Abstract.** This paper describes an approach to automatically obtain an HTN planning domain from a well structured learning objects repository and also to apply an HTN planner to obtain IMS Learning Designs adapted to the features and needs of every student.

## 1 Introduction

Nowadays, distance learning is positioning as a key tool not only for graduate courses but also for professionals continuing education. In these areas, the heterogeneity of students, their different performance and needs and previous studies force current e-learning platforms to highlight the issue of customizing learning designs so that every student may optimally exploit the contents of a given course. This is not new, and the need to adapt learning designs is carefully described in current standards for learning management systems (LMS). Educational metadata (IEEE-LOM [1] or IMS-MD [5]) allows instructors to classify learning resources according to a set of variables. Student profiles (IMS-LIP [5]) are also represented to gather information about their features.And, finally, learning designs (IMS-LD [5]) allow instructors to adapt the learning path and the use of learning resources to the features and capabilities of every student.

The use of these standards, amongst others, is fostering a common language and new interoperability capabilities between all the entities involved in e-learning activities. Even more, different learning objects could be potentially shared between different platforms. However, the process of building a learning design is a very complex task, that must be manually developed by the instructor.

This paper focuses on making the life of instructors easier, thanks to the use of artificial intelligence planning techniques [4,3] able to automatically obtain a learning design customized to every student needs and features. These techniques have been usually employed to help experts of different fields to define their strategic plans like in aerospatial domains , civil emergencies or military campaigns . However, they are also specially useful for the design of learning paths, since they can both explore all the possibilities of the available learning

D. Borrajo, L. Castillo, and J.M. Corchado (Eds.): CAEPIA 2007, LNAI 4788, pp. 40–49, 2007.

resources, its different learning objects and their features, and also take into account the features and needs of every student in order to elaborate, like in those strategic plans, the best learning path for every student.

We must say that the use of artificial intelligence planning techniques in real applications imply a great knowledge engineering effort in order to acquire and validate the available know-how of every domain and to encode this knowledge into a set of rules or protocols which is usually named the planning domain. A planning domain is the core of any planning application that guides the search effort of the planner and it is usually written in the Planning Domain Description Language [6] or any of its flavours [3]. This important effort has been an obstacle for the practical application of planning techniques and the technical part of this paper is devoted to show that this planning domain may be automatically generated from a well structured domain like the learning objects repository of a LMS. In order to do that, we propose an exhaustive labeling of learning objects making use of the IMS-MD or IEEE-LOM standards and an inference procedure that explores all the metadata and relations to generate a valid planning domain. Later on, a state-of-the art planning algorithm might be used to obtain a customized learning design for every student. Given that most LMS are intended to use these standard metadata, our approach could be directly used in any of them just by checking for a correct labeling of learning objects. These contributions are aligned towards an important horizon: enable end users (instructors and students) to easily adopt e-learning standards at a low cost.

## 2   HTN Planning Foundations

In order to better understand the main contributions of this paper, a brief introduction to HTN planning techniques [4] is presented first. HTN (Hierarchical Task Network) planning is a family of artificial intelligence planners that have shown to be very powerful in practical applications on very different domains. HTN planning paradigm is based on the same three concepts that any other planning approach. The initial state is a set of literals that describe the facts that are true at the beginning of the problem; this would be the students' profile. The goal is a description of what we want to achieve with a plan, that is, the learning goals. The domain is the set of available actions or rules to achieve the goals. In our case, the available learning objects.

### 2.1   HTN Planning Domains

HTN planning domains are designed in terms of a hierarchy of compositional activities. Lowest level activities, named actions or primitive operators, are non-decomposable activities which basically encode changes in the environment of the problem. In our approach, these primitive operators are represented as PDDL 2.1 level 3 durative actions. On the other hand, high level activities, named tasks, are compound actions that may be decomposed into lower level activities. Depending on the problem at hand, every task may be decomposed following different schemes, or methods, into different sets of sub-activities. These sub-activities may be either tasks, which could be further decomposed, or just actions. Tasks and their, possibly multiple, decompositions encode domain dependent rules for obtaining a plan, that can only be composed of primitive actions. Unlike non HTN planners, HTN goals are not specified as a well formed formula that must be made true by the plan from the initial state. Instead, goals are described as a partially ordered set of tasks that need to be carried out. And finally, the main HTN planning algorithm takes the set of tasks to be achieved, explores the space of possible decompositions replacing a given task by its component activities, until the set of goal tasks is transformed into a set of only primitive actions that make up the plan.

HTN planning domains are usually written after a knowledge engineering stage in which the know-how of the problem is studied and formally represented [10,3]. This stage requires a strong commitment of domain's experts and a deep knowledge of planning techniques, so it is not an easy task. However, in problems with an underlying strongly structured knowledge like a learning objects repository with an exhaustive metadata labeling, this domain could be automatically extracted as will be shown in the following sections.

## 3   Our Approach

The main idea behind this approach is that AI planning techniques may be used to automatically generate a customized learning design based on the following assumptions: (1) The learning objects repository is labeled using a extensive set of standard metadata that is described along this section. (2) The instructor explores the repository and define the learning objectives of a given course. (3) Our system explores the different databases of users profiles, learning objects and learning objectives and generates the necessary PDDL files [6,3] for our HTN planner to run. The planner is executed and a customized learning plan is obtained for every student registered at the same course. (4) The learning plan is translated into a form playable or understandable by the LMS. (5) The plan is executed (or played) by the student to follow the course adapted to its own features and needs.

In order to guarantee a valid extraction of an HTN planning domain and a successful adaptation of the learning path, at least the following set of metadata are required to be present in the labeling of the learning objects[1]:

**Hierarchical structure.** Hierarchical relations of the form chapter/sub-chapter/ lesson, being lesson the atomic part of the hierarchy, are encoded by means of the `is-part-of` relational metadata. This allows to encode hierarchical dependencies between learning objects. A learning path, that is, the sequence of learning objects that is to be followed by student will only be made up of atomic objects. This means that compound objects might

---
[1] There is a wider variety of metadata that allow for a greater adaptation capability to the features of every student. They have not been included due to lack of space.

have no content, except those included in their constituent atomic objects and they primarily act as the underlying structure of the course. (Figure 1).

**Ordering relations.** The order relation or sequence between learning objects defined by the instructor, in the case that they exist, are encoded by means of the `is-based-on` relational metadata. Figure 1 shows a simple example so far.

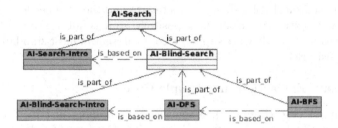

**Fig. 1.** A simple labeling of learning objects showing a piece of a classic Artificial Intelligence course chapter devoted to search: After a brief introduction, the sections about depth-first search (DFS) and breadth-first search (BFS) exactly in this order. Lowest level objects (atomic) appear shadowed.

**Content dependencies.** Sometimes, the content of a given chapter or sub-chapter depends on other chapters of the same repository. Since the student may or may not have background knowledge on these dependencies, they are encoded my means of the relational metadata `requires`. For example, the chapter `AI-Search` depends on knowledge about graphs, that belongs to a learning object of another course. This dependency is encoded to allow the planning algorithm to reason about the convenience or not of including a chapter about graphs in a given learning path: if the student does not know about graphs, it would be strongly required to pass first this chapter, otherwise, it would be ignored. (Figure 3)

**Optional lessons.** These are lessons that may be included or not in a learning path depending on some conditions, usually the global time span of the course. This is encoded by means of the general metadata `coverage` that is labeled with the constant `optional`. If this metadata is empty, then the learning object is intended to be mandatory.

**Different languages.** Our approach is also intended to cope with repositories handling different languages so that the planner may or may not may select some learning objects depending on a student's knowledge of other languages. It is encoded with the general metadata `language`.

**Typical Learning Time.** The educational metadata is a very important issue to successfully encode a learning path given the temporal constraints imposed by the course, the student or both.

**Type of resources.** Every resource, that is, a learning object, in the repository must be labeled with the educational metadata `learning-resource-type` (a lesson, an example, an excercise, etc).

**Hardware/Software requirements.** In the case that a given learning object would require special hardware or software features (like multimedia files, for example) this could be used for the planner to reason about its inclusion or not in the learning path depending on the declared HW/SW platform of every student. This is encoded in the technical metadata other-platform-requirements.

These are standard IEEE-LOM [1] metadata and they are needed to ensure a correct domain extraction from the repository, so it is not a heavy requirement of our approach, since they are supposed to be present in most standard learning objects repositories.

## 3.1   Domain Extraction in a Simple Case

In the simplest case (Figure 1), a repository containing just hierarchical and sequencing metadata may be intuitively translated into an HTN domain as those presented earlier just by exploring these relations. Compound objects (those with any "child object") would be translated into a compound task and simple objects (those with no children) would be translated into non-decomposable actions. Therefore, the simple repository shown in Figure 1 would be translated into the HTN domain shown in Figure 2

```
(:task AI-Search
 :parameters (?student)
 (:method One
  :tasks (
          (AI-Search-Intro ?student)
          (AI-Blind-Search ?student))))
(:task AI-Blind-Search
 :parameters (?student)
 (:method One
  :tasks (
          (AI-Blind-Search-Intro ?student)
          (AI-DFS ?student)
          (AI-BFS ?student))))
```

```
(:durative-action AI-Search-Intro
 :parameters(?student)
 :duration (= ?duration
             (typical-learning-time AI-Search-Intro))
 :condition()
 :effect(passed ?student AI-Search-Intro))
(:durative-action AI-DFS
 :parameters(?student)
 :duration (= ?duration
             (typical-learning-time AI-DFS))
 :condition()
 :effect(passed ?student AI-DFS))
```

**Fig. 2.** Part of the domain extracted from the sample repository of Figure 1

## 3.2   Domain Extraction in Complex General Cases

The simple domain extraction procedure roughly sketched before is too simple and it does not allow for a full adaptation of the learning path, taking into account the full set of metadata present in the repository (Figure 3). This section fully describes a domain extraction procedure that completely fits into the expected adaptation scheme represented in these metadata. Let us consider the repository shown in Figure 3

**Extracting Primitive Actions.** HTN primitive actions are extracted from those learning objects that have no children. These actions will take into account the following issues. The duration of the action will be its typical learning time. If there are some special hardware requirements or it has been written in a language different than the common language of the course, then the list of preconditions

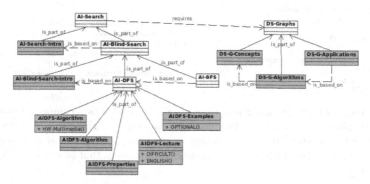

**Fig. 3.** A labeling of learning objects slightly more complex than Figure 1. Lowest level objects (atomic) appear shadowed.

will include these conditions for the action to be included. Figure 4 shows two actions that exhibit these preconditions so they will only be included in the learning path if the profile of the student meets these conditions.

```
(:durative-action AIDFS-Algorithm
 :parameters(?student)
 :duration (= ?duration
    (typical-learning-time AIDFS-Algorithm))
 :condition(hardware ?student multimedia)
 :effect(passed ?student AIDFS-Algorithm))
```

```
(:durative-action AIDFS-Lecture
 :parameters(?student)
 :duration (= ?duration
    (typical-learning-time AIDFS-Lecture))
 :condition(>= (mark ?student english) 50)
 :effect(passed ?student AIDFS-Lecture))
```

**Fig. 4.** Action `AIDFS-Algorithm` requires the student hardware platform to have multimedia capabilities. Action `AIDFS-lecture` is written in english, a foreign language for the student, and it requires the student to have a satisfactory mark registered in its profile (at least 50 out of 100).

For every atomic learning object labeled as "optional", a new task is created with two different methods, one of them includes its corresponding action and the other does not. For example, Figure 5 shows how the optional object `AIDFS-Examples` is treated.

As may be seen in Figure 3, there may be more than one atomic object with the same name (i.e. there are two objects with name `AIDFS-Algorithm`). This means that they are different ways of performing the same learning act and, probably, under different conditions. This allows the student to follow a given lesson although the lesson offered to each student might be different depending on their context. This is encoded as an additional compound task that includes a unique method containing a single action. There will be a primitive action for each atomic object so that, the compound task forces the introduction of one of these actions that will be found by the planner by search and backtracking in the case that the conditions of the actions are not met (see Figure 6).

**Extracting Compound Tasks.** The previous domain extraction procedure allows to generate the primitive actions of an HTN domain and some additional

```
(:task OPTIONAL-AIDFS-Examples
 :parameters (?student)
 (:method Yes                                    (:durative-action AIDFS-Examples
  :precondition ()                                :parameters(?student)
  :tasks (                                        :duration (= ?duration
          (AIDFS-Examples ?student)))                       (typical-learning-time AIDFS-Example))
 (:method No                                      :condition()
  :precondition ()                                :effect(passed ?student AIDFS-Example))
  :tasks ()))
```

**Fig. 5.** Action `AIDFS-Examples` is optional. This is encoded as a compound task with two alternative decompositions. The first one, labeled as "Yes" tries to include the object `AIDFS-Examples`. If a backtracking is produced during the search, then the method labeled as "No" introduces an empty decomposition, that is, it does not include the object.

```
                                                 (:durative-action AIDFS-Algorithm
                                                  :parameters(?student)
                                                  :duration (= ?duration
(:task MULTIPLE-AIDFS-Algorithm                     (typical-learning-time AIDFS-Algorithm))
 :parameters (?student)                            :condition(hardware ?student multimedia)
 (:method Unique                                   :effect(passed ?student AIDFS-Algorithm))
  :precondition ()                                (:durative-action AIDFS-Algorithm
  :tasks (                                          :parameters(?student)
          (AIDFS-Algorithm ?student))))             :duration (= ?duration
                                                      (typical-learning-time AIDFS-Algorithm))
                                                    :condition()
                                                    :effect(passed ?student AIDFS-Algorithm))
```

**Fig. 6.** Part of the domain extracted from the sample repository of Figure 3. Action `AIDFS-Algorithm` may be included in any of the forms present in the domain to adapt the learning path to the existing conditions

compound tasks to encode part of the adaptation scheme. This will enable the planner to adapt a learning path to the individual features of every student. However, there are still more possibilities to encode additional adaptation schemes in the repository so that the search capability of the planner is increased. They are related to the decomposition of a compound task. There may be compound actions, like `DS-Graphs` in Figure 3 whose constituents parts are fully ordered and, therefore, they will always be included in the same order in any learning path. However, other compound tasks like `AI-DFS` do not have its constituents objects fully ordered. This means that the order in which these objects will be included in a learning path is not always the same and it may depend on some external conditions. In order to represent this, implicit ordering relations are defined in our approach to encode different orderings for every compound task based on the `learning-resource-type` of every object. For example, the following rule

((TRUE) (Problem-statement Simulation Experiment Exercise Lecture))

would mean that in every possible situation in which the order of the component objects is not explicitly defined by the instructor, the ordering in which they appear in the task will be the following: first the object labeled with `learning-resource-type` equal to `problem-statement`, then those labeled as`simulation`, those labeled as `experiment`, the objects labeled as `exercise` and at the end, those labeled as `lecture`.These other rules encode a more interesting example:

```
((Honey-Alonso-Learning-Type ?student Theorist)
  (Problem-statement Simulation Experiment Exercise Lecture))
((Honey-Alonso-Learning-Type ?student Pragmatic)
  (Simulation Experiment ExerciseProblem-statement Lecture))
```

They mean that the decomposition of a compound object depends on the registered Honey-Alonso learning profile of every student. For example, these two previous rules would produce the decomposition scheme for task AI-DFS shown in Figure 7.

```
(:task AI-DFS
  :parameters (?student)
  (:method Pragmatic                                      (:method Theorist
    :precondition (learning-type ?student pragmatic)        :precondition (learning-type ?student theorist)
    :tasks (                                                :tasks (
(MULTIPLE-AIDFS-Algorithm ?student)                              (AIDFS-Properties ?student)
      (AIDFS-Examples ?student)                            (MULTIPLE-AIDFS-Algorithm ?student)
      (AIDFS-Properties ?student)                               (AIDFS-Examples ?student)
      (AIDFS-Lecture ?student)))                                (AIDFS-Lecture ?student))))
```

**Fig. 7.** Task AI-DFS is decomposed depending on the Honey-Alonso learning profile of the student

And finally, there is the case that a compound object requires another object that belong to any other course. Figure 3 shows that the object AI-Search depends on the object DS-Graphs that belongs to another course, let say Data Structures. In this case, the task AI-Search includes two different decompositions, one of then for the case that the student has successfully passed this required object, and the other one for the case that the student has not passed this object and thus, will have to be included in his/her learning path.

In summary, this section has shown that a valid HTN domain may be extracted from a well structured learning objects repository just by exploring a set of standard metadata present in most LMS[2].

## 4  Obtaining a Plan

The application of this procedure to a learning objects repository would produce a file named "domain.pddl" that is one of the components for any PDDL-compliant planner. This file will be the same for every student since it only contains the translation of the learning objects repository into a PDDL domain. However, for the planner to run, there is another file that must be present. It is usually named "problem.pddl" and it encodes, both, the initial state and the goal of the problem. In terms of a LMS, the initial state encodes student profiles and the goal encodes the learning goals.

Students profiles are extracted from the LMS' databases following the IMS-LIP [5] standard or any other equivalent formalism. These profiles will contain all

---

[2] There is a preamble of the HTN planning domain in PDDL, but it is practically always the same and it is not included here.

the available information about the student that will make the planner to search and backtrack amongst the available tasks and actions in the translated domain and, therefore, to optimally adapt the desired learning path to its features and needs.

Learning goals are defined by the instructor amongst the list of compound tasks available in the domain (i.e. the highest level learning objects) and they will appear totally ordered in the goal section of the pddl problem. Figure 8 shows a piece of this problem. As may be seen, there are two students, Peter and Clark, Peter doest not have any temporal constraint[3] to end the course, but Clark needs to end the course in less than 320 minutes.

```
(define (problem simple)
(:domain test)
(:objects                              (:tasks-goal
  Peter, Clark - student)                :tasks [
(:init                                     (AI-Search Peter)
  (learning-type Peter pragmatic)          ((<= ?end 320) (AI-Search Clark))
  (= (mark Peter english) 50)            ]
  (passed Peter DS-Graphs)             )
  (hardware Peter multimedia) ...))
```

**Fig. 8.** The problem of the PDDL scenario is also automatically extracted from the LMS databases, both the initial state (students profiles) and the goal (learning goals asserted by the instructor)

Once the domain and the problem have been translated from the LMS repository and databases into PDDL compliant files, the HTN planner [3] is executed and an adapted learning path is obtained for each of the students included in the problem. This plan may be easily encoded in a IMS-LD, packaged in a IMS-CP that contains all the involved learning objects and delivered for execution in most LMS. The procedure described along this paper has been implemented in Python and fully integrated in the ILIAS LMS [9], which embeds a SOAP (Simple Object Access Protocol) server, so that several Python scripts implement the extraction procedures described so far, just by using the available SOAP functions, and obtain the domain and problem files. The SIADEX HTN planner [3] is then executed and a plan is obtained. ILIAS does not support IMS-LD specification yet, so in order to make the plan available to student, we have translated the plan into a follow up guideline that appears over the student' ILIAS desktop.

## 5   Related Work

There are several approaches in the literature that shows the relative success of AIP&S technologies for the assisted design of learning paths, either for HTN planners [2] or non HTN planners [8]. In all these approaches, the planning domain cannot be encoded by the instructor, but by a person with deep knowledge on AIP&S and PDDL. This means that any change in the learning objects repository has to be recoded again, making the instructor to depend on third persons. Our approach clearly grants the independence of instructors and reduces the cost of using AIP&S to zero.

# 6   Concluding Remarks

This paper has presented an integrated approach able to extract a planning domain from a well structured learning objects repository just by exploring the standard metadata labeling present in the objects. This is just a first step towards the automatic use of an HTN planner able to obtain customized learning paths adapted to every student' needs and features. The use of an artificial intelligence HTN planner allows for a fast and robust generation of adapted learning designs with respect to typical learning designs that had to be manually encoded in a long and boring process. The main obstacle for the practical use of AI HTN planners, i.e. the design of the planning domain, has also been overcome without any intervention of instructors.

However there is still an issue that needs further study: the adaptation of the learning path to run-time information like the result of intermediate evaluations during the development of a course. We are pursuing a continual planning approach [7] in which the planning of a whole course with intermediate evaluations is neglected in favour of a sequence of planning episodes, each planning episode happening between every two consecutive evaluations. It is clear that if a course has no intermediate evaluations, then the continual planning approach is not necessary and a unique plan is enough to cover the whole development of a course.

# References

1. ANSI/IEEE. IEEE Standard for Learning Object Metadata.
   http://ltsc.ieee.org/wg12/
2. Ullrich, C.: Course Generation Based on HTN Planning. In: Proceedings of 13th Annual Workshop of the SIG Adaptivity and User Modeling in Interactive Systems, pp. 74–79 (2005)
3. Castillo, L., Fdez-Olivares, J., García-Pérez, O., Palao, F.: Efficiently handling temporal knowledge in an HTN planner. In: Sixteenth International Conference on Automated Planning and Scheduling, ICAPS (2006)
4. Ghallab, M., Nau, D., Traverso, P.: Automated planning: theory and practice. Morgan Kaufmann, San Francisco (2004)
5. IMS-GLC. IMS Global Learning Consortium. http://www.imsglobal.org/
6. Long, D., Fox, M.: PDDL2.1: An Extension to PDDL for Expressing Temporal Planning Domains. Journal of Artificial Intelligence Research 20, 61–124 (2003)
7. Myers, K.L.: CPEF: A continuous planning and execution framework. AI Magazine 20(4), 63–69 (1999)
8. R-Moreno, M.D., Camacho, D.: AI techniques for Automatic Learning Design. In: International electronic Conference on Computer Science (IeCCS-2006) (2006)
9. ILIAS Learning Management System. ILIAS website.
   http://www.ilias.de/ios/index-e.html
10. Wilkins, D.E., DesJardin, M.: A call for knowledge-based planning. AI Magazine 22(1), 99–115 (2001)

# On the Initialization of Two-Stage Clustering with Class-GTM

Raúl Cruz-Barbosa[1,2] and Alfredo Vellido[1]

[1] Universitat Politècnica de Catalunya, Jordi Girona, 08034, Barcelona, Spain
{rcruz,avellido}@lsi.upc.edu
www.lsi.upc.edu/dept/investigacion/sectia/soco
[2] Universidad Tecnológica de la Mixteca, Car. Acatlima km. 2.5, 69000, Huajuapan, Oaxaca, México

**Abstract.** Generative Topographic Mapping is a probabilistic model for data clustering and visualization. It maps points, considered as prototype representatives of data clusters, from a low dimensional latent space onto the observed data space. In semi-supervised settings, class information can be added resulting in a model variation called class-GTM. The number of class-GTM latent points used is usually large for visualization purposes and does not necessarily reflect the class structure of the data. It is therefore convenient to group the clusters further in a two-stage procedure. In this paper, class-GTM is first used to obtain the basic cluster prototypes. Two novel methods are proposed to use this information as prior knowledge for the K-means-based second stage. We evaluate, using an entropy measure, whether these methods retain the class separability capabilities of class-GTM in the two-stage process, and whether the two-stage procedure improves on the direct clustering of the data using K-means.

## 1 Introduction

Amongst density-based methods, Finite Mixture Models have established themselves as a flexible and robust tool for multivariate data clustering [1]. In many practical data analysis scenarios, though, the available knowledge concerning the cluster structure of the data may be quite limited. In these cases, data exploration techniques are valuable tools and, amongst them, multivariate data visualization can be of great help by providing the analyst with intuitive cues about data structural patterns. In order to endow Finite Mixture Models with data visualization capabilities, certain constraints must be enforced. One alternative is forcing the model components to be centred in a low-dimensional manifold embedded into the usually high-dimensional observed data space. Such approach is the basis for the definition of Generative Topographic Mapping (GTM) [2], a flexible manifold learning model for simultaneous data clustering and visualization whose probabilistic nature makes possible to extend it to perform tasks such as missing data imputation [3], robust handling of outliers [4], and unsupervised feature selection [5], amongst others.

D. Borrajo, L. Castillo, and J.M. Corchado (Eds.): CAEPIA 2007, LNAI 4788, pp. 50–59, 2007.

Finite Mixture Models can also be used beyond unsupervised learning in order to account for class-related information in supervised or semi-supervised settings [6]. Class information can be integrated as part of the GTM training to enrich the cluster structure definition provided by the model [7,8]. The resulting class-GTM model is the basis of this paper.

GTM in general and class-GTM in particular do not place any strong restriction on the number of mixture components (or clusters), in order to achieve an appropriate visualization of the data. This richly detailed cluster structure does not necessarily match the more global cluster and class distributions of the data. For that reason, a two-stage clustering procedure may be useful in this scenario [9]. Class-GTM can be used in the first stage to generate a detailed cluster partition in the form of a mixture of components. The centres of these components, also known as prototypes, can be further clustered in the second stage. For that role, the well-known K-means algorithm is used in this study. The issue remains of how we should initialize K-means in the second clustering stage. Random initialization, with the subsequent choice of the best solution, was the method selected in [9]. This approach, though, does not make use of the prior knowledge generated in the first stage of the procedure. Here, we propose two different ways of introducing such prior knowledge in the initialization of the second stage K-means, without compromising the final clusterwise class separation capabilities of the model. This fixed initialization procedures allow significant computational savings.

The outline of the remaining of the paper is as follows: In section 2, we summarily introduce the GTM and its class-GTM variant, as well as the two-stage clustering procedure with its alternative initialization strategies. Several experimental results are provided and discussed in section 3, while a final section outlines some conclusions and directions for future research.

## 2  Two-Stage Clustering

The two-stage clustering procedure outlined in the introduction is described in this section. The first stage model, namely class-GTM, is introduced first. This is followed by the details of different initialization strategies for the second stage. We propose two novel second stage fixed initialization strategies that take advantage of the prior knowledge obtained in the first stage.

### 2.1  The Class-GTM Model

The standard GTM is a non-linear latent variable model defined as a mapping from a low dimensional latent space onto the multivariate data space. The mapping is carried through by a set of basis functions generating a constrained mixture density distribution. It is defined as a generalized linear regression model:

$$\mathbf{y} = \phi(\mathbf{u})\mathbf{W}, \tag{1}$$

where $\phi$ is a set of $M$ basis functions $\phi(\mathbf{u}) = (\phi_1(\mathbf{u}), ..., \phi_M(\mathbf{u}))$. For continuous data of dimension $D$, spherically symmetric Gaussians

$$\phi_m(\mathbf{u}) = \exp\left\{-1/2\sigma^2 \|\mathbf{u} - \mu_m\|^2\right\} \tag{2}$$

are an obvious choice of basis function, with centres $\mu_m$ and common width $\sigma$; $\mathbf{W}$ is a matrix of adaptive weights $w_{md}$ that defines the mapping, and $\mathbf{u}$ is a point in latent space. To avoid computational intractability a regular grid of $K$ points $\mathbf{u}_k$ can be sampled from the latent space. Each of them, which can be considered as the representative of a data cluster, has a fixed prior probability $p(\mathbf{u}_k) = 1/K$ and is mapped, using (1), into a low dimensional manifold non-linearly embedded in the data space. This latent space grid is similar in design and purpose to that of the visualization space of the SOM. A probability distribution for the multivariate data $\mathbf{X} = \{\mathbf{x}_n\}_{n=1}^{N}$ can then be defined, leading to the following expression for the log-likelihood:

$$L(\mathbf{W}, \beta | \mathbf{X}) = \sum_{n=1}^{N} \ln \left\{ \frac{1}{K} \sum_{k=1}^{K} \left(\frac{\beta}{2\pi}\right)^{D/2} \exp\left\{-\beta/2 \|\mathbf{y}_k - \mathbf{x}_n\|^2\right\} \right\} \tag{3}$$

where $\mathbf{y}_k$, usually known as *reference* or *prototype* vectors, are obtained for each $\mathbf{u}_k$ using (1); and $\beta$ is the inverse of the noise variance, which accounts for the fact that data points might not strictly lie on the low dimensional embedded manifold generated by the GTM. The EM algorithm is an straightforward alternative to obtain the Maximum Likelihood (ML) estimates of the adaptive parameters of the model, namely $\mathbf{W}$ and $\beta$.

The class-GTM model is an extension of GTM and therefore inherits most of its properties. The main goal of this extension is to improve class separability in the clustering results of GTM. For this purpose, we assume that the clustering model accounted for the available class information. This can be achieved by modelling the joint density $p(C, \mathbf{X})$, instead of $p(\mathbf{X})$, for a given set of classes $\{T_i\}$. For the Gaussian version of the GTM model [7,8], such approach entails the calculation of the posterior probability of a cluster representative $\mathbf{u}_k$ given the data point $\mathbf{x}_n$ and its corresponding class label $c_n$, or class-conditional *responsibility* $\hat{z}_{kn}^c = p(\mathbf{u}_k | \mathbf{x}_n, c_n)$, as part of the E step of the EM algorithm. It can be calculated as:

$$\hat{z}_{kn}^c = \frac{p(\mathbf{x}_n, c_n | \mathbf{u}_k)}{\sum\limits_{k'=1}^{K} p(\mathbf{x}_n, c_n | \mathbf{u}_{k'})} = \frac{p(\mathbf{x}_n | \mathbf{u}_k)p(c_n | \mathbf{u}_k)}{\sum\limits_{k'=1}^{K} p(\mathbf{x}_n | \mathbf{u}_{k'})p(c_n | \mathbf{u}_{k'})} = \frac{p(\mathbf{x}_n | \mathbf{u}_k)p(\mathbf{u}_k | c_n)}{\sum\limits_{k'=1}^{K} p(\mathbf{x}_n | \mathbf{u}_{k'})p(\mathbf{u}_{k'} | c_n)}, \tag{4}$$

and, being $T_i$ each class,

$$p(\mathbf{u}_k | T_i) = \frac{\sum_{n;c_n=T_i} p(\mathbf{x}_n | \mathbf{u}_k) / \sum_n p(\mathbf{x}_n | \mathbf{u}_k)}{\sum_{k'} \sum_{n;c_n=T_i} p(\mathbf{x}_n | \mathbf{u}_{k'}) / \sum_n p(\mathbf{x}_n | \mathbf{u}_{k'})}. \tag{5}$$

Equation (4) differs from the standard responsibility $\hat{z}_{kn}$ of GTM in that, instead of imposing a fixed prior $p(\mathbf{u}_k) = 1/K$ on latent space, we consider a class-conditional prior $p(\mathbf{u}_k|T_i)$. Once the class-conditional responsibility is calculated, the rest of the model's parameters are estimated following the standard EM procedure.

## 2.2 Two-Stage Clustering Based on GTM

In the first stage of the proposed two-stage clustering procedure, a class-GTM is trained to obtain the representative prototypes (detailed clustering) of the observed dataset $\mathbf{X}$. As mentioned in the introduction, the number of prototype vectors is usually chosen to be large for visualization purposes, and does not necessarily reflect the global cluster and class structure of the data. In this study, the resulting prototypes $\mathbf{y}_k$ of the class-GTM are further clustered using the K-means algorithm. In a similar two-stage procedure to the one described in [9], based on SOM, the second stage K-means initialization in this study is first randomly replicated 100 times, subsequently choosing the best available result, which is the one that minimizes the error function

$$E = \sum_{k=1}^{C} \sum_{\mathbf{x} \in G_k} \|\mathbf{x} - \mu_k\|^2, \tag{6}$$

where $C$ is the final number of clusters in the second stage and $\mu_k$ is the centre of cluster $G_k$. This approach seems somehow wasteful, though, as the use of GTM instead of SOM can provide us with richer a priori information to be used for fixing the K-means initialization in the second stage.

Two novel fixed initialization strategies that take advantage of the prior knowledge obtained by class-GTM in the first stage are proposed. They are based on two features of the model, namely: the Magnification Factors (MF) and the Cumulative Responsibility (CR). The Magnification Factors measure the level of distorsion of the mapping from the latent to the data spaces. Areas of low data concentration correspond to high distorsions of the mapping (i.e., high MF), whereas areas of high data density correspond to low MF. The MF is described in terms of the derivatives of the basis functions $\phi_j(\mathbf{u})$ in the form:

$$\frac{dA'}{dA} = \det{}^{1/2} \left( \psi^{\mathbf{T}} \mathbf{W}^{\mathbf{T}} \mathbf{W} \psi \right), \tag{7}$$

where $\psi$ has elements $\psi_{ji} = \partial\phi_j/\partial u^i$ [10]. If we choose $C$ to be the final number of clusters for K-means in the second stage, the first proposed fixed initialization strategy will consist on the selection of the class-GTM prototypes corresponding to the $C$ non-contiguous latent points with lowest MF for K-means initialization. That way, the second stage algorithm is meant to start from the areas of highest data density.

As its name suggests, the CR is the sum of responsibilities over all data points in $\mathbf{X}$ for each cluster $k$:

$$CR_k = \sum_{n=1}^{N} \hat{z}_{kn}^c \ . \tag{8}$$

The second proposed fixed initialization strategy, based on CR, is similar in spirit to that based on MF. Again, if we choose $C$ to be the final number of clusters for K-means in the second stage, the fixed initialization strategy will now consist on the selection of the class-GTM prototypes corresponding to the $C$ non-contiguous latent points with highest CR. That is, the second stage algorithm is meant to start from those cluster prototypes that are found to be most responsible for the generation of the observed data.

## 3    Experiments

In this section, we first describe the experimental design and settings. This is followed by a presentation and discussion of the corresponding results.

### 3.1    Experimental Design and Settings

The class-GTM model was implemented in MATLAB®. For the experiments reported next, the adaptive matrix **W** was initialized, following a procedure described in [2], as to minimize the difference between the prototype vectors $y_k$ and the vectors that would be generated in data space by a partial PCA, $m_k = V_2 u_k$, where the columns of matrix $V_2$ are the two principal eigenvectors (given that the latent space considered here is 2-dimensional). Correspondingly, the inverse variance $\beta$ was initialised to be the inverse of the $3^{rd}$ PCA eigenvalue. This ensures the replicability of the results. The value of parameter $\sigma$, describing the common width of the basis functions, was set to 1. The grid of latent points $u_k$ was fixed to a square 13x13 layout for the *ecoli* dataset and to a 20x20 layout for the *oil flow* dataset. Both datasets are summarily described in section 3.2. The corresponding grid of basis functions $\phi$ was equally fixed to a 5x5 square layout for both datasets.

The goals of these experiments are twofold. First, we aim to assess whether a two-stage clustering procedure, where the first stage involves class-GTM and the second stage involves K-means, improves on the class separation capabilities of the straight clustering of the data using the K-means algorithm alone. Secondly, we aim to test whether the second stage initialization procedures based on the Magnification Factors and the Cumulative Responsibility of the class-GTM, described in section 2.2, retain the class separability capabilities of the two-stage clustering procedure in which K-means is randomly initialized. If this is the case, a fixed second stage initialization strategy should entail a substantial reduction of computational time compared to a random second stage initialization requiring a large number (100 in the reported experiments and also in [9]) of algorithm runs.

Beyond the visual exploration that could be provided by class-GTM, the second stage clustering results should be explicitly quantified in terms of class separability. For that purpose, the following entropy-like measure is proposed:

$$E_{C_k}(\{T_i\}) = -\sum_{\{C_k\}} P(C_k) \sum_{\{T_i\}} P(T_i|C_k) \ln P(T_i|C_k) = -\sum_{k=1}^{K} \frac{N_k}{N} \sum_{i=1}^{|\{T_i\}|} p_{ki} \ln p_{ki}\ .$$

(9)

Sums are performed over the set of classes $\{T_i\}$ and the class-GTM clusters $\{C_k\}$; $N$ is the total number of prototypes; $N_k$ is the number of prototypes assigned to the $k^{th}$ cluster; $p_{ki} = \frac{n_{ki}}{N_k}$, where $n_{ki}$ is the number of prototypes from class $i$ assigned to cluster $k$; and, finally, $|\{T_i\}|$ is the cardinality of the set of classes. The minimum possible entropy value is 0, which corresponds to the case of no clusters being assigned prototypes corresponding to more than one class.

Given that the use of a second stage in the clustering procedure is intended to provide final clusters that best reflect the overall structure of the data, the problem remains of what is the most adequate number of clusters. This is a time-honoured matter of debate, which goes beyond the scope of this paper, and many cluster validity indices have been defined over the years. In this paper we use the widely known Davies-Bouldin (DB) index [11,9] to provide us with some indication of what the adequate number of final clusters might be. According to the DB index, the best clustering minimizes

$$\frac{1}{C} \sum_{k=1}^{C} \max_{l \neq k} \left\{ \frac{S_c(G_k) + S_c(G_l)}{d_{ce}(G_k, G_l)} \right\},$$

(10)

where $C$ is the number of clusters; $S_c$ is a within-cluster distance named centroid distance and is calculated as $S_c = \frac{\sum_{\mathbf{y}_i \in G_k} \|\mathbf{y}_i - \mu_k\|}{N_k}$, $N_k$ is the number of samples in cluster $G_k$; and $d_{ce}$ is a between-clusters distance named centroid linkage defined as $d_{ce}(G_k, G_l) = \|\mu_k - \mu_l\|$.

## 3.2 Results and Discussion

In the first stage of the two-stage clustering procedure, class-GTM was trained to model two datasets taken, in turn, from the UCI and the Pattern Recognition and Machine Learning book[1] repositories: *ecoli* and *oil flow*. The resulting prototypes $\mathbf{y}_k$ were then clustered in the second stage using the K-means algorithm. This last stage was performed in three different ways, as described in section 2. In the first one, K-means was randomly initialized 100 times, selecting the results corresponding to the minimum of the error function in (6). In the second, we used the Magnification Factors of class-GTM as prior knowledge for the initialization of K-means. In the third, Cumulative Responsibility was used as prior knowledge. In all cases, K-means was forced to yield a given number of final clusters, from 2 up to 13. The DB index and the final entropy were calculated for all the above procedures and numbers of clusters.

The DB index results for the experiments with *ecoli*, including the direct clustering of the data with K-means alone, are reported in Fig. 1. *Ecoli* consists of 336 7-dimensional points belonging to 8 classes representing protein location

---

[1] http://research.microsoft.com/~cmbishop/PRML/webdatasets/datasets.htm

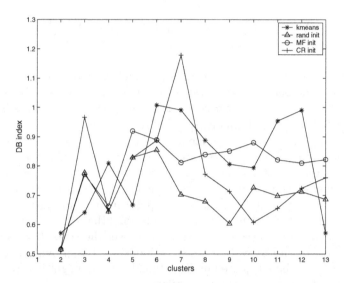

**Fig. 1.** DB index for the clustering of *ecoli* using two-stage clustering with different initializations (based on Magnification Factors (MF init), Cumulative Responsibility (CR init) and random (rand init)), and K-means alone

sites, 3 of which are very small, i.e., the data set is strongly class-unbalanced. It is therefore unsurprising that the results in Fig. 1 do not provide a clear pattern. They nevertheless suggest that no more of 4 clusters (for two-stage clustering) or 5 (for direct K-means) represent an adequate solution. In fact, there are only 4 main groups in *ecoli*, namely: cytoplasm, periplasm, inner membrane and outer membrane. Some relatively good solutions are also suggested for 8 or 9 clusters using the two-stage procedure.

The entropy results for *ecoli* are shown in Fig. 2. Two immediate conclusions can be drawn: First, all the two-stage clustering procedures based on class-GTM perform much better than direct K-means clustering in terms of class separation in the resulting clusters. Second, random initialization in the second stage of the clustering procedure does not entail any significant advantage over the proposed fixed initialization strategies across the whole range of possible final number of clusters, while being far more costly in computational terms.

The DB index results for the experiments with *oil flow*, also including the direct clustering of the data with K-means, are reported in Fig. 3. *Oil flow*, firstly used in [12], simulate non-intrusive measurements by gamma densitometry from a pipeline transporting a mixture of gas, oil, and water. It consists of 1000 points described by 12 attributes. Three types of flow configuration are used as class information labels. The results in Fig. 3 do not indicate any clear number of clusters when data are grouped directly by K-means without any class information. Instead, for the two-stage procedure based on class-GTM there is no indication that more than 4 clusters would provide any substantial improvement.

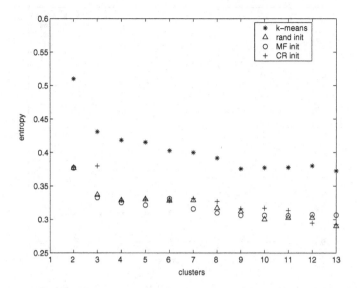

**Fig. 2.** Entropy measurements for two stage and K-means alone clusterings of *ecoli*. Legend as in Fig. 1.

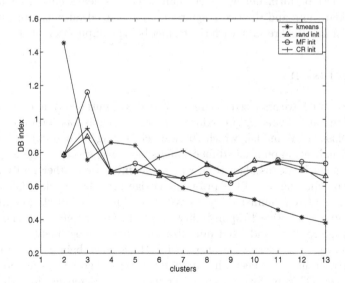

**Fig. 3.** DB index for the clustering of *oil flow* using two-stage clustering with different initializations and K-means alone. Legend as in Fig. 1.

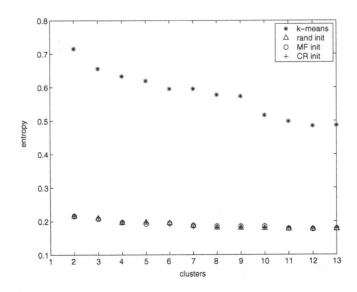

**Fig. 4.** Entropy measurements for two stage and K-means alone clusterings of *oil flow*.
Legend as in Fig. 1.

The entropy results for *oil flow* are shown in Fig. 4 and they are fully consistent with the results for *ecoli*. Again, the two-stage clustering procedures based on class-GTM perform much better than direct K-means clustering in terms of class separation, and the two-stage random and fixed initialization strategies yield almost identical results, with the former being computationally more costly.

## 4    Conclusion

In this paper we have analysed different strategies of initialization for a two-stage multivariate data clustering procedure. The first stage is based on the manifold learning class-GTM model, which, besides clustering, also provides data and clusters visualization on a low-dimensional space. The second stage is based on the well-known K-means algorithm, which was initialized either multiple times randomly or, making use of the prior knowledge provided by class-GTM in the first stage, in a fixed manner using a novel procedure based on its Magnification Factors and Cumulative Responsibility. Several experiments have shown that the two-stage random and fixed initializations yield almost identical results in terms of clusterwise class separation, with the former being computationally more costly. It has also been shown that the two-stage clustering procedures based on class-GTM perform much better than direct K-means clustering of the data in terms of this clusterwise class separation.

Future research should expand the reach of the analyses to assess whether the class information-enriched class-GTM model performs better than the standard GTM as first stage clustering method. Different cluster validity indices could also be used in order to obtain further guidance on the choice of an appropriate final number of clusters.

**Acknowledgements.** Alfredo Vellido is a researcher within the Ramón y Cajal program of the Spanish MEC and acknowledges funding from the MEC I+D project TIN2006-08114. Raúl Cruz-Barbosa acknowledges SEP-SESIC (PROMEP program) of México for his PhD grant.

# References

1. Figueiredo, M.A.T., Jain, A.K.: Unsupervised learning of finite mixture models. IEEE Transactions on Pattern Analysis and Machine Intelligence 24(3), 381–396 (2002)
2. Bishop, C.M., Svensén, M., Williams, C.K.I.: The Generative Topographic Mapping. Neural Computation 10(1), 215–234 (1998)
3. Vellido, A.: Missing data imputation through GTM as a mixture of t-distributions. Neural Networks 19(10), 1624–1635 (2006)
4. Vellido, A., Lisboa, P.J.G.: Handling outliers in brain tumour MRS data analysis through robust topographic mapping. Computers in Biology and Medicine 36(10), 1049–1063 (2006)
5. Vellido, A., Lisboa, P.J.G., Vicente, D.: Robust analysis of MRS brain tumour data using t-GTM. Neurocomputing 69(7-9), 754–768 (2006)
6. Hastie, T., Tibshirani, R.: Discriminant analysis by Gaussian mixtures. Journal of the Royal Statistical Society (B) 58, 155–176 (1996)
7. Cruz, R., Vellido, A.: On the improvement of brain tumour data clustering using class information. In: Proceedings of the 3rd European Starting AI Researcher Symposium (STAIRS'06), Riva del Garda, Italy (2006)
8. Sun, Y., Tiňo, P., Nabney, I.T.: Visualization of incomplete data using class information constraints. In: Winkler, J., Niranjan, M. (eds.) Uncertainty in Geometric Computations, pp. 165–174. Kluwer Academic Publishers, The Netherlands (2002)
9. Vesanto, J., Alhoniemi, E.: Clustering of the Self-Organizing Map. IEEE Transactions on Neural Networks (2000)
10. Bishop, C.M., Svensén, M., Williams, C.K.I.: Magnification Factors for the GTM algorithm. In: Proceedings of the IEE fifth International Conference on Artificial Neural Networks, pp. 64–69 (1997)
11. Davies, D.L., Bouldin, D.W.: A cluster separation measure. IEEE Trans. on Pattern Analysis and Machine Intelligence 1(2), 224–227 (1979)
12. Bishop, C.M., James, G.D.: Analysis of multiphase flows using dual-energy gamma densitometry and neural networks. Nuclear Instruments and Methods in Physics Research A327, 580–593 (1993)

# Three-Dimensional Anisotropic Noise Reduction with Automated Parameter Tuning: Application to Electron Cryotomography

J.J. Fernández[1,2], S. Li[1], and V. Lucic[3]

[1] MRC Laboratory of Molecular Biology, Hills Road, Cambridge CB2 2QH, UK
[2] Dept. Computer Architecture, University of Almería, Almería 04120, Spain
jjfdez@ual.es
[3] Dept. Structural Biology, Max Planck Institute of Biochemistry, Martinsried, Germany

**Abstract.** This article presents an approach for noise filtering that is based on anisotropic nonlinear diffusion. The method combines edge-preserving noise reduction with a strategy to enhance local structures and a mechanism to further smooth the background. We have provided the method with an automatic mechanism for parameter self-tuning and for stopping the iterative filtering process. The performance of the approach is illustrated with its application to electron cryotomography (cryoET). CryoET has emerged as a leading imaging technique for visualizing the molecular architecture of complex biological specimens. A challenging computational task in this discipline is to increase the extremely low signal-to-noise ratio (SNR) to allow visualization and interpretation of the three-dimensional structures. The filtering method here proposed succeeds in substantially reducing the noise with excellent preservation of the structures.

## 1 Introduction

In many disciplines, raw data acquired from instruments are substantially corrupted by noise. Filtering techniques are then indispensable for a proper interpretation or post-processing. Standard linear filtering techniques based on local averages or Gaussian kernels succeed in reducing the noise, but at expenses of blurring edges and features. Nonlinear filtering techniques achieve better feature preservation as they try to adaptively tune the strength of the smoothing to the local structures found in the image.

Anisotropic nonlinear diffusion (AND) is currently one of the most powerful noise reduction techniques in the field of image processing and computer vision [1]. This technique takes into account the local structures found in the image to filter noise, preserve edges and enhance some features, thus considerably increasing the signal-to-noise ratio (SNR) with no significant quantitative distortions of the signal. Pioneered in 1990 by Perona and Malik [2], in the last decade AND has grown up to become a well-established tool for denoising multidimensional images [1,3,4,5,6] .

Electron cryotomography (cryoET) has emerged as a leading imaging technique for structural analysis of large complex biological specimens at molecular resolution, which is critical to understand the cellular function [7]. CryoET allows the elucidation of the three-dimensional (3D) structure of specimens in their native state, but produces

D. Borrajo, L. Castillo, and J.M. Corchado (Eds.): CAEPIA 2007, LNAI 4788, pp. 60–69, 2007.

extremely low contrast 3D density maps (known as "tomograms" in the field). The poor signal-to-noise ratio (SNR) that tomograms present, around 0.1, severely hinders their visualization and interpretation, and precludes the application of automatic image analysis techniques, such as segmentation or pattern recognition. Therefore sophisticated filtering techniques are indispensable for a proper interpretation of tomograms [6].

In this article an approach to anisotropic nonlinear filtering for cryoET is presented. The method combines structure-preserving noise reduction with a strategy for enhancement of planar and curvilinear local structures, and a mechanism to further filter the background. The method is provided with capability for automatic parameter tuning and for objectively stopping the iterative filtering process. We illustrate the method with its application to several 3D maps of biological specimens obtained by cryoET.

## 2 Review of Anisotropic Nonlinear Diffusion

AND accomplishes a sophisticated edge-preserving denoising that takes into account the structures at local scales. Conceptually speaking, AND tunes the strength of the smoothing along different directions based on the local structure estimated at every point of the multidimensional image.

### 2.1 Estimation of Local Structure

The *structure tensor* is the mathematical tool that allows us to estimate the local structure in a multidimensional image. The structure tensor of a 3D image $I$ is a symmetric positive semi-definite matrix given by:

$$\mathbf{J}(I) = \begin{bmatrix} I_x^2 & I_x I_y & I_x I_z \\ I_x I_y & I_y^2 & I_y I_z \\ I_x I_z & I_y I_z & I_z^2 \end{bmatrix} \tag{1}$$

where $I_x = \frac{\partial I}{\partial x}$, $I_y = \frac{\partial I}{\partial y}$, $I_z = \frac{\partial I}{\partial z}$ are the derivatives of the image with respect to $x$, $y$ and $z$, respectively. The components of $\mathbf{J}$ are usually averaged with an Gaussian convolution kernel in order to represent the local structure at a higher scale.

The eigen-analysis of the structure tensor allows determination of the local structural features in the image [1]:

$$\mathbf{J}(I) = [\mathbf{v_1}\, \mathbf{v_2}\, \mathbf{v_3}] \cdot \begin{bmatrix} \mu_1 & 0 & 0 \\ 0 & \mu_2 & 0 \\ 0 & 0 & \mu_3 \end{bmatrix} \cdot [\mathbf{v_1}\, \mathbf{v_2}\, \mathbf{v_3}]^T \tag{2}$$

The orthogonal eigenvectors $\mathbf{v_1}$, $\mathbf{v_2}$, $\mathbf{v_3}$ provide the preferred local orientations, and the corresponding eigenvalues $\mu_1$, $\mu_2$, $\mu_3$ (assume $\mu_1 \geq \mu_2 \geq \mu_3$) provide the average contrast along these directions. The first eigenvector $\mathbf{v_1}$ represents the direction of the maximum variance, whereas $\mathbf{v_3}$ points to the direction with the minimum variance. Based on the relative values of $\mu_i$, basic local structures can be characterized (Fig. 1):

– Line-like structures have a preferred direction ($\mathbf{v_3}$) exhibiting a minimum variation whose eigenvalue is much lower than the other two, i.e. $\mu_1 \approx \mu_2 \gg \mu_3$. $\mathbf{v_1}$ and $\mathbf{v_2}$ are directions perpendicular to the line.

– Plane-like structures have two preferred directions exhibiting similar small contrast variation, whose eigenvalues are much lower than the first one, i.e. $\mu_1 \gg \mu_2 \approx \mu_3$. $v_1$ represents the direction perpendicular to the plane-like structure, whereas $v_2$ and $v_3$ define the plane that better fits the local structure.

– Isotropic structures. When the two previous conditions do not hold, then the local structure is considered isotropic or unstructured. In general, for these structures, the eigenvalues have values of similar magnitude or order, i.e. $\mu_1 \approx \mu_2 \approx \mu_3$.

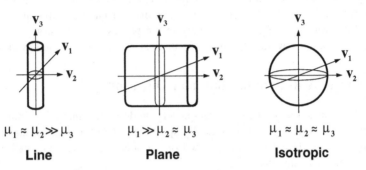

**Fig. 1.** Basic local structures found by eigen-analysis of the structure tensor. $\mu_1$, $\mu_2$, $\mu_3$ are the eigenvalues. $v_1$, $v_2$, $v_3$ are the corresponding eigenvectors.

## 2.2 Concept of Diffusion in Image Processing

Diffusion is a physical process that equilibrates concentration differences as a function of time, without creating or destroying mass. In image processing, density values play the role of concentration. This observation is expressed by the *diffusion equation* [1]:

$$I_t = \text{div}(\mathbf{D} \cdot \nabla I) \qquad (3)$$

where $I_t = \frac{\partial I}{\partial t}$ denotes the derivative of the image $I$ with respect to the time $t$, $\nabla I$ is the gradient vector, $\mathbf{D}$ is a square matrix called *diffusion tensor* and div is the *divergence* operator.

The diffusion tensor $\mathbf{D}$ allows us to tune the smoothing (both the strength and direction) across the image. $\mathbf{D}$ is defined as a function of the structure tensor $\mathbf{J}$:

$$\mathbf{D} = [\mathbf{v_1}\,\mathbf{v_2}\,\mathbf{v_3}] \cdot \begin{bmatrix} \lambda_1 & 0 & 0 \\ 0 & \lambda_2 & 0 \\ 0 & 0 & \lambda_3 \end{bmatrix} \cdot [\mathbf{v_1}\,\mathbf{v_2}\,\mathbf{v_3}]^T \qquad (4)$$

where $v_i$ denotes the eigenvectors of the structure tensor. The values of the eigenvalues $\lambda_i$ define the strength of the smoothing along the direction of the corresponding eigenvector $v_i$. The values of $\lambda_i$ rank from 0 (no smoothing) to 1 (strong smoothing). In AND, the $\lambda_i$s are normally set up independently so that the smoothing is anisotropically adapted to the local structure of the image. Consequently, AND allows smoothing on the edges: Smoothing runs along the edges so that they are not only preserved but smoothed and enhanced. AND has turned out, by far, the most effective denoising method by its capabilities for structure preservation and feature enhancement [1,5,6].

## 2.3  Common Diffusion Approaches

AND may function differently, by either filtering noise or enhancing some structural features, depending on the definition of $\lambda_i$ of the diffusion tensor $\mathbf{D}$. Currently, the most common ways of setting up $\mathbf{D}$ give rise to the following diffusion approaches:

- **EED: Edge Enhancing Diffusion.**
  The primary effects of EED are edge preservation and enhancement [1]. Here strong smoothing is applied along the direction corresponding to the minimum change (the third eigenvector, $\mathbf{v_3}$), while the strength of the smoothing along the other eigenvectors depends on the gradient: the higher the value is, the lower the smoothing strength is. The $\lambda_i$s are then set up as:

$$\begin{cases} \lambda_1 = g(|\nabla I|) \\ \lambda_2 = g(|\nabla I|) \\ \lambda_3 = 1 \end{cases} \tag{5}$$

  with $g$ being a monotonically decreasing function, such as [1]:

$$g(x) = 1 - \exp\left(\frac{-3.31488}{(x/K)^8}\right)$$

  where $K > 0$ is a contrast threshold constant; Structures with $|\nabla I| > K$ are regarded as edges, otherwise as the interior of a region.

- **CED: Coherence Enhancing Diffusion.**
  CED is able to connect interrupted lines and improve flow-like structures [3] and also enhance plane-like structures [6]. The strength of the smoothing along $\mathbf{v_2}$ must be tightly coupled to the plane-ness, given by $(\mu_1 - \mu_2)$, whereas the smoothing along $\mathbf{v_3}$ depends on the anisotropy $(\mu_1 - \mu_3)$. So, the $\lambda_i$s are then set up as:

$$\begin{cases} \lambda_1 \approx 0 \\ \lambda_2 = h(\mu_1 - \mu_2) \\ \lambda_3 = h(\mu_1 - \mu_3) \end{cases} \tag{6}$$

  with $h$ being a monotonically increasing function, such as [3]:

$$h(x) = \alpha + (1 - \alpha)\exp(-C/x^2)$$

  where $\alpha$ is a regularization constant (typically $10^{-3}$) and $C > 0$ is a threshold. Plane-like structures have $(\mu_1 - \mu_2)^2 > C$ and line-like ones have $(\mu_1 - \mu_3)^2 > C$.

# 3  Anisotropic Nonlinear Diffusion in cryoET

## 3.1  Diffusion Approach

In cryoET a hybrid diffusion approach is used in order to combine the advantages of both EED and CED simultaneously [5,8,6]. The strategy is based on the fact that the anisotropy $(\mu_1 - \mu_3)$ reflects the local relation of structure and noise. Therefore, we use this value as a switch: CED is applied if the anisotropy is larger than a suitably chosen threshold, otherwise EED is applied. The threshold $t_{ec}$ is derived *ad hoc* as the maximum anisotropy found in a subvolume of the image containing only noise. This approach carries out an efficient denoising which highlights the edges and connects lines and enhances flow-like and plane-like structures.

## 3.2 Smoothing the Background with Gaussian Filtering

In our diffusion approach, we have included a strategy to further smooth out the background. Since the interesting structural features usually have higher density levels than the background, those voxels with density values below a threshold are considered as background, and hence linear Gaussian filtering is applied. The threshold $t_g$ is computed from the average grey level in a subvolume of the tomogram that contains only noise, i.e. only background. As a consequence, those voxels that are considered background are significantly smoothed thanks to the Gaussian filtering.

## 3.3 Numerical Discretization of the Diffusion Equation

The diffusion equation, Eq. (3), can be numerically solved using finite differences. The term $I_t = \frac{\partial I}{\partial t}$ can be replaced by an Euler forward difference approximation. The resulting explicit scheme allows calculation of subsequent versions of the image iteratively:

$$\begin{aligned} I^{(k+1)} = I^{(k)} + \tau \cdot ( & \tfrac{\partial}{\partial x}(D_{11}I_x) + \tfrac{\partial}{\partial x}(D_{12}I_y) + \tfrac{\partial}{\partial x}(D_{13}I_z) + \\ & \tfrac{\partial}{\partial y}(D_{21}I_x) + \tfrac{\partial}{\partial y}(D_{22}I_y) + \tfrac{\partial}{\partial y}(D_{23}I_z) + \\ & \tfrac{\partial}{\partial z}(D_{31}I_x) + \tfrac{\partial}{\partial z}(D_{32}I_y) + \tfrac{\partial}{\partial z}(D_{33}I_z)) \end{aligned} \qquad (7)$$

where $\tau$ denotes the time step size, $I^{(k)}$ denotes the image at time $t_k = k\tau$ and the $D_{mn}$ terms represent the components of the diffusion tensor $\mathbf{D}$.

In this work, we have approximated the spatial derivatives ($\frac{\partial}{\partial x}$, $\frac{\partial}{\partial y}$ and $\frac{\partial}{\partial z}$) by means of filters with optimally directional invariance due to their better capabilities for structural preservation [4,8]. This discretization scheme is much more stable [4] and allows up to four times larger time step size ($\tau = 0.4$) than the traditional explicit scheme based on central differences ($\tau = 0.1$). Our scheme may thus require up to 4 times less iterations to obtain similar improvement in SNR.

## 3.4 The Stopping Criterion: Noise Estimate Variance

AND works iteratively, yielding successive smoother versions of the image, gradually removing noise and details. The process should stop before the signal in the image is significantly affected. In this work, we use the *noise estimate variance* (NEV) stopping criterion [6]. Here, the noise that has been filtered at time $t$ is estimated as the difference between the original noisy image, $I^0$, and its current filtered version, $I^t$. The variance of this noise estimate increases monotonically from 0 to $\text{var}(I^0)$ during diffusion. The optimal stopping time is the time slot where $\text{var}(I^0 - I^t)$ reaches the variance of the noise subvolume in the original noisy image $\text{var}(I_N^0)$:

$$t_{\text{stop}} = \arg\min_t \{|\text{var}(I_N^0) - \text{var}(I^0 - I^t)|\}$$

## 3.5 Automatic Parameter Tuning

The diffusion process is controlled by a number of parameters. Some of them are automatically tuned based on the statistics of a subvolume, extracted from the tomogram, that only contains noise: in particular, the NEV threshold $\text{var}(I_N^0)$, and the thresholds $t_{ec}$ and $t_g$. However, setting up the parameters $K$ and $C$ controlling the EED and CED diffusion processes, respectively, is far from trivial [5,8,6]. So far, they were set up manually based on the density range of the input tomogram, and they were fixed for the whole diffusion process [5,8,6]. In this work, we present a strategy to tune these parameters automatically based on the statistics of the noise subvolume previously mentioned. $K$ and $C$ can be set up as the average gradient and square anisotropy $(\mu_1 - \mu_3)^2$, respectively, found in the noise subvolume at each iteration. With this strategy, the parameters $K$ and $C$ do not keep fixed for the whole process any more. Instead, they evolve with iterations according to the noise and local structure remaining in the tomogram.

## 3.6   Scheme of Our Diffusion Approach

The outline of our AND approach is the following:

---

**(0.) Compute NEV threshold from the subvolume containing noise.**
It computes the threshold $\text{var}(I_N^0)$ used for the stopping criterion.
- $\text{var}(I_N^0)$ is the variance found in the noise subvolume.

**(1.) Compute statistics of the subvolume containing noise.**
Based on the statistics, it computes:
- the threshold $t_{ec}$ used to switch between EED and CED.
  - $t_{ec}$ is the maximum anisotropy $(\mu_1 - \mu_3)$ in the noise subvolume.
- the threshold $t_g$ used to apply Gaussian filtering.
  - $t_g$ is the average grey level in the noise subvolume.
- the parameter $K$ used for EED.
  - $K$ is the average gradient in the noise subvolume.
- the parameter $C$ used to CED.
  - $C$ is the average square anisotropy $(\mu_1 - \mu_3)^2$ in the noise subvolume.

**(2.) Compute the structure tensor J.**

**(3.) Compute the diffusion tensor D.**
For every voxel:

**(3.1.) Analysis of the local structure.**
It decides if the voxel is to be processed as EED, CED or background.
- The voxel is considered background if its grey level is lower than $t_g$.
- CED is to be applied, if the local anisotropy $(\mu_1 - \mu_3)$ is larger than $t_{ec}$.
- Otherwise, EED is to be applied.

**(3.2.) Computation:**
- Linear Diffusion.
  If background, linear diffusion (i.e. Gaussian filtering) is applied.
- EED: Edge Enhancing Diffusion.
  If EED, the diffusion tensor **D** is computed according to Eqs. (4) and (5).
- CED: Coherence Enhancing Diffusion.
  If CED, the diffusion tensor **D** is computed according to Eqs. (4) and (6).

**(4.) Solve the partial differential equation of diffusion, Eqs. (3) and (7).**

**(5.) Iterate: go to step (1.)**

---

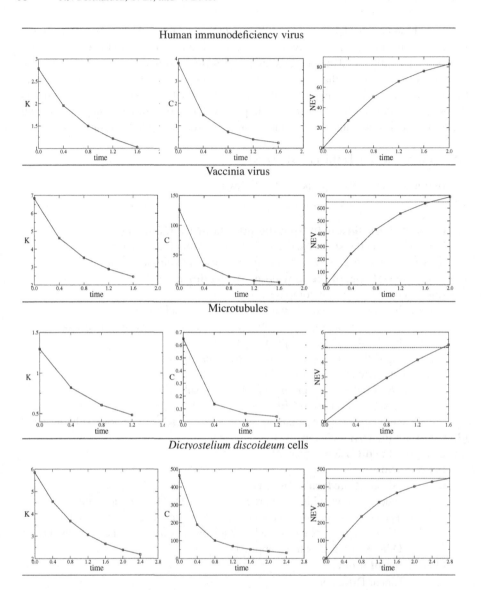

**Fig. 2.** Evolution of the denoising parameters with the iterations. The little squares in the graphs represents the values at the iterations, whereas X axis represents denoising time. The curves for K and C show the values used for the corresponding iteration. The NEV curve show the NEV measured at the corresponding iteration and the dashed-line represents the threshold to stop the process.

## 4   Experimental Applications

The AND approach presented here has been applied to tomograms of four different biological specimens: human immunodeficiency virus (HIV) [9], vaccinia virus (VV) [10], microtubules (MTs) [11] and *Dictyostelium discoideum* cells (DDC) [12].

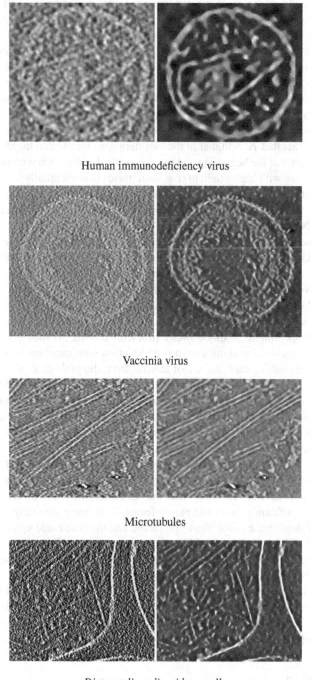

Human immunodeficiency virus

Vaccinia virus

Microtubules

*Dictyostelium discoideum* cells

**Fig. 3.** Visual results from denoising. Left: a slice extracted from the original tomogram. Right: the same slice extracted from the denoised tomogram.

Fig. 2 shows the evolution of the denoising parameters during the iterative process for all the tomograms. The curves on the right show the evolution of the NEV and the iteration where the denoising process stopped because the NEV threshold (shown with dashed lines) was reached. For HIV, VV, MTs and DDC, the number of iterations used was 5, 5, 4, 7, respectively. These numbers of iterations correspond to a denoising time of 2.0, 2.0, 1.6 and 2.8, respectively, using a time step size of $\tau = 0.4$. In general, the NEV curves are logarithm-like, exhibiting a larger reduction of noise variance at the first iterations and becoming progressively smaller.

The evolution of $K$ with the iterations, as seen in Fig. 2, shows a negative exponential-like curve. The fact that $K$ is higher at the first iterations means that the strength of the smoothing is higher at the beginning and progressively decays down with the iterations. Furthermore, noise with high gradient (e.g. shot noise) is substantially smoothed at the beginning. Then, the denoising process gradually focuses on more homogeneous areas. This behaviour is consistent with the progressively smaller reduction of noise variance as seen in the NEV curves.

Fig. 2 shows that the evolution of $C$ with the iterations also follows a negative exponential-like curve. The fact that $C$ is higher at the first iterations means that the strength of the enhancement is lower at the beginning and progressively goes up as the iterations evolve. This behaviour reflects that the enhancement of the features increases gradually, as the local structures are reinforced with the iterations.

Fig. 3 shows visual results obtained from noise reduction applied to the tomograms of the different specimens. A single slice extracted from the 3D tomograms is shown. All the results clearly show significant noise reduction with excellent structure preservation. The structural features that are of interest from the biological point of view are smoothed and enhanced substantially thanks to the hybrid EED/CED diffusion process. In particular, the CED approach plays an essential role in the enhancement of the membranes and other linear and planar features of the specimens. The strategy to further smooth the background has a remarkable performance whereby the specimens' features are successfully highlighted over the background.

Fig. 3 clearly shows the benefits of denoising for interpretation of the biological structures. In the case of HIV, there is strong enhancement of the outer membrane and the core's surface, as well as some other bodies inside the core. In the case of VV, denoising has significantly improved planar features, allowing the interpretation of the architecture of the virus, e.g. the outer membrane and the core made up of a membrane and a palisade. With regard to the MTs, the continuity along them and their interactions are apparent. Finally, denoising has emphasized the membranes of the cell and the fibrous structures that compose the cell's cytoplasm in the DDC tomogram.

The ability to parameter self-tuning provided in the denoising method has allowed high levels of autonomy. Apart from the input tomogram and the coordinates of the noise subvolume used for parameter tuning, no other parameters were needed. This makes this method very appropriate for users non-expert in the details of denoising.

# 5   Conclusion

We have presented a method to perform structure-preserving denoising based on anisotropic nonlinear diffusion. The AND approach relies on a hybrid strategy that combines noise reduction and feature enhancement. A strategy to further smooth out the background and highlight structural features has been included. We have provided a mechanism for automatic parameter tuning and for stopping the iterative denoising process. This anisotropic noise reduction method has been applied to CryoET, and the results show that it succeeds in filtering noise and emphasizing the features of interest. Therefore, this method facilitates interpretation of the structural information concealed in the noisy cryo-tomograms. The parameter self-tuning provided in the method allows high levels of autonomy and no user intervention required. This ability makes this method well suited for structural biologists working in cryoET, usually non-experts in AND.

## Acknowledgments

The authors thank Dr. R.A Crowther for fruitful discussions; Drs. O. Medalia for the *D. discoideum* dataset; Drs. J.L. Carrascosa for the VV dataset. The HIV dataset was obtained from the EBI-MSD database. Work partially supported by the MRC and grants MEC-TIN2005-00447, EU-FP6-LSHG-CT-2004-502828, JA-P06-TIC1426.

## References

1. Weickert, J.: Anisotropic Diffusion in Image Processing. Teubner (1998)
2. Perona, P., Malik, J.: Scale space and edge detection using anisotropic diffusion. IEEE Trans. Patt. Anal. Mach. Intel. 12, 629–639 (1990)
3. Weickert, J.: Coherence-enhancing diffusion filtering. Int. J. Computer Vision 31, 111–127 (1999)
4. Weickert, J., Scharr, H.: A scheme for coherence-enhancing diffusion filtering with optimized rotation invariance. J. Visual Comm. Imag. Repres. 13, 103–118 (2002)
5. Frangakis, A.S., Stoschek, A., Hegerl, R.: Wavelet transform filtering and nonlinear anisotropic diffusion assessed for signal reconstruction performance on multidimensional biomedical data. IEEE Trans. BioMed. Engineering 48, 213–222 (2001)
6. Fernandez, J.J., Li, S.: Anisotropic nonlinear filtering of cellular structures in cryo-electron tomography. Computing in Science and Engineering 7(5), 54–61 (2005)
7. Sali, A., Glaeser, R., Earnest, T., Baumeister, W.: From words to literature in structural proteomics. Nature 422, 216–225 (2003)
8. Fernandez, J.J., Li, S.: An improved algorithm for anisotropic nonlinear diffusion for denoising cryo-tomograms. J. Struct. Biol. 144, 152–161 (2003)
9. Briggs, J., Grunewald, K., Glass, B., Forster, F., Krausslich, H., Fuller, S.: The mechanism of HIV-1 core assembly: Insights from 3D reconstructions of authentic virions. Structure 14, 15–20 (2006)
10. Cyrklaff, M., Risco, C., Fernandez, J.J., Jimenez, M.V., Esteban, M., Baumeister, W., Carrascosa, J.L.: Cryo-electron tomography of vaccinia virus. Proc. Natl. Acad. Sci. USA 102, 2772–2777 (2005)
11. Hoog, J., Schwartz, C., Noon, A., O'Toole, E., Mastronarde, D., McIntosh, J., Antony, C.: Organization of interphase microtubules in fission yeast analyzed by electron tomography. Dev. Cell 12, 349–361 (2007)
12. Medalia, O., Weber, I., Frangakis, A.S., Nicastro, D., Gerisch, G., Baumeister, W.: Macromolecular architecture in eukaryotic cells visualized by cryoelectron tomography. Science 298, 1209–1213 (2002)

# A Middle-Ware for the Automated Composition and Invocation of Semantic Web Services Based on Temporal HTN Planning Techniques

Juan Fdez-Olivares[1], Tomás Garzón[2], Luis Castillo[1], Óscar García-Pérez[2], and Francisco Palao[2]

[1] Dpto. Ciencias de la Computación e I.A., University of Granada, Spain
[2] IActive Intelligent Solutions
http://www.iactive.es

**Abstract.** This work presents a middle-ware able to translate OWL-S web services descriptions into a temporal HTN domain in order to automatically compose and execute sequences of web service invocations, including parallel branches and complex synchronizations, based on the combination of HTN planning and temporal reasoning techniques.

## 1 Introduction

Semantic web services (SWS) techniques [11] support the way in which already existing "syntactic" web services (usually described in WSDL [10]) can be extended with a semantic layer in order to be automatically discovered, composed and invoked. The main goal of such representation is to provide a logical framework in order for a software system to be capable of both *interpreting* SWS descriptions and, given a service request, *reasoning* about them in order to automatically compose and execute a sequence of web service invocations that provides the resquested service. The main long-term goal of SWS is getting the Semantic Web in its full potential by semantically annotating both data and web processes, but there is a short-term goal that is concerned with the semantic annotation of business web services deployed on service oriented enterprise architectures. In this case SWS may help to leverage the Business Process Management (BPM)[2] life cycle in which *business processes* (workflow schemes designed to specify the operation of business web services) of a company are at present manually composed and orchestrated in order to be executed by standard commercial BPM engines. The application of SWS techniques may lead to a more agile and flexible BPM life cycle by automating the composition and orchestration of business processes while keeping human intervention to a minimum.

Although there are several standard proposals of SWS languages [1], OWL-S [4] is a language that may serve to this purpose for two reasons: firstly, it allows to represent web services as *processes* with typed input/output parameters, preconditions and effects, as well as their data model on the basis of an OWL ontology. And, second, the core concept of OWL-S is the *Process Model*: an

D. Borrajo, L. Castillo, and J.M. Corchado (Eds.): CAEPIA 2007, LNAI 4788, pp. 70–79, 2007.

OWL ontology that allows to describe both the semantics of web services as a compositional hierarchy of atomic (that represent already existing WSDL web services) and composite processes (that represent high-level services), and the operation of every composite process as a *workflow scheme* that specifies both order constraints (by using **sequence, unordered, split, and join** structs) and the control flow logic (by using conditional, **if-then-else**, and iterative, **while and repeat-until** control structs) that sub-processes should follow in order to obtain an executable sequence of web services.

From the point of view of OWL-S, web service composition consists on finding a suitable sequence of atomic processes (that is, web services invocations) that provides a high-level service-request expressed as a composite process, and considering the process model as a *guideline* to be followed by the composition process. Regarding the automated composition of web services as OWL-S processes, although several techniques may be applied to this problem [12], AI Planning and Scheduling (P&S)[7] seems to be the most promising one since during the last 40 years it has dealt with the development of planning systems capable of interpreting a planning domain as a set of actions schemes (i.e. a process model) and reasoning about them in order to compose a suitable plan (i.e. a sequence of actions) such that its execution reaches a given goal (that can be seen as a service request) starting from an initial state. Concretely, HTN planning [5,3] becomes the most suitable AI P&S technique since it supports the modeling of planning domains in terms of a compositional hierarchy of tasks representing compound and primitive tasks by describing how every compound task may be decomposed into (compound/primitive) sub-tasks and the order that they must follow, by using different methods, and following a reasoning process that is guided by the knowledge encoded in the HTN domain.

Therefore, considering this previous discussion, in this work we present a middle-ware able to both *interpret* OWL-S web services descriptions, by translating them into an HTN domain and problem description, and *carry out a reasoning process* based on HTN planning techniques in order to automatically compose a sequence of executable web services. This sequence is obtained by following the workflow scheme defined in the OWL-S process model and provides a high-level service request introduced as a problem. The cornerstone of this architecture is SIADEX, an own developed HTN planner [3,6] that receives as input an HTN domain automatically translated from an OWL-S process model and a planning problem representing both, a goal extracted from a high-level service request, and an initial state extracted from the instances of the OWL-S' underlying OWL data model. In the following section we will describe in detail the main features of SIADEX that make it suitable in its application to web service composition as well as its related aspects with the OWL-S Process Model. Then, a mapping algorithm that translates a OWL-S Process Model into a SIADEX domain will be illustrated. Finally, the architecture of the middle-ware will be shown and we will briefly describe a service oriented enterprise application in a simulated scenario where this middle-ware has been tested in order to interpret and execute business processes modeled as OWL-S processes.

## 2    SIADEX in a Nutshell

SIADEX is an AI Planning and Scheduling system that uses as its planning domain and problem description language an HTN extension of the PDDL standard in such a way that primitive tasks are encoded as PDDL 2.2 level 3 durative actions (see [3] for details). In addition, methods used to decompose tasks into sub-tasks include a precondition that must be satisfied by the current world state in order for the decomposition method to be applicable by the planner. The basic planning process of SIADEX is a state-based forward HTN planning algorithm that, starting from the initial state and a goal expressed as a high-level task, iteratively decomposes that top-level task and its sub-tasks by selecting their decomposition methods according to the current state and following the order constraints posed in tasks decomposition schemes as a search-control strategy (See Figure 1).

This process makes possible to know the current state of the world at every step in the planning process and, concretely, when preconditions of both methods and primitive actions are evaluated, what allows to incorporate significant inferencing and reasoning power as well as the ability to call external programs (that in this case might be web services) to infer new knowledge by requesting information to external sources. For this purpose, SIADEX uses two mechanisms: on the one hand,

**(a)**

```
(:derived (vip_user ?u - User)
 (and (> (salary ?u) 3000)
       (genre ?u F)))
(:task GetPrice
 :parameters (?c - Car ?u - User)
 (:method is_vip_user
  :precondition (vip_user ?u)
  :tasks (
         (getPrice ?c ?p)
         (getDisccount ?c ?d)
         (final_price ?p ?d ?f)
         (:inline () (price ?c ?u ?f))))
 (:method not_vip_user
  :precondition (not (vip_user ?u))
  :tasks (
         (getPrice ?c ?p)
         (final_price ?p 0 ?f)
         (:inline () (price ?c ?u ?f)))))
```

**(b)**

```
(:derived (vat_applied ?p ?v)
   {import math
    ?v = ?p * 1.16
    return 1}))

(:durative-action final_price
 :parameters(?p ?d ?f - number)
 :duration (= ?duration 3)
 :condition(and (vat_applied ?p ?v)
 :effect(and (assign ?f (- ?v ?d)))))

(:task while-loop
  :parameters (?x - Number)
  (:method base case
   :precondition (and not (> ?x 0))
   :tasks ())
  (:method loop
   :precondition (and (> ?x 0))
   :tasks ((do-something ?x)
          (:inline ()
          (assign ?x (- ?x 1)))
          (while-loop ?x))))
```

**Fig. 1.** The basics of HTN planning domains in SIADEX' domain language: (a) A derived literal inferring whether a given user is or not a vip user and a compound *task* with two different *methods* of decomposition, describing how to compute the price of a car depending on the profile of a given user. The decomposition method uses an *inline task* to assert in the current state the price of the car for that user . (b) A primitive *action* that computes a final-price with discount, it is preconditioned with a derived literal that infers, by using a Python script, the VAT applied to a price. The task while-loop exploits the capability of recursive decompositions in order to describe repetitive tasks.

deductive inference tasks of the form (:inline <p> <c>) that may be fired, in the context of a decomposition scheme, when the logical expression <p>(condition) is satisfied by the current state, providing additional bindings for variables or asserting/retracting literals into the current state, depending on the logical expression described in <c>(consequent); on the other hand, abductive inference rules represented as PDDL 2.2 derived literals of the form (:derived <lit> <expr>), that allow to satisfy a literal <lit>when it is not present in the current state by evaluating the expression <expr>that may be either a logical expression or a Python script that both binds its inputs with variables of that literal and returns information that might be bound to some of the variables of <literal>. This one is a crucial capability since, as it will be detailed in the following sections, supports the way in which SIADEX interacts with external web services.

Furthermore, the domain description language of SIADEX and the planning algorithm support to explicitly represent and manage time and concurrency in both compound and primitive tasks, thanks to the handling of metric time over a Simple Temporal Network (See [3] for more details). This temporal representation provides enough expressivity power to represent OWL-S workflow schemes such as sequence, unorder, split and join. Finally, the search control strategy followed by SIADEX allows to represent other patterns like conditional or iterative control constructs, giving support to fully represent an OWL-S process model. This will be seen in next section where the translation process from OWL-S to the domain description language of SIADEX is illustrated.

## 3  Mapping an OWL-S Process Model into a SIADEX Domain

**Mapping Overview.** The translation process first maps the OWL data model into the PDDL data model by translating OWL classes, properties and instances into PDDL types, predicates and objects, respectively[1]. Then it maps the OWL-S process model into a SIADEX HTN domain that represents the operation of both atomic and composite processes as primitive tasks and task decomposition schemes, respectively. Atomic processes are mapped as PDDL durative actions (see below) and the workflow pattern of every composite process is mapped into a method-based task decomposition scheme that expresses the operational semantics of the control structs found in that composite process. In that section it will be shown how the mapping process exploits (1) the order between sub-tasks in order to represent sequence and unordered control structs, (2) the management of temporal constraints to represent split, join and split-join of processes, and (3) the search control used to decompose tasks in order to represent conditional structs and the possibility of describing recursive decompositions as the basis to represent iterative control structs. However, firstly we will start by illustrating how to map an atomic OWL-S process into primitive actions managed by SIADEX.

---

[1] Space limitations prevents detailing this ontology mapping process, although a similar one on a frame-based ontology is described in [6].

**Atomic processes as PDDL durative actions.** The header of an atomic process (i.e. its name, input and output properties, See Figure 2 ) is directly mapped into the header of a PDDL durative-action with typed parameters (these types correspond to classes of the OWL data model). This is also the case for preconditions/effects, since there is also a direct correspondence between expressions inside preconditions and effects of any atomic process and preconditions/effects of PDDL actions[2].

This direct translation works for world-altering only atomic processes (i.e. only alter internal states in processes) and that don't need to manage external information. However, atomic processes might be associated to WSDL information-providing web services in such a way that atomic process' outputs might be filled with information sent back by the web service once it has been invoked. This real need reveals as a key issue the management of information gathering at planning (i.e. composition) time since a considerable part of the knowledge needed by SIADEX to reason about methods and primitive actions' preconditions might not be contained either in the initial or the current state, but accessible from external information sources. In this case it becomes necessary to represent in the SIADEX domain both, the atomic process structure and the web service invocation, since it will be needed to obtain information at planning time. This is done by translating the correspondence (defined in the *Service Grounding*) between the atomic process and the WSDL service as an inference rule represented as a *derived literal*. This inference rule has the general form (:derived <header> <call>) where <header> is a literal automatically generated from the header of the atomic process (that corresponds with the "header" of the WSDL web service) and <call> is a Python script (also automatically generated) that invokes the web service by passing the input parameters of the composite process and provides a bind for the output parameters with the information sent-back by the web service. Finally, the literal <header> is added to the preconditions of the PDDL action in order to be evaluated when the action is applied in the planning process. The example shows

```
<process:AtomicProcess rdf:ID="#GetPrice">
<process:hasInput rdf:resource="#CarModel"/>
<process:hasInput rdf:resource="#User_Car"/>
<process:hasOutput rdf:resource="#Price"/>
<process:hasPrecondition rdf:resource="#AlwaysTrue"/>
<process:hasEffect> Price(User_Car Price) />
</process:AtomicProcess>
```

**Fig. 2.** An OWL-S atomic process that returns the price of a car

how the correspondence between the atomic process getPrice(input:Model input:Car output:Price) and it associated WSDL web service is translated into a derived literal which is added to the preconditions of the action

---

[2] We have used the Protege OWL-S tab plug-in for editing OWL-S process models. This tab allows to represent preconditions an effects in several formats like SWRL or KIF. We have chosen to represent them as strings with the KIF format, a similar representation to the one of PDDL.

```
(:derived (d_getPrice ?m ?c ?p)
 {i1 = ?m
  i2 = ?c                              (:durative-action ActiongetPrice
  <invoke wsdl#getPrice i1 i2 o1>       :parameters (?m - Model ?c - Car ?p - Number)
  ?p = o1})                             :precondition (d_getPrice ?m ?c ?p)
                                        :effect (Price ?c ?p))
```

**Fig. 3.** The correspondence between the atomic process `GetPrice` and the web service
`wsdl#GetPrice` described as a primitive action and a derived literal, respectively

```
(:task Purchase
  :parameters (?m - CarModel ?user_car - Car)
  (:method
   :precondition ()
   :tasks ((getAvailability ?m)
           [(getPrice ?m ?user_car ?p)
             (getDiscount ?m ?user_car ?d)]
           (bookCar ?m ?user_car)
           (payCar ?user_car))))
```

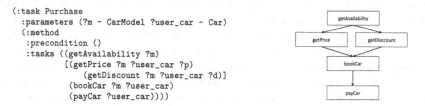

**Fig. 4.** The decomposition scheme of action `Purchase` and its associated plan implementing a split-joint construct

`ActionGetPrice` corresponding tho the atomic process. This representation allows, on the one hand, to bind the variable `?p` (for price) with a value coming
from an external source through a web service invocation and, on the other hand,
when the action is applied to the current state, to incorporate this binding at
planning time when asserting the effect of the action in the current state.

**Composite processes and management of time-order constraints.** The
translation algorithm maps every OWL-S composite process and its sub-
processes into a SIADEX task decomposition scheme where sub-tasks (corresponding to sub-processes) are structured in methods depending on the control structure
that is modeled in the composite process. This is done in two steps: firstly, process parameters are mapped into task parameters as in atomic processes, process
preconditions are added to the preconditions of every method of the corresponding task and, since HTN domain descriptions do not allow to explicitly describe
effects in a tasks, process' effects are mapped into an *in-line inference task* of the
form (`:inline () <consequent>`) where () stands for an empty condition part
(representing a condition that is always true) and the consequent contains the logical expression of the effects of that composite process. This allows to assert, at
planning time, the effects (if any) of the translated composite process in the current state. The second step considers the control struct of the composite process
making a distinction between control structs that define the execution order between processes (sequencing, unordering, splitting or join), and those that define
the control flow logic of processes (conditional an iterative ones.)

In the former case the translation process generates one single method that expresses such control structures by describing order constraints between its component sub-tasks. For this purpose SIADEX allows sub-tasks in a method to be
either sequenced, and then their signature appears between parentheses (T1,T2) ,
or splitted, appearing between braces [T1,T2]. Furthermore, an appropriate combination of these syntactics forms may result in split, join or split-join control

structs. For example, the decomposition method of task purchase (?m - Model ?user_car - Car) in Figure 4 specifies that, in a plan for the composition of web services, in order to purchase a car of a model, before to invoke booking and paying web services, it is firstly necessary getting the availability of cars of that model and, concurrently, obtaining the price and discount of that model.

Current state-based forward planners (HTN and non-HTN, like SHOP2[5] or OWLSXPLan[8]) with application to web service composition lack of the required expressivity for representing web services execution paths as the one shown in the previous example. The reason is that these planners return plans as a totally ordered sequence of actions and, as opposed to them, SIADEX is capable of obtaining plans with true parallel branches of execution due to the handling of metric time over a Simple Temporal Network (STN). At planning time, SIADEX deploys its partially generated plan over a STN that associates a pair of start and end time-points to either every compound or primitive task. All the time points and constraints of the STN are posted and propagated automatically, observing the order constraints defined in the decomposition scheme, every time that a compound or primitive task is added to the plan. Therefore, the control construct initially modeled in OWL-S contains implicit temporal constraints that, when translated, are automatically explicited and managed by SIADEX. This is a clear advantage of SIADEX with respect to other approaches, since despite OWL-S does not support time-related information in processes, the planning process of SIADEX is aware of these temporal constraints between processes, and capable of automatically manage and infer them from qualitative order relations like those above illustrated.

Conditional and iterative control constructs are translated into task decomposition schemes that exploit the main search control technique of SIADEX. Briefly, a composite process $p$ that contains a conditional struct *if c then p1 else p2* is translated into a task decomposition scheme (:task $p$ (:method :precondition c :tasks (*p1*)) (:method :precondition (not c) :tasks (p2))) describing that if $c$ holds in the current state then decompose the task *p1* else decompose the task *p2*. A composite process $p$ that contains an iterative struct *while c p1* is translated into a task decomposition scheme (:task $p$ (:method :precondition *(not c)* :tasks ()) (:method :precondition c :tasks (*p1 p*))), describing that the task *p1* should be repeatedly performed (and so recursively decomposed) while $c$ holds in the current state.

Finally, it is important to recall that given an OWL-S process model and its associated service grounding the translation process[3] above described allows to automatically generate a planning domain represented as a hierarchical extension of PDDL2.2, capable of representing information providing actions by invoking external web services, which is fully ready to use (without human intervention) by SIADEX in order to solve problems of web services composition. On the basis of this translation process we have also developed an architecture

---

[3] The sources and java. jar files can be downloaded from
   http://decsai.ugr.es/~faro/OwlsTranslator

for the dynamical composition and execution of semantic web services described in OWL-S, that is shown in the next section.

# 4 Middle-Ware for the Composition and Execution of Web Services

Figure 5 shows the architecture of the middle-ware here presented able to both *interpret* OWL-S web services descriptions, by translating them into an HTN domain as explained in the previous section, and *carry out a reasoning process* based on HTN planning techniques in order to automatically compose and execute a sequence of executable web services. This sequence is obtained by following the workflow scheme defined in the OWL-S process model and provides a high-level service request introduced as a problem. The proposed architecture has the following components: a **Translator** that maps an initial service-request (through a java interface) into both, an HTN goal (represented as a high-level task that is an instance of a composite process already modeled in OWL-S), and an initial state which is made from OWL instances of the OWL-S data model (any way, most of the information needed to planning resides in external sources and recall that the planner can access to it by means of web services invocations). The problem together with the translated OWL-S process model are sent to the **Web Services Composer**(SIADEX), the cornerstone of this architecture, in order to start the composition (planning) process. Then the planner makes use of the knowledge encoded in the domain (representing the OWL-S process model) as a guide to find a sequence of temporally annotated primitive actions that represents a suitable composition (with possibly parallel branches) of atomic processes. This sequence is sent to the **Monitor** that is in charge of both scheduling the execution of atomic processes according to their temporal information and sending execution orders to the **Executive**. This module is in charge of executing web services invocations (requested at either planning or plan execution time) and sending back the information. At planning time, the requested information may result in a fail when the web service requested is not available or the information returned gets a precondition unsatisfied. In that case SIADEX performs a backtracking process that may lead to select a different web service (thus carrying out a form of web service discovery) or even a completely different way to compose the high-level service (if so encoded in the OWL-S process model). At execution time, the execution of a web service might raise an exception the notification of which is sent to the Monitor that raises a **Re-planning process**. This module is in charge of manage the uncertainty when executing web services and at present is in development, but it is being designed in order to fastly, locally repair the composed sequence. Any way, at present and in case of an exception is raised, the Monitor informs to the user that the service requested is unfeasible and a new composition episode is initiated.

This middle-ware has been tested in the framework of a geographically distributed, service oriented enterprise application devoted to car sales. In this simulated scenario the above described middle-ware plays the role of a semantically extended Business Process Engine that bridges the gap between business

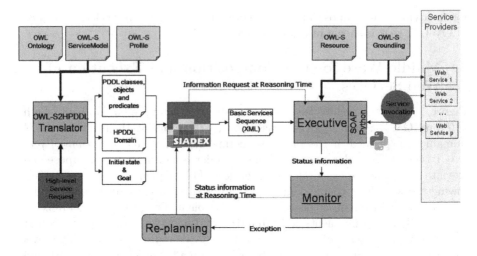

**Fig. 5.** A middle-ware where an HTN planner (SIADEX) plays the role of a web services composer for the automated composition of OWL-S semantic web services

process modeling and web services execution phases, by automatically interpreting, composing and enacting them. Furthermore, apart from this application we have developed a standalone Protégé plug-in (called ProblemEditor [4]) in order to locally edit, visualize and test HTN planning problems and domains automatically extracted from an OWL-S process model.

## 5   Related Work

Regarding the application of AI P&S to the composition of OWL-S web services in [5] can be found a translation process from OWL-S to SHOP2 domains that inspired the work here presented. Nevertheless, SHOP2 authors neglect the management of temporal constraints what prevents to translate fully OWL-S process models containing split and join constructs, what limits its real application to web composition problems as the ones here faced by SIADEX. Furthermore, in [3] we show a detailed experimentation proving that SIADEX clearly outperforms SHOP2. OWLSXPlan [8] is a planner that faces the composition of OWL-S *service profiles* with non-HTN planning techniques what makes impossible to interpret full OWL-S process models (indeed it is focused on automatically discovering and composing non-hierarchical OWL-S service profiles already published in the web, a different approach to the one here presented). Authors of OWLSXPlan recognize that, due to the absence of temporal reasoning, control structs like *unordered sequence* are not realizable. Recall that, apart from its time performance, the main advantage of SIADEX is the capability of making explicit the management of implicit temporal constraints found in every OWL-S process model, allowing to

---

[4] This plug-in and the complete OWL-S model can be downloaded from
http://decsai.ugr.es/~faro/OwlsTranslator

represent parallel branches of execution as well as complex synchronization mechanisms. Finally [9] translates OWL-S process models into conditional web services sequences ready to be interpreted by standard workflow engines what allows to manage the uncertainty at execution time by establishing conditional courses of execution. However this approach has a high computational cost that might be reduced with the alternative approach here presented that allows both to incorporate and manage external information at planning time and to fast and dynamically repair a sequence that raises an execution exception.

## 6   Conclusions

In this work we present three significative advances regarding web services composition and its relation with AI Planning and business process management: first, we have introduced a novel and fully automated translation process from OWL-S process models to a hierarchical extension of the PDDL standard that allows a temporal HTN planner to automatically compose and execute OWL-S web services. Secondly, plans obtained represent sequences of web services invocations including parallel and synchronization mechanisms what makes the middle-ware here presented to be considered as an important step forward in the application of AI Planning techniques to real SWS composition problems. Finally, a full application has been developed where business processes are modeled as OWL-S processes that are used to automatically compose and orchestrate business web services of a simulated virtual enterprise. At present we are working in the management of execution exceptions based on an HTN plan repairing process.

## References

1. W3c standard submissions. http://www.w3c.org/
2. Workflow management coalition. http://www.wfmc.org/
3. Castillo, L., Fdez-Olivares, J., García-Pérez, O., Palao, F.: Efficiently handling temporal knowledge in an HTN planner. In: Proc. ICAPS (2006)
4. Martin, D., Burstein, M., et al.: Describing web services using owl-s and wsdl (October 2003), http://www.daml.org/services/owl-s/1.0/owl-s-wsdl.html
5. Sirin, E., Parsia, B., Wu, D., Hendler, J., Nau, D.: Htn planning for web service composition using shop2. Journal of Web Semantics 1(4) (2004)
6. Fdez-Olivares, J., Castillo, L., García-Pérez, O., Palao, F.: Bringing users and planning technology together. Experiences in SIADEX. In: Proc. ICAPS (2006)
7. Ghallab, M., Nau, D., Traverso, P.: Automated Planning: Theory and Practice. Elsevier, Amsterdam (2004)
8. Klusch, M., Gerber, A., Schmidt, M.: Semantic web service composition planning with owl-sxplan. In: Int. AAAI Fall Symp. on Agents and Semantic Web (2005)
9. Traverso, P., Pistore, M.: Automated composition of semantic web services into executable processes. In: International Semantic Web Conference (2004)
10. Graham, S., Davis, D., et al.: Building Web Services with Java (2005)
11. McIlraith, S.A., Son, T.C., Zeng, H.: Semantic web services. IEEE Intelligent Systems 2(16), 46–53 (2001)
12. Charif, Y., Sabouret, N.: An overview of semantic web services composition approaches. In: Proc. Int. Workshop on Context for Web Services (2005)

# A Multiobjective Approach to Fuzzy Job Shop Problem Using Genetic Algorithms

Inés González-Rodríguez[1], Jorge Puente[2], and Camino R. Vela[2]

[1] Department of Mathematics, Statistics and Computing,
University of Cantabria, (Spain)
ines.gonzalez@unican.es
[2] A.I. Centre and Department of Computer Science,
University of Oviedo, (Spain)
{puente,crvela}@uniovi.es
http://www.aic.uniovi.es/Tc

**Abstract.** We consider a job shop problem with uncertain durations and flexible due dates and introduce a multiobjective model based on lexicographical minimisation. To solve the resulting problem, a genetic algorithm and a decoding algorithm to generate possibly active schedules are considered. The multiobjective approach is tested on several problem instances, illustrating the potential of the proposed method.

## 1 Introduction

In the last decades, scheduling problems have been subject to intensive research due to their multiple applications in areas of industry, finance and science [1]. To enhance the scope of applications, fuzzy scheduling has tried to model the uncertainty and vagueness pervading real-life situations, with a great variety of approaches, from representing incomplete or vague states of information to using fuzzy priority rules with linguistic qualifiers or preference modelling [2],[3].

The complexity of problems such as shop problems means that practical approaches to solving them usually involve heuristic strategies, such as genetic algorithms, local search, etc [1]. It is not trivial to extend these strategies to fuzzy scheduling. Indeed, incorporating uncertainty to scheduling usually requires a significant reformulation of the problem and solving methods. In the literature, we find some attempts to extend heuristic methods for job shop solving to the fuzzy case. For instance, 6-point fuzzy numbers and simulated annealing are used for single objective problem in [4], while triangular fuzzy numbers and genetic algorithms are considered for multiobjective problems in [5], [6] and [7]. The latter also proposes a semantics for solutions to job shop with uncertainty.

In the sequel, we describe a fuzzy job shop problem with uncertain durations and flexible due dates. A leximin approach is taken to define an objective function that combines minimisation of the expected fuzzy makespan and maximisation of due-date satisfaction. The resulting problem is solved by means of a genetic algorithm (GA) based on permutations with repetitions that searches in the space of possibly active schedules. We analyse the performance of the resulting multiobjective GA on a set of problem instances.

D. Borrajo, L. Castillo, and J.M. Corchado (Eds.): CAEPIA 2007, LNAI 4788, pp. 80–89, 2007.
© Springer-Verlag Berlin Heidelberg 2007

## 2  Uncertain Processing Times and Flexible Constraints

In real-life applications, it is often the case that the exact duration of a task is not known in advance. However, based on previous experience, an expert may have some knowledge about the duration, thus being able to estimate, for instance, an interval for the possible processing time or its most typical value. In the literature, it is common to use fuzzy numbers to represent such processing times, as an alternative to probability distributions, which require a deeper knowledge of the problem and usually yield a complex calculus.

When there is little knowledge available, the crudest representation for uncertain processing times would be a human-originated confidence interval. If some values appear to be more plausible than others, a natural extension is a a fuzzy interval or a fuzzy number. The simplest model of fuzzy interval is a *triangular fuzzy number* or *TFN*, using only an interval $[a^1, a^3]$ of possible values and a single plausible value $a^2$ in it. For a TFN $A$, denoted $A = (a^1, a^2, a^3)$, the membership function takes the following triangular shape:

$$\mu_A(x) = \begin{cases} \frac{x-a^1}{a^2-a^1} & : a^1 \leq x \leq a^2 \\ \frac{x-a^3}{a^2-a^3} & : a^2 < x \leq a^3 \\ 0 & : x < a^1 \text{ or } a^3 < x \end{cases} \tag{1}$$

Two arithmetic operations on TFNs are of interest herein. The first one is *fuzzy number addition*, which in the case of TFNs $A = (a^1, a^2, a^3)$ and $B = (b^1, b^2, b^3)$ is reduced to adding three pairs of real numbers so $A + B = (a^1 + b^1, a^2 + b^2, a^3 + b^3)$. The second one is the *maximum* $A \vee B$, obtained by extending the lattice operation max on real numbers using the Extension Principle. Computing the membership function is not trivial and the result is not guaranteed to be a TFN, so in practice we approximate $A \vee B$ by a TFN, $A \sqcup B = (a^1 \vee b^1, a^2 \vee b^2, a^3 \vee b^3)$. This approximation was first proposed in [4] for 6-point fuzzy numbers, a particular case of which are TFNs. The approximated maximum can be trivially extended to the case of $n > 2$ TFNs.

When a TFN models an uncertain duration, its membership function may be interpreted as a possibility distribution on the values that the duration may take. Given this interpretation and based on credibility theory, the *expected value* [8] of a TFN $A$ is given by $E[A] = \frac{1}{4}(a^1 + 2a^2 + a^3)$.

In practice, if due-date constraints exist, they are often flexible. For instance, customers may have a preferred delivery date $d^1$, but some delay will be allowed until a later date $d^2$, after which the order will be cancelled. The satisfaction of a due-date constraint becomes a matter of degree, our degree of satisfaction that a job is finished on a certain date. A common approach to modelling such satisfaction levels is to use a fuzzy set $D$ with linear decreasing membership function:

$$\mu_D(x) = \begin{cases} 1 & : x \leq d^1 \\ \frac{x-d^2}{d^1-d^2} & : d^1 < x \leq d^2 \\ 0 & : d^2 < x \end{cases} \tag{2}$$

Such membership function expresses a flexible threshold "less than", representing the satisfaction level $sat(t) = \mu_D(t)$ for the ending date $t$ of the job [2]. When the job's completion time is no longer a real number $t$ but a TFN $C$, the degree to which $C$ satisfies the due-date constraint $D$ may be measured using the following *agreement index* [9],[5]:

$$AI(C, D) = \frac{area(D \cap C)}{area(C)} \tag{3}$$

## 3   The Job Shop Scheduling Problem

### 3.1   Description of the Problem

The *job shop scheduling problem*, also denoted *JSP*, consists in scheduling a set of jobs $\{J_1, \ldots, J_n\}$ on a set of physical resources or machines $\{M_1, \ldots, M_m\}$, subject to a set of constraints. There are *precedence constraints*, so each job $J_i$, $i = 1, \ldots, n$, consists of $m$ tasks $\{\theta_{i1}, \ldots, \theta_{im}\}$ to be sequentially scheduled. Also, there are *capacity constraints*, whereby each task $\theta_{ij}$ requires the uninterrupted and exclusive use of one of the machines for its whole processing time. In addition, we may consider *due-date constraints*, where each job has a maximum completion time and all its tasks must be scheduled to finish before this time. A solution to this problem is a schedule (a starting time for all tasks) which, besides being *feasible*, in the sense that due precedence and capacity constraints hold, is optimal according to some criteria, for instance, that due-date satisfaction is maximal or makespan is minimal.

A schedule $s$ for a job shop problem of size $n \times m$ ($n$ jobs and $m$ machines) is fully determined by a decision variable representing a task processing order $\boldsymbol{x} = (x_1, \ldots, x_{nm})$, where $1 \leq x_l \leq n$ for $l = 1, \ldots, nm$ and $|\{x_l : x_l = i\}| = m$ for $i = 1, \ldots, n$. This is a permutation with repetition as proposed by Bierwirth [10]; a permutation of the set of tasks, where each task is represented by the number of its job. Thus a job number appears in such decision variable as many times as different tasks it has. The order of precedence among tasks requiring the same machine is given by the order in which they appear in the decision variable $\boldsymbol{x}$. Hence, the decision variable represents a task processing order that uniquely determines a feasible schedule. This permutation should be understood as expressing partial schedules for every set of operations requiring the same machine.

Let us assume that the processing time $p_{ij}$ of each task $\theta_{ij}$, $i = 1, \ldots, n$, $j = 1, \ldots, m$ is a fuzzy variable (a particular case of which are TFNs). Let $\boldsymbol{\xi}$ be the matrix of fuzzy processing times such that $\xi_{ij} = p_{ij}$, let $\boldsymbol{\nu}$ be a machine matrix such that $\nu_{ij}$ is the machine required by task $\theta_{ij}$, let $C_i(\boldsymbol{x}, \boldsymbol{\xi}, \boldsymbol{\nu})$ denote the completion time of job $J_i$ and let $C_{ij}(\boldsymbol{x}, \boldsymbol{\xi}, \boldsymbol{\nu})$ denote the completion time of task $\theta_{ij}$, $i = 1, \ldots, n$ $j = 1, \ldots, m$. Clearly, the completion time of a job is the completion time of its last task, that is: $C_i(\boldsymbol{x}, \boldsymbol{\xi}, \boldsymbol{\nu}) = C_{im}(\boldsymbol{x}, \boldsymbol{\xi}, \boldsymbol{\nu})$, $i = 1, \ldots, n$. The starting time for task $\theta_{ij}$, $i = 1, \ldots, n$, $j = 1, \ldots, m$ will be the maximum between the completion times of the tasks preceding $\theta_{ij}$ in its job and its machine. Hence, the completion time of task $\theta_{ij}$ is given by the following:

$$C_{ij}(\boldsymbol{x}, \boldsymbol{\xi}, \boldsymbol{\nu}) = \big(C_{i(j-1)}(\boldsymbol{x}, \boldsymbol{\xi}, \boldsymbol{\nu}) \sqcup C_{rs}(\boldsymbol{x}, \boldsymbol{\xi}, \boldsymbol{\nu})\big) + p_{ij}$$

where $\theta_{rs}$ is the task preceding $\theta_{ij}$ in the machine according to the processing order given by $\boldsymbol{x}$. $C_{i0}(\boldsymbol{x}, \boldsymbol{\xi}, \boldsymbol{\nu})$ is assumed to be zero and, analogously, $C_{rs}(\boldsymbol{x}, \boldsymbol{\xi}, \boldsymbol{\nu})$ is taken to be zero if $\theta_{ij}$ is the first task to be processed in the corresponding machine. Finally, the *fuzzy makespan* $C_{max}(\boldsymbol{x}, \boldsymbol{\xi}, \boldsymbol{\nu})$ is the maximum completion time of jobs $J_1, \ldots, J_n$ as follows:

$$C_{max}(\boldsymbol{x}, \boldsymbol{\xi}, \boldsymbol{\nu}) = \sqcup_{1 \leq i \leq n} (C_i(\boldsymbol{x}, \boldsymbol{\xi}, \boldsymbol{\nu}))$$

## 3.2   A Multiobjective Model

It is not trivial to optimise a schedule in terms of fuzzy makespan, since neither the maximum $\vee$ nor its approximation $\sqcup$ define a total ordering in the set of TFNs. In the literature, this problem is tackled using some ranking method for fuzzy numbers, lexicographical orderings, comparisons based on $\lambda$-cuts or defuzzification methods. Here the modelling philosophy is similar to that of stochastic scheduling, which optimises some expected objective functions subject to some expected constraints. For this purpose, we use the concept of expected value for a fuzzy variable, so the objective is to minimise the expected makespan $E[C_{max}(\boldsymbol{x}, \boldsymbol{\xi}, \boldsymbol{\nu})]$, a crisp value. In the absence of due-date constraints, this provides an *expected makespan model* for fuzzy job shop scheduling problems [11].

If flexible due dates $D_i$ exist for jobs $J_i$, $i = 1, \ldots, n$, the agreement index $AI(C_i(\boldsymbol{x}, \boldsymbol{\xi}, \boldsymbol{\nu}), D_i)$, denoted $AI_i(\boldsymbol{x}, \boldsymbol{\xi}, \boldsymbol{\nu})$ for short, is a crisp value measuring to what degree the due date is satisfied. The degree of overall due-date satisfaction for schedule $s$ may be obtained by combining the satisfaction degrees $AI_i(\boldsymbol{x}, \boldsymbol{\xi}, \boldsymbol{\nu})$, $i = 1, \ldots, n$. We may expect due dates to be satisfied in average or, being more restrictive, expect that all due dates be satisfied. The degree to which schedule $s$, determined by an ordering $\boldsymbol{x}$, satisfies due dates is then given, respectively, by the following:

$$AI_{av}(\boldsymbol{x}, \boldsymbol{\xi}, \boldsymbol{\nu}) = \frac{1}{n} \sum_{i=1}^{n} AI_i(\boldsymbol{x}, \boldsymbol{\xi}, \boldsymbol{\nu}), \quad AI_{min}(\boldsymbol{x}, \boldsymbol{\xi}, \boldsymbol{\nu}) = \min_{i=1,\ldots,n} AI_i(\boldsymbol{x}, \boldsymbol{\xi}, \boldsymbol{\nu}) \quad (4)$$

Clearly, both $AI_{av}(\boldsymbol{x}, \boldsymbol{\xi}, \boldsymbol{\nu})$ and $AI_{min}(\boldsymbol{x}, \boldsymbol{\xi}, \boldsymbol{\nu})$ should be maximised. Notice however that they model different requirements and encourage different behaviours.

In order to maximise both measures of due-date satisfaction and minimise the expected makespan, we may formulate a multiobjective problem as a fuzzy goal programming model according to a priority structure and target levels established by the decision makers as follows:

**Priority 1.** $f_1(\boldsymbol{x}, \boldsymbol{\xi}, \boldsymbol{\nu}) = E[C_{max}(\boldsymbol{x}, \boldsymbol{\xi}, \boldsymbol{\nu})]$ should be minimised and should not exceed a given target value $b_1$, i.e. we have the following goal constraint:

$$f_1(\boldsymbol{x}, \boldsymbol{\xi}, \boldsymbol{\nu}) + d_1^- - d_1^+ = b_1 \quad (5)$$

where $d_1^+$, the positive deviation from the target, should be minimised.

**Priority 2.** $f_2(\boldsymbol{x}, \boldsymbol{\xi}, \boldsymbol{\nu}) = AI_{av}(\boldsymbol{x}, \boldsymbol{\xi}, \boldsymbol{\nu})$ should be maximised and should not be less than a given target value $b_2$, i.e. we have the following goal constraint:

$$f_2(\boldsymbol{x}, \boldsymbol{\xi}, \boldsymbol{\nu}) + d_2^- - d_2^+ = b_2 \qquad (6)$$

where $d_2^-$, the negative deviation from the target, should be minimised.

**Priority 3.** $f_3(\boldsymbol{x}, \boldsymbol{\xi}, \boldsymbol{\nu}) = AI_{min}(\boldsymbol{x}, \boldsymbol{\xi}, \boldsymbol{\nu})$ should be maximised and should not be less than a given target value $b_3$, i.e. we have the following goal constraint:

$$f_3(\boldsymbol{x}, \boldsymbol{\xi}, \boldsymbol{\nu}) + d_3^- - d_3^+ = b_3 \qquad (7)$$

where $d_3^-$, the negative deviation from the target, should be minimised.

Thus, we have the following *lexmin scheduling model* for the fuzzy job shop problem (FJSP):

$$\begin{cases} \text{lexmin} & (d_1^+, d_2^-, d_3^-) \\ \text{subject to:} \\ & f_i(\boldsymbol{x}, \boldsymbol{\xi}, \boldsymbol{\nu})] + d_i^- - d_i^+ = b_i, \quad i = 1, 2, 3, \\ & b_i \geq 0, \quad i = 1, 2, 3, \\ & d_i^-, d_i^+ \geq 0, \\ & 1 \leq x_l \leq n, \quad l = 1, \dots, nm, \\ & |\{x_l : x_l = i\}| = m, \quad i = 1, \dots, n, \\ & x_l \in \mathbb{Z}^+, \quad l = 1, \dots, nm. \end{cases} \qquad (8)$$

where lexmin denotes lexicographically minimising the objective vector.

## 4   Using Genetic Algorithms to Solve FJSP

The crisp job shop problem is a paradigm of constraint satisfaction problem and has been approached using many heuristic techniques. In particular, genetic algorithms have proved to be a promising solving method [10],[12],[13]. The structure of a conventional genetic algorithm for the FJSP is described in Algorithm 1. First, the initial population is generated and evaluated. Then the genetic algorithm iterates for a number of steps or generations. In each iteration, a new population is built from the previous one by applying the genetic operators of selection, recombination and acceptance.

To codify chromosomes we use the decision variable $\boldsymbol{x}$, a permutation with repetition, which presents a number of interesting characteristics [14]. The quality of a chromosome is evaluated by the fitness function, which is taken to be the objective function of the leximin problem lexmin($d_1^+, d_2^-, d_3^-$) as defined above.

In the selection phase, chromosomes are grouped into pairs using tournament. Each of these pairs is mated to obtain two offsprings and acceptance consists in selecting the best individuals from the set formed by the pair of parents and their offsprings. For chromosome mating we consider the *Job Order Crossover*

---

**Require:** an instance of fuzzy JSP, $P$
**Ensure:** a schedule $H$ for $P$
  1. Generate the initial population;
  2. Evaluate the population;
**while** No termination criterion is satisfied **do**
  3. Select chromosomes from the current population;
  4. Apply the recombination operator to the chromosomes selected at step 3. to generate new ones;
  5. Evaluate the chromosomes generated at step 4;
  6. Apply the acceptance criterion to the set of chromosomes selected at step 3. together with the chromosomes generated at step 4.;
  **return** the schedule from the best chromosome evaluated so far;

---

**Algorithm 1.** Conventional Genetic Algorithm

(JOX) [10]. Given two parents, JOX selects a random subset of jobs, copies their genes to the offspring in the same positions as they appear in the first parent, and the remaining genes are taken from the second parent so as to maintain their relative ordering. This operator has an implicit mutation effect. Therefore, no explicit mutation operator is actually necessary and parameter setting is simplified, as crossover probability is 1 and mutation probability need not be specified.

From a given decision variable $x$ we may obtain a *semi-active* schedule as explained in Section 3, meaning that for any operation to start earlier, the relative ordering of at least two tasks must be swapped. However, other possibilities may be considered. For the crisp job shop, it is common to use the G&T algorithm [15], which is an active schedule builder. A schedule is *active* if one task must be delayed for any other one to start earlier. Active schedules are good in average and, most importantly, the space of active schedules contains at least an optimal one, that is, the set of active schedules is *dominant*. For these reasons it is worth to restrict the search to this space. Moreover, the G&T algorithm is complete for the job shop problem.

In Algorithm 2 we propose an extension of G&T to the case of fuzzy processing times. It should be noted nonetheless that, due to the uncertain durations, we cannot guarantee that the produced schedule will indeed be active when it is actually performed (and tasks have exact durations). We may only say that the obtained fuzzy schedule is *possibly active*. Throughout the algorithm, given any task $\theta$, its starting and completion times will be denoted by $S_\theta$ and $C_\theta$ respectively.

Recall that operator JOX tries to maintain for each machine a subsequence of tasks in the order as they appear in parent 1 and the remaining tasks in the same order as they are in parent 2. It often happens that these two subsequences are not compatible with each other in order to obtain an active schedule, so the decoding algorithm given in Algorithm 2 has to exchange the order of some operations. This new order is translated to the chromosome, for it to be passed

---

**Require:** a chromosome $x$ and a fuzzy JSP $P$
**Ensure:** the schedule $s$ given by chromosome $x$ for problem $P$
1. $A = \{\theta_{i1}, i = 1, \ldots, n\}$; /*set of first tasks of all jobs*/
2. **while** $A \neq \emptyset$ **do**
3.    Determine the task $\theta' \in A$ with minimum earliest completion time $C_{\theta'}^1$ if scheduled in the current state;
4.    Let $M'$ be the machine required by $\theta'$ and $B \subseteq A$ the subset of tasks requiring machine $M'$;
5.    Remove from $B$ any task $\theta$ that starts later than $C_{\theta'}$: $C_{\theta'}^i \leq S_\theta^i$, $i = 1, 2, 3$;
6.    Select $\theta^* \in B$ such that it is the leftmost operation in the sequence $x$;
7.    Schedule $\theta^*$ as early as possible to build a partial schedule;
8.    Remove $\theta^*$ from $A$ and insert in $A$ the task following $\theta^*$ in the job if $\theta^*$ is not the last task of its job;
9. **return** the built schedule;

---

**Algorithm 2.** Extended G&T for triangular fuzzy times

onto subsequent offsprings. In this way, the GA exploits the so called lamarckian evolution. As mentioned above, an implicit mutation effect is obtained.

The GA described above has been successfully used to minimise the expected makespan using semi-active schedules, comparing favourably to a simulated annealing algorithm from the literature [4]. Also, the GA combined with the extended G&T improves the expected makespan results obtained by a niche-based GA where chromosomes are matrices of completion times and recombination operators are based on fuzzy G&T [11].

## 5   Experimental Results

For the experimental results, we follow [4] and generate a set of fuzzy problem instances from well-known benchmark problems: FT06 of size $6 \times 6$ and LA11, LA12, LA13 and LA14 of size $20 \times 5$. For a given crisp processing time $x$, a symmetric fuzzy processing time $p(x)$ is generated such that its centre value, $p^2$, is equal to $x$. The value of $p^1$ is selected at random so that the TFN's maximum range of fuzziness is 30% of $p^2$, taking into account that $p^3$ is the symmetric point to $p^1$ with respect to $p^2$, $p^3 = 2p^2 - p^1$. In [4], only uncertain durations are considered. To generate a flexible due date for a given job $J_i$, let $\iota_i = \sum_{j=1}^m p_{i,j}^2$ be the sum of most typical durations across all its tasks. Also, for a given task $\theta_{i,j}$ let $\rho_{i,j}$ be the sum of most typical durations of all other tasks requiring the same machine as $\theta_{i,j}$, $\rho_{i,j} = \sum_{r \neq i, s \neq j: \nu_{rs} = \nu_{ij}} p_{r,s}^2$, where $p_{r,s}^2$ denotes the most typical duration of task $\theta_{r,s}$. Finally, let $\rho_i = \max_{j=1,\ldots,m} \rho_{i,j}$ be the maximum of such values across all tasks in job $J_i$. The earlier due date $d^1$ is a random value from $[d_m, d_M]$, where $d_m = \iota_i + 0.5\rho_i$ and $d_M = \iota_i + \rho_i$, and the later due date $d^2$ is a random value from $[d^1, int(1.3d^1)]$, where $int(x)$ denotes the smallest integer greater than or equal to $x$. [16].

For each problem instance, we have run the GA 30 times, using the three single-objective functions $f_1, f_2$ and $f_3$ and the multi-objective function proposed in this work $lexmin(d_1^+, d_2^-, d_3^-)$. The configuration parameters of the GA are population size 100 and number of generations 200. To fix the target value for the expected makespan $b_1$, we use our experience obtained with previous experimentation using $f_1$ as single objective and set $b_1$ equal to the makespan's average value across 30 runs of the single-objective GA (see Table 1). The target values for due date satisfaction are in all cases $b_2 = b_3 = 1$. Finally, we also include results obtained with a different multi-objective function based on fuzzy decision making, proposed in [7] and denoted $f$ hereafter. In this approach, the decision maker must define gradual satisfaction degrees for each objective. The results shown herein are obtained with maximum satisfaction for each objective equal to the above target values; the minimum satisfaction degrees for makespan are $int(1.1b_1)$ and, in all cases, the minimum satisfaction for $f_2$ and $f_3$ is achieved at 0. For each fitness function we measure $E[C_{max}]$, $AI_{av}$ and $AI_{min}$ of the obtained schedule and compute the best, average and worst of these values across the 30 executions of the GA. The results are shown in Table 1; under each problem name and between brackets we include optimal value of the makespan for the original crisp problem, which provides a lower bound for the expected makespan of the fuzzified version [4].

Let us first analyse the results obtained by the proposed multiobjective approach, compared to the results obtained when optimising a single criterion. For the most prioritary objective, minimisation of makespan, we see that the multiobjective approach obtains exactly the same expected makespan values than the single-objective function. These expected values also coincide with the optimal value for the crisp problem in all cases except LA12. For this problem, the fuzzy makespan for the 30 runs of the GA is $C_{max} = (972, 1039, 1110)$, so the most typical value coincides with the optimal value of the crisp problem, but $E[C_{max}] = 1040$. Besides, there is a clear improvement in due date satisfaction.

Regarding the second objective, $AI_{av}$, the results obtained by lexmin compared to $1 - f_2$ yield a relative error lower than 1%, except for FT06, where the relative error is close to 6%. Notice however that, for this problem, the single objective $1 - f_2$ has a relative error w.r.t. the best expected makespan values up to 36%. The use of multiobjective optimisation sets this error to 0, at the expense of reasonably worse results for the second objective. In the remaining problems, the benefits of multiobjective optimisation are even clearer: the makespan errors (w.r.t. the best values) go from 2.26%-28.12% when using $1 - f_2$ to zero using the multiobjective approach and, at the same time, the multiobjective approach has notably higher values of $AI_{av}$ than when only makespan ($f_1$) is optimised, at the same computational cost.

The behaviour for the third objective, $AI_{min}$ is similar. There is a slight worsening in the value of $AI_{min}$ when lexmin is used instead of $1 - f_3$ (with the exception of FT06, where worsening is higher), but this is largely compensated by the improvement in makespan. Notice as well that the errors obtained in $AI_{min}$ when only makespan minimisation is considered may be up to 100% and they are reduced by lexmin between 60% and 100%, with an average reduction of 77.72%, again with the exception of FT06.

**Table 1.** Results obtained by the GA

| Problem | Fitness | $f_1$ | | | $f_2$ | | | $f_3$ | | |
|---------|---------|-------|-----|-------|-------|-----|-------|-------|-----|-------|
| | | Best | Avg | Worst | Best | Avg | Worst | Best | Avg | Worst |
| FT06 (55) | $f_1$ | 55 | 55 | 55 | 0.94 | 0.94 | 0.94 | 0.64 | 0.64 | 0.64 |
| | $1 - f_2$ | 59 | 70.47 | 75 | 1 | 1 | 1 | 1 | 1 | 1 |
| | $1 - f_3$ | 61 | 72.28 | 75 | 1 | 1 | 1 | 1 | 1 | 1 |
| | lexmin | 55 | 55 | 55 | 0.94 | 0.94 | 0.94 | 0.64 | 0.64 | 0.64 |
| | $f$ | 59 | 69.07 | 87 | 0.98 | 0.89 | 0.68 | 0.89 | 0.51 | 0 |
| LA11 (1222) | $f_1$ | 1222 | 1222 | 1222 | 0.93 | 0.83 | 0.74 | 0.37 | 0.07 | 0 |
| | $1 - f_2$ | 1238 | 1326.91 | 1371 | 1 | 1 | 1 | 1 | 1 | 1 |
| | $1 - f_3$ | 1241 | 1327.88 | 1372.50 | 1 | 1 | 1 | 1 | 1 | 1 |
| | lexmin | 1222 | 1222 | 1222 | 1 | 1 | 0.98 | 1 | 0.99 | 0.80 |
| | $f$ | 1279.75 | 1339.22 | 1488.75 | 0.86 | 0.75 | 0.61 | 0.32 | 0.03 | 0 |
| LA12 (1039) | $f_1$ | 1040 | 1040 | 1040 | 0.95 | 0.88 | 0.82 | 0.64 | 0.15 | 0 |
| | $1 - f_2$ | 1084 | 1112.53 | 1212.75 | 1 | 1 | 1 | 1 | 1 | 1 |
| | $1 - f_3$ | 1084 | 1102.16 | 1192.25 | 1 | 1 | 1 | 1 | 1 | 1 |
| | lexmin | 1040 | 1040 | 1040 | 1 | 0.99 | 0.99 | 0.93 | 0.92 | 0.90 |
| | $f$ | 1064.50 | 1145.97 | 1293 | 0.91 | 0.84 | 0.77 | 0.47 | 0.08 | 0 |
| LA13 (1150) | $f_1$ | 1150 | 1150 | 1150 | 0.96 | 0.92 | 0.88 | 0.80 | 0.54 | 0.34 |
| | $1 - f_2$ | 1198 | 1291.62 | 1359.25 | 1 | 1 | 1 | 1 | 1 | 1 |
| | $1 - f_3$ | 1151 | 1272.12 | 1363 | 1 | 1 | 1 | 1 | 1 | 1 |
| | lexmin | 1150 | 1150 | 1150 | 1 | 1 | 1 | 1 | 1 | 1 |
| | $f$ | 1185.75 | 1289.16 | 1378.25 | 0.96 | 0.87 | 0.80 | 0.75 | 0.24 | 0 |
| LA14 (1292) | $f_1$ | 1292 | 1292 | 1292 | 0.95 | 0.86 | 0.81 | 0.60 | 0.04 | 0 |
| | $1 - f_2$ | 1292 | 1321.21 | 1432.75 | 1 | 1 | 1 | 1 | 1 | 1 |
| | $1 - f_3$ | 1292 | 1315.63 | 1445 | 1 | 1 | 1 | 1 | 1 | 1 |
| | lexmin | 1292 | 1292 | 1292 | 1 | 1 | 1 | 1 | 1 | 1 |
| | $f$ | 1292 | 1337.54 | 1427.50 | 0.94 | 0.86 | 0.79 | 0.47 | 0.05 | 0 |

Finally, if we compare the two multiobjective approaches, lexmin is clearly better than $f$. The latter, based on fuzzy decision making, uses the minimum to aggregate the objectives' satisfaction degrees and this operator might be too coarse in some cases, for instance, when one objective is more difficult to achieve than the others or when objectives are partially incompatible.

## 6    Conclusions and Future Work

We have considered a job shop problem with uncertain durations, modelled using TFNs, and flexible due dates, also modelled with fuzzy sets. The goal is to find an ordering of tasks that yields a feasible schedule with minimal makespan and maximum due-date satisfaction. We propose to formulate the multiobjective problem as a fuzzy goal programming model according to a priority structure and target levels established by the decision maker, using the expected value of the makespan and lexicographical minimisation. The resulting problem is solved using a GA with codification based on permutations with repetitions. Experimental results on fuzzy versions of well-known problem instances illustrate the potential of both the proposed multiobjective formulation and the GA. Indeed, in most cases the expected makespan values coincide with optimal values for the original problems and due-date satisfaction is maximal.

In the future, the multiobjective approach will be further analysed on varied set of problem instances, incorporating the semantics proposed in [7]. Also, the GA may be hybridised with other heuristic techniques such as local search, which implies further studying task criticality when durations are fuzzy.

# References

1. Brucker, P., Knust, S.: Complex Scheduling. Springer, Heidelberg (2006)
2. Dubois, D., Fargier, H., Fortemps, P.: Fuzzy scheduling: Modelling flexible constraints vs. coping with incomplete knowledge. European Journal of Operational Research 147, 231–252 (2003)
3. Słowiński, R., Hapke, M. (eds.): Scheduling Under Fuzziness. Studies in Fuzziness and Soft Computing, vol. 37. Physica-Verlag, Heidelberg (2000)
4. Fortemps, P.: Jobshop scheduling with imprecise durations: a fuzzy approach. IEEE Transactions of Fuzzy Systems 7, 557–569 (1997)
5. Sakawa, M., Kubota, R.: Fuzzy programming for multiobjective job shop scheduling with fuzzy processing time and fuzzy duedate through genetic algorithms. European Journal of Operational Research 120, 393–407 (2000)
6. Fayad, C., Petrovic, S.: A fuzzy genetic algorithm for real-world job-shop scheduling. In: Ali, M., Esposito, F. (eds.) IEA/AIE 2005. LNCS (LNAI), vol. 3533, pp. 524–533. Springer, Heidelberg (2005)
7. González Rodríguez, I., Puente, J., Vela, C.R., Varela, R.: Semantics of schedules for the fuzzy job shop problem. IEEE Transactions on Systems, Man and Cybernetics, Part A, Accepted for publication (2007)
8. Liu, B., Liu, Y.K.: Expected value of fuzzy variable and fuzzy expected value models. IEEE Transactions on Fuzzy Systems 10, 445–450 (2002)
9. Celano, G., Costa, A., Fichera, S.: An evolutionary algorithm for pure fuzzy flowshop scheduling problems. Fuzziness and Knowledge-Based Systems 11, 655–669 (2003)
10. Bierwirth, C.: A generalized permutation approach to jobshop scheduling with genetic algorithms. OR Spectrum 17, 87–92 (1995)
11. González Rodríguez, I., Vela, C.R., Puente, J.: A memetic approach to fuzzy job shop based on expectation model. In: Proceedings of FUZZ-IEEE 2007 (2007)
12. Mattfeld, D.C.: Evolutionary Search and the Job Shop Investigations on Genetic Algorithms for Production Scheduling. Springer, Heidelberg (1995)
13. Varela, R., Vela, C.R., Puente, J., Gómez, A.: A knowledge-based evolutionary strategy for scheduling problems with bottlenecks. European Journal of Operational Research 145, 57–71 (2003)
14. Varela, R., Serrano, D., Sierra, M.: New codification schemas for scheduling with genetic algorithms. In: Mira, J.M., Álvarez, J.R. (eds.) IWINAC 2005. LNCS, vol. 3562, pp. 11–20. Springer, Heidelberg (2005)
15. Giffler, B., Thomson, G.L.: Algorithms for solving production scheduling problems. Operations Research 8, 487–503 (1960)
16. González Rodríguez, I., Vela, C.R., Puente, J.: Study of objective functions in fuzzy job-shop problem. In: Rutkowski, L., Tadeusiewicz, R., Zadeh, L.A., Zurada, J.M. (eds.) ICAISC 2006. LNCS (LNAI), vol. 4029, pp. 360–369. Springer, Heidelberg (2006)

# CTC: An Alternative to Extract Explanation from Bagging

Ibai Gurrutxaga, Jesús Mª Pérez, Olatz Arbelaitz, Javier Muguerza, José I. Martín, and Ander Ansuategi

Dept. of Computer Architecture and Technology, University of the Basque Country
M. Lardizabal, 1, 20018 Donostia, Spain
{i.gurrutxaga,txus.perez,
olatz.arbelaitz,j.muguerza,j.martin}@ehu.es
aansuategui001@ikasle.ehu.es
http://www.sc.ehu.es/aldapa

**Abstract.** Being aware of the importance of classifiers to be comprehensible when using machine learning to solve real world problems, bagging needs a way to be explained. This work compares Consolidated Tree's Construction (CTC) algorithm with the Combined Multiple Models (CMM) method proposed by Domingos when used to extract explanation of the classification made by bagging. The comparison has been done from two main points of view: accuracy, and quality of the provided explanation. From the experimental results we can conclude that it is recommendable the use of CTC rather than the use of CMM. From the accuracy point of view, the behaviour of CTC is nearer the behaviour of bagging than CMM's one. And, analysing the complexity of the obtained classifiers, we can say that Consolidated Trees (CT trees) will give simpler and, therefore, more comprehensible explanation than CMM classifiers. And besides, looking to the stability of the structure of the built trees, we could say that the explanation given by CT trees is steadier than the one given by CMM classifiers. As a consequence, the user of the classifier will feel more confident using CTC than using CMM.

## 1 Introduction

The main objective of machine learning techniques when used to solve real world problems is to automate knowledge acquisition for performing useful tasks. The most pursued objective is probably accurate prediction (error or guess), but there are real domains such as fraud detection, illness diagnosis, etc., where it is not enough to obtain the right classification and the users wish to gain insight into the domain [5]. To solve this kind of problems, the learner's output needs to be comprehensible. In other situations where comprehensibility is not necessary, it will also be an advantage for classifiers because it will help in processes of refinement.

In this context, classifiers can be divided in two main groups: classifiers with no comprehensible output and classifiers with comprehensible output. In the first group we can find artificial neural networks, support vector machines, multiple classifiers,

D. Borrajo, L. Castillo, and J.M. Corchado (Eds.): CAEPIA 2007, LNAI 4788, pp. 90–99, 2007.

etc., that, due to their complexity and structure do not provide an explanation to the classification. The second group includes classifiers that focus on representation, such as decision trees and rule sets. Comprehensible methods are usually very dependent on the training data. That is to say, classifiers induced from slightly different samples of the same data set are very different in accuracy and structure [6]. As Turney found when working on industrial applications of decision tree learning, not only to give an explanation but the stability of that explanation is of capital importance: "the engineers are disturbed when different batches of data from the same process result in radically different decision trees. The engineers lose confidence in the decision trees even when we can demonstrate that the trees have high predictive accuracy" [14].

Decision trees have been chosen as paradigm with comprehensive output in this work. Since in a decision tree the explanation is given by its structure, if we want to obtain a convincing explanation we need a way to build structurally steady trees with small complexity. Multiple classifiers such as bagging and boosting [1][2][4][7][13] reduce the error rate, but, even when the used weak classifiers are decision trees, a set of them needs to be combined to make a decision on the whole, and, as a consequence, comprehensibility disappears. Domingos explained it very clearly in [5]: "while a single decision tree can easily be understood by a human as long as it is not too large, fifty such trees, even if individually simple, exceed the capacity of even the most patient". Domingos proposes Combined Multiple Models (CMM) algorithm [5] to extract explanation from bagging or any other multiple classifier.

We have developed a methodology for building classification trees based on several subsamples, Consolidated Trees' Construction Algorithm (CTC), which is less sensitive to changes in the training set from a structural point of view. Therefore the classification is contributed with a more steady explanation. The aim of this work is to show that CTC algorithm can be used to extract explanation from bagging achieving better results than CMM from three points of view: accuracy, complexity of the built classifiers and stability in explanation.

The paper proceeds describing the two alternatives used to extract explanation from bagging, CTC and CMM, in Section 2. Details about the experimental methodology are described in Section 3. In Section 4 we present an analysis of the experimental results: comparison in accuracy, complexity and structural stability of CTC and CMM algorithms. Finally Section 5 is devoted to show the conclusions and further work.

## 2   Two Alternatives to Extract Explanation from Bagging

The alternatives we are going to compare in this work, CTC and CMM, propose different strategies to combine the knowledge of the $m$ classifiers used in bagging in a single one in order to maintain the explaining capacity of the final classifier.

### 2.1   CMM Algorithm

CMM proposes to recover the comprehensibility loss in bagging using the learning algorithm to model the produced data partitioning. The learning is done from randomly generated examples that are classified using the bagging. Finally these examples will be used to build a classifier with comprehensible output. CMM is a general algorithm that can be used with different learners and ensemble methods but in this work we will use it to extract explanation from bagging when the selected learning algorithm is classification trees, specifically C4.5 release 8 of Quinlan [12]. The knowledge of this multi-classifier will be transmitted to CMM using it to artificially generate and label the examples that will be used to build it.

Algorithm 1 shows Domingo's CMM proposal adapted to the concrete implementation. $N\_S$ bootstrap samples are extracted from $S$, the original training set, and one C4.5 tree is built from each of them. $n$ new examples are generated using the probability distribution implicit in the generated C4.5 trees ($n/N\_S$ examples from each component C4.5 tree). The corresponding class ($c$) is assigned to each example based on the class the bagging of all the generated C4.5 trees assigns them ($c=$ bagging $_{M_{1},...,\ M_{N\_S}}(x)$). This way, the examples will be representative of the combination of basic classifiers. The CMM classifier will be the C4.5 tree built from the new sample obtained adding the $n$ randomly generated examples to the original training set.

**Algorithm 1.** CMM Algorithm for bagging and C4.5

---

Inputs:
   $S$ training set
   *C4.5* classifier with comprehensible output
   *bagging* procedure for combining models
   $N\_S$ (*Number_Samples*) number of component models to generate
   $n$ number of new examples to generate

Procedure CMM ($S$, *C4.5*, *bagging*, $N\_S$, $n$)

   **for** $i := 1$ to $N\_S$
      Let $S^i$ be a bootstrap sample of $S$
      Let $M^i$ be the model produced by applying *C4.5* to $S^i$
   **end for**

   **for** $j := 1$ to $n$
      Let $x$ be the randomly generated example
      Let $c$ be the class assigned to $x$ by *bagging* $_{M_{1},...,\ M_{N\_S}}(x)$
      Let $T = T \cup \{(x,c)\}$
   **end for**

   Let $M$ be the model produced by applying *C4.5* to $S \cup T$

---

## 2.2  CTC Algorithm

CTC algorithm was created to solve a fraud detection problem where the class distribution needed to be changed and explanation was required. In this kind of problems, classification trees built from different subsamples are very different in structure and accuracy. CTC draws together the information of a set of subsamples building a single tree [10]. The structural consensus is achieved at each step of the tree's building process. The different subsamples are used to make proposals about the feature that should be used to split in the current node, and, only one feature is selected. The repetition of this process in every node leads to the construction of a single tree. In order to make the CTC comparable to CMM, the split function used is the gain ratio criterion (the same used by Quinlan in C4.5 [12]). The iterative process is described in Algorithm 2.

CTC algorithm uses several subsamples to induce a single tree, therefore, if we want to use it to explain the classification made by bagging, the same subsamples used for bagging will be used to build the CT tree.

The algorithm starts extracting a set of subsamples ($N\_S$) from the original training set. The subsamples are obtained based on the desired resampling technique. In this case the bootstrap samples used for bagging will be used. $LS^i$ contains all the data partitions created from each subsample $S^i$. When the process starts, the only existing partitions are the bootstrap subsamples of bagging. The pair $(X,B)^i$ is the split proposal for the first data partition in $LS^i$. $X$ is the feature selected to split and $B$ indicates the proposed branches or criteria to divide the data in the current node. In the consolidation step, $X_c$ and $B_c$ are the feature and branches selected by a voting process among all the proposals. The process is repeated while $LS^i$ is not empty. The Consolidated Tree's generation process finishes when, in the last subsample in all the partitions in $LS^i$, most of the proposals are not to split it, so, to become it a leaf node. When a node is consolidated as a leaf node, the a posteriori probabilities associated to it are calculated averaging the a posteriori obtained from the data partitions related to that node in all the subsamples. Once the consolidated tree has been built it works the same way a decision tree does.

**Algorithm 2.** CTC Algorithm

---

Generate $N\_S$ *bootstrap* samples ($S^i$) from $S$
$CurrentNode := RootNode$
**for** $i := 1$ to $N\_S$
  $LS^i := \{S^i\}$
**end for**
**repeat**
  **for** $i := 1$ to $N\_S$
    $CurrentS^i := First(LS^i)$
    $LS^i := LS^i - CurrentS^i$
    Induce the best split $(X,B)^i$ for $CurrentS^i$
  **end for**
  Obtain the consolidated pair $(X_c, B_c)$ based on $(X,B)^i$, $1 \le i \le N\_S$
  **if** $(X_c, B_c) \ne Not\_Split$
    Split $CurrentNode$ based on $(X_c, B_c)$
    **for** $i := 1$ to $N\_S$
      Divide $CurrentS^i$ based on $(X_c, B_c)$ to obtain $n$ subsamples $\{S_1^i, ..., S_n^i\}$
      $LS^i := \{S_1^i, ..., S_n^i\} \cup LS^i$
    **end for**
  **else** consolidate $CurrentNode$ as a leaf
  **end if**
  $CurrentNode := NextNode$
  **until** $\forall i$, $LS^i$ is empty

---

## 3 Experimental Methodology

Eleven databases of real applications from the UCI Repository benchmark [9] have been used for the experimentation: *Breast-W, Iris, Heart-C, Glass, Segment, Voting, Lymph, Hepatitis, Hypo, Soybean-L,* and *KDDcup99.* For *KDDcup99,* in order to reduce the experimentation cost, we have used a stratified sample of 4,941 examples where the number of classes has been reduced to two (attack / not attack). The used domains have a wide range of characteristics: the number of patterns goes from 148 to 4,941; the number of features from 4 to 41; and the number of classes from 2 to 15.

The validation methodology used in this experimentation has been to execute 5 times a 10-fold stratified cross validation [8]. In each of the folds of the cross-validation we have obtained 200 bootstrap samples. These subsamples have been used to explore the effect of the $N\_S$ parameter (12 values: 3, 5, 10, 20, 30, 40, 50, 75, 100, 125, 150 and 200) in the particular implementation of bagging. So in each one of the 50 folds of the cross validations 12 bagging classifiers have been built. We have selected for each database the value of $N\_S$ that minimizes error rate. Once this parameter has been fixed it has been used to build CT trees and CMM classifiers and compare them from two points of view: accuracy and quality of the explanation. The quality of explanation has been evaluated based on complexity and stability of the given explanation. Complexity has been measured as the number of internal nodes of the tree, and, the stability in explanation as structural stability of the tress which has been measured by *Common* parameter (number of identical nodes —level, variable and division— among two trees). *Common* has been normalized in respect to the complexity so that the parsimony principle was taken into account. We will call this measure *%Common* and it will quantify the identical fraction of two or more trees [11].

In both cases, error and explanation, an analysis of the statistically significant differences has been done based on the recent work of Demšar [3].

For building CMM classifiers the number of randomly generated examples ($n$) needs to be fixed. Taking into account the process used to generate examples ($n/N\_S$ examples are generated from each component C4.5 tree) and that the number of component C4.5 trees goes from 3 to 200, this number needs to be large enough to generate a minimum set of examples from each one of the C4.5 trees and, as the original sample is added to these examples to build the CMM, it also needs not to be too small compared to it. Domingos generated 1,000 artificial examples but the databases used for the experimentation were smaller than the ones used in our experimentation. As a consequence, the number has been fixed to max (1,000; ($NPT$ * 1.5)) being *NPT* the number of patterns of the training set.

## 4 Experimental Results

CTC and CMM algorithms have been compared from three points of view: error, complexity, and structural stability (measured based on *Common* and *%Common*). From a practical point of view, the complexity quantifies how simple the given explanation is, *Common* and *%Common* quantify structural stability of the trees, whereas the error would quantify the "quality" of the explanation given by the tree. Evidently an improvement in comprehensibility must be supported with a reasonable error rate. As a consequence, we will start the comparison from the accuracy point of view.

## 4.1  Discriminating Capacity

In the first step, the effect of $N\_S$ in bagging has been analyzed so that for each database the best number of samples could be selected. Table 1 shows the obtained results. We can observe that even if the use of several basic classifiers provides bagging with stability, the results are not exactly the same for different values of $N\_S$. Minimum error rates for each database are marked in bold. It can be observed that the smallest average error is achieved when $N\_S$ is 100. The values of $N\_S$ obtaining best results have been selected to build CTC and CMM classifiers.

**Table 1.** Error values for bagging in 11 databases and different values of $N\_S$

| $N\_S$ | Bagging | | | | | | | | | | | |
|---|---|---|---|---|---|---|---|---|---|---|---|---|
| | 03 | 05 | 10 | 20 | 30 | 40 | 50 | 75 | 100 | 125 | 150 | 200 |
| *Breast-w* | 5.61 | 5.24 | 5.35 | 4.64 | 4.84 | 4.78 | 4.78 | 4.75 | 4.64 | **4.61** | 4.64 | 4.70 |
| *Iris* | 5.87 | 6.40 | 5.87 | 6.53 | 6.13 | 5.87 | 5.73 | 5.47 | 5.47 | **5.33** | 5.47 | 5.33 |
| *Heartc* | 24.34 | 23.41 | 21.91 | 21.58 | 21.97 | 21.50 | 21.44 | 20.91 | **20.39** | 20.53 | 20.53 | 20.46 |
| *Glass* | 29.68 | 27.47 | 26.45 | 24.59 | 24.69 | 24.37 | 23.70 | 23.62 | **23.13** | 24.18 | 23.71 | 23.85 |
| *Segment* | 3.75 | 3.18 | 2.80 | 2.64 | 2.57 | 2.48 | 2.47 | **2.38** | 2.40 | 2.42 | 2.39 | 2.43 |
| *Voting* | 4.05 | 3.82 | 3.73 | 3.50 | 3.59 | 3.54 | 3.50 | 3.59 | 3.45 | 3.46 | **3.41** | 3.50 |
| *Lymph* | 21.10 | 20.77 | 20.29 | 19.38 | 18.85 | 19.56 | 19.41 | 19.07 | 18.82 | 19.17 | 19.17 | **18.60** |
| *Hepatitis* | 20.11 | 18.05 | 17.80 | 17.88 | 17.89 | 18.36 | 17.37 | 16.96 | 16.97 | 17.08 | **16.61** | 16.83 |
| *Hypo* | 0.82 | **0.75** | 0.78 | 0.77 | 0.75 | 0.76 | 0.76 | 0.76 | 0.76 | 0.75 | 0.76 | 0.75 |
| *Soybean_large* | 13.24 | 11.24 | 10.41 | 10.00 | 9.17 | 9.38 | 9.45 | 9.24 | **9.03** | 9.10 | 9.10 | 9.38 |
| *kddcup* | 0.37 | 0.31 | 0.36 | 0.33 | 0.32 | 0.32 | 0.30 | 0.32 | 0.30 | 0.28 | 0.28 | **0.28** |
| **Average** | 11.72 | 10.97 | 10.52 | 10.17 | 10.07 | 10.08 | 9.90 | 9.73 | **9.58** | 9.72 | 9.64 | 9.65 |

Before starting with the comparison of CTC and CMM we compare in Table 2 error rates achieved for both algorithms, C4.5 (as base classifier) and bagging, so that we situate CTC and CMM in respect to them. Results in Table 2 show that as we expected bagging is the algorithm achieving the smallest error rates, whereas the largest ones are achieved with C4.5. CTC and CMM are situated among these two algorithms, being the error of CMM slightly smaller in average.

The multiple test proposed by Demšar in [3] has been used to deeper analyse the differences among the four algorithms. With this aim, we need to rank each algorithm for every database. Average rank values are: bagging (1.36), CTC (2.50), C4.5 (3.05) and CMM (3.09). Even if in results in Table 2 we could see that in average CMM achieves smaller error rate than CTC, this was an effect of the average. Rank values show that, if instead of analysing absolute values we analyse the rank, CTC is in second position, whereas CMM is in the 4th one, even behind C4.5.

**Table 2.** Error values for C4.5, bagging, CTC and CMM in 11 databases. *N_S* fixed based on best results obtained for bagging.

|  | **C4.5** | **N_S** | **Bagging** | **CMM** | **CTC** |
|---|---|---|---|---|---|
| *Breast-w* | 5.63 | 125 | 4.60 | 5.26 | 5.60 |
| *Iris* | 5.75 | 125 | 5.33 | 5.34 | 4.14 |
| *Heartc* | 23.96 | 100 | 20.39 | 22.85 | 23.42 |
| *Glass* | 31.55 | 100 | 23.13 | 28.16 | 29.85 |
| *Segment* | 3.24 | 75 | 2.38 | 3.27 | 3.33 |
| *Voting* | 3.41 | 150 | 3.41 | 3.69 | 3.36 |
| *Lymph* | 20.44 | 200 | 18.60 | 20.77 | 20.19 |
| *Hepatitis* | 20.29 | 150 | 16.61 | 18.51 | 20.95 |
| *Hypo* | 0.71 | 5 | 0.75 | 0.78 | 0.73 |
| *Soybean_large* | 11.02 | 100 | 9.03 | 11.57 | 10.67 |
| *kddcup* | 0.46 | 200 | 0.28 | 0.50 | 0.46 |
| **Average** | **11.50** |  | **9.50** | **10.97** | **11.16** |

Next step is to analyse whether significant differences among the 4 algorithms exist using Friedman test [3]. The critical value ($\alpha$=0.05) is 2.9223 and the achieved value has been $F_F$= 6.3293. As a consequence significant differences exist. And we need to use a post-hoc test. We will use Nemenyi test [3] to compare all classifiers to each other and Bonferroni-Dunn test [3] to compare all classifiers with a control classifier (C4.5 in our work). Nemenyi test (for 4 algorithms, 11 databases and $\alpha$=0.05) says that if the difference among average ranks is smaller than 1.4142 there is not significant difference among the compared algorithms, whereas the critical value for Bonferroni-Dunn is 1.3179.

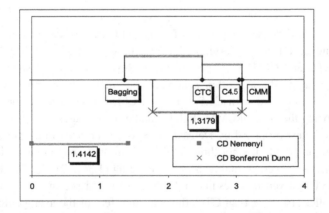

**Fig. 1.** Results for Nemenyi and Bonferroni-Dunn for C4.5, bagging, CTC and CMM

Figure 1 shows graphically results for these tests based on CD ((*Critical Difference*)) diagrams. In Nemenyi's test (upper line in the figure) two algorithms are connected by a line if no significant differences exist whereas for Bonferroni-Dunn test (lower line in the figure) there are significant differences with the control classifier only if the corresponding point is outside the line. Graphs show that based on both kind of tests, there are not significant differences among bagging and CTC (there are significant differences among bagging and the rest of the algorithms) but neither among CTC and the rest of the algorithms.

To make a deeper analysis of CTC and CMM we will make the statistical tests proposed by Demšar for two algorithms (Sign Test and Wilcoxon Signed-Ranks Test). We can use the signs obtained when calculating relative improvements of CTC with respect to CMM presented in Table 3 for the Sign Test. Results in Table 3 show that CTC has smaller error than CMM in 6 databases out of 11 (in bold) obtaining an average relative improvement of 2.28%. However, none of the two tests finds significant differences ($\alpha$=0.05) in the set of 11 databases we have used (for the Sign test the statistic should be at least 9 and it should be smaller than 10 for Wilcoxon test). As a consequence we could say that even if in accuracy the behaviour of CTC and CMM is similar, it is slightly better for CTC.

**Table 3.** Relative improvement of CTC with respect to CMM for each database; average relative improvement and values of the statistics of the Sing Test and Wilcoxon Test

|  | **CTC - CMM** |
| --- | --- |
| *Breast-w* | 6.46% |
| *Iris* | **-22.46%** |
| *Heartc* | 2.52% |
| *Glass* | 6.00% |
| *Segment* | 1.89% |
| *Voting* | **-8.84%** |
| *Lymph* | **-2.81%** |
| *Hepatitis* | 13.18% |
| *Hypo* | **-6.15%** |
| *Soybean_large* | **-7.73%** |
| *kddcup* | **-7.20%** |
| **Average** | **-2.28%** |
| Sign Test | 6 |
| Wilcoxon Test | 31 |

## 4.2  Explaining Capacity

Comprehensibility or explaining capacity of classification trees and quality of the given explanation can be measured by complexity and stability (*common & %common*). These values are shown in Table 4. If we analyse the complexity, results show that in 10 databases out of 11, trees obtained with CTC are simpler than the ones obtained with CMM with a relative average improvement of 32.08%. Similar behaviour is found when analysing the stability. In most of the databases *Common* and *%Common* are larger for CTC than for CMM (with average relative improvements of 36.33% and 118.41%). If we look to the statistics for the Sign Test and Wilcoxon Test (in the two last rows in Table 4) we find that there are significant differences in favour of CTC in the three parameters. So, we can state that from the explanation point of view CT classifiers are simpler and more stable than CMM classifiers.

**Table 4.** Explanation related values: Complexity, *Common* and *%Common* for CTC and CMM

|  | Complexity | | Common | | %Common | |
| --- | --- | --- | --- | --- | --- | --- |
|  | CTC | CMM | CTC | CMM | CTC | CMM |
| *Breast-w* | 4.02 | **3.52** | **2.71** | 2.56 | 68.41 | **74.10** |
| *Iris* | **3.42** | 5.42 | 1.81 | **2.87** | 53.02 | **53.15** |
| *Heartc* | **22.51** | 34.54 | **1.91** | 1.55 | **8.49** | 4.47 |
| *Glass* | **34.71** | 54.14 | **4.97** | 3.56 | **14.34** | 6.58 |
| *Segment* | **62.64** | 100.24 | **14.79** | 12.95 | **23.51** | 12.94 |
| *Voting* | **5.13** | 6.74 | **4.35** | 3.11 | **84.74** | 46.35 |
| *Lymph* | **12.33** | 21.74 | **4.12** | 2.29 | **33.28** | 10.56 |
| *Hepatitis* | **10.16** | 28.30 | **2.14** | 1.57 | **21.04** | 5.57 |
| *Hypo* | **5.98** | 7.38 | **2.83** | 2.52 | **48.44** | 34.72 |
| *Soybean_large* | **25.98** | 39.36 | **9.42** | 4.52 | **36.25** | 11.48 |
| *kddcup* | **15.80** | 25.42 | **5.42** | 3.04 | **34.27** | 11.82 |
| **Average** | **18.43** | 29.71 | **4.95** | 3.69 | **38.71** | 24.70 |
| Sign Test | 10 | | 10 | | 9 | |
| Wilcoxon Test | 1 | | 5 | | 4 | |

## 5 Conclusions

Being aware of the importance of classifiers to be comprehensible when using machine learning to solve real world problems, we propose in this work CTC algorithm as an alternative to the Combined Multiple Models (CMM) algorithm proposed by Domingos to extract explanation from bagging. We have compared both proposals from three points of view: accuracy, complexity of the built classifiers and stability in explanation.

From the experimental results we can conclude that it is recommendable the use of CTC rather than the use of CMM. From the accuracy point of view, the behaviour of both algorithms, CTC and CMM, is similar, although the behaviour of CTC is nearer to bagging's one than the behaviour of CMM. Based on Demšar proposal for statistical analysis we can say that there are not significant differences among bagging and CTC whereas these differences exist if we compare bagging with CMM or C4.5. After analysing the complexity of both kinds of trees, we can say that CT trees will give simpler and as a consequence more comprehensible explanation than CMM classifiers. We could say this explanation is 32.08% simpler. And besides, looking to how steady the structure of the built trees is, we could say that the explanation fraction maintained common in Consolidated Trees at least twice as big as the one maintained CMM classifiers. As a consequence, the explanation given to bagging using CTC will be simpler and more stable than the one given by CMM.

There are many things that can be done in the future related to this work. Firstly the experimentation can be extended to more databases. The way the classification is made in CTC can be changed: it can be seen as a multiple classifier system that classifies the same way bagging does but with a single structure. Related to the measure of stability in explanation, other structural measures can be tried.

## Acknowledgments

This work was partly funded by the Diputación Foral de Gipuzkoa and the E.U.

The *lymphography* domain was obtained from the University Medical Centre, Institute of Oncology, Ljubljana, Yugoslavia. Thanks go to M. Zwitter and M. Soklic for providing the data.

## References

1. Bauer, E., Kohavi, R.: An Empirical Comparison of Voting Classification Algorithms: Bagging, Boosting, and Variants. Machine Learning 36, 105–139 (1999)
2. Breiman, L.: Bagging Predictors. Machine Learning 24, 123–140 (1996)
3. Demšar, J.: Statistical Comparisons of Classifiers over Multiple Data Sets. Journal of Machine Learning Research 7, 1–30 (2006)
4. Dietterich, T.G.: An Experimental Comparison of Three Methods for Constructing Ensembles of Decision Trees: Bagging, Boosting, and Randomization. Machine Learning 40, 139–157 (2000)
5. Domingos, P.: Knowledge acquisition from examples via multiple models. In: Proc. 14th International Conf. on Machine Learning Nashville, TN, pp. 98–106 (1997)
6. Drummond, C., Holte, R.C.: Exploiting the Cost (In)sensitivity of Decision Tree Splitting Criteria. In: Proc. of the 17th Int. Conf. on Machine Learning, pp. 239–246 (2000)
7. Freund, Y., Schapire, R.E.: Experiments with a New Boosting Algorithm. In: Proceedings of the 13th International Conference on Machine Learning, pp. 148–156 (1996)
8. Hastie, T., Tibshirani, R., Friedman, J.: The Elements of Statistical Learning. Springer, Heidelberg (2001)
9. Newman, D.J., Hettich, S., Blake, C.L., Merz, C.J.: UCI Repository of machine learning databases. University of California, Department of Information and Computer Science, Irvine, CA (1998), http://www.ics.uci.edu/ mlearn/MLRepository.html
10. Pérez, J.M., Muguerza, J., Arbelaitz, O., Gurrutxaga, I., Martín, J.I.: Combining multiple class distribution modified subsamples in a single tree. Pattern Recognition Letters 28(4), 414–422 (2007)
11. Pérez, J.M., Muguerza, J., Arbelaitz, O., Gurrutxaga, I., Martín, J.I.: Consolidated Trees: an Analysis of Structural Convergence. In: Williams, G.J., Simoff, S.J. (eds.) Data Mining. LNCS (LNAI), vol. 3755, pp. 39–52. Springer, Heidelberg (2006)
12. Quinlan, J.R. (eds.): C4.5: Programs for Machine Learning. Morgan Kaufmann Publishers Inc., San Mateo, California (1993)
13. Skurichina, M., Kuncheva, L.I., Duin, R.P.W.: Bagging and Boosting for the Nearest Mean Classifier: Effects of Sample Size on Diversity and Accuracy. In: Roli, F., Kittler, J. (eds.) MCS 2002. LNCS, vol. 2364, pp. 62–71. Springer, Heidelberg (2002)
14. Turney, P.: Bias and the quantification of stability. Machine Learning 20, 23–33 (1995)

# Ranking Attributes Using Learning of Preferences by Means of SVM

Alejandro Hernández-Arauzo[1], Miguel García-Torres[2],
and Antonio Bahamonde[1]

[1] Universidad de Oviedo, Centro de Inteligencia Artificial Gijón, España
{alex,antonio}@aic.uniovi.es
[2] Universidad de La Laguna, Dpto. Estadística, I. O. y Computación,
La Laguna, España
mgarciat@ull.es

**Abstract.** A relaxed setting for Feature Selection is known as Feature Ranking in Machine Learning. The aim is to establish an order between the attributes that describe the entries of a learning task according to their utility. In this paper, we propose a method to establish these orders using Preference Learning by means of Support Vector Machines (SVM). We include an exhaustive experimental study that investigates the virtues and limitations of the method and discusses, simultaneously, the design options that we have adopted. The conclusion is that our method is very competitive, specially when it searchs for a ranking limiting the number of combinations of attributes explored; this supports that the method presented here could be successfully used in large data sets.

## 1 Introduction

In Machine Learning, the *Feature Selection* problem in classification or regression tasks can be formulated as a combinatorial problem. The aim is to find the subset of attributes from which can be induced the best hypothesis; throughout this paper we will use feature and attribute as synonyms, both terms will mean the descriptors used to represent the entries of a data set. Frequently, in classification tasks, the quality of a hypothesis is measured by the estimation of the success rate in the prediction of new (unseen in training) cases; although it is also possible to consider other kind of indicators. For instance, the complexity of the learned model, or some measurements that combine the successes and errors costs when these are available in the context of the problem. In any case, the optimization of a set of attributes tries to improve both the quality of the hypothesis learned, as well as to reduce the cost of the training and acquisition of new cases to classify, as it was pointed out by Guyon and Elisseeff in [4].

When the selection of features is faced using a searching approach, the space, which represents the set of attribute subsets, has an exponential size with respect to the number of attributes. Therefore, in practice to solve the problem, the use of heuristics is required to guide the search through a reasonable number of

D. Borrajo, L. Castillo, and J.M. Corchado (Eds.): CAEPIA 2007, LNAI 4788, pp. 100–109, 2007.

subsets. Eventually, these heuristics may lead to measure the usefulness of each feature by means of some function that only considers the values of the attribute and the class to learn. This is the case of *filters* that, in general, are less effective than methods that somehow evaluate the usefulness of subsets of more than one attribute [9]. The task of establishing an attribute *ranking* based on its prediction power is a relaxed formalization of the selection of features [8] since it leaves the effective selection of a subset of features to a later phase.

In this paper we present a method to determine an attribute ranking that is inspired by the strategies LEM (Learnable Evolution Model) [11] of Michalski, and BAYES-OPT (Bayessian Classifier based Optimization) [12] of Miquélez et al. These two methods start sampling a collection of subsets of attributes (called *population*) and estimating their quality. The next step consists in learning a pattern able to explain the improvements in quality measurements. In order to search for this pattern, the algorithms LEM and BAYES-OPT assign a label to each subset (each *individual*), in a qualitative scale. The subsets of attributes are labeled according to the estimation of quality of the hypothesis that can be learned using them to describe the entries of the learning task. So, LEM divides the subsets of attributes in three categories called *good, regular* and *bad*; the aim is to allow a set of rules, learned by an inducer of classification rules, to distinguish between *good* and *bad* individuals. On the other hand, BAYES-OPT uses a hybrid strategy between EDAs (Estimation of Distribution Algorithms) and LEM; it only considers the categories *good* and *bad* to induce a probabilistic graphical model. Once these methods have learned the way to distinguish between those subsets, and following an evolutionary strategy, both methods generate new populations using the knowledge just learned.

In the method presented in this article, only one sample of subsets of attributes is built. The core idea is that subsets of attributes can be ordered according to a quality measure, and then we can establish that we *prefer* those of better quality. Thus we only need to learn, from these *preference judgments*, a function that tries to assign higher values to more preferable objects, that is, subsets of attributes. In other words, we propose to tackle the problem of constructing a ranking of features as a preference learning task that will be finally solved using Support Vector Machines [5, 1, 7].

The rest of the paper is organized as follows. In section 2 we present the formal framework of the problem and we describe the proposed method to create an attribute ranking. Throughout this section we introduce two strategies that are simpler than our proposal. Next, we report the experimental results obtained to evaluate our proposal. Here, following the evaluation methodology used in [8] and [14], we will use artificial data sets described in section 3. Finally, the paper is closed with section 4 where we discuss the achievements and draw the conclusions of the article.

## 2  Computation of Feature Ranking

### 2.1  General Framework

Let $\mathcal{T} = \{(\mathbf{x}_1, y_1), \ldots, (\mathbf{x}_n, y_n)\}$ be a data set that represents a classification learning task, where vectors $\mathbf{x}_i \in \mathbb{R}^d$ are the objects to be classified, and they are described by $d$ attributes or features; on the other hand, $y_i$ are the labels of a finite set of classes.

In order to construct a ranking depending on the usefulness in a classification learning task, we will construct a function able to assign a value

$$At(i) \in \mathbb{R}, \forall\, i = 1, \ldots, d. \tag{1}$$

The attribute ranking will be given by the list of attributes ordered according to the values $At(i)$.

As it was explained in the Introduction, our approach starts from a sample of attribute subsets endowed with a quality measurement. This measurement is an estimation of the performance that can be reached in the task $\mathcal{T}$. Formally, we build a set $\mathcal{M} = \{(\mathbf{z}_1, a_1), \ldots, (\mathbf{z}_m, a_m)\}$, where $\mathbf{z}_j$ are binary vectors that represent subsets of $\{1, \ldots, d\}$ randomly selected, while $a_j$ are quality measurements estimated with an external learning algorithm that had the set $\mathcal{T}$ as input but considering only the attributes in $\mathbf{z}_j$.

A first attempt at searching for a pattern in $\mathcal{M}$, that we will call *Simple Method* from now on, consists in defining, as the value associated to each attribute $i$, the average qualities measurements that appear in $\mathcal{M}$ in the cases where the $i$-th attribute is present. In symbols:

$$Simple\_At(i) = \frac{\sum_{j=1}^m a_j z_j(i)}{\sum_{j=1}^m z_j(i)}, \forall\, i = 1, \ldots, d. \tag{2}$$

Later we will see that this is an excessively naive method: obviously it can not capture all complex relationships among attributes. However we will verify that this method yields quite good results in some kind of problems. In any case, all ranking approaches should have to outperform the Simple Method.

A second criterion for attribute ranking can be drawn from a regression model. In fact, notice that $\mathcal{M}$ can be read as a regression task where the attributes values would be, in this case, binary. In order to approximate the $a_j$ values independently of the dimension of $\mathbf{z}_j$ we can use a Support Vector Regression (SVR) [16]. Then, if the learned function from $\mathcal{M}$ is

$$f(x) = \sum_{j=1}^d w_j x_j + b, \tag{3}$$

we define the value for each attribute as the absolute value of the weight of that attribute in the previous regression function. That is,

$$Reg\_At(i) = |\mathbf{w}_i|, \forall\, i = 1, .., d. \tag{4}$$

## 2.2   Support Vector Machines to Learn Preferences

The target of a preference learning task is a function able to order a set of objects. Training examples may have different origins, but in our case they will be pairs of entries of $\mathcal{M}$ $(\mathbf{z}_i, \mathbf{z}_j)$ such that the first one has an higher estimation of quality than the second one; that is, $a_i > a_j$. Such pairs will be called a *preference judgment* and they all form a set that we will denote by

$$PJ = \{(\mathbf{z}_i, \mathbf{z}_j) : a_i > a_j, (\mathbf{z}_i, a_i), (\mathbf{z}_j, a_j) \in \mathcal{M}\}. \tag{5}$$

In this context, the aim of preference learning is to find a valuation function

$$f : \mathbb{R}^d \to \mathbb{R} \tag{6}$$

such that maximizes the probability that $f(u) > f(v)$ whenever $(u, v) \in PJ$. We will call $f$ a *preference, ranking* or *utility* function.

Although non-linear functions could had been used, as we will see in the experimental results reported in section 3, in this case linear functions are good enough to obtain competitive scores. Thus, in the linear case, $f$ is determined by a vector $\mathbf{w}$ called weight or director vector. The value of the function in a vector $\mathbf{z}$ will be the scalar product

$$f(\mathbf{z}) = \langle \mathbf{w}, \mathbf{z} \rangle = \sum_{j=1}^{d} w_j z_j. \tag{7}$$

In order to determine the function $f$ or the weight vector $\mathbf{w}$, we will follow the approach found in [5, 1, 7]; that is to say, we will consider each preference judgment as a constraint for a binary classification since for $(\mathbf{u}, \mathbf{v}) \in PJ$,

$$f(\mathbf{u}) > f(\mathbf{v}) \Leftrightarrow 0 < f(\mathbf{u}) - f(\mathbf{v}) = f(\mathbf{u} - \mathbf{v}) = \mathbf{w}(\mathbf{u} - \mathbf{v}). \tag{8}$$

Thus, the ranking function can be induced by a Support Vector Machine (SVM) [15] that seeks the hyperplane (with director vector $\mathbf{w}$) that pass through the origin and leaves, with the maximum separation margin, in the positive semispace most of the vectors $\mathbf{u} - \mathbf{v}$, with $(\mathbf{u}, \mathbf{v}) \in PJ$. Finally, to get a ranking of attributes, as in the case of regression, we define

$$Pref\_At(i) = |\mathbf{w}_i|, \forall\ i = 1, .., d. \tag{9}$$

To apply this method we have to notice that the number of preference judgments that can be created from $\mathcal{M}$ is on the order of the square of the size of $\mathcal{M}$, in our case $O(m^2)$. In practice, fortunately, not all preference judgments are necessary and so we will consider different heuristics, that will be explained in the next section, to select a sample of pairs from $\mathcal{M}$ in order to build a reduced but representative set of preference judgments.

## 3   Experimental Results

### 3.1   Evaluation of Methods for Building Ranking of Attributes

To evaluate and compare algorithms for attribute ranking, sometimes are used collections of classification tasks taken from a well known and accepted by the community repository, as it is the case of the UCI Machine Learning Repository. In these cases, the evaluation of ranking algorithms must be done by means of indirect methods. Since the *correct* order of the attributes is not known, the comparison is performed using the success rate in cross validation achieved for instance with the best 25, 50 or 100 attributes according to the order given by the algorithms involved in the comparison. Nevertheless this comparison method is not suitable: a good classification inducer could *fix* small errors of a ranking algorithm.

In order to overcome this problem we will use a direct method that evaluates the order given by each algorithm. This comparison method was previously used, for example, in [8] and [14]. The evaluation will be done considering only artificially generated data sets whose classification rules are known beforehand. The order given by ranking algorithms will then be compared with the correct order using the Area Under ROC Curve (AUC): the so called ROC-FS [8] that we will define later.

**Specifications and Construction of Data Sets.** We constructed data sets $T$ with $n$ examples described by pairs $(\mathbf{x}_i, y_i)$, where each $\mathbf{x}_i$ is a vector described by $d$ quantitative variables, and its corresponding $y_i \in \{-1, +1\}$ is a qualitative attribute that stands for the associated class to the vector. So $x_{ij}$ will represent the $j$-th component of the $i$-th example.

The definition of the data sets were based on 5 parameters (see [8]) that specify the nature and difficulty of the corresponding learning tasks. Thus a data set is defined by means of the tuple $(n, d, r, l, \sigma)$, where $n$ represents the number of examples, $d$ the total number of attributes, $r$ the number of relevant attributes, $l$ the type of classification rule, and $\sigma$ the noise rate in the attributes.

An attribute is considered to be relevant to the learning task if it is present in the classification rule definition. In this case we considered two types of classification rules: linear ($l = 1$) and non-linear. For an example $i$ of the set $T$, the definition of the linear classification rule [8] is:

$$y_i = \begin{cases} +1 \text{ if } \sum_{j=1}^{r} x_{ij} > \mu \\ -1 \text{ otherwise} \end{cases} \tag{10}$$

where $\mu$ is the threshold given by $\mu = r/2$. For the non-linear case [14], we generated a $r \times 2$ ($c_{j,m}$) random matrix with coefficients in $[-2, -1] \cup [+1, +2]$. We used this range to avoid coefficients with values close to 0, which would falsify the subset of relevant attributes. Then, we build a polynomial of degree 2, and for each example $i$ we define:

$$p_i = \prod_{k=1}^{2} \left( \sum_{j=1}^{r} (c_{jk} x_{ij}) + b_k \right); \quad y_i = \begin{cases} +1 \text{ if } p_i > \mu \\ -1 \text{ otherwise} \end{cases} \tag{11}$$

where $b_k$ is a random independent term to assure that all monomials of degree 1 and 2 are generated, and $\mu$ is the median of $p_i, i = 1, \ldots, n$.

Each element $x_{ij}$ were drawn uniformly in $[0, 1]$. The label $y_i$ of each example $\mathbf{x}_i$ was assigned considering the equations 10 and 11.

For the experiments carried out in this article, we used data sets with $n = 200$ examples, while the number of attributes varied from 25 to 700. The number of relevant attributes was fixed to $r = 10$ for all data sets. Additionally, in order to increase the difficulty, the input values of the data sets were perturbed by adding Gaussian noise drawn after $\mathcal{N}(\mu, \sigma)$, with average $\mu = 0$ and variance $\sigma = 0$, 0.05, and 0.10. We generated samples with $|\mathcal{M}| = 100$ and $|\mathcal{M}| = 200$. To take into account the stochastic nature of data, for each data set specification (set of parameters values), 20 different random data sets were constructed. Thus, a total of 3600 data sets were used for the experiments reported in this article. To estimate the quality of the hypothesis learned with each subset of attributes, we used the average classification success in a test set independently generated with the same size of the training set. The learning algorithm employed was Naïve Bayes [2].

**Area Under the ROC Curve.** ROC (Receiver Operating Characteristics) curves allow us to see and measure the performance of classifiers. Inspired by these curves, Jong et al. [8] propose to evaluate the correctness of an attribute ranking by means of the curves that they call ROC-FS. However, we will use a slight variant: ROC-FR [14], where FR stands for Feature Ranking.

Given a ranking of $m$ attributes, the ROC-FR curve is defined by the set of points

$$\{(FPR(i), TPR(i)) : i = 1, \ldots, d\}, \tag{12}$$

where $TPR(i)$ (respectively $FPR(i)$) stands for True (False) Positive Rate and it is calculated as the fraction of true (false) relevant variables whose position in the ranking is higher than $i$. The curve starts at position $(0, 0)$, and for each index the curve will advance in vertical if in that position of the ranking it is placed a relevant attribute; on the other hand, the curve will advance in horizontal whenever the $i$-th attribute of the ranking is an irrelevant one. Finally, the curve will end when the point $(1, 1)$ is reached. A perfect ordering would imply that all relevant attributes fill the highest positions of the ranking over any irrelevant attribute. In this case the Area Under this Curve would be $AUC = 1$. Let us remark that a random ordenation would have $AUC = 0.5$.

## 3.2 Two Comparison Stages

We have performed two types of comparisons. In the first one we compared different versions of the strategy proposed in this paper; the aim is to ratify the options selected during the design of the method. These versions are defined by the heuristic strategy employed to choose the pairs of examples to become preference judgments. The general approach consisted in dividing the examples of the sample according to the quality values $\{a_1, \ldots, a_m\}$. Then, the preference judgment were constructed comparing each example from a group with a (randomly selected) example from other group. We studied three heuristics; the first one divides the sample in 4 groups (or bins) with equal frequency: we called it $SVM_{quartiles}$. The other two heuristics built 4 and 10 bins in $[min\{a_j\}, max\{a_j\}]$ of equal length; we call them $SVM_{4Bins}$ and $SVM_{10Bins}$ respectively.

Once the *inner* comparisons were performed and the best version was selected, we compared it with a well-known ranking strategies: an evolutionary algorithm based on EDAs. The version considered was FSSEBNA [6], where the stopping criterion was modified so that it only evaluate a fixed number of individuals. It is necessary to remember that this method assigns a probability to each attribute based on the quality of the solutions in which it appears and this is done by means of probabilistics models. We considered that the higher is that probability for an attribute, the higher is the ranking position of the attribute. Additionally, we also included a simplified version of the approach proposed in this paper that uses regression (SVR from now on) as it was described in section 2.1. The objective is to show that it is not enough the estimations of qualities, in fact it is necessary to consider in the model the ordering relations among them. We called *outer* comparisons to this group experiments.

The Simple Method (see equation 2) was used in all comparisons as a reference to emphasize the results that can be obtained without any theoretical sophistication. Only results significantly higher than those reached by this method are worthwhile to be considered.

All differences reported in both types of comparisons are statistically significant according to a one tail t-test with threshold $p < 0.05$

### 3.3   Inner Comparisons

In figures 1(a) and 1(b), for each ranking method based on learning preferences with SVM, we show the evolution of the AUC values depending on the number of input attributes. As was pointed out in the previous section, the *Simple Method* was included as a baseline. We can observe that the version $SVM_{10Bins}$ significantly outperforms the other strategies, and it reaches AUC values higher than 0.8 for datasets of least or equal 400 attributes. For more than 400 attributes, $SVM_{10Bins}$ does not improve the scores of the *Simple Method*. This is the case both for samples of size $|\mathcal{M}| = 100$ and $|\mathcal{M}| = 200$.

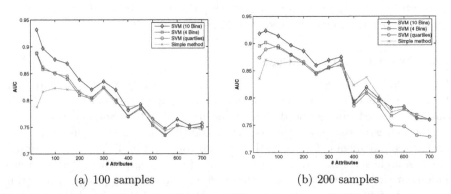

(a) 100 samples                    (b) 200 samples

**Fig. 1.** Comparison between different versions based on learning preferences with an SVM and the *Simple Method*

## 3.4   Outer Comparisons

In the previous subsection we have seen that SVM$_{10Bins}$ outperforms the other heuristics. Therefore, now we will compare the scores attained by preferences SVM endowed with this heuristic against other strategies not based on preferences that were already mentioned in sections 2 and 3.2.

Figures 2(a) and 2(b) show the comparison between SVM$_{10Bins}$, the raking based on EDA of Inza et al. [6], and the SVR version (recall Eq[4]). Again the *Simple Method* will be the baseline.

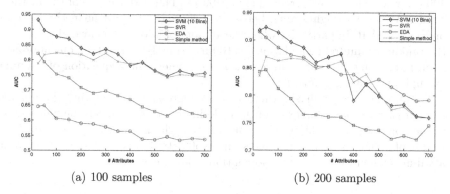

(a) 100 samples                         (b) 200 samples

**Fig. 2.** Comparison between the SVM$_{10Bins}$ and the methods based on EDA and SVR

With samples of size $|\mathcal{M}| = 100$ (figure 2(a)), the scores of the SVM and the *Simple Method* significatively outperform those obtained by EDA and SVR. Since the results of EDA and SVR are worse than those achieved by the *Simple Method*, we can conclude that they require much more individuals to produce quality results, specially in the case of EDA. Nevertheless the SVM method reaches AUC higher than 0.8 until data sets have 400 attributes; then the differences between SVM and the *Simple Method* are not significant. In general, we can say that the behaviour of the SVM is quite good when the sample size is small, getting results that significantly outperform those obtained with other strategies.

With 200 samples (figure 2(b)) the SVR method improves its scores slightly, but still they are too far from those achieved by the *Simple Method*; therefore, the regression is not suitable for these kind of problems. On the other hand, the EDA has noticeably improved the scores obtained when the sample size was $|\mathcal{M}| = 100$, (see figure 2(a)). In fact, for up to 150 attributes, the EDA provides better results than the *Simple Method*; nevertheless for data sets in the interval [150, 450], there are no significant differences. Finally, for higher dimensional data sets the EDA becomes the algorithm with the best performance, providing AUC values higher than 0.75; moreover, the differences are statistically significant. Thus, we acknowledge that the EDA works well with data sets with a high number of irrelevant attributes. The SVM based on preferences is the best strategy for data sets up to 400 attributes as in the case of $|\mathcal{M}| = 100$. If the number of attributes increases, the results are similar to those of the *Simple Method*.

# 4   Conclusions

We have presented a method to induce a ranking of attributes based on learning preferences with an SVM. Given a classification learning task, the method starts with a population of attribute subsets endowed with a measurement of the quality of the hypothesis that can be induced using those attributes.

The benefits of the method were measured with an exhaustive collection of artificially generated data sets that cover both linear and nonlinear classification rules. The method has exhibited a very competitive behavior in data sets of up to 400 (10 relevant and 390 irrelevant) attributes. The performance of the method attains AUC values significantly better than those reached by the methods based on EDA or SVR. In particular when the amount of information available to learn the ranking is limited (populations of 100 individuals). Therefore, our approach is an interesting alternative in learning tasks where the acquisition of training examples is costly or difficult.

We would like to emphasize that the use of regression in these kind of problems can not capture the complexity of the ordering relations between the individuals of the population. Finally we can conclude that the EDA has a good behaviour in case of high dimensional problems (up to 500 attributes) with only 10 relevant attributes when the size of the population is large enough.

## Acknowledgments

We want to thank to the EDA authors [6] for providing us the code of the version of the algorithm based on EDAs that was used in the experimentation described in this article. This research has been partially supported under grants TIN2005-08288, TIN2005-08404-C04-03 from the MEC (Ministerio de Educación y Ciencia), and PI042004/088 from the Gobierno de Canarias.

## References

[1] Bahamonde, A., Bayón, G.F., Díez, J., Quevedo, J.R., Luaces, O., del Coz, J.J., Alonso, J., Goyache, F.: Feature subset selection for learning preferences: A case study. In: Greiner, R., Schuurmans, D. (eds.) Proceedings of the International Conference on Machine Learning (ICML '04), Banff, Alberta (Canada), pp. 49–56 (July 2004)

[2] Duda, R., Hart, P.: Pattern Classification and Scene Analysis. Wiley, Chichester (1973)

[3] Egan, J.P.: Signal Detection Theory and ROC Analysis. Series in Cognition and Perception. Academic Press, New York (1975)

[4] Guyon, I., Elisseeff, A.: An introduction to variable and feature selection. Journal of Machine Learning Research 3, 1157–1182 (2003)

[5] Herbrich, R., Graepel, T., Obermayer, K.: Large margin rank boundaries for ordinal regression. In: Advances in Large Margin Classifiers, MIT Press, Cambridge, MA (2000)

[6] Inza, I., Larrañaga, P., Etxeberria, R., Sierra, B.: Feature subset selection by Bayesian networks based optimization. Artificial Intelligence 123(1-2), 157–184 (2000)

[7] Joachims, T.: Optimizing search engines using clickthrough data. In: Proceedings of the ACM Conference on Knowledge Discovery and Data Mining (KDD). ACM, New York (2002)

[8] Jong, K., Mary, J., Cornuéjols, A., Marchiori, E., Sebag, M.: Ensemble feature ranking. In: Boulicaut, J.-F., Esposito, F., Giannotti, F., Pedreschi, D. (eds.) PKDD 2004. LNCS (LNAI), vol. 3202, pp. 267–278. Springer, Heidelberg (2004)

[9] Kohavi, R., John, G.H.: Wrappers for feature subset selection. Artificial Intelligence 97(1-2), 273–324 (1997)

[10] Larrañaga, P., Lozano, J.: Estimation of Distribution Algorithms. A New Tool for Evolutionary Computation. Kluwer Academic Publishers, Norwell, MA (2001)

[11] Michalski, R.: Learnable evolution model: Evolutionary processes guided by machine learning. Machine Learning, 9–40 (2000)

[12] Miquélez, T., Bengoetxea, E., Larrañaga, P.: Evolutionary computations based on bayesian classifiers. International Journal of Applied Mathematics and Computer Science 14(3), 101–115 (2004)

[13] Larrañaga, P., Lozano, J.A.: Synergies between evolutionary computation and probabilistic graphical models. International Journal of Approximate Reasoning, 155–156 (2002)

[14] Quevedo, J.R., Bahamonde, A., Luaces, O.: A simple and efficient method for variable ranking according to their usefulness for learning. In: Computational Statistics and Data Analysis (to appear, 2007)

[15] Vapnik, V.: Statistical Learning Theory. John Wiley, Chichester (1998)

[16] Vapnik, V., Golowich, S., Smola, A.: Support vector method for function approximation, regression estimation, and signal processing. In: Mozer, M.C., Jordan, M.I., Petsche, T. (eds.) Advances in Neural Information Processing Systems, vol. 9, pp. 281–287. MIT Press, Cambridge, MA (1997)

# Improving HLRTA*(k)*

Carlos Hernández[1] and Pedro Meseguer[2]

[1] UCSC, Caupolicán 491, Concepción, Chile
chernan@ucsc.cl
[2] IIIA, CSIC, Campus UAB, 08193 Bellaterra, Spain
pedro@iiia.csic.es

**Abstract.** Real-time search methods allow an agent to move in unknown environments. We provide two enhancements to the real-time search algorithm HLRTA*(k). First, we give a better way to perform bounded propagation, generating the HLRTA*$_{LS}$(k) algorithm. Second, we consider the option of doing more than one action per planning step, by analyzing the quality of the heuristic found during lookahead, producing the HLRTA*(k, d) algorithm. We provide experimental evidence of the benefits of both algorithms, with respect to other real-time algorithms on existing benchmarks.

## 1 Introduction

The classical heuristic search approach assumes that a solution can be computed off-line (i.e., by a systematic traversal of the search space), and once the whole solution is available, it is executed on-line. This approach is valid for some tasks (typically without uncertainty, with state spaces perfectly defined, in totally controlled environments). But it is not valid for other tasks when either (i) there is not enough information to compute a solution off-line (for instance, in unknown environments), or (ii) even if a complete solution could be computed, the task has some timing requirements and it cannot wait to compute the complete solution (for instance, a state space too large to be systematically explored). In some cases, both conditions hold (imagine a character in a video game, who has to react almost instantly to changes in a mostly unknown environment).

Real-time heuristic search is an alternative approach. Real-time search interleaves planning and action execution phases in an on-line manner, with an agent that performs the intended task. In the planning phase, one or several actions are planned, which are performed by the agent in the action execution phase. The planning phase has to be done in a limited, short amount of time. To satisfy this, real-time methods restrict search to a small part of the state space around the current state, which is called the *local space*. The size of the local space is small and independent of the size of the complete state space. Searching in the local space is feasible in the limited planning time. As result, the best trajectory inside the local space is found, and the corresponding action (or actions) are

---

* Supported by the Spanish REPLI-III project TIC-2006-15387-C03-01.

D. Borrajo, L. Castillo, and J.M. Corchado (Eds.): CAEPIA 2007, LNAI 4788, pp. 110–119, 2007.

performed in the next action execution phase. The whole process iterates with new planning and action execution phases until a goal state is found.

This approach gives up the optimality of the computed solution. Obviously, if search is limited to a small portion of the state space, there is no guarantee to produce an optimal global trajectory. However, some methods guarantee that after repeated executions on the same problem instance (each execution is called a *trial*), the trajectory converges to an optimal path. To prevent cycling, real-time search methods update the heuristic values of the visited states.

The initial algorithms for real-time search were RTA* and LRTA* [9]. While RTA* performs reasonably well in the first trial, it does not converge to optimal paths. On the contrary, LRTA* converges to optimal paths with a worse performance in the first trial. Both approaches are combined in the HLRTA* algorithm [10]. Including the idea of bounded propagation, which propagates recursively a change in the heuristic of the current state up to a maximum of $k$ states, the new HLRTA*(k) algorithm was proposed [6]. HLRTA*(k) keeps all good properties of HLRTA*, improving largely its performance in practice.

In this paper, we present further improvements to HLRTA*(k). First, we present an alternative method for bounded propagation. This new method implements propagation more efficiently than the initially proposed method. For instance, if a state should be updated, the initial method performs elementary updates, allowing the state to enter several times in the propagation queue. Now, all the updating is joined in a single operation. With this new method, we produce the new HLRTA*$_{LS}(k)$, which keeps all good properties of its predecessor and improves significantly its performance. Second, we consider the option of doing more than one action per planning step. There is some debate about the relative performance of planning one single action versus several actions per planning step, with the same lookahead. Our contribution is to consider the quality of the heuristic found during lookahead. If we find some evidence that the heuristic is not accurate, we plan one action only. Otherwise, we allow to plan several actions in this step. In addition, if some inaccuracy is detected during lookahead, it is repaired although it is not located at the current state.

The structure of the paper is as follows. First, we define precisely the problem, summarizing some of the most popular algorithms and explaining bounded propagation for the initial HLRTA*. We present our first contribution, the new HLRTA*$_{LS}(k)$ algorithm, which performs a single move per planning step. Then, we present and discuss our second contribution, the HLRTA*$(k, d)$ algorithm that performs bounded propagation up to $k$ states and is able to compute up to $d$ moves per planning step. Both algorithms are experimentally evaluated on two benchmarks. Finally, we extract some conclusions from this work.

## 2  Background

**Problem Definition.** The state space is defined as $(X, A, c, s, G)$, where $(X, A)$ is a finite graph, $c : A \mapsto [0, \infty)$ is a cost function that associates each arc with a positive finite cost, $s \in X$ is the start state, and $G \subset X$ is a set of goal states.

$X$ is a finite set of states, and $A \subset X \times X \setminus \{(x, x)\}$, where $x \in X$, is a finite set of arcs. Each arc $(v, w)$ represents an action whose execution causes the agent to move from state $v$ to state $w$. The state space is undirected: for any action $(x, y) \in A$ there exists its inverse $(y, x) \in A$ with the same cost $c(x, y) = c(y, x)$. The cost of the path between state $n$ and $m$ is $k(n, m)$. The successors of a state $x$ are $Succ(x) = \{y | (x, y) \in A\}$. A heuristic function $h : X \mapsto [0, \infty)$ associates to each state $x$ an approximation $h(x)$ of the cost of a path from $x$ to a goal $g$ where $h(g) = 0$ and $g \in G$. The exact cost $h^*(x)$ is the minimum cost to go from $x$ to any goal. $h$ is admissible iff $\forall x \in X, h(x) \leq h^*(x)$. $h$ is consistent iff $0 \leq h(x) \leq c(x, w) + h(w)$ for all states $w \in Succ(x)$. A path $\{x_0, x_1, .., x_n\}$ with $h(x_i) = h^*(x_i), 0 \leq i \leq n$ is optimal.

**RTA\*/LRTA\*.** The pioneer and reference algorithms for real-time search are RTA\* and LRTA\* [9]. From the current state $x$, RTA\* performs lookahead at depth $d$, and updates $h(x)$ to the max $\{h(x), \text{2nd min } [k(x, v) + h(v)]\}$, where $v$ is a frontier state and $k(x, v)$ is the cost of the path from $x$ to $v$. Then, the agent moves to $y$, successor of $x$, with minimum $c(x, y) + h(y)$. State $y$ becomes the current state and the process iterates, until finding a goal. In finite state spaces with positive edge costs, finite heuristic values and where a goal state is reachable from every state, RTA\* is correct, complete and terminates [9]. However, it does not converge to optimal paths when solving repeatedly the same instance, because of its updating strategy. Alternatively, the LRTA\* algorithm behaves like RTA\*, except that $h(x)$ is updated to the max $\{h(x), \text{min } [k(x, v) + h(v)]\}$. This updating assures admissibility, provided the original heuristic was admissible, so the updated heuristic can be reused for the next trial. LRTA\* is a correct and complete algorithm, that converges to optimal paths when solving repeatedly the same instance, keeping the heuristic estimates of the previous trial.

**HLRTA\*.** RTA\* works fine in the first trial but it does not converge to optimal paths. LRTA\* converges but it performs worse than RTA\* in the first trial. The HLRTA\* algorithm [10] combines them as follows. It keeps for each visited state two heuristic values, $h_1$ and $h_2$, which correspond to the heuristic updating of LRTA\* and RTA\* respectively. In addition, it keeps in $d(x)$ the state where the agent moved from $x$ (that is, $d(x)$ is the next current state from $x$). The interesting result here is that when search has passed through $x$, and it backtracks to $x$ from $d(x)$ (that is, when it goes back to $x$ through the same arc it used to leave) then $h_2$ estimate is admissible and it can be used instead of $h_1$ [10]. HLRTA\* uses a heuristic $H(x) = max\{h_1(x), h_2(x)\}$ when $h_2$ is admissible, otherwise $H(x) = h_1(x)$. Since HLRTA\* searches using admissible heuristics which are stored between trials, it converges to optimal paths in the same way that LRTA\* does. Experimentally, HLRTA\* does better than LRTA\* in the first trial but it requires more trials than LRTA\* to converge [2].

**Bounded Propagation.** Originally, real-time search algorithms updated the heuristic estimate of the current state only. In [5], the idea of *bounded propagation* was presented. Basically, it consists of propagating the change in the heuristic of the current state to its successor states. If some of them change their heuristic, these changes are propagated to its own successor states, and so on and so forth. Since the whole process could be long for a real-time context, a limit was proposed: after the first change, up to $k$ states could be considered for further changes. Since propagation is limited up to $k$ states, it is meaningful to consider which states are the most adequate to be updated. An option is to limit propagation to states already expanded. Other alternatives are discussed in [4].

This simple idea can be easily included in existing algorithms like LRTA* producing the LRTA*(k) version [5] (in fact, LRTA* is just a particular case of LRTA*(k) with $k = 1$). In practice, it has been shown to be very beneficial considering the effort to reach a solution in the first trial, and the number of trials to convergence. It also increases the solution stability before convergence. However, bounded propagation requires longer planning steps, since propagating to $k$ states is computationally more expensive than propagating to one (the current) state. Nevertheless, benefits are important and the extra requirements on planning time are moderate, so if the application can accommodate longer planning steps, the use of bounded propagation is strongly recommended.

Considering HLRTA*, bounded propagation generates HLRTA*(k) [6] (again, HLRTA* is the particular case HLRTA*($k = 1$)) with similar benefits. Since HLRTA* keeps two heuristic estimates per visited state, it is worth noting that propagation is done on $h_1$, the heuristic that correspond to the updating of LRTA*. Performing propagation on $h_2$ may cause to lose the heuristic admissibility. This is due to the following fact. Let $x$, $y$ and $z$ be states. During propagation, $h_2(x)$ may go into $h_1(y)$, which after some steps is used to update $h_1(z)$. If propagation is long enough, $h_1(z)$ may go into $h_1(x)$, so the second minimum contribution appears in the first minimum without satisfying the conditions of admissibility for $h_2$ [10] (realize that the agent does not move during propagation). Without admissibility, convergence to optimal paths is not guaranteed.

## 3   HLRTA*$_{LS}(k)$

Bounded propagation was initially implemented using a propagation queue $Q$ [6]. This implementation presented some weak points:

1. A state $y$ may enter $Q$ but, after reconsideration it may happen that $h(y)$ does not change. This is a wasted effort.
2. A state may enter $Q$ more than once, making several updatings before reaching its final value. Would it not be possible to perform a single operation?
3. The order in which states enter $Q$, combined with the value of $k$ parameter, may affect the final result.

These points are partially solved using a new implementation of bounded propagation, based on the notion of *local space* [7]. Formally, a local space is a pair $(I, F)$, where $I \subset X$ is a set of interior states and $F \subset X$ is the set of frontier states, satisfying that $F$ surrounds $I$ immediate and completely, so $I \cap F = \emptyset$. The procedure to find the local space around the current state is as follows:

1. Set $I = \emptyset, Q = \{x\}$, where $x$ is the current state.
2. Loop until $Q$ is empty or $|I| = k$ Extract a state $w$ from $Q$. If $w$ is a goal, exit loop. Otherwise, check by looking at $succ(w)$ that are not in $I$ if $h(w)$ is going to change (if $h(w) < min_{v \in succ(w)-I} h(v) + c(w, v)$, we call this expression the updating condition). If so, include $w$ in $I$, and $succ(w) - I$ in $Q$.
3. The set $F$ surrounds $I$ immediate and completely.

This procedure is called when $x$, the current state, satisfies the updating condition. Then, a local space $(I, F)$ is computed around $x$. Observe that the number of interior states is upper bounded by $k$. Once the local space is determined, it is updated using a Dijkstra shortest paths procedure, updating the heuristic $h_1$

**procedure HLRTA\*-LS(k)**$(X, A, c, s, G, k)$
  **for each** $x \in X$ **do** $h_1(x) \leftarrow h_0(x)$; $h_2(x) \leftarrow 0$; $d(x) \leftarrow null$;
  **repeat**
    **HLRTA-LS(k)-trial**$(X, A, c, s, G, k)$;
  **until** $h_1$ does not change;
**procedure HLRTA-LS(k)-trial**$(X, A, c, s, G, k)$
  $x \leftarrow s$;
  **while** $x \notin G$ **do**
    **if** Changes?$(x)$ **then**
      $(I, F) \leftarrow$ SelectLS$(x, k)$;
      Dijkstra-shortest-paths$(I, F)$;
    HLRTA-LookaheadUpdate2min$(x)$;
    $y \leftarrow$ argmin$_{w \in Succ(x)}[c(x, w) + H(w, x)]$;
    execute$(a \in A$ such that $a = (x, y))$; $d(x) \leftarrow y$; $x \leftarrow y$;
**function SelectLS**$(x, k)$: **pair of sets**;
  $Q \leftarrow \langle x \rangle$; $F \leftarrow \emptyset$; $I \leftarrow \emptyset$; $cont \leftarrow 0$;
  **while** $Q \neq \emptyset \wedge cont < k$ **do**
    $v \leftarrow$ extract-first$(Q)$;
    $y \leftarrow$ argmin$_{w \in Succ(v) \wedge w \notin I}[c(v, w) + H(w, v)]$;
    **if** $h_1(v) < c(v, y) + H(y, v)$ **then**
      $I \leftarrow I \cup \{v\}$; $cont \leftarrow cont + 1$;
      **for each** $w \in Succ(v)$ **do**
        **if** $w \notin I \wedge w \notin Q$ **then** $Q \leftarrow$ add-last$(Q, w)$;
    **else if** $I \neq \emptyset$ **then** $F \leftarrow F \cup \{v\}$;
  **if** $Q \neq \emptyset$ **then** $F \leftarrow F \cup Q$;
  **return** $(I, F)$;
**procedure HLRTA-LookaheadUpdate2min**$(x)$
  $z \leftarrow$ arg 2nd min$_{v \in Succ(x)}[c(x, v) + H(v, x)]$;
  **if** $h_2(x) < c(x, z) + H(z, x)$ **then** $h_2(x) \leftarrow c(x, z) + H(z, x)$;
**function Changes?**$(x)$: **boolean**;
  $y \leftarrow$ argmin$_{v \in Succ(x)}[c(x, v) + H(v, x)]$;
  **if** $h_1(x) < c(x, y) + H(y, x)$ **then return** *true*; **else return** *false*;
**function H**$(v, from)$: **real**;
  **if** $d(v) = from$ **then return** $max\{h_1(v), h_2(v)\}$; **else return** $h_1(v)$;

**Fig. 1.** The HLRTA\*$_{LS}(k)$ algorithm

of interior states from the heuristic $H$ of frontier states. If the initial heuristic is admissible, this updating process keeps admissibility [8].

When HLRTA* includes this form of bounded propagation, it is called HLRTA*$_{LS}(k)$. Its code appears in Figure 1. When $I$ admits previously visited states only, this version is called HLRTA*$_{LS-path}(k)$. It not difficult to see that HLRTA*$_{LS}(k)$ inherits the good properties of HLRTA*($k$), that is, it is correct, complete and terminates. Since admissibility is maintained, it also converges to optimal paths.

## 4   HLRTA*($k, d$)

There is some debate about planning one action versus several actions per planning step, with the same lookahead. Typically, single-action planning produces trajectories of better quality (minor cost). However, the overall CPU time in single-action planning is usually longer than in the other approach, since the whole effort of lookahead produces a single move. Nevertheless, planning several actions is an attractive option that has been investigated [8], [1].

In unknown environments, the visibility range of an agent is the set of states around the current state that can be sensed by the agent. When planning several actions in unknown environments, moves are computed using the "free space assumption": if a state is not in the visibility range of the agent and there is no evidence that contains an obstacle, it is assumed to be feasible. When moves are performed, if an obstacle is found in one of these assumed feasible states, execution stops and a new planning phase starts.

Planning a single action per step is a conservative strategy. The agent has searched the local space and it has found the best trajectory in it. But from a global perspective, the agent is unsure whether this best trajectory effectively brings the agent closer to a goal state, or it follows a wrong path that will become apparent later. In this situation, the least commitment strategy is to plan a single action: the best move from the current state.

Planning several actions per step is a more risky strategy. Following the best trajectory in the local space is risky because (i) it might not be good at global level, and (ii) if it is finally wrong, since it includes several actions, it will require some effort to come back. Otherwise, if the trajectory is good, performing several moves in one step will bring the agent closer to the goal than a single move.

These strategies are two extremes of a continuum of possible planning strategies. We propose an intermediate option, that consist on taking into account the quality of the heuristic found during lookahead. If there is some evidence that the heuristic quality is not good at local level, we do not trust the heuristic values and plan one action only. Otherwise, if the heuristic quality is good in the local space, we trust it and plan for several actions. Specifically, we propose not to trust the heuristic when one of the following conditions holds:

1. the final state for the agent (= first state in OPEN when lookahead is done using A*) satisfies the updating condition,
2. there is a state in the local space that satisfies the updating condition.

**procedure** HLRTA*(k,d)$(X, A, c, s, G, k, d)$
  **for each** $x \in X$ **do** $h_1(x) \leftarrow h_0(x); h_2(x) \leftarrow 0; d(x) \leftarrow null;$
  **repeat**
    HLRTA(k,d)-trial$(X, A, c, s, G, k, d);$
    **until** $h_1$ does not change;
**procedure** HLRTA*(k,d)-trial$(X, A, c, s, G, k, d)$
  $x \leftarrow s;$
  **while** $x \notin G$ **do**
    $path \leftarrow$ A*$(x, d, G); z \leftarrow$ last$(path);$
    **if** Changes?$(z)$ **then**
      $(I, F) \leftarrow$ SelectLS$(z, k);$
      Dijkstra-shortest-paths$(I, F);$
      HLRTA-LookaheadUpdate2min$(x);$
      $y \leftarrow$ argmin$_{w \in Succ(x)}[c(x, w) + H(w, x)];$
      execute$(a \in A$ such that $a = (x, y)); d(x) \leftarrow y; x \leftarrow y;$
    **else**
      $x \leftarrow$ extract-first$(path);$
      **while** $path \neq \emptyset$ **do**
        HLRTA-LookaheadUpdate2min$(x);$
        $y \leftarrow$ extract-first$(path);$
        execute$(a \in A$ such that $a = (x, y)); d(x) \leftarrow y; x \leftarrow y;$

**Fig. 2.** The HLRTA*$(k, d)$ algorithm. Missing procedures/functions appear in Fig. 1.

In both cases, we repair the inaccuracy of the heuristic, that is, we generate a local space around that state, we update the heuristic and this change is propagated by bounded propagation. This is an important point in our approach: as soon as one heuristic inaccuracy is detected, it is repaired and propagated.

These ideas are implemented in the HLRTA*$(k, d)$ algorithm. It is based on HLRTA*, and it propagates heuristic updates up to $k$ states [6]. In addition, it is able to plan either 1 or up to $d$ actions per planning step. It includes:

- Lookahead using A*. Following [8], the lookahead required to plan more than one action per step is done using the well-known A* algorithm [3].
- Local space selection. When $h(x)$ of a state $x$ in the lookahead changes, the local space around $x$ is computed by the SelectLS procedure (Section 3).
- Propagation in local space. Once the local space is selected, propagation of heuristic changes into the local space is done using the Dijkstra shortest paths algorithm, as done by [8].

HLRTA*$(k, d)$ is more that a novel combination of existing techniques. As new element, the algorithm determines the number of actions to plan depending on the quality of the heuristic found in the lookahead. If the heuristic value of some state found during lookahead satisfies the updating condition, lookahead stops, this change is propagated up to $k$ states and one action is planned only. If no heuristic value satisfies the updating condition in the lookahead states, a sequence of $d$ actions are planned. These actions are executed in the execution phase, taking into account that if an obstacle is found, the execution stops and a new planning phase starts.

The code of HLRTA*($k, d$) appears in Figure 2. The central procedure is HLRTA*(k,d)-trial, that is executed once per trial until finding a solution. This procedure works at follows. First, it performs lookahead from the current state $x$ using the A* algorithm. A* performs lookahead until (i) it finds an state which heuristic value satisfies the updating condition, (ii) if finds a state $w$ such that $g(w) = d$, or (iii) it finds a solution state. In any case, it returns the sequence of states, *path*, that starting with the current state $x$ connects with (i) the state which heuristic value satisfies the updating condition, (ii) a state $w$ such that $g(w) = d$, or (iii) a solution state. Observe that *path* has at least one state $x$, and the only state that might change its heuristic value is last(*path*). If this state satisfies the updating condition, then this change is propagated: the local space is determined and updated using the shortest paths algorithm. Then, one action is planned, executed and the loop iterates. If last(*path*) does not change its heuristic value, then up to $d$ actions are planned and executed.

Since the heuristic always increases, HLRTA*($k, d$) completeness is guaranteed. If the heuristic is initially admissible, updating the local space with shortest paths algorithm keeps admissibility, so convergence to optimal paths is guaranteed. So HLRTA*($k, d$) inherits the good properties of HLRTA*.

One might expect that HLRTA*($k, d$) collapses into HLRTA*$_{LS}(k)$ when $d = 1$. However, this is not the case. When $d = 1$, these two algorithms basically differ in the following. If the heuristic of the current state satisfies the updating condition, HLRTA*$_{LS}(k)$ updates it and propagates this change in a local space constructed around the current state. In this case, HLRTA*($k, 1$) behaves exactly like HLRTA*$_{LS}(k)$. But if the heuristic of the current state does not change, HLRTA*($k, 1$) generates a local space using the A* algorithm, and if the heuristic of some state of this local space satisfies the updating condition, it is updated and this change is propagated in a local space around that state.

## 5   Experimental Results

We compare the performance of HLRTA*$_{LS}(k)$ and HLRTA*($k, d$) with HLRTA*($k$) [6] and LRTA* (version of Koenig) [8]. Parameter $k$ is the size of the local space, where bounded propagation is performed; it is usually taken as the lookahead parameter for LRTA*. We have used the values $k = 5, 10, 20, 40, 80$. Parameter $d$ is the upper limit on the number of planned actions per step for HLRTA*($k, d$). We have used the values $d = 1, 2, 4, 6$. Benchmarks are four-connected grids where an agent can move one cell north, south, east or west, on which we use Manhattan distance as the initial heuristic. We use the following benchmarks:

1. Grid35. Grids of size 301 × 301 with a 35% of obstacles placed randomly. Here, Manhattan distance tends to provide a reasonably good advice.
2. Maze. Acyclic mazes of size 181 × 181 whose corridor structure was generated with depth-first search. Here, Manhattan distance could be very misleading.

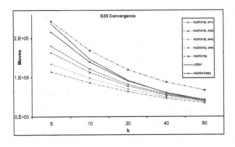
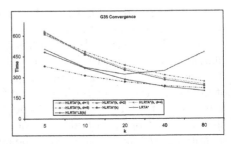

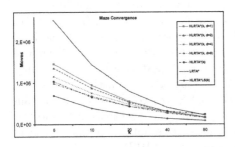
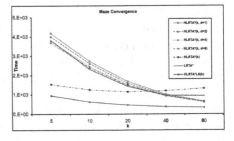

**Fig. 3.** Experimental results on Grid35 and Maze benchmarks: solution cost (left) and total planning time (right) for convergence of Grid35 (1st row) and Maze (2nd row)

In both benchmarks, the start and goal states are chosen randomly assuring that there is a path from the start to the goal. All actions have cost 1. The agent visibility radius is 1. We have obtained results for first trial and convergence to optimal trajectories. For space reasons, only convergence results are shown in Figure 3: solution cost (number of actions to reach the goal) and total planning time (in milliseconds), plotted against $k$, averaged over 1500 different instances.

Results for convergence on Grid35 indicate that solution cost decreases monotonically as $k$ increases, and for HLRTA*$(k, d)$ it also decreases monotonically as $d$ increases. HLRTA*$(k, d)$ versions obtain the best results for low lookahead, and all algorithms have a similar cost for high lookahead (except HLRTA*$(k)$ which has a higher cost). Considering total planning time, all algorithms decrease monotonically with $k$ except LRTA*, which first decreases and from $k = 20$ increases again. HLRTA*$(k, d)$ versions require more time than HLRTA*$(k)$ and HLRTA*$_{LS}(k)$, which are the fastest algorithms in the whole $k$ range.

Results for convergence on Maze exhibit a slightly different behavior. Regarding solution cost, all algorithms decrease as $k$ increases. HLRTA*$_{LS}(k)$ obtains the best cost for the whole $k$ range. Regarding total planning time, for HLRTA*$(k, d)$ versions it decreases monotonically as $k$ increases, with little difference for $d$ parameter. The interesting point here is that HLRTA*$_{LS}(k)$ is again the fastest algorithm in the whole $k$ range.

From these results, we conclude that the main parameter is $k$, the lookahead size. For high lookahead ($k = 40, 80$), HLRTA*$(k, d)$ with a low number of moves

$(d = 1, 2)$ or HLRTA*$_{LS}(k)$ offer the best trade-off between solution cost and planning time. For low lookahead $(k = 5, 10)$, HLRTA*$(k, d)$ versions offer the best solution cost, while HLRTA*$_{LS}(k)$ has better time requirements.

The Maze benchmark deserves special analysis. For this problem, the best algorithm is HLRTA*$_{LS}(k)$, unbeaten by the more sophisticated HLRTA*$(k, d)$. We believe that this is due to the special structure of the benchmark, with many corridors that finalize in dead-ends. Apparently, a relatively simple strategy using the second min updating is enough to obtain very good results. More research is required to confirm this hypothesis.

# 6    Conclusions

We have presented two contributions to improve HLRTA*$(k)$. First, a new method to implement bounded propagation, producing the new HLRTA*$_{LS}(k)$ algorithm. Second, a new approach to plan more than one action per step, analyzing the quality of the heuristic found during lookahead. This approach generates the new HLRTA*$(k, d)$ algorithm. Both algorithms are correct, complete, terminate and converge to optimal trajectories after repeated executions on the same problem instance. Experimentally, we have observed that they achieve a good performance, improving over LRTA (version of Koenig) and HLRTA*$(k)$. Apparently, the ability to plan a few moves per step is beneficial, provided these moves are of good quality. This is done by assessing the quality of the heuristic. We believe that the results on the Maze are due to its special structure.

# References

1. Bulitko, V., Lee, G.: Learning in real time search: a unifying framework. Journal of Artificial Intelligence Research 25, 119–157 (2006)
2. Furcy, D., Koenig, S.: Combining two fast-learning real-time search algorithms yields even faster learning. In: Proc. 6th European Conference on Planning (2001)
3. Hart, P., Nilsson, N., Raphael, B.: A formal basis for the heuristic determination of minimum cost paths. IEEE Trans. Sys. Science & Cybernetics 2, 100–107 (1968)
4. Hernandez, C., Meseguer, P.: Improving convergence of lrta(k). In: IJCAI 2005 Work on Planning and Learning in a Priori Unknown or Dynamic Domains (2005)
5. Hernandez, C., Meseguer, P.: Lrta*(k). In: Proc. IJCAI 2005, pp. 1238–1243 (2005)
6. Hernandez, C., Meseguer, P.: Propagating updates in real-time search: Hlrta*(k). In: Marín, R., Onaindía, E., Bugarín, A., Santos, J. (eds.) CAEPIA 2005. LNCS (LNAI), vol. 4177, pp. 379–388. Springer, Heidelberg (2006)
7. Hernandez, C., Meseguer, P.: Improving lrta*(k). In: Proc. IJCAI 2007, pp. 2312–2317 (2007)
8. Koenig, S.: A comparison of fast search methods for real-time situated agents. In: Proc. AAMAS 2004, pp. 864–871 (2004)
9. Korf, R.E.: Real-time heuristic search. Artificial Intelligence 42, 189–211 (1990)
10. Thorpe, P.E.: A hybrid learning real-time search algorithm. Master's thesis, Computer Science Dep. UCLA (1994)

# Sliding Mode Control of a Wastewater Plant with Neural Networks and Genetic Algorithms

Miguel A. Jaramillo-Morán[1], Juan C. Peguero-Chamizo[2],
Enrique Martínez de Salazar[1], and Montserrat García del Valle[1]

[1] E. de Ingenierías Industriales, University of Extremadura,
Avda. de Elvas s/n. 06071 Badajoz, Spain
miguel@unex.es, dsalazar@unex.es, montse@nernet.unex.es
[2] Centro Universitario de Mérida, S. Joaquina de Jornet, s/n. 06800 Mérida, Spain
jcpeguero@unex.es

**Abstract.** In this work a simulated wastewater treatment plant is controlled with a sliding mode control carried out with softcomputing techniques. The controller has two modules: the first one performs the plant control when its dynamics lies inside an optimal working region and is carried out by a neural network trained to reproduce the behavior of the technician who controls an actual plant, while the second one drives the system dynamics towards that region when it works outside it and is carried out by a corrective function whose parameters have been adjusted with a genetic algorithm. The controller so defined performs satisfactory even when extreme inputs are presented to the model.

**Keywords:** Sliding Mode Control, Neural Networks, Genetic Algorithms.

## 1 Introduction

Sliding Mode Control [1] is a control technique whose aim is to drive the dynamics of a nonlinear system towards a certain surface and then force the dynamics to remain inside it. To do so, the control has two different laws: the first one, usually named corrective control, tries to drive the system evolution towards a surface defined in the state space of the system where it is to be kept, while the second one tries to control the system dynamics inside that surface and is usually named equivalent control.

Nevertheless, this technique has two important drawbacks. The first one relates to the mathematical definition of the surface where the system must converge, which, as it is usually very complex, makes the corresponding control law that keeps the system dynamics inside it be also very complex. This definition may become impossible when a precise representation of the system or the surface is not provided. The second drawback arises from the fact that the corrective control will act whenever the system dynamics goes outside the optimal surface, what will repeatedly happen because of the inability of the equivalent control to retain the system dynamics inside the optimal surface. So undesired high frequency oscillations will appear in the control signal. The use of switching functions as corrective controllers will boost this effect.

D. Borrajo, L. Castillo, and J.M. Corchado (Eds.): CAEPIA 2007, LNAI 4788, pp. 120–129, 2007.

To solve the first problem both neural networks [2] and fuzzy sets [3] have been used, because of their ability to identify the dynamics of complex systems, specially when their models are unknown.

To solve the second problem, saturating functions that allow a smooth transition between active and inactive states of the corrective control have been used. Neural networks [2] or fuzzy sets [3] also provide an easy solution to this problem.

Generally, the development of a sliding mode control needs a very precise definition of the sliding surface where the systems is to be driven, nevertheless, there are systems whose dynamics may be driven to a region instead of a surface. In many cases this region may have an imprecise definition. This kind of system will be even more difficult to control with algorithmic techniques because of that lack of accuracy in the definition of the sliding surface. Nevertheless, these are the kind of systems neural networks or fuzzy sets were designed to deal with. In this work such a system, a Wastewater Treatment Plant (WTP), will be controlled with a sliding mode control, in which the equivalent control will be carried out by a neural network trained to reproduce a plant technician's experience while the corrective control will be performed with a simple function which measures the distance from the system to an optimal region and whose parameters will be adjusted with a genetic algorithm. This controller represents a modification of another sliding mode controller developed in an author's previous work [4] where two neural networks carried out both the predictive and the corrective controls. The modifications proposed in this work provides a simpler and more effective controller behavior than that obtained in [4].

The rest of the work is organized as follows. A description of the plant to be used is presented in Section 2. The sliding mode control is developed in Section 3. In Section 4 the genetic algorithm used to adjust the parameters of the corrective control is described. Finally, in Section 5, the results obtained in simulation are presented.

## 2 Plant Description

WTP are systems where urban and industrial wastewaters are processed to eliminate as much pollution as possible. When these wastewaters enter the plant they are driven to an aeration tank where they are mixed with a sludge made up of bacteria. After they have "eaten" most of the organic matter, water and sludge are driven to a settling tank where they are separated. The sludge flows downwards while the water stays at the top of the tank and flows over an overflow weir to be released to nearby rivers. The sludge is withdrawn from the tank and then split into two streams: one is driven to the aeration tank to keep the sludge concentration at an appropriate level while the other is eliminated. A diagram of a WTP is shown in Fig. 1., where the parameters defining the real plant whose data has been used in this work, that of the city of Mérida [5], also appear.

The definition of a model of the whole system to be used in simulation is very difficult as biological processes are involved in the plant dynamics. Therefore a simplification must be applied in order to obtain a computational treatable structure. A good approximation to the behavior of the plant may be obtained with the description of only the aeration tank, the main element of the whole system. It may be simulated with a set of two differential equations describing the evolution of sludge (microorganisms) and output pollution concentrations [6]:

$$\frac{dSe}{dt} = -\frac{Qf}{V} Se - k\, Xva\, Se + Sf\, \frac{Qf}{V} \; , \tag{1}$$

$$\frac{dXva}{dt} = -\left[\frac{Qf}{V}(1+r) + kd\right] Xva - \frac{Qf}{V} Y\, Se + \frac{Qf}{V} r\, Xvu + \frac{Qf}{V} Y\, Sf \; , \tag{2}$$

$$r = \frac{Qo - Qf}{Qf} = \frac{Qr}{Qf} \cong \frac{Xva}{Xvu - Xva} \; . \tag{3}$$

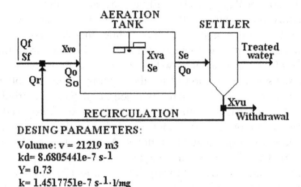

**DESING PARAMETERS:**
Volume: v = 21219 m3
kd= 8.6805441e-7 s-1
Y= 0.73
k= 1.4517751e-7 s-1·l/mg

**Fig. 1.** Diagram of a Wastewater Treatment Plant and values of the parameters of the actual plant used for simulation

In this model $Qf$ represents the "Influent Flowrate", $Sf$ the "Influent Pollution Concentration", $Xva$ the "Sludge Concentration" in the aeration tank and $Se$ the "Output Pollution Concentration". $Xvu$, the "Sludge Concentration" in the settler, is assumed to be a process parameter that will be provided at every time step, as only the aeration tank is modeled. It defines the sludge concentration in the settler, a portion of which will be recirculated to the aeration tank to keep the sludge concentration at an appropriate level. This recirculation is defined by a flowrate, $Qr$, which is adjusted by the technician supervising the plan dynamics. It is represented by a parameter, $r$, which provides the ratio between this "Recirculation Flowrate" and the "Influent Flowrate". It is adjusted to adapt the plant dynamics to "mean" values of pollution input, so that it is usually adjusted daily in response to daily mean variations of the system variables or inputs. In actual plants aeration is also controlled by technicians to adjust the system dynamics to fluctuations in the pollution input, so that the microorganisms have oxygen enough to "eat" that pollution. It may be then considered as a short-time control in opposition to the recirculation control, which may be assumed as a long-term one. As they are usually independently adjusted, only one of them will be studied in his work: that based on recirculation. Daily mean data of all the aforementioned variables and parameters corresponding to years 1998 and 1999 were obtained from the exploitation and maintenance reports of the plant of the city of Mérida [5].

In order to ensure an optimal behavior of the plant operation, the model here used [6] defines a new parameter, the relation between "food" and "microorganisms":

$$F/M \cong \frac{Qf \; Sf}{Xva \; V} \; . \tag{4}$$

For a plant to work properly this parameter ought to be close to an optimal value, which may be different for different types of plants. For those known as "low charge", as the actual plant used in this work, that value is $F/Mopt=0.133$. It is usually assumed that a value between 0.098 and 0.168 may be considered as optimum [6].

As weather conditions may influence the system behavior, the available data have been split into two groups: hot and cold. The first is formed with months from October through March, and the second with the remaining months. Two different simulations will be carried out, one for each group. Year 1998 will be used to train the controller and 1999 to test its performance.

## 3  Plant Control

The plant control will be carried out by the combined action of an equivalent control which works when the system has a value of $F/M$ inside the optimal interval [0.098, 0.168] and a corrective control which drives the system dynamics towards that region when $F/M$ has a value outside it. The first one will be carried out with a neural network trained to reproduce the actions of the technician controlling the actual plant used in this work [4]. It will provide a value for $r$ that will be used in the simulation of the system represented with equations (1)-(3). The second controller will be defined by a function that measures the distance of the value of $F/M$ obtained in simulation from its optimal value, providing a correction that depends on that distance. If this value falls outside the optimal interval a correction will be added to $r$ and a new value will be so obtained, which will be used to carry out a new simulation of the system. Then $F/M$ will be measured again and the process will be repeated until the value of $F/M$ falls inside the desired interval. So the value of $r$ may be defined as:

$$r = ro + \delta r + \delta r F/M \; . \tag{5}$$

In this expression $ro$ is a constant term, $\delta r$ the contribution of the neural network (equivalent control) and $\delta r F/M$ that corresponding to the correction added when $F/M$ falls outside the optimal interval (corrective control). The constant term $ro$ has been included in order to define the control action as a fluctuation around a constant value of the recirculation, as this is the way technicians of actual plants use to work. This constant has been assumed to be the mean value of $r$ in the actual plant used in this work throughout the whole period of available data: $ro=1.74$.

## 3.1  Equivalent Control

The neural model used to learn the technician's behavior is a Multilayer Perceptron [7]. The network has five inputs: the product of $Qf$ and $Sf$, the system variables $Xva$ and $Se$, the inner variable $Xvu$, they all measured in the present time step, and the control signal $\delta r$, measured a time step before. We have considered the product of the input flowrate and its concentration instead of their separated values because that product represents the value of the total pollutant mass, which have a more direct influence on the sludge evolution than their separated values. Simulations have been carried out with both options and the best performance was obtained with the product. The network output is the correction $\delta r$.

The neural network structure has been selected by trial and error testing several configurations. The best results were obtained with two hidden layers: the first with 15 elements and the second with 10. Their activation functions were the logistic ones, while that of the neuron in the output layer was the arctangent, whose output ranges between $-1$ and $+1$ to provide the desired fluctuation around $ro$.

The network training process was carried out with the Levenberg-Maquart version of the Backpropagation algorithm [7]. Two neural networks will be trained, one for hot months and the other for cold months, with the data of year 1998.

## 3.2  Corrective Control

This control will be carried out by a function which will provide a correction to the value of the recirculation whenever a value of $F/M$ outside the optimal interval is obtained. This function ought to increase the value of the recirculation when $F/M>F/Mopt=0.133$ and decrease it when $F/M<F/Mopt$. Then the system will be simulated again and a new value of $F/M$ will be obtained. If it falls inside the optimal interval the value of $r$ obtained will be assumed as an adequate recirculation, otherwise the process will be repeated adding new corrections to $r$ until such a value will be obtained. The whole process may be defined as:

$$r = ro + \delta r + \sum_i \gamma_i (F/M) , \tag{6}$$

where subscript $i$ represents the $i$th iteration of the process, and $\gamma_i(x)$ the correction added to the recirculation in the $i$th iteration, whose value is obtained from:

$$\gamma(F/M) = \frac{-1}{1+e^{P1(F/M-G1)}} + \frac{1}{1+e^{-P2(F/M-G2)}} , \tag{7}$$

which accomplish with the previously stated specifications for the function performing the corrective control (Fig. 2).

The value of this correction is determined by parameters P1, G1, P2 and G2. P1 and P2 control the function slope, while G1 and G2 represent the inputs which respectively generate the values -0.5 and +0.5 as function output (Fig. 2). So they must be carefully defined in order to provide an adequate correction to the recirculation. A too small correction will not drive the system dynamics inside the desired interval, forcing the controller to repeat the iterative process defined by (6), while, on the other hand, a too big one could force the system, in the worst case, to provide a value of *F/M* in the non-optimum interval opposite to that where the system initially was, or, in the best case, an unnecessary too big modification of the recirculation which will augment the electric consumption. So the values of those parameters must be carefully defined to provide a correction which will be big enough to drive the system inside the optimum interval in an as low as possible number of iterations but not too high to produce an unnecessary electric consumption.

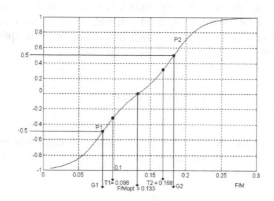

**Fig. 2.** Plot of function $\gamma_i(x)$

It is necessary to notice that, as the dynamics of the biological process of the aeration tank is very slow (a perturbation in the inputs takes about half an hour to affect the plant dynamics), a modification in the recirculation will also needs a long time period to modify the plant evolution. So the use of a too high value could not be corrected in time to compensate for their effects, while a low value may be easily corrected following the plant evolution with successive corrections of *r*. This conservative behavior accomplish with the aforementioned control strategy in actual wastewater treatment plants, where sudden variations in the plant inputs are compensated with air pumping adjustment, while recirculation is only modified to compensate for mean variations along several hours or days.

As the definition of the function parameters of (7) must be done taking into account all the aforementioned facts, it is not possible to adjust them with a classical adjustment algorithm. Genetic algorithms [8],[9] represent an option which allows those parameters to be obtained taking into account all those facts. So they will be used in this work. Bounds have been imposed to those parameters: $G1 \in (0.07, 0.12)$, $G1 \in (0.14, 0.197)$ and $P1, P2 \in (25, 75)$.

## 4   Genetic Adjustment of the Corrective Control

The parameters of equation (7) have been arranged to form a chromosome. It was 40 bits long, ten for each one. The population was formed with 20 individuals defined by their corresponding chromosomes. The algorithm starts with a randomly obtained initial population, which will undergo crossover and mutation operations. Then the system will be simulated with each individual (set of parameters of (7)) along 6 months of year 1998 (one simulation for hot months and another for cold months) and a fitness function will be calculated in order to carry out a selection process. Those individuals performing the best will be selected to form a new population and the whole process will be repeated until the fitness function of some individual reaches a predetermined minimum or a maximum number of iterations is carried out.

There are a plenty of possible fitness functions depending on the system considered. In that used in this work the control law looks for the system dynamics to produce a value of $F/M$ inside an optimal interval, so the fitness function may be defined as the distance of the value obtained in simulation to its optimal value. The root mean squared error (RMSE) is the selected function:

$$\sigma_m = \left[ \frac{1}{N} \sum_{i=1}^{N} \left( F/M_i - F/M_{opt} \right)^2 \right]^{1/2},$$  (8)

where $m$ defines each individual and $N$ is the number of days simulated (6 months). Nevertheless this function is not usually used as fitness function. Instead of it its relative value is preferred:

$$P_m = \frac{\sigma_m}{\sum\limits_{i=1}^{Pop\_size} \sigma_i}.$$  (9)

The individuals performing the best will be those with a lower value of $P_m$.

This function will be also used as a base to define the selection method used in this work to select individuals for reproduction: the "roulette wheel". To carry it out each individual will be associated with its cumulative fitness:

$$C_i = \sum_{j=1}^{i} P_j.$$  (10)

To select an individual a series of $M$ (number of individuals of the population) random numbers $n_k$ with values between 0 and 1 is generated. They will be compared with the whole population, so that the $i$-th individual will be selected when $C_i < n_k \leq C_{i+1}$. 20 individuals were selected for crossover, as an individual may be picked several times.

A "double point" crossover will be carried out with the 10 couples of parents. Those two crossover points will be randomly selected. A "reduced surrogate" operator has been included to avoid generating individuals identical to their parents. Only the best 70% of the offspring will be added to the population, which will then suffer a mutation process. The probability an individual is mutated is very low: $P_{mut} = 0.7/Lind$, where $Lind$ is the length of the chromosome, 40 bits in this work.

Once crossover and mutation and have been performed the fitness function (9) of each individual will be obtained and 20 of them, those with a lower value, will be selected to repeat the whole process until a fixed performance is obtained or a high enough number of iterations have been done. As in this work performance is a "fuzzy" concept (the system must work inside an optimal region, no matter how close to the optimal value of $F/M$) the definition of a performance limit has been discarded and the only stop condition is the number of iteration. Simulations have proved that 100 was high enough to obtain appropriate values for the parameters of (7).

The values of those parameters obtained after running the genetic algorithm were, for cold months: $G1 = 0.11863$, $G2 = 0.16374$, $P1 = 61.755$, $P2 = 53.006$. For hot months they were: $G1 = 0.11316$, $G2 = 0.155521$, $P1 = 42.2043$, $P2 = 36.2903$.

## 5  Simulation and Results

The plant model along with the controller defined by (6) have been simulated twice: one for cold months and another for hot months. The data corresponding to 1998 have been used to train the controllers while those corresponding to 1999 have been used to validate them. The results obtained have been compared with those provided by the operation reports of the actual plant used as reference [4].

For the sake of space availability only the results of one month of each simulation have been presented: January 1999 for cold months (Fig 3.) and August 1999 for hot months (Fig.4). The $F/M$s obtained are presented along with those obtained from the data of the actual plant. In both Figures the total number of iterations needed to drive the system dynamics inside the optimum interval is also presented.

As it may be seen many values of $F/M$ (both actual data and those obtained when only the neural network works) are outside the optimum interval and the inclusion of the correction to recirculation defined by (7) drives the system to generate a proper value. These results prove that the control so designed is able to force the system dynamics inside its optimal working region.

In actual plants recirculation has an upper and a lower limit: the former defined by the maximum pumping power and the latter zero. This fact has been taken into account in the design of the controller. When a lower than zero recirculation is provided by the controller a value of zero will be assigned to it. The upper limit was fixed to $r=3.74$ as this is the highest value which may be obtained from the sum of the three terms of expression (6) (assuming that only one correction to recirculation is done). If the iterative process defined with (6) provides a higher value it will be fixed to $r=3.74$. So if a recirculation outside those limits is needed to drive the system inside the optimal region, the controller will not be able to provide it and the system will be outside that region. In such a case only the time evolution of the system may drive it inside that region, what from the viewpoint of simulation means that added iterations (with $r$ fixed to an extreme value: $r=0$ or $r=3.74$) will be needed. This effect will be more noticeable when a lower than the optimum value of $F/M$ is obtained, as the controller will not able to reduce the concentration of microorganisms, it may only avoid its increase.

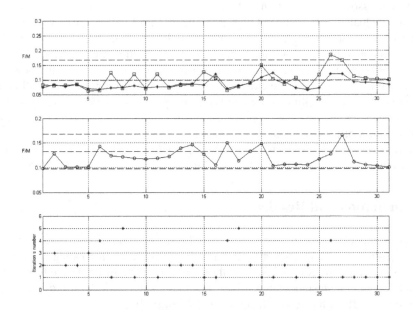

**Fig. 3.** January 1999. Values of F/M provided by simulation without correction of recirculation (square) and actual data (asterisk) (first plot). Final value of F/M when the controller defined by (6) is applied (second plot). Number of corrections to recirculation (1 when a proper value of *F/M* was obtained only with the neural controller, 2 if a correction was needed and so on).

To test the good performance of the controller developed in this work the system has been forced to work under extreme working conditions. The inputs of some days have been modified to abnormally high or low values in order to test the controller behavior. In November 1999 three days (6, 7, 8) were raised from their values (220 mg/l) to other abnormally high (350, 400, 300). The controller was able to drive the system to the optimum region, although it needed to increase the number of iteration of equation (6) (4, 7, 1). The same days, but in February 1999, suffered a sudden decrease in their input conditions from 300 mg/l to (200, 150, 150). The controller was able to drive the system inside the desired region with (2, 2, 2) iterations. These results prove the capability of the controller to manage sudden modifications of the system input conditions. Although in some extreme cases the controller needed a high number of iterations to drive the system inside its optimal region it did it at last.

The results obtained prove the great capability of the neural structure proposed in this work to carry out the same tasks the technicians controlling WTP do, and the capability of the whole controller to provide a reliable control which drives the system dynamics inside its optimal region. These results point out that the controller defined may be a valuable tool to help technicians in WTPs to control them. Further research is to be done to use models more complex than that defined by (1)-(3) which allow more sophisticated controllers to be defined in order to provide a reliable tool to be used by technicians in actual WTPs.

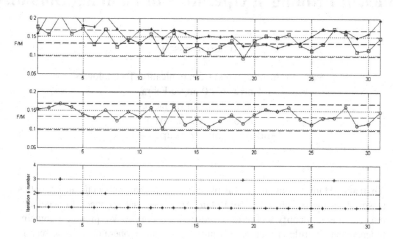

**Fig. 4.** August 1999. All the symbols have the same meaning as those in Fig. 3.

## References

1. DeCarlo, R.A., Zak, S.H., Drakunov, S.V.: Variable Structure, Sliding-Mode Controller design. In: Levine, S.W. (ed.) The Control Handbook. CRC Press-IEEE Press, pp. 941–951 (1996)
2. Tsai, C.H., Chung, H.Y., Yu, F.M.: Neuro-Sliding Mode Control with its Applications to Seesaw Systems. Trans. on Neural Networks 15(1), 124–134 (2004)
3. Wang, J., Rang, A.B., Chang, P.T.: Indirect Adaptive Fuzzy Sliding Mode Control: Part I: Fuzzy Switching. Fuzzy Sets and Systems 122, 21–30 (2001)
4. Jaramillo-Morán, M.A., Peguero-Chamizo, J.C., Martínez de Salazar, E., García del Valle, M.: Sliding Mode Control of a Wastewater Treatment Plant with Neural Networks. In: Marín, R., Onaindía, E., Bugarín, A., Santos, J. (eds.) CAEPIA 2005. LNCS (LNAI), vol. 4177, pp. 409–418. Springer, Heidelberg (2006)
5. Aguas, E.D.A.R., de Mérida, S.L.: Exploitation and maintenance report (1998 and 1999)
6. Ramalho, R.S.: Introduction to Wastewater Treatment Processes. Academic Press, London (1983)
7. Bishop, C.M.: Neural networks for pattern recognition. Oxford University Press, Oxford (1995)
8. Mitchell, M.: An Introduction to Genetic Algorithms. MIT Press, Cambridge (1998)
9. Houck, C., Joines, J., Kay, M.: A Genetic Algorithm for Function Optimization: A Matlab Implementation. NCSU-IE TR 95-09 (1995)

# Efficient Pruning of Operators in Planning Domains

Anders Jonsson

Dept. of Information and Communication Technologies
Universitat Pompeu Fabra
Passeig de Circumval·lació, 8
08003 Barcelona, Spain
anders.jonsson@upf.edu

**Abstract.** Many recent successful planners use domain-independent heuristics to speed up the search for a valid plan. An orthogonal approach to accelerating search is to identify and remove redundant operators. We present a domain-independent algorithm for efficiently pruning redundant operators prior to search. The algorithm operates in the domain transition graphs of multi-valued state variables, so its complexity is polynomial in the size of the state variable domains. We prove that redundant operators can always be replaced in a valid plan with other operators. Experimental results in standard planning domains demonstrate that our algorithm can reduce the number of operators as well as speed up search.

## 1 Introduction

Planning is the problem of finding a sequence of operators for moving from a start state to a goal state. The search space is usually very large, so most research in planning has focused on making search faster. The most successful approach has been to devise domain-independent heuristics for guiding the search along promising paths. Another approach, which has been explored less, is to identify redundant operators and remove them prior to search. There are usually several ways to reach the goal, and under certain conditions, some of these may be immediately discarded. Reducing the number of operators means reducing the branching factor, typically making search faster.

We present a domain-independent algorithm for identifying and pruning redundant operators in planning domains. We use the SAS$^+$ formalism [1] to represent planning domains using multi-valued state variables. The algorithm constructs domain transition graphs of individual state variables and performs search in the graphs to identify redundant operators. We prove that redundant operators can always be replaced in a valid plan with other operators. Thus, it is safe to prune the redundant operators. Experiments in standard planning domains demonstrate the utility of our approach.

Several other researchers have exploited domain knowledge to simplify the planning problem prior to search. Nebel et al. [2] designed an algorithm for removing irrelevant facts and operators, which works well in certain planning problems but is not solution-preserving. Scholz [3] defined a concept of redundant sequences of actions, restricted to sequences of length 2, and used it as a constraint to exclude plans that contained redundant sequences. Haslum and Jonsson [4] defined redundant operators as operators that

D. Borrajo, L. Castillo, and J.M. Corchado (Eds.): CAEPIA 2007, LNAI 4788, pp. 130–139, 2007.
© Springer-Verlag Berlin Heidelberg 2007

can be replaced by operator sequences, and designed an algorithm for identifying and pruning redundant operators. Scholz [5] developed a technique for pruning operators similar to ours, using information about the local effect of operators. However, the author reported that the approach did not work well in LOGISTICS and BLOCKSWORLD, two domains in which our approach achieves good results. Vidal and Geffner [6] used inference to solve simple planning problems without performing search.

## 2   Notation

Let $V = \{v_1, \ldots, v_n\}$ be a set of state variables, and let $\mathcal{D}(v_i)$ be the finite domain of state variable $v_i \in V$. Let $\mathcal{D}_C = \times_{v_i \in C} \mathcal{D}(v_i)$ be the joint domain of a subset $C \subseteq V$ of state variables. We define a *context* $c \in \mathcal{D}_C$ as an assignment of values to the subset $C$ of state variables. Let $c[v_i] \in \mathcal{D}(v_i)$ be the value that context $c$ assigns to state variable $v_i \in C$. We use the convention of capitalizing a context to denote its associated subset of state variables. For example, $C$ is the subset of state variables associated with context $c$. A *state* $s \in \mathcal{D}_V$ assigns a value to each state variable in $V$.

We define two operations on contexts. Let $f_W(c)$ be the projection of context $c$ onto the subset $W \subseteq V$ of state variables. The result of $f_W(c)$ is a context $x$ such that $X = C \cap W$ and $x[v_i] = c[v_i]$ for each $v_i \in X$. Also, let $c \oplus w$ be the composition of contexts $c$ and $w$. The result of $c \oplus w$ is a context $x$ such that $X = C \cup W$, $x[v_i] = w[v_i]$ for each $v_i \in W$ and $x[v_i] = c[v_i]$ for each $v_i \in C - W$. Note that the right operand overrides the values of the left operand.

A SAS$^+$ planning problem is a tuple $\mathcal{P} = \langle V, s_I, c_G, A \rangle$, where $V$ is the set of state variables, $s_I$ is an initial state, $c_G$ is a goal context, and $A = \{a_1, \ldots, a_m\}$ is a set of grounded operators. Each operator $a_j \in A$ has the form $\langle \mathbf{pre}_j, \mathbf{post}_j, \mathbf{prv}_j \rangle$, where the contexts $\mathbf{pre}_j$, $\mathbf{post}_j$, and $\mathbf{prv}_j$ denote the pre-, post- and prevail-condition of $a_j$, respectively. For each $a_j \in A$, $\mathbf{Pre}_j = \mathbf{Post}_j$ and $\mathbf{Pre}_j \cap \mathbf{Prv}_j = \emptyset$. Operator $a_j$ is applicable in state $s$ if $f_{\mathbf{Pre}_j}(s) = \mathbf{pre}_j$ and $f_{\mathbf{Prv}_j}(s) = \mathbf{prv}_j$. The result of successfully applying $a_j$ in state $s$ is $s \oplus \mathbf{post}_j$. The objective is to find a plan, i.e., a sequence of operators in $A^*$, where $*$ is the Kleene star, for moving the system from the initial state $s_I$ to a state $s$ such that $f_{C_G}(s) = c_G$. In this paper, we study the class of planning problems with unary operators, i.e., for each operator $a_j \in A$, $|\mathbf{Pre}_j| = |\mathbf{Post}_j| = 1$. In this case, it is possible to form the set $A_i = \{a_j \in A \mid \mathbf{Pre}_j = \mathbf{Post}_j = \{v_i\}\}$ of operators that change the value of state variable $v_i \in V$.

## 3   Context Subsumption

To prune operators, we are interested in determining when the prevail-condition of one operator causes the prevail-condition of another operator to hold. We formalize this idea using context subsumption:

**Definition 1.** *A context* $c$ *subsumes a context* $z$, *which we denote* $c \sqsupseteq z$, *if and only if* $C \subseteq Z$ *and* $f_C(z) = c$.

If a context subsumes another, any state that satisfies the latter will also satisfy the former. In other words, if $c \sqsupseteq z$, for any state $s$ such that $f_Z(s) = z$ it follows that $f_C(s) = c$.

We also introduce the idea of context paths, which are sequences of contexts.

---

**Algorithm 1.** SUBSUMES $(\mathcal{C}^{\mathcal{A}}, \mathcal{C}^{\mathcal{A}'}, i, j)$

1: $subsumes \leftarrow i > |\mathcal{C}^{\mathcal{A}}|$
2: **for** $(k \leftarrow 0; \mathbf{not}(subsumes)$ **and** $k \leq (|\mathcal{C}^{\mathcal{A}'}| - j) - (|\mathcal{C}^{\mathcal{A}}| - i); k \leftarrow k + 1)$
3:      **if** SUBSUMES$(\mathbf{c}_i^{\mathcal{A}}, \mathbf{c}_{j+k}^{\mathcal{A}'})$
4:          $subsumes \leftarrow$ SUBSUMES $(\mathcal{C}^{\mathcal{A}}, \mathcal{C}^{\mathcal{A}'}, i + 1, j + k + 1)$
5: **return** $subsumes$

---

**Definition 2.** *A context path* $C = \{\mathbf{c}_1, \ldots, \mathbf{c}_k\}$ *is a sequence of* $|\mathcal{C}| = k$ *contexts* $\mathbf{c}_i$ *such that for each* $i \in [2, \ldots, k]$, $\mathbf{c}_{i-1} \not\sqsupseteq \mathbf{c}_i$ *and* $\mathbf{c}_i \not\sqsupseteq \mathbf{c}_{i-1}$.

In other words, no two neighboring contexts in a context path subsume each other. We extend the idea of context subsumption to context paths:

**Definition 3.** *A context path* $C$ *subsumes a context path* $\mathcal{Z}$, *which we denote* $C \sqsupseteq \mathcal{Z}$, *if and only if* $|\mathcal{C}| \leq |\mathcal{Z}|$ *and there exist* $j_1, \ldots, j_k$, $k = |\mathcal{C}|$, *such that for each* $i \in [2, \ldots, k]$, $j_{i-1} < j_i$, *and such that for each* $i \in [1, \ldots, k]$, $\mathbf{c}_i \sqsupseteq \mathbf{z}_{j_i}$.

In other words, there exists a subsequence of $|\mathcal{C}|$ contexts in $\mathcal{Z}$, preserving their internal order, such that each of them is subsumed by the corresponding context in $C$. Algorithm 1 describes a subroutine for determining whether a context path $\mathcal{C}^{\mathcal{A}}$ subsumes a context path $\mathcal{C}^{\mathcal{A}'}$. When calling the algorithm, the indices $i$ and $j$ should be initialized to 1.

Let $\mathcal{A} = \{a_1, \ldots a_l\}$ be a sequence of operators in $A_i^*$. Given $\mathcal{A}$, $\{\mathbf{prv}_1, \ldots, \mathbf{prv}_l\}$ is the sequence of prevail-conditions of the operators in $\mathcal{A}$. Since neighboring prevail-conditions may subsume each other, this sequence may not be a context path. However, it is easy to convert it into a context path by merging neighboring prevail-conditions that subsume each other using the $\oplus$ operator. Let $\mathcal{C}^{\mathcal{A}}$ denote the context path of prevail-conditions derived from the operator sequence $\mathcal{A}$. Each context $\mathbf{c}_i^{\mathcal{A}}$ in $\mathcal{C}^{\mathcal{A}}$ corresponds to one or several operators in $\mathcal{A}$ that are applicable in states that satisfy $\mathbf{c}_i^{\mathcal{A}}$.

**Theorem 1.** *Let* $\mathcal{A} = \{a_1, \ldots a_l\}$ *and* $\mathcal{A}' = \{a'_1, \ldots a'_m\}$ *be two valid sequences of operators in* $A_i^*$ *such that* $\mathbf{pre}_1 = \mathbf{pre}'_1$ *and* $\mathbf{post}_l = \mathbf{post}'_m$. *Assume that* $\mathcal{A}'$ *is part of a valid plan and that for each* $j \in [1, \ldots, m-1]$, *operator* $a'_j$ *is not in the support of the prevail-condition of any operator in the plan. Then if* $\mathcal{C}^{\mathcal{A}} \sqsupseteq \mathcal{C}^{\mathcal{A}'}$ *it is possible to substitute* $\mathcal{A}$ *for* $\mathcal{A}'$ *in the plan without invalidating the plan.*

*Proof.* From the definition of $\mathcal{C}^{\mathcal{A}} \sqsupseteq \mathcal{C}^{\mathcal{A}'}$ it follows that there exists $j_1, \ldots, j_k$, $k = |\mathcal{C}^{\mathcal{A}}|$, such that for each $i \in [1, \ldots, k]$, $\mathbf{c}_i^{\mathcal{A}} \sqsupseteq \mathbf{c}_{j_i}^{\mathcal{A}'}$. For each $\mathbf{c}_{j_i}^{\mathcal{A}'}$, there is some operator $a'_j \in \mathcal{A}'$ that is only applicable in context $\mathbf{c}_{j_i}^{\mathcal{A}'}$. Therefore, when $a'_j$ is applied in the plan, $\mathbf{c}_{j_i}^{\mathcal{A}'}$ must hold. But since $\mathbf{c}_i^{\mathcal{A}} \sqsupseteq \mathbf{c}_{j_i}^{\mathcal{A}'}$, this means that $\mathbf{c}_i^{\mathcal{A}}$ also holds, which makes all operators corresponding to $\mathbf{c}_i^{\mathcal{A}}$ applicable. Thus, at some point in the plan, each operator in $\mathcal{A}$ is applicable, making it possible to replace all operators in $\mathcal{A}'$ with the operators in $\mathcal{A}$. Since $\mathcal{A}$ and $\mathcal{A}'$ begin and end with the same value for $v_i$, this does not compromise operators that change the value of $v_i$ at earlier or later points in the plan. Since no operator in $\mathcal{A}'$ (except possibly the last) is in the support of the prevail-condition of any other operator in the plan, the substitution does not invalidate the plan.

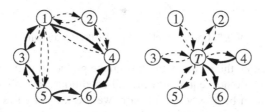

**Fig. 1.** Domain transition graphs for $v_T$ and $v_P$

## 4   Pruning Operators

Using Theorem 1, we devise an algorithm for pruning operators from the planning domain. First, construct the domain transition graph for each state variable. The domain transition graph for state variable $v_i \in \mathbf{V}$ is a graph with one node per value in $\mathcal{D}(v_i)$. For each operator $a_j \in A_i$, add an edge in the domain transition graph from $\mathbf{pre}_j$ to $\mathbf{post}_j$. Go through the remaining operators of the planning domain to determine the subset of values $\mathcal{Q}_i \subseteq \mathcal{D}(v_i)$ that appear in the prevail-condition of any operator in $A$.

Starting from the projected initial state $\mathbf{s}_I[v_i] \in \mathcal{D}(v_i)$, do a breadth-first search over the domain transition graph. For each $d \in \mathcal{Q}_i$ visited during search, store the different operator sequences in $A_i^*$ for reaching $d$ from $\mathbf{s}_I[v_i]$. If the context path of one operator sequence subsumes the context path of another, it follows from Theorem 1 that we can replace the latter operator sequence with the former. If two context paths subsume each other (i.e., they are equal), we break ties by preferring the shorter of the two.

For each value $d \in \mathcal{Q}_i$ visited during the search from $\mathbf{s}_I[v_i]$, repeat breadth-first search starting at $d$. If the goal context $\mathbf{c}_G$ specifies a value for $v_i$, it is also necessary to determine the possible operator sequences for reaching the value $\mathbf{c}_G[v_i] \in \mathcal{D}(v_i)$. We are left with a minimal set of operator sequences necessary to move between any two values in $\mathcal{Q}_i$ (possibly starting in $\mathbf{s}_I[v_i]$ and/or ending in $\mathbf{c}_G[v_i]$). Any operator that does not appear in any of these operator sequences can be safely pruned.

To illustrate the algorithm for pruning operators we use a problem from the LO-GISTICS domain. In LOGISTICS, trucks and airplanes are used to move one or several packages to designated locations. We choose a problem with one truck and one package, which can be modelled as a SAS$^+$ instance with two state variables $v_T$ and $v_P$, representing the location of the truck and the package, respectively. The problem has six locations $1, \ldots, 6$, so $\mathcal{D}(v_T) = \{1, \ldots, 6\}$ and $\mathcal{D}(v_P) = \{1, \ldots, 6, T\}$, where $T$ denotes that the package is inside the truck. Figure 1 shows the domain transition graphs of $v_T$ and $v_P$. The initial state is $(v_T = 3, v_P = 4)$ and the goal context is $(v_P = 6)$.

First run the algorithm on the domain transition graph for $v_P$. The projected initial state is 4, and no operator of the problem has a prevail-condition on $v_P$, so the only target value is the projected goal context 6. One operator sequence for reaching 6 from 4 is $(pickup(4), putdown(6))$ with associated context path $((v_T = 4), (v_T = 6))$. Any other operator sequence for reaching 6 drops the package in an intermediate location along the way, so its associated context path is subsumed by $((v_T = 4), (v_T = 6))$. Thus, we can prune all operators other than $pickup(4)$ and $putdown(6)$.

Next run the algorithm on the domain transition graph for $v_T$. After pruning operators for $v_P$, only $(v_T = 4)$ and $(v_T = 6)$ appear as prevail-conditions of other operators.

**Fig. 2.** Causal graph of the LOGISTICS domain

Thus, we need to reach the values 4 and 6 from the projected initial state 3. Operators for moving the truck do not require any prevail-conditions, so each associated context path will by definition be empty. In this case, we break ties by selecting the shortest operator sequences: from 3 via 1 to 4, and from 3 via 5 to 6. We repeat the search from 4 and 6 to find the shortest operator sequences for reaching 6 and 4, respectively.

The pruned operators appear as broken edges in Figure 1. In this problem, our algorithm prunes 20 out of 28 operators. An advantage of the algorithm is that it handles each state variable separately. Typically, the domain transition graph of a single state variable has limited size, which bounds the complexity of the algorithm.

Note, however, that the order of pruning is important. If we start pruning operators for $v_T$, each value of $v_T$ appears in the prevail-condition of other operators, since we can pick up and put down the package anywhere. Thus, we would not prune any operator for $v_T$. To determine the order of pruning operators, we construct the causal graph of the domain. The causal graph has one node per state variable $v_i$, and an edge between $v_j$ and $v_i$ indicates that there exists an operator in $A_i$ with a prevail-condition on $v_j$.

To get rid of cycles in the causal graph, we compute the strongly connected components of the graph. We construct a component graph with the strongly connected components as nodes and edges mapped from the causal graph. The component graph is by definition acyclic. Figure 2 shows the causal graph of the LOGISTICS domain in our example. Since the causal graph is acyclic, each node is its own strongly connected component, so the component graph is identical to the causal graph in this case.

Operators that affect state variables in a strongly connected component have prevail-conditions on state variables in parent strongly connected components. Therefore, it makes sense to prune operators for the strongly connected components in inverse topological order. In the example, that means first pruning operators for $v_P$, then for $v_T$. Algorithm 2 describes the final algorithm for pruning operators.

Theorem 1 ensures that our algorithm preserves a valid solution. In the following theorem, we prove that in many cases our algorithm also preserves the optimal solution.

---

**Algorithm 2.** PRUNE($\mathcal{P}$)

---
1: construct the causal graph of the domain
2: compute strongly connected components (**SCC**) of graph
3: construct component graph of **SCC**s
4: **for each SCC** in inverse topological order
5:  **repeat** until convergence
6:   **for each** $v_i \in$ **SCC**
7:    determine set $\mathcal{Q}_i \subseteq \mathcal{D}(v_i)$ of prevail-condition values
8:    let $L \leftarrow \{\mathbf{s}_I[v_i]\} \cup \mathcal{Q}_i$
9:    **for each** $d \in L$
10:     do breadth-first search in domain transition graph
11:     find minimal operator sequences to $\mathcal{Q}_i \cup \{\mathbf{c}_G[v_i]\}$
12:     prune any operator not in a minimal operator sequence

---

**Theorem 2.** *If redundant operator sequences are always at least as long as the operator sequences with which they can be replaced, the pruned operator set generated by our algorithm preserves the optimal solution.*

*Proof.* Assume that a pruned operator is part of a valid plan. To be pruned, this operator has to be part of a redundant operator sequence. From Theorem 1 it follows that we can replace the redundant operator sequence with a sequence of non-redundant operators without invalidating the plan. If the redundant operator sequence is at least as long as the replacing operator sequence, the transformed plan is shorter or equal in length to the original plan. Thus, it is always possible to generate an optimal plan using only operators that are not pruned.

Note that the condition in Theorem 2 does not always hold. When we derive the context path of prevail-conditions associated with an operator sequence, we use the $\oplus$ operator to merge neighboring contexts that subsume each other. Thus, a long operator sequence may have a short associated context path. In particular, it is possible that a redundant operator sequence is shorter than the replacing operator sequence.

## 5 Extended Operators

When translating planning problems to multi-valued representations, it is sometimes possible to infer the truth value of certain predicates. The translated operators may be applicable for a subset of values of a state variable. We introduce the notion of extended operators, which are operators whose prevail-conditions specify sets of values on state variables. Extended operators can compactly represent activities that it would otherwise take many regular operators to represent.

Let $2^{\mathbf{C}} = \times_{v_i \in \mathbf{C}} 2^{\mathcal{D}(v_i)}$ be the joint domain power set of a subset $\mathbf{C} \subseteq \mathbf{V}$ of state variables. An *extended* context $\mathbf{c}^e \in 2^{\mathbf{C}}$ assigns a subset of values $\mathbf{c}^e[v_i] \subseteq \mathcal{D}(v_i)$ to each state variable $v_i \in \mathbf{C}$. An extended operator $a_j^e = \langle \mathbf{pre}_j, \mathbf{post}_j, \mathbf{prv}_j^e \rangle$ has an extended context $\mathbf{prv}_j^e$ describing the prevail-condition. The extended operator $a_j^e$ is applicable in any state $\mathbf{s}$ such that for each $v_i \in \mathbf{Prv}_j^e$, $\mathbf{s}[v_i] \in \mathbf{prv}_j^e[v_i]$.

We illustrate the benefit of using extended operators using the BLOCKSWORLD domain. In BLOCKSWORLD a robot hand has to rearrange a group of blocks to achieve a designated target configuration. Helmert [7] showed how to translate planning problems from PDDL to multi-valued formulations. The idea is to identify invariants, which are sets of predicates such that precisely one predicate in each set is true at any point. Table 1 shows the invariants of an instance of BLOCKSWORLD with four blocks.

To obtain a multi-valued planning problem, define a state variable for each invariant with the set of predicates as its domain. Once a predicate has been included in the domain of a variable, it is excluded from all other invariants. In the example, this creates four state variables $v_1$ through $v_4$ whose domains equal invariants 1-4. The remaining five invariants now contain a single predicate (clear(x) and handempty, respectively), since all others have been excluded.

Helmert introduces five binary state variables corresponding to invariants 5-9. However, it is possible to infer the true predicate of these invariants from the first four state variables. For example, if on(b, a) holds in invariant 2, clear(a) is false in invariant 5. If

**Table 1.** Invariants in BLOCKSWORLD with four blocks

1. $holding(a), ontable(a), on(a, a), on(a, b), on(a, c), on(a, d)$
2. $holding(b), ontable(b), on(b, a), on(b, b), on(b, c), on(b, d)$
3. $holding(c), ontable(c), on(c, a), on(c, b), on(c, c), on(c, d)$
4. $holding(d), ontable(d), on(d, a), on(d, b), on(d, c), on(d, d)$
5. $holding(a), clear(a), on(a, a), on(b, a), on(c, a), on(d, a)$
6. $holding(b), clear(b), on(a, b), on(b, b), on(c, b), on(d, b)$
7. $holding(c), clear(c), on(a, c), on(b, c), on(c, c), on(d, c)$
8. $holding(d), clear(d), on(a, d), on(b, d), on(c, d), on(d, d)$
9. $holding(a), holding(b), holding(c), holding(d), handempty$

no block is on top of c and c is not held, $clear(c)$ is true in invariant 7. Thus, the problem is completely specified by state variables $v_1$ through $v_4$.

When translating a PDDL operator to the multi-valued representation, we can simply ignore add and delete effects on inferred predicates. However, we cannot ignore inferred predicates in the pre-condition. As an example, consider the operator $stack(a, b)$ with pre-condition $holding(a)$ and $clear(b)$. The operator deletes $holding(a)$ and $clear(b)$ and adds $on(a, b)$, $clear(a)$ and $handempty$. Delete and add effects on $clear(b)$, $clear(a)$ and $handempty$ can be ignored since they are inferred. Consequently, the pre-condition of the translated operator is $v_1 = holding(a)$ and the post-condition is $v_1 = on(a, b)$.

In contrast, the inferred predicate $clear(b)$ in the pre-condition cannot be ignored. Since $clear(b)$ is true, it follows from invariant 6 that $holding(b)$ is false and no block is on top of b. Since $holding(a)$ is true, it follows from invariant 5 that no block is on top of a, and from invariant 9 that no other block is held. Thus, the prevail-condition of the translated operator is an extended context on $\{v_2, v_3, v_4\}$ such that $v_2 \in \{ontable(b), on(b, c), on(b, d)\}$, $v_3 \in \{ontable(c), on(c, c), on(c, d)\}$ and $v_4 \in \{ontable(d), on(d, c), on(d, d)\}$. This operator could be represented using $3^3 = 27$ regular SAS$^+$ operators, but the extended operator is clearly more compact.

It is easy to modify our pruning algorithm to planning problems with extended operators. First, we modify the definition of subsumption to include extended contexts:

**Definition 4.** *An extended context $\mathbf{c}^e$ subsumes an extended context $\mathbf{z}^e$, which we denote $\mathbf{c}^e \sqsupseteq \mathbf{z}^e$, if and only if $\mathbf{C} \subseteq \mathbf{Z}$ and for each $v_i \in \mathbf{C}$, $\mathbf{z}^e[v_i] \subseteq \mathbf{c}^e[v_i]$.*

As before, if $\mathbf{c}^e \sqsupseteq \mathbf{z}^e$, any state s that satisfies $\mathbf{z}^e$ also satisfies $\mathbf{c}^e$. The definitions of extended context paths and subsumption of extended context paths are analogous to Definitions 2 and 3.

In the domain transition graph for a state variable, the only difference is that prevail-conditions are now sets of nodes. Starting from the projected initial state, determine the minimal operator sequences for reaching any node in each prevail-condition. Store each node reached this way and repeat the process from each such node.

Figure 3 shows the domain transition graph of state variable $v_1$ in BLOCKSWORLD. Block a can either be held ($H$), on the table ($T$) or on top of blocks $a - d$. Suppose that the initial state is $v_1 = on(a, b)$ and that the goal context specifies $v_1 = on(a, d)$. It turns out that $ontable(a)$ is part of every extended prevail-condition on variable $v_1$. In addition, the prevail-condition of the operator for putting block a on the table subsumes the prevail-condition of any operator that stacks block a on top of another block.

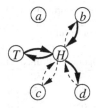

**Fig. 3.** Domain transition graph for BLOCKSWORLD

The modified algorithm finds that it is always possible to put block a on the table instead of stacking a on top of another block. In addition, putting a on the table satisfies the prevail-condition of each extended operator of the domain. Thus, the operator sequences for stacking block a on an intermediate block are redundant. The minimal operator sequences only include the solid edges in the figure. All broken edges correspond to operators that are pruned by the algorithm.

## 6   Experimental Results

We ran experiments with our algorithm in three domains taken from the International Planning Competition: LOGISTICS, BLOCKSWORLD and DRIVERLOG. DRIVERLOG is an extension of LOGISTICS that includes the problem of allocating drivers to trucks. All three domains can be translated to $SAS^+$ with extended unary operators. In each domain, we ran the algorithm across a range of problem instances. We used the translator of Helmert [7] to identify invariants, and wrote our own code to translate the PDDL code into $SAS^+$ with extended operators. Table 2 shows the number of state variables, operators, and operators pruned in each of the problem instances.

In LOGISTICS, the algorithm pruned about half of the operators. In BLOCKSWORLD, the algorithm did very well, pruning up to 95% of the operators. Finally, in DRIVER-LOG, the algorithm did not do as well, pruning 10-30% of the operators. For comparison, Haslum and Jonsson [4] reported a minimal reduced set of 420 operators in Blocks15, whereas our algorithm found a reduced set of 48 operators in the same problem instance, guaranteed to preserve solution existence.

For each problem instance, we tested how the reduced operator set affects search. We ran the Fast Downward planner [8] on the original problem instance and the problem instance with pruned operators. Since Fast Downward cannot handle extended operators, we reverted to Fast Downward's multi-valued translation prior to search. Table 2 shows the search time (in seconds) and the resulting plan length in the two cases.

Unsurprisingly, the speedup in search time was largest in BLOCKSWORLD. In the largest instance of BLOCKSWORLD, Fast Downward failed to solve the problem with the original operator set, but solved the problem quickly with the pruned operator set. In LOGISTICS, the pruned operator set cut the search time roughly in half, while in DRIVERLOG it did not have a significant effect. Overall, the reduction in search time seems proportional to the number of operators pruned. This is to be expected since the planner spends most of its time evaluating heuristics along different branches. Reducing the branching factor should reduce search time by an equivalent factor. More surprising

Table 2. Results of operator pruning and Fast Downward search

| Problem | Variables | Operators | Pruned | Original Time | Original Length | Pruned Time | Pruned Length |
|---|---|---|---|---|---|---|---|
| Logistics5 | 9 | 78 | 50 | 0.01 | 32 | 0.00 | 32 |
| Logistics10 | 17 | 308 | 254 | 0.05 | 55 | 0.02 | 55 |
| Logistics15 | 22 | 650 | 370 | 0.21 | 97 | 0.10 | 97 |
| Logistics20 | 30 | 1274 | 714 | 0.53 | 135 | 0.24 | 137 |
| Logistics25 | 39 | 2664 | 1300 | 1.85 | 190 | 0.94 | 181 |
| Logistics30 | 43 | 3290 | 1452 | 2.92 | 230 | 1.60 | 237 |
| Logistics35 | 51 | 4740 | 2420 | 5.12 | 233 | 2.63 | 232 |
| Blocks5 | 5 | 50 | 36 | 0.01 | 12 | 0.00 | 12 |
| Blocks10 | 10 | 200 | 166 | 0.07 | 48 | 0.03 | 34 |
| Blocks15 | 15 | 450 | 402 | 0.45 | 228 | 0.09 | 52 |
| Blocks20 | 20 | 800 | 728 | 0.60 | 192 | 0.12 | 74 |
| Blocks25 | 25 | 1250 | 1160 | 1.95 | 326 | 0.41 | 84 |
| Blocks30 | 30 | 1800 | 1696 | 3.27 | 284 | 1.04 | 104 |
| Blocks35 | 35 | 2450 | 2322 | 10.67 | 404 | 1.95 | 134 |
| Blocks40 | 40 | 3200 | 3054 | unsolved | | 1.35 | 138 |
| DriverLog3 | 8 | 120 | 24 | 0.01 | 15 | 0.01 | 15 |
| DriverLog6 | 11 | 222 | 78 | 0.05 | 13 | 0.04 | 13 |
| DriverLog9 | 11 | 384 | 108 | 0.13 | 63 | 0.10 | 39 |
| DriverLog12 | 11 | 948 | 90 | 1.61 | 108 | 1.62 | 102 |

was the fact that the resulting plan length in BLOCKSWORLD was significantly reduced, sometimes by as much as 75%.

## 7   Conclusion

We have presented a novel algorithm for identifying and pruning operators in planning problems prior to search. The algorithm constructs domain transition graphs of multi-valued state variables and performs search in the graphs to identify redundant operator sequences. The pruned operator set generated by the algorithm is solution-preserving, and under certain conditions it also preserves the optimal solution. We modified the algorithm to allow for extended operators whose prevail-conditions specify sets of values on state variables. Experimental results indicate that our approach can significantly speed up search in some planning problems.

In the future, we would like to extend the algorithm to planning problems with non-unary operators. Most planning problems cannot be translated to a multi-valued representation with unary operators, even when extended operators are used. The trick is to handle non-unary operators without significantly increasing the complexity of the algorithm. Ideally, the algorithm should still be able to identify redundant operator sequences using the domain transition graphs of individual state variables.

Another interesting approach to explore is the notion of objects in multi-valued representations. For example, in LOGISTICS, two trucks that operate within the same area are perceived as two different objects, so our algorithm will consider their operator sequences to be different. However, transporting a package using one truck is functionally equivalent to transporting the packing using the other truck. Even though the PDDL language includes a notion of objects, this notion is not preserved during the translation to multi-valued representations. If the $SAS^+$ formalism included a notion of objects, our algorithm could potentially prune even more operators.

# References

1. Bäckström, C., Nebel, B.: Complexity results for $SAS^+$ planning. Computational Intelligence 11(4), 625–655 (1995)
2. Nebel, B., Dimopoulos, Y., Koehler, J.: Ignoring irrelevant facts and operators in plan generation. In: Proceedings of the 4th European Conference on Planning, pp. 338–350 (1997)
3. Scholz, U.: Action constraints for planning. In: Proceedings of the 5th European Conference on Planning, pp. 148–158 (1999)
4. Haslum, P., Jonsson, P.: Planning with Reduced Operator Sets. In: Proceedings of the 5th International Conference on Automated Planning and Scheduling, pp. 150–158 (2000)
5. Scholz, U.: Reducing Planning Problems by Path Reduction. Ph.D Thesis, Darmstadt University of Technology, Darmstadt, Germany (2004)
6. Vidal, V., Geffner, H.: Solving Simple Planning Problems with More Inference and No Search. In: Proceedings of the 11th International Conference on Principles and Practice of Constraint Programming, pp. 682–696 (2005)
7. Helmert, M.: Solving Planning Tasks in Theory and Practice. Ph.D Thesis, Albert-Ludwigs-Universität, Freiburg, Germany (2006)
8. Helmert, M.: The Fast Downward Planning System. Journal of Artificial Intelligence Research 26, 191–246 (2006)

# Heuristics for Planning with Action Costs

Emil Keyder[1] and Hector Geffner[2]

[1] Universitat Pompeu Fabra
Passeig de Circumvalació 8
08003 Barcelona Spain
keyder@upf.edu
[2] ICREA & Universitat Pompeu Fabra
Passeig de Circumvalació 8
08003 Barcelona Spain
hector.geffner@upf.edu

**Abstract.** We introduce a non-admissible heuristic for planning with action costs, called the *set-additive heuristic*, that combines the benefits of the *additive heuristic* used in the HSP planner and the *relaxed plan heuristic* used in FF. The set-additive heuristic $h_a^s$ is defined mathematically and handles non-uniform action costs like the additive heuristic $h_a$, and yet like FF's heuristic $h_{FF}$, it encodes the cost of a specific *relaxed plan* and is therefore compatible with FF's helpful action pruning and its effective enforced hill climbing search. The definition of the set-additive heuristic is obtained from the definition of the additive heuristic, but rather than propagating the value of the best supports for a precondition or goal, it propagates the supports themselves, which are then combined by set-union rather than by addition. We report then empirical results on a planner that we call FF($h_a^s$) that is like FF except that the relaxed plan is extracted from the set-additive heuristic. The results show that FF($h_a^s$) adds only a slight time overhead over FF but results in much better plans when action costs are not uniform.

## 1 Motivation

The additive heuristic used in HSP [1] and the relaxed plan heuristic used in FF [2] are two of the best known heuristics in classical planning. While both are based on the delete-relaxation, the latter produces more accurate estimates along with information in the form of 'helpful actions' that is exploited in the 'enforced hill climbing' search, where non-helpful actions are ignored. Better estimates, helpful action pruning, and enforced hill climbing search are actually the three reasons that make FF a more effective planner than HSP [2]. The additive heuristic used in HSP, however, has some advantages as well. In particular, it is defined mathematically rather than procedurally, resulting in a formulation that handles non-uniform actions costs.

In this work, we introduce a new non-admissible heuristic for planning that we call the *set-additive heuristic*, that combines the benefits of the *additive* and *relaxed plan* heuristics. The set-additive heuristic $h_a^s$ is defined mathematically

D. Borrajo, L. Castillo, and J.M. Corchado (Eds.): CAEPIA 2007, LNAI 4788, pp. 140–149, 2007.
© Springer-Verlag Berlin Heidelberg 2007

and handles non-uniform action costs like the additive heuristic $h_a$, and yet like FF's heuristic $h_{FF}$, it encodes the cost of a specific *relaxed plan* and thus is compatible with FF's helpful action pruning and its effective enforced hill climbing search. The motivation is similar to the works in [3,4] which also aim to make the FF planner sensitive to cost information, yet rather than modifying the planning graph construction or extraction phases to take action costs into account, we modify the cost-sensitive additive heuristic to yield relaxed plans.

The paper is organized as follows. We first review the cost model and the definitions of the additive heuristic and the planning graph heuristic used by FF. We then introduce the new set-additive heuristic and present empirical results.

## 2   Planning Model and Heuristics

We consider planning problems $P = \langle F, I, O, G \rangle$ expressed in Strips, where $F$ is the set of relevant atoms or fluents, $I \subseteq F$ and $G \subseteq F$ are the initial and goal situations, and $O$ is a set of (grounded) actions $a$ with preconditions, add, and delete lists $Pre(a)$, $Add(a)$, and $Del(a)$ respectively, all of which are subsets of $F$.

For each action $a \in O$, there is also a *non-negative cost* $cost(a)$. In classical planning this cost is assumed to be positive and uniform for all actions, normally equal to 1. In such a case, the cost of a plan is given by the number of actions in the plan. More generally, we take the cost $cost(\pi)$ of a plan $\pi = a_0, \ldots, a_n$ to be

$$cost(\pi) = \sum_{i=0,n} cost(a_i)$$

The search for plans is guided by heuristics that provide an estimate of the cost-to-go that are extracted automatically from the problem encoding $P$. Two of the most common heuristics are the *additive heuristic* used in the HSP planner [1] and the *relaxed plan heuristic* used in FF. Both are based on the delete-relaxation $P^+$ of the problem, and they both attempt to approximate the optimal delete-relaxation heuristic $h^+$ which is well-informed but intractable. Heuristics that are not based on the delete-relaxation and are admissible are used in Graphplan [5] and HSPr* [6]. These heuristics, however, are not as informed as their non-admissible counterparts.

We review some of these heuristics below. In order to simplify the definition of some of the heuristics, we introduce in some cases a new dummy $End$ action with *zero cost*, whose preconditions $G_1, \ldots, G_n$ are the goals of the problem, and whose effect is a dummy atom $G$. In such cases, we will obtain the heuristic estimate $h(s)$ of the cost from state $s$ to the goal, from the estimate $h(G; s)$ of achieving the 'dummy' atom $G$ from $s$.

## 3   The Additive Heuristic

Since the computation of the optimal delete-free heuristic $h^+$ is intractable, HSP introduces a polynomial approximation where all subgoals are assumed to be *independent* in the sense that they can be achieved with no 'side effects'. This assumption is false normally (as is that of the delete-relaxation) but results in a simple heuristic function $h_a(s) = h_a(G; s)$ that can be computed efficiently in every state $s$ visited in the search:

$$h_a(p; s) = \begin{cases} 0 & \text{if } p \in s \\ \min_{a \in O(p)}[h_a(a; s)] & \text{otherwise} \end{cases}$$

where $h_a(p, s)$ stands for an estimate of the cost of achieving the atom $p$ from $s$, $O(p)$ is the set of actions in the problem that add $p$, and

$$h_a(a; s) = cost(a) + \sum_{q \in Pre(a)} h_a(q; s)$$

stands for the cost of applying the action $a$ after achieving its preconditions.

The additive heuristic, as its name implies, makes the assumption that the cost of achieving a set of atoms is equal to the *sum* of the costs of achieving each of the atoms separately. When this assumption is true, either because action preconditions and subgoals can be achieved with *no side effects*, or because the goal and action preconditions contain *one atom at most*, $h_a$ is equal to $h^+$, and hence the additive heuristic is optimal in the delete relaxation. Most often this is not the case, yet as shown early in [7] and later in the HSP planner [1], the additive heuristic $h_a$ can often guide the search for plans fairly well. Versions of the additive heuristic appear also in [8,3,9], where the cost of joint conditions in action preconditions or goals is set to the sum of the costs of each condition in isolation. The additive heuristic $h_a$ for classical planning is obtained simply by setting the action costs $cost(a)$ all to 1 (except for the 'dummy' End action).

## 4   The Relaxed Planning Graph Heuristic

The planner FF improves HSP along two dimensions: the heuristic and the basic search algorithm. Unlike $h_a$, the **heuristic** $h_{FF}$ used in FF makes no independence assumption for approximating $h^+$, instead computing one plan for $P^+$ which is not guaranteed to be optimal. This is done by a Graphplan-like procedure [5], which due to the absence of deletes, constructs a planning graph with no mutexes, from which a plan $\pi_{FF}(s)$ is extracted backtrack-free [2]. The heuristic $h_{FF}(s)$ is then set to $|\pi_{FF}(s)|$. The basic **search procedure** in FF is not $WA^*$ as in HSP but (enforced) *hill-climbing* (EHC), in which the search moves from the current state $s$ to a neighboring state $s'$ with smaller heuristic value by performing a *breadth first search*. This breadth first search is carried out with a *reduced branching factor* where actions $a$ that are not found to be 'helpful' in a state $s$ are ignored. The 'helpful actions' in a state $s$ are the actions applicable in $s$ that add a relevant subgoal $p$, as judged from the computation of the relaxed plan $\pi_{FF}(s)$. The more accurate relaxed plan heuristic, along with the reduced branching factor in the breadth first search that follows from the exclusion of non-helpful actions, make the FF planner scale up better than HSP [2].

An advantage of HSP over FF, however, is the ability to naturally take into account non-uniform actions costs. While the additive heuristic $h_a$ extends naturally to such cases, the relaxed plan extraction procedure and the layered planning graph construction on which it is based do not. Some recent attempts to modify the planning graph construction in order to take cost information into account can be found in [3,4]. Here we take a different approach that avoids planning graphs entirely, relying instead on a simple modification of the additive heuristic to compute *relaxed plans*.

The new *set-additive heuristic* modifies the formulation of the additive heuristic slightly, so that rather than expressing *numbers* $h_a(p; s)$ it expresses 'relaxed plans' $\pi_a(p; s)$, i.e., sets of actions that can be ordered into plans for $p$ from the state $s$ in the delete-relaxation $P^+$.

## 5    The Set-Additive Heuristic

The definition of the additive heuristic can be rewritten as

$$h_a(p; s) \stackrel{\text{def}}{=} \begin{cases} 0 & \text{if } p \in s \\ h_a(a_p; s) & \text{otherwise} \end{cases}$$

where

$$a_p = \operatorname{argmin}_{a \in O(p)} h_a(a; s)$$

is the *best supporting action* for $p$ in $s$, and $h(a; s)$ is

$$h_a(a; s) = cost(a) + \sum_{q \in Pre(a)} h_a(q; s)$$

In the additive heuristic, the value of the best supporter $a_p$ of $p$ in $s$, $h_a(a_p; s)$, is propagated into the heuristic value of $p$, $h_a(p; s)$. The *set-additive* heuristic can be understood in terms of a small change: rather than propagating *the value* $h_a(a_p; s)$ of the best supporter $a_p$ of $p$, it propagates *the supporter* $a_p$ itself. In addition, unlike values, such supports are not combined by *sums* but by *set-unions*, resulting in a function $\pi_a(p; s)$ that represents a *set of actions*, which in analogy to $h_a(p; s)$ is defined as:[1]

$$\pi_a(p; s) = \begin{cases} \{\} & \text{if } p \in s \\ \pi_a(a_p; s) & \text{otherwise} \end{cases}$$

where

$$a_p = \operatorname{argmin}_{a \in O(p)} Cost(\pi_a(a; s))$$

$$\pi_a(a; s) = \{a\} \bigcup \{\cup_{q \in Prec(a)} \pi_a(q; s)\}$$

---

[1] The value of the set-additive heuristic $h_a^s(s)$, unlike the value of the normal additive heuristic, depends on the way ties are broken. We assume that among several supports $a_p$ with the same costs $Cost(a_p; s)$, the one containing fewer actions, i.e., smallest $|\pi_a(a_p; s)|$, is preferred.

$$Cost(\pi_a(a;s)) = \sum_{a' \in \pi_a(a;s)} cost(a')$$

That is, the best supporter $a_p$ for $p$ is propagated into $p$, and supports for joint preconditions and goals are combined by set-union. The best-supporter is selected in turn as the action $a_p$ for which the 'plan' made up of the supports of each of its preconditions along with the action itself has minimum cost. The *set-additive heuristic* $h_a^s(s)$ for the state $s$ is then defined as

$$h_a^s(s) = Cost(\pi_a(G;s))$$

While $\pi_a(p;s)$ is a *set* and not a *sequence* of actions, its definition ensures that the actions it contains can be ordered into an action sequence that is a *plan* for $p$ in the relaxed problem $P^+$ from state $s$. Indeed, one such parallel plan can be obtained by scheduling in a 'first layer' $A_0$, the actions $a$ in $\pi_a(p;s)$ with empty supports; i.e., with $\pi_a(a;s) = \{\}$, then in a 'second layer', the actions $a$ with supports in the first layer only, i.e., with $\pi_a(a;s) \subseteq A_0$, and so on. Within each layer, the actions can be serialized in any way as there are no deletes in $P^+$. As a result, and provided that there is a (relaxed) plan for each atom $p$ in the delete-relaxation $P^+$,[2] we have that:

**Proposition 1.** $\pi_a(p;s)$ *represents a* relaxed plan *for $p$ from $s$.*

This means that $\pi_a(G;s)$ for the dummy goal $G$ can play the role of the *relaxed plan* in FF in place of the planning graph extraction procedure that is not sensitive to cost information. The rest of FF's machinery, such as helpful actions, enforced hill climbing, and so on, can be kept in place. We will call the resulting planner $FF(h_a^s)$.

Notice that since $\pi_a(G;s)$ is a *set* of actions, there are *no action duplicates* in the corresponding relaxed plan. This property is true also of the relaxed plan computed by FF, following from the NO-OP first heuristic [2].[3]

We have implemented the set-additive heuristic $h_a^s$ on top of the code that computes the normal additive heuristic $h_a$ in HSP, which is a Bellman-Ford algorithm that solves shortest-path problems [10,11,12]. For the set-additive heuristic, the label of a 'node' $p$ in the graph must represent both the set of actions $\pi_a(p;s)$ and its cost $Cost(\pi_a(p;s))$. The sets of actions are represented as sparse, ordered lists so that the union of two such sets is done in time linear in the sum of their sizes. In the additive heuristic, the analogous operation is a sum which is certainly cheaper, yet as the experiments below show the computational cost of these unions is not prohibitive.

---

[2] This condition is easily enforced by adding 'dummy' actions $a_p'$ with very high cost that add $p$ for each $p$. Thus, if $h(p;s)$ is $h(a_p')$, it means that there is no plan for achieving $p$ from $s$ in the relaxation.

[3] No action duplicates are needed in plans for the delete-relaxation of Strips problems. For problems involving conditional effects, however, this is no longer true. For applying the set-additive heuristic in such cases, conditional effects must be compiled exactly or approximately into action preconditions.

# 6    Additive and Set-Additive Heuristics Compared

The normal additive heuristic can be understood as the *bag* or *multiset* additive heuristic, which is exactly like the set-additive heuristic above, but with the expressions $\pi_a(p; s)$ combined as *bags* or *multisets* rather than *sets* [13]. A *bag* or *multiset* is a collection *with repetitions*, where each element can have a *multiplicity* greater than 1. E.g., in the the multiset $A = \{a, a, a, b, b, c\}$, the element $a$ has multiplicity 3, $b$ has multiplicity 2, and $c$ has multiplicity 1 (all other elements have multiplicity 0). If $B = \{a, c\}$ is another multiset, then the multi-set union of $A$ and $B$, is $\{a, a, a, a, b, b, c, c, \}$. If $\pi_a(p; s)$ is a *multiset*, then it may include duplicate actions that lead to *overcounting* when the costs of each of the actions in the multiset are added up. From this perspective, the *set-additive* heuristic eliminates the overcounting that arises from the *multiset-additive* heuristic, which is equivalent to the normal additive heuristic, by replacing *multisets* by *sets*. The result is a heuristic that like $h_{FF}$ does not 'overcount' [2] and that like $h_a$ is sensitive to cost information.

# 7    The FF($h_a^s$) Planner

The FF($h_a^s$) planner analyzed below is FF but with the relaxed plan $\pi_{FF}(s)$ computed from the relaxed planning graph replaced by the one computed with the *set-additive heuristic*: $\pi_a(G; s)$. The resulting heuristic $h_a^s(s)$ is thus cost-sensitive, and furthermore, remains optimal in problems in which the normal additive heuristic is optimal as well, such as when preconditions and goals involve one atom at most. Two other small changes have been made to take action costs into account in the enforced hill-climbing procedure (EHC).

First, while a single step of EHC in FF ends as soon as a state $s'$ is found by breadth-first search from $s$ such that $h(s') < h(s)$, in FF($h_a^s$) this is not true in the first level of the search. Instead, all states $s'$ resulting from applying a helpful action $a$ in $s$ are evaluated, and among those for which $h(s') < h(s)$ holds, the action minimizing the expression $cost(a) + h(s')$ is selected.[4]

Second, while helpful actions in FF are defined as $H(s) = \{a \in A | add(a) \cap G_1 \neq \emptyset\}$, where $G_1$ denotes the set of atoms in the first layer of the planning graph arising from the extraction of the plan $\pi_{FF}(s)$, in FF($h_a^s$), $G_1$ is defined as the set of atoms $p$ achievable in one step, i.e., $|\pi_a(p; s)| = 1$, such that $p$ is a precondition of some action in the relaxed plan $\pi_a(G; s)$.

# 8    Experimental Results

We tested three heuristics in combination with two search algorithms. The heuristics are the additive heuristic $h_a$, the set-additive heuristic, and FF's

---

[4] Actually, when an action $a$ maps $s$ into a state $s'$ in the first level such that $h(s') = h(s) - cost(a)$ and the size of the computed relaxed plan is decreased by 1, such an action is selected right away.

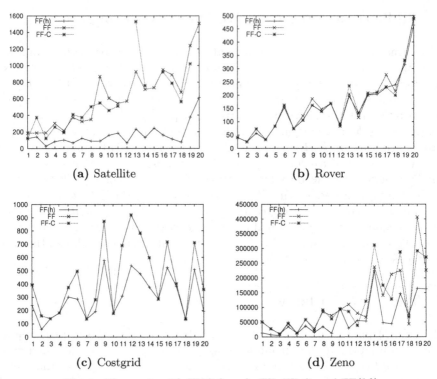

**Fig. 1.** Plan costs with EHC Search: FF, FF-C, and FF($h_a^s$)

heuristic $h_{FF}$. The search algorithms are EHC and WA* with evaluation function $f(n) = g(n) + Wh(n)$ with $W = 5$. The only combination we did not try was $h_a$ with EHC, as EHC requires the notion of a relaxed plan that the heuristic $h_a$ does not provide.

The five combinations were implemented on top of Metric-FF, an extension of the FF planner that handles numeric fluents [14]. This is because the current accepted syntax for non-uniform action costs is expressed through numeric fluents and metric expressions that Metric-FF can handle. Numeric fluents, however, are only used to encode such cost information, and once the cost information is obtained from the input, numeric fluents are eliminated from the problem, leaving a boolean planning problem with cost information.

Experiments were performed with six domains with non-uniform action costs and five STRIPS domains. Four of these were versions of the domains Satellite, Rovers, Depots, and Zenotravel from the Third International Planning Competition (IPC3), modified as discussed above. The fifth domain, Driverlog, needed no modification as no numeric variables occur in preconditions of actions or goals. The sixth domain, Costgrid, is a simple grid domain in which movements between squares are randomly assigned costs between 0 and 100. It is possible to prove that in such a domain, the additive and set-additive heuristics are optimal as preconditions and goals involve a single atom. The five STRIPS domains used were the STRIPS versions of the five IPC3 domains.

All experiments were run on a grid consisting of 76 nodes, each a dual-processor Xeon "Woodcrest" dual core computer, with a clock speed of 2.33 GHz and 8 Gb of RAM. Execution time was limited to 1,800 seconds.

**FF vs. FF($h_a^s$): Quality.** EHC with the set-additive heuristic often yields better plans than with FF's heuristic. This can be seen from the curves in Figure 1 that display plan costs over four domains. The differences are significant in Satellite, Zeno, and CostGrid, where we have found that the heuristic values computed by the two heuristics in the initial state are also the most different. On the other hand, the values produced by the two heuristics in Rovers, Depots, and Driverlog are closer, leading to plans with similar costs.

**FF vs. FF($h_a^s$): Time.** FF($h_a^s$) often takes longer than normal FF. The reasons are two: the overhead of propagating sets in the heuristic computation, and the fact that the plans that FF($h_a^s$) finds are sometimes longer but with better overall cost. The times for the four domains above are shown in Figure 2. This overhead, however, does not affect coverage: FF and FF($h_a^s$) in EHC mode solve all 20 instances of Satellite, Rovers, Zenotravel, and Costgrid, and both fail only in 2 of the 22 instances in Depots, and in 3 and 4 instances respectively of Driverlog.

**FF with Costs vs. FF($h_a^s$).** Aside from the curves for FF and FF($h_a^s$), Figures 1 and 2 show a third curve. This curve, labeled FF-C, corresponds to the combination of the modified EHC procedure used in FF($h_a^s$) with a version of the FF heuristic that takes action costs into account. While $h_{FF}(s)$ is $|\pi_{FF}(s)|$, where $\pi_{FF}(s)$ is the relaxed plan computed by FF from $s$, the heuristic $h_{FF}^c(s)$ used in FF-C is the result of adding up the cost of the actions in $\pi_{FF}(s)$. As it can be seen from the curves, FF-C improves FF in terms of plan quality in a few cases but not as often as FF($h_a^s$) and not as much. This is because the relaxed plan extraction remains cost-insensitive. At the same time, FF-C is slower than FF, which by ignoring action costs completely, searches for the goal more greedily.

**Heuristics in WA\* Search.** When the heuristics $h_a$, $h_a^s$, and $h_{FF}$ are used in the context of the WA\* search, the first two heuristics do better than the latter one. The coverage of the three heuristics is shown in Table 1, where the additive heuristic $h_a$ does slightly better than the set-additive heuristic $h_a^s$ (because it is cheaper to compute), and both do better than $h_{FF}$. On the other hand, the set-additive heuristic with EHC solves many more problems than the additive heuristic with WA\*.

**Table 1.** Coverage of the three heuristics combined with a WA\* search. There are 20 problems in each domain except for Depots with 22.

| $h$ | Satellite | Rovers | Zenotravel | Depots | Driverlog | Costgrid |
|-----|-----------|--------|------------|--------|-----------|----------|
| $h_a$ | 0 | 4 | 14 | 13 | 11 | 20 |
| $h_a^s$ | 0 | 4 | 11 | 13 | 9 | 20 |
| $h_{FF}$ | 0 | 5 | 8 | 10 | 6 | 20 |

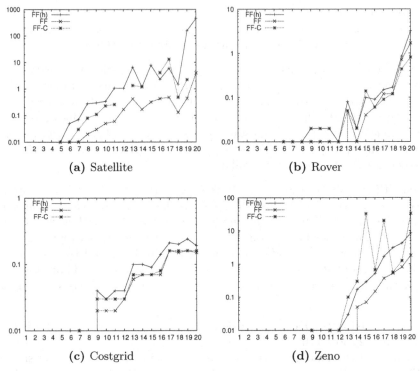

**Fig. 2.** Times in EHC Search: FF, FF-C, and FF($h_a^s$)

**Uniform vs. Non-Uniform Costs.** The heuristic values computed by $h_a^s$ and $h_{FF}$ when costs are uniform are not necessarily equal, yet we have found them to be very much alike over these domains, leading to plans with roughly the same costs. We omit the corresponding graphs due to lack of space. This suggests that when costs are uniform, the overhead in the computation of the set-additive heuristic does not pay off. For non-uniform costs, on the other hand, $h_a^s$ used with EHC search appears to yield the best tradeoff.

## 9  Summary

We have introduced a new non-admissible heuristic for planning, the *set-additive heuristic*, that combines the benefits of the *additive* and *relaxed plan* heuristics. The motivation is similar to the work in [3,4] which also aims to make the FF planner sensitive to cost information, but rather than modifying the plan graph construction or extraction phase to take action costs into account, we have modified the cost-sensitive additive heuristic to yield relaxed plans. The resulting formulation sheds light also on the normal additive heuristic, which can now be as the *multiset-additive* heuristic, and suggests further refinements that can result from the propagation of symbolic labels (supports) rather than numbers in the basic formulation.

# Acknowledgements

We thank the anonymous reviewers for useful comments. H. Geffner is partially supported by Grant TIN2006-15387-C03-03 from MEC, Spain.

# References

1. Bonet, B., Geffner, H.: Planning as heuristic search. Artificial Intelligence 129(1–2), 5–33 (2001)
2. Hoffmann, J., Nebel, B.: The FF planning system: Fast plan generation through heuristic search. Journal of Artificial Intelligence Research 14, 253–302 (2001)
3. Sapena, O., Onaindia, E.: Handling numeric criteria in relaxed planning graphs. In: Lemaître, C., Reyes, C.A., González, J.A. (eds.) IBERAMIA 2004. LNCS (LNAI), vol. 3315, pp. 114–123. Springer, Heidelberg (2004)
4. Fuentetaja, R., Borrajo, D., Linares, C.: Improving relaxed planning graph heuristics for metric optimization. In: Proc. 2006 AAAI Workshop on Heuristic Search, Memory Based Heuristics and its Applications, pp. 79–86 (2006)
5. Blum, A., Furst, M.: Fast planning through planning graph analysis. In: Proceedings of IJCAI 1995, pp. 1636–1642. Morgan Kaufmann, San Francisco (1995)
6. Haslum, P., Geffner, H.: Admissible heuristics for optimal planning. In: Proc. of the Fifth International Conference on AI Planning Systems (AIPS-2000), pp. 70–82 (2000)
7. Bonet, B., Loerincs, G., Geffner, H.: A robust and fast action selection mechanism for planning. In: Proceedings of AAAI 1997, pp. 714–719. MIT Press, Cambridge (1997)
8. Do, M.B., Kambhampati, S.: Sapa: A domain-independent heuristic metric temporal planner. In: Proc. ECP 2001, pp. 82–91 (2001)
9. Smith, D.E.: Choosing objectives in over-subscription planning. In: Proc. ICAPS 2004, pp. 393–401 (2004)
10. Bertsekas, D.: Linear Network Optimization: Algorithms and Codes. MIT Press, Cambridge (1991)
11. Cormen, T.H., Leiserson, C.E., Rivest, R.L.: Introduction to Algorithms. MIT Press, Cambridge (1989)
12. Liu, Y., Koenig, S., Furcy, D.: Speeding up the calculation of heuristics for heuristic search-based planning. In: Proc AAAI 2002, pp. 484–491 (2002)
13. Blizard, W.D.: Multiset theory. Notre Dame J. Formal Logic 30(1), 36–66 (1988)
14. Hoffmann, J.: The metric-ff planning system: Translating "ignoring delete lists" to numeric state variables. J. Artif. Intell. Res (JAIR) 20, 291–341 (2003)

# Mixed Narrative and Dialog Content Planning Based on BDI Agents

Carlos León, Samer Hassan, Pablo Gervás, and Juan Pavón

Departamento de Ingeniería del Software e Inteligencia Artificial
Universidad Complutense de Madrid
{cleon,samer}@fdi.ucm.es, {pgervas,jpavon}@sip.ucm.es

**Abstract.** There exist various narrative systems, focused on different parts of the complex process of story generation. Some of them are oriented to *content planning*, and some to *sentence planning*, with different properties and characteristics. In this paper we propose a system based on BDI agents that generates stories (creating content, performing *content planning* and simple *sentence planning*) with narrative parts and dialogs. The content for the story is generated in a multiagent social simulation system, and the *content planning* is based on rules and a state space search algorithm based on the system representation of the reader's perception of the story.

## 1 Introduction

It is possible to find in the literature several types of narrative systems. These systems try to emulate the human activity of creating readable texts from a set of stored facts or data, organised in several possible ways. There are proposals mainly focused on narrative generation for storytelling, with different characteristics.

In storytelling, dialogs carry much information not present in simple narrative text. Dialogs show many aspects of the characters in a very different way that descriptive sentences do, because literal sentences in dialogs show exactly what the character says, and the form it expresses the content. Then, for a story to be fully descriptive, it is necessary to include dialogs that show interaction based on communication between the characters.

There exist various approaches to story generation, and they are focused on different stages of the generation process. There are systems that propose alternatives for *content planning*, like those in [1,2], but they do not offer dialog generation, and do not address *sentence planning*. Other systems, like [3], can handle dialog generation, but they do not perform *content planning* operations, as they are only focused on *sentence planning*.

In this paper we propose a system that addresses *content planning* for *dialogs* together with *narrative text*, in a coherent way. The work presented is divided in two main applications: a multiagent system that simulates social interaction between a set of characters in a fantastic medieval domain, modelled as intelligent agents with *beliefs*, *desires* and *intentions*, and an automatic story generation system, that receives the set of facts that happened in the simulation, and creates a textual representation of the main events.

D. Borrajo, L. Castillo, and J.M. Corchado (Eds.): CAEPIA 2007, LNAI 4788, pp. 150–159, 2007.

## 2    Previous Work

In this section we briefly review research relevant for the work presented in this paper: BDI model, Multiagent Social Systems, and Natural Language Generation.

### 2.1    Social Systems and BDI Model

Social phenomena are extremely complicated and unpredictable, since they involve complex interaction and mutual interdependence networks. A social system consists of a collection of individuals that interact among them, evolving autonomously and motivated by their own beliefs and personal goals, and the circumstances of their social environment.

A multi-agent system (MAS) consists of a set of autonomous software entities (the agents) that interact among them and with their environment. Autonomy means that agents are active entities that can take their own decisions. The agent paradigm assimilates quite well to the individual in a social system, so it can be used to simulate them, exploring the complexity of social dynamics. In fact, there are numerous works in agent theory on organisational issues of MAS. Also, theories from the field of Psychology have been incorporated to design agent behaviour, the most extended being the Beliefs-Desires-Intentions (BDI) model, in the work of [4].

The MAS described in this paper has been developed as an extension of an existing one by enriching it with additional features to support dialogs between agents. In this MAS, as explained in [5], the agents have been developed with several main attributes: from simple ones such as gender or age, to complex ones, like for example ideology or educational level. The population in the agents' society (as in real societies) also experiments demographic changes: individuals are subject to a life-cycle: they get married, reproduce and die. Moreover, the agents/individuals can build and be part of relational groups with other agents: they can communicate with other close agents, leading to friendship relationships determined by the rate of similarity. Or, on the other hand, they can build family nuclei as children are born close to their parents.

The system has an underlying sociological model, which can be configured (i.e. changing the mean of male average age of death). It deals with hundreds of agents, all of them interacting with their neighbourhood in each time-step of the execution. As we simulate thousands of time-steps, so many dynamic factors are involved, and as any other complex systems, it is not subject to laws, but to trends, which can affect individuals in a probabilistic way.

As we will see in a further section, these simple agents will be transformed into BDI model agents. In this model, Beliefs represent the knowledge of the agent about his world, including his own actual state and the environment state. To use the term "belief" implies that what the agent beliefs does not have to be necessarily true (and in fact it can change through time). It is "what I know and believe". The Desires (objectives) represent the state that the agent is trying to reach, the situations that it is seeking: "What I want". The Intentions (plans) are the means that the agent choose to accomplish its objectives, what the agent has chosen to do: its goal. The BDI of a single agent is its mental state.

We can refer to multiple works that use this psychological modelling perspective. A review comparison between several modelling techniques can be found in [6]. A very useful approach to sociologic agents using BDI, with deep and sophisticated social behaviour, was studied by [7]. A common problem using BDI is the huge gap between a clear theoretical model and its implementation. An effort on this subject was done in [8], trying to clarify how to turn BDI theory concepts to the practical complex system.

## 2.2   The Multiagent System: Fantastic Society

The ideas expressed in section 2.1 concerning social simulations using multiagent systems are the core of action from which we have built the whole narrative system. Several changes to the original MAS have to be made in the perspective of execution to be able to generate "life logs" of the individuals, which will be the basis for the texts describing the storyline. It is necessary to shift the point of view from trends data acquisition to vital biographies. We do not need numerical data, but semantic content that can be interpreted by the rules as we interpret them, because we want the story generation to be as close as possible to what humans might have done faced with similar sets of events.

In this framework, it was necessary to adapt the designed MAS to a new environment: a Fantasy Medieval World far from the previous Post-Modern context. This deep change of context meant the introduction of several minor changes, and a twist in the meaning and interpretation of some facts. This evolution is explained in depth in [9].

Thus, now the agents have a name, an inheritable last name, a race (elf, orc, dwarf...). For each agent now exists a random possibility of dying, allowing the possibility that we can relate this early death to the betrayal of a friend, poisoning by a wife, a mysterious accident...

Following the cited objective of emulating real life behaviours, in this new MAS context dependent relationships and life events has been introduced: usual life events were not exciting enough to build a fantasy adventure. And so, an individual can have friends and enemies. Along his path, he can get married and have children, but he also can, randomly, suffer several spells, kill monsters, get lost in mazes or dark forests, or find treasures and magic objects in dangerous dungeons. In this way we can build a more interesting story, with several characters that evolve and interact among them.

## 2.3   Natural Language Generation

Natural Language Generation is important for a study of storytelling because it involves both a model of the task that need to be carried out to generate a valid text - therefore partially modelling the activity of an author - and a model of the story as linguistic artifact - a story model. The general process of text generation is defined in [10] as taking place in several stages, during which the conceptual input is progressively refined by adding information that will shape the final text. During the initial stages the concepts and messages that will appear in the final content are decided and these messages are organised into a specific order and structure (*content planning*). A number of stages after that deal with *sentence planning*, where each message resulting from the previous stage is progressively enriched with all the linguistic information required to realize it. A final stage of *surface realization* assembles all the relevant pieces into linguistically and typographically correct text.

The Natural Language Generation work presented in this paper is mainly centered around *content planning*. The subtask of building a set of messages from the input is always heavily dependent on the particular domain of operation, and tightly coupled with the particular kind of input being processed. A slightly more generic subtask determines the ordering and rhetorical relations of the logical messages, hereafter called facts, that the generated document is intended to convey. Related work with *content planning* this paper can be found on [11].

Research on storytelling has been a classic since the early days of Artificial Intelligence. In recent times, two approaches stand out as worth mentioning in contrast with the one followed in this paper. MEXICA [2] follows a cognitive approach to build story plots about the ancient inhabitants of Mexico City, paying special attention to evolution of the emotional links and the tensions between the characters of a story. A different approach [1] relies on planning techniques to build stories from an initial world state and a set of goals to be fulfilled by the end of the story. Both are comparable to the *content planning* presented here - rather than the application as a whole - in the sense that they concentrate solely on building a conceptual representation, with only schematic transcription as text intended to make the plots understandable. None of them includes dialogs as part of the content they handle. The STORYBOOK system [3] - at the opposite extreme - considers only the production of text from an input corresponding to the conceptual representation of a given plot. It relies on having an external planner that defines the outline of the intended story, and it carries out elaborated sentence planning to produce input for a surface realizer, and it is capable of dealing with fragments of dialogue represented conceptually in the input.

# 3   BDI Model in Storytelling

In this section we explain the ideas we have followed for developing a system based on BDI agents. We describe the agents, and how their beliefs, desires and intentions guide their behaviour and the story generation. In the next two Sections (4 and 5), we explain how this BDI model is used in the multi-agent system and the *content planner*.

We have introduced new changes in the system described in Section 2.2, changing the structure of the original simple agents. In this way the interactions will be more complex and we will have much more contents to tell in our stories. Thus, we take as base system the previously defined fantastic world, with its events and enemies. The new objective is to make agents evolve in time (internally, not just in terms of the relationships between them). First, we force agents'

**Table 1.** Example rules from transition between reader's perception of the story

| Fact | Agent's mental state |
|------|----------------------|
| know_where | Agent now knows some location (belief) |
| want_find | Agent wants to find something (desire) |
| do_trick | Agent tricks somebody (intention) |

characteristics to change internally depending on the events that happened in their lives. For example, if an agent finds a treasure, his economy will be dramatically increased.

But the really deep change is the use of a BDI model inside the agents. Now the agents will have "What I know/believe" (like "I know where a treasure is"), "What I want" ("I want a treasure") and "What I am going to do" ("I am going to the mountain to find the treasure"). With these ideas, we have agents with specific knowledge, with objectives to accomplish and with actions to do. Table 1 shows a little example of how facts in the story affect the BDI state of the character, and thus, reader's perception of the story.

To guide the content planner, we consider that in each stage of the discourse, as the reader sees it, we have to know, at least, the information about characters in the story, at every stage of the discourse. This information evolves as the story is being told, in such a way that the reader's concept of each character changes during the narration. For this purpose we store, in each stage of the narration, the BDI state of the characters as the reader should have understood it from what has been communicated so far. In Section 5 more detail about this is given.

## 4    Agent Planning

With the BDI model, each agent is "more intelligent", taking his own decisions, and building a real story. Thus, for example, if a character wants (desire) to kill a dragon, he will ask his friends about information related to dragons (asking if they have such beliefs). When he finds someone that knows something, his friend will tell it to him (that agent will throw a "say" event), and he will have the new belief (for ex. "where to find a dragon"), changing his mental state (and throwing a "know" event, that as all events will be recorded in the XML file). When he discovers (after gathering the info between his friends) enough information about dragons, (their weak points, their types and where he can find one) he will be able to generate the intentions associated to that desire. Those intentions could be "travel to the north", "go to the highest mountain" and "kill the dragon". When he generates those events ("do" events), his desire will be satisfied and will disappear.

This ideas guide the planning and the generation of the characters' story, during the execution of the multiagent system. We can see that the planning of the agents is very simple, but it is enough for the prototype to generate coherent and linked content, in the sense that the facts in the story are not just random and unlinked events.

# 5   Content Planner

In this section we present the *content planner* of the story generation system. This generator receives data from the Multiagent System described in Section 2.2. The Multiagent System outputs a XML file that stores the full log of every agent in the simulation, each log representing the set of facts of a character in the story, and the *content planner* imports that file.

Along with the facts that happened during the simulation, we need relations between them, like "at the same time", or "because of that". The relations between facts of the story are computed when the XML from the multiagent system is loaded. Knowing the domain rules (when some fact is the cause of another, or when two statements are consecutive facts), we can infer when two facts are related by a *causal relation*, a *temporal relation*, and so on. This is done by hard–coding the domain model in the XML loader, creating the relations during the import stage. Of course, this approach is far from being general, and it is possible to infer the relations between facts in a more generalistic manner, although it is not addressed in this work.

To handle dialogs in the narration, we consider that each element of communication between two agents, like "saying where" or "asking how" is indeed another fact, like "jumping" or "going somewhere". Each one of these facts has particular relations with other facts, that can be dialog facts, or narrative facts. With this approach, dialogs and narrative parts can be mixed inside the text, thus getting a richer narrative output.

## 5.1   System Representation of the Reader's Perception of the Story

Of course, nowadays the task of modelling the human brain is far from being possible. There are many scientific (and not only scientific) disciplines involved in such task, and to propose a model is not the objective of this work. However, we have made a lot of relaxations in the formalism of the model, and we have adjusted it to be very particular to the domain of this study. In this manner, it is possible to approximate to a kind of mental state model that does not try to emulate human's.

We present an algorithm for *content planning* based on the reader's perception of the story. In the system we present in this paper, the process of creating the discourse of a story takes into account what the potential reader of the text thinks and knows, using the model of the characters, about the world we are describing, and tries to give the reader the information he should receive at each stage of the story. The system chooses, in this way, which set of facts are going to appear in the final realization, and which relations connect them.

With this model of the characters, the *content planner* decides to choose some relations or others, depending on the BDI state of some characters. In this way, the state of the characters during the story guides the generation. We have created rules for computing the new state, and they are dependent on the previous state and the new sentence that the reader is going to read. These rules are based on the BDI structure and rules of the agents, as explained in Section 3.

## 5.2   State Space Search

Once we have defined a perception model and the guidelines that hold the information we need for writing the story, we have the basic data structures we need to work. The next step, then, is to create the discourse. We propose a simple approach based on state space search algorithms. What we have done is to define a initial state, with no information, and start, from it, a `backtracking` algorithm that explores the solution space, by creating different stories, using *relations between statements* as operators. Figure 1 depicts these ideas.

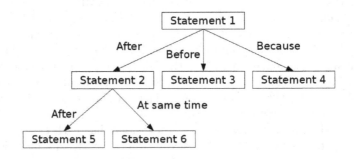

**Fig. 1.** Search tree for *content planning*

## 5.3   Generation Goals

When running the space state search, many possible stories are generated. However, we need a method to chose which of them is the best one. For this purpose we define *objectives*, that are data structures holding several attributes of the story draft. These attributes are the *linearity* of the text, or the level of sequentiality the story has; the *theatricality* of the story, counting the percentage of dialogue parts in the text; and the *causality*, or how important it is for the final story to contain "cause–effect" relations. This values are computed with rules and simple algorithms.

Then we can compute the similarity between a story generated during the search and an *objective* previously established by the user. The system will select that story with higher similarity to the *objective*. This similarity is computed by calculating the euclidean distance between the values of the attributes previously explained.

## 6   An Example

We can see an example of the *content planner* execution, from a set of ten agents during fifty years in Figure 2. It is a fragment of a generated story. It is important to note that *sentence planning* and *surface realization* are not addressed in a formal way. Instead, our proposal is to create simple template based text creation. From the discourse that has been generated, we apply a simple algorithm that fills the gaps in text templates.

*It was a man. And His name was Deron. And His last name was Cairnbreaker. And Deron Cairnbreaker desired to become a great wizard. After that, the spell of memory was cast upon Deron Cairnbreaker. Because of that, its education decreased. After that, Deron Cairnbreaker and Parbagar Greatcutter talked:*
*- Do you know who has the one ring?*
*- Yes, I can tell you who has the one ring - said Deron Cairnbreaker, and it told where.*
*- Are you sure? Then I'll go and talk with it. - said Parbagar Greatcutter - Farewell.*
*Before that, Deron Cairnbreaker and Georgia Houston talked:*
*- Do you know where can I find another wizard?*
*- Yes, I do. I will tell you. - said Deron Cairnbreaker. Then, Deron Cairnbreaker showed the place.*
*- Ok, now I have this useful information. - said Georgia Houston - Thank you!*

**Fig. 2.** Example of a story

However, these templates are not only filled with the statement that is going to be added: Not only the sentence is important for the template: also the reader's mental state influences the final text output. What the reader thinks about a character can change the way we produce the sentences. For example, if the mental state says that the reader knows nothing about the gender of a character, we can not use pronominal references that would require implicit mention of gender.

# 7   Comparison with Other Systems

The work in HERODOTUS [9] presents a *content planning* system which performs content determination assigning an heuristic value (*interest*) to facts, removing those facts whose *interest* falls below a given threshold, and discourse planning using templates. Compared to the system presented in this paper, the template system is too rigid, and it only allows to create a defined fixed set of types of stories. Although the rules it uses for *content planning* give some flexibility to the system, the resulting discourse is not good enough. Creating new stories is hard, and the system is not "very intelligent". There is much effort on *content determination*, and the main advantage was the ability of filtering a huge amount of information, and displaying it in a more human readable manner.

In MEXICA [2], emotional links are followed for planning the story and the present work follows a mental state model of the reader, although these concepts are not the same, there are some similar ideas between them. The work of Riedl and Young [1] shows a *content planning* system that creates stories from an initial state, and trying to reach some goals in the final story. None of these works addresses *sentence planning*.

The work presented adds dialog generation, mixed with the narrative content of the story, and simple final text generation. With dialogs we try to create richer and more complex stories, because dialogs show aspects of the story not present in plain narrations. Dialogs usually describe characters and action in such a way that the resulting story, together with narrated parts, becomes more interesting for the reader.

## 8    Conclusions and Future Work

A multiagent social system with intelligent agents based on BDI model has been presented. This system simulates the life of several fantastic characters living and communicating between them. Also, a storytelling system able to generate text with narrative content and dialogs has been shown and explained. This two parts, taken as a whole system, try to create stories with focus on characters interacting.

The BDI model for the planning system is still not good enough. It follows very simple ideas, and thus the agent system and the story generator do not produce very good output. However, there are many possible solutions. An easy but useful change could be to add a percentage number for each Belief, Desire and Intention. For the Beliefs, the number would represent its certainty: how sure the agent is about what he knows. In this way we could introduce the possibility of being confused, doubting or even lying.

Another way of introducing complexity in the system is by improving the agents' dialogs, thus making then able to negotiate in a more complex way. Now agents have just basic conversations: if one agent asks, the other agent answers, if he knows, what the first one wants to know. But this could be highly more sophisticated. They may ask about their own interests, see what they have in common, and share their knowledge about those things.

The natural text generation system has some advantages with respect to other systems, as it has been show in the comparison (Section 7), but it has also many disadvantages that must be taken into account to evolve the system. First, it is necessary, following this research line, to improve the model of the mental state. Although creating a mental model is a very ambitious task, it is possible to develop simpler prototypes, thus obtaining some aspects of the main characteristics of the understanding of a text by the reader.

A more effective reasoner is necessary. The algorithm presented is very inefficient, and it would be very interesting to add new reasoning capabilities, perhaps with the use of knowledge systems, like ontologies.

Another main point to be improved in the narrative system is the *sentence planner*. It has been addressed from a very simple and direct point of view, but better quality in the process can give much better output. Also, this *sentence planner* is fully domain dependent, and it only can produce text for the multiagent system logs. Concerning the work of STORYBOOK [3], which has dialogs, perhaps it would be interesting to connect the output or our system with that storytelling system.

## Acknowledgements

This research is funded by the Spanish Ministry of Education and Science (projects TIN2006-14433-C02-01 and TIN2005-08501-C03-01).

# References

1. Riedl, M., Young, R.M.: From linear story generation to branching story graphs. IEEE Journal of Computer Graphics and Applications, 23–31 (2006)
2. Pérez y Pérez, R., Sharples, M.: Mexica: a computer model of a cognitive account of creative writing. Experim. and Theo. Artif. Intell. 13(2), 119–139 (2001)
3. Callaway, C.B., Lester, J.C.: Narrative prose generation. Artif. Intell. 139(2), 213–252 (2002)
4. Bratman, M.E.: Intentions, Plans, and Practical Reason. Harvard University Press, Cambridge, MA, USA (1987)
5. Pavon, J., Arroyo, M., Hassan, S., Sansores, C.: Simulacion de sistemas sociales con agentes software. In: CMPI-2006. Actas del Campus Multidisciplinar en Percepcion e Inteligencia, vol. I, pp. 389–400 (2006)
6. Sanz, J.J.G.: Metodologías para el desarrollo de sistemas multi-agente. Inteligencia Artificial, Revista Iberoamericana de Inteligencia Artificial 18, 51–63 (2003)
7. Dignum, F., Morley, D., Sonenberg, L., Cavedon, L.: Towards socially sophisticated BDI agents. In: ICMAS 2000. Proceedings of the Fourth International Conference on MultiAgent Systems, Boston, USA, pp. 111–118 (2000)
8. Rao, A., Georgeff, M.: BDI agents: From theory to practice. In: Proceedings of the International Conference on Multi-Agent Systems (1995)
9. León, C., Hassan, S., Gervas, P.: From the event log of a social simulation to narrative discourse: Content planning in story generation. In: AISB Annual Convention, Newcastle University, Newcastle upon Tyne, UK, pp. 402–409 (April 2007)
10. Reiter, E., Dale, R.: Building Natural Language Generation Systems. Cambridge University Press, Cambridge (2000)
11. Young, R.M., Moore, J.D., Pollack, M.E.: Towards a principled representation of discourse plans. In: Proceedings of the Sixteenth Conference of the Cognitive Science Society, Atlanta, GA (1994)

# NMUS: Structural Analysis for Improving the Derivation of All MUSes in Overconstrained Numeric CSPs

R.M. Gasca, C. Del Valle, M.T. Gómez-López, and R. Ceballos

Departmento de Lenguajes y Sistemas Informáticos. Escuela Técnica Superior de
Ingeniería Informática. Universidad de Sevilla. (Spain)
{gasca,carmelo,mayte,ceballos}@lsi.us.es

**Abstract.** Models are used in science and engineering for experimentation, analysis, model-based diagnosis, design and planning/sheduling applications. Many of these models are overconstrained Numeric Constraint Satisfaction Problems ($NCSP$), where the numeric constraints could have linear or polynomial relations. In practical scenarios, it is very useful to know which parts of the overconstrained NCSP instances cause the unsolvability.

Although there are algorithms to find all optimal solutions for this problem, they are computationally expensive, and hence may not be applicable to large and real-world problems. Our objective is to improve the performance of these algorithms for numeric domains using structural analysis. We provide experimental results showing that the use of the different strategies proposed leads to a substantially improved performance and it facilitates the application of solving larger and more realistic problems.

## 1 Introduction

A lot of Artificial Intelligence problems can be cast in terms of Numeric Constraint Satisfaction Problems ($NCSPs$), and a large number of systems have been developed to compute efficiently solutions of these problems. $NCSPs$ are more and more often used to solve engineering problems arisen in different areas such as qualitative reasoning, diagnosis, planning, scheduling, configuration, distributed artificial intelligence, etc... This work focuses on problems related to engineering field, what play a prominent role in industrial applications. Generally, these problems are formed by a set of constraints among variables whose domains are real interval values. Usually, the numeric constraints are linear or polynomial relations (equations or inequations).

However, not every set of numeric constraints is satisfiable. Different researchers have proposed methods for the identification of Minimally Unsatisfiable Subsets of Constraints ($MUSes$) or Conflict Sets ($CS$) as they are also named in overconstrained $CSPs$. Determining $MUSes$ can be very valuable in many industrial applications, because it describes what is wrong in a $NCSP$

D. Borrajo, L. Castillo, and J.M. Corchado (Eds.): CAEPIA 2007, LNAI 4788, pp. 160–169, 2007.

instance. They represent the smallest explanations -in terms of the number of involved constraints- of infeasibility. Indeed, when we check the consistency of a $NCSP$, we prefer knowing which constraints are contradicting one another rather than only knowing that the whole $NCSP$ is inconsistent.

In the bibliography, different types of $CSPs$ have been treated in order to obtain the $MUSes$. They are related to Satisfiability Problems [8] [2] [13] [7], Disjunctive Temporal Problem ($DTP$) [11] [9] [12] and model-based diagnosis and debugging problems [10] [5] [6] [1] [3]. Due to the high computational complexity of these problems, the goal of most of these approaches was to reduce the amount of satisfaction checking and subsets examined. However, some approaches were designed to derive only some $MUSes$ and no all $MUSes$ of these overconstrained $CSPs$.

To derive $MUSes$ in overconstrained $NCSP$, we are aware of very few technical works. In [4], Irreducible Infeasible Subsets (IIS) was studied for only linear and integer domains, but not all MUSes are obtained. These problems may contain multiple MUSes, and all of them must be resolved by constraint relaxation before the $NCSP$ can be solved. Also, other authors of the model-based diagnosis community have treated the high complexity of these problems using constraint databases [6] and new concepts such as constraint clusters and nodes [3].

In this paper, a set of new derivation techniques are presented to obtain efficiently $MUSes$ of a overconstrainted $NCSP$. These techniques improve the complete technique in several ways depending on the structure of the constraint network. It makes use of the powerful concept of the structural lattice of the constraints and neighborhood-based structural analysis to boost the efficiency of the exhaustive algorithms. As systematic methods for solving hard combinatorial problems are too expensive, structural analysis offers an alternative approach for quickly generating all $MUSes$. Accordingly, experimental studies of these new techniques outperform the best exhaustive ones. They avoid to solve a high number of $NCSPs$ with exponential complexity, however they add some new procedures with polynomial complexity.

The rest of the article is organized as follows. In Section 2, we start presenting some examples of overconstrained $NCSPs$ to introduce the problem domain. Section 3 presents some definitions and notations. Section 4 exposes different neighborhood concepts based on the structural analysis of the constraint network. Afterwards, we propose different search algorithms for deriving numeric $MUSes$ in a efficient way and their experimental results are argued in Section 5. Finally, in the last section we present our conclusions and future work.

## 2  Motivating Examples

The parts of an overconstrained $NCSP$ instance that could cause the unsolvability are the variables domains or constraints of the problem. Only this last cause will be treated in this article.

In the following subsections, we specify some different $NCSP$ instances to motivate this work. The specification of a $NCSP$ instance is represented by $\Psi$,

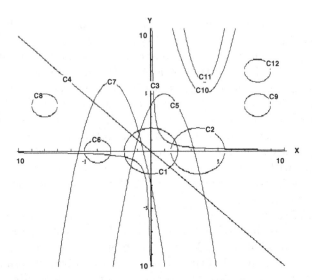

**Fig. 1.** Overconstrained NCSP with same real variables for all constraints

the variables by $X^{\Psi}$, the domains by $D^{\Psi}$, the constraints by $C^{\Psi}$ and the goals by $G^{\Psi}$. In this last item, the modeler could also specify which constraints would be preferred for relaxing.

### 2.1  $NCSP$ with the Same Real Variables for All Constraints

An example is the following geometrical problem, where the overconstrained $NCSP$ instance has linear equations and polynomial equations/inequations:

$$
\Psi \equiv
\begin{cases}
X^{\Psi} = \{x, y\} \\
D^{\Psi} = \{x, y \in [-10, +10]\}, \\
C^{\Psi} = \{c_1 \equiv x^2 + y^2 < 4, c_2 \equiv (x - 7/2)^2 + y^2 < 4, c_3 \equiv x * y > 1, \\
\quad c_4 \equiv x + y = 0, c_5 \equiv y + (x - 1)^2 = 5, c_6 \equiv (x + 4)^2 + y^2 = 1, \\
\quad c_7 \equiv y = 6 - (x + 3)^2, c_8 \equiv (x + 8)^2 + (y - 4)^2 = 1, \\
\quad c_9 \equiv (x - 8)^2 + (y - 4)^2 = 1, c_{10} \equiv y = 5 + (x - 4)^2, \\
\quad c_{11} \equiv y = 6 + 2 * (x - 4)^2, c_{12} \equiv (x - 8)^2 + (y - 7)^2 = 1\} \\
G^{\Psi} = Solutions(X)? \quad Why?
\end{cases}
$$

This problem has no solution, but the question is what cause it. In this case, $\Psi$ exhibits the following MUSes, namely $\{c_1, c_2, c_5\}$, $\{c_{10}, c_{11}\}$, $\{c_9, c_{12}\}$, etc...

### 2.2  $NCSP$ with Some Different Variables for the Numeric Constraints

The following example is extracted from a recent work in the model-based diagnosis community [3], where the $m_i$ and $a_i$ constraints corresponds to multipliers and adders respectively. This is a very illustrative example to show the utility of the structural analysis:

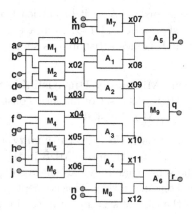

**Fig. 2.** Overconstrained NCSP with different real variables for all constraints

$$
\Psi \equiv
\begin{cases}
X^{\Psi} = \{a, b, c, d, e, f, g, h, i, j, k, m, n, o, p, q, r, x_i (i \in \{1, ..., 12\})\} \\
D^{\Psi} = \{x_i \in (-\infty, +\infty), \\
\quad a, b, c, d, e, f, g \in [2, 4] \ \ k, m, n, o \in [3, 5] \\
\quad p, q, r \in [15, 18])\} \\
C^{\Psi} = \{m_1 \equiv a * c = x_{01}, \ a_1 \equiv x_{01} + x_{02} = x_{08}, \\
\quad etc...\} \\
G^{\Psi} = Solutions(X)? \ \ Why?
\end{cases}
$$

## 3    Definitions and Notations

In the previous section, some overconstrained $NCSPs$ in terms of examples have been shown. This section presents some necessary definitions to formalize and clarify the derivation of all $MUSes$ in these problems.

**Definition 3.1 (Numeric Variable).** A variable of the $NCSP$ whose domain is a real interval value. The set of numeric variables of the problem is denoted by $X^{\Psi}$ and $X^{\Psi}(c_i)$ stands for the set of variables of a constraint $c_i$.

**Definition 3.2 (Numeric Constraint).** It is a linear or polynomial relation (equations or inequations) involving a finite subset of numeric variables.

**Definition 3.3 (Goal).** A predicate that denotes the users' preferences to search why the $NCSP$ is overconstrained.

**Definition 3.4 (Numeric Constraint Satisfaction Problem).** A four-tuple $\Psi = (X, D, C, G)$ where $X^{\Psi} = \{x_1, ..., x_n\}$ is a set of variables, whose continuous domains are respectively $D^{\Psi} = \{d_1, ..., d_n\} (n \geq 1)$, $C^{\Psi} = \{c_1, ..., c_m\} (m \geq 1)$ is a set of numeric constraints and $G^{\Psi}$ is the goal.

**Definition 3.5 (Overconstrained NCSP).** It is a $NCSP$ with no solution caused by some of the domains or constraints contradicting others.

When a $NCSP$ instance is unsatisfiable, it has at least one *Numeric Minimally Unsatisfiable SubSet*, in short one *NMUS*. It is a set of numeric constraints which is unsatisfiable, but becomes satisfiable as soon as we remove any of its constraints.

**Definition 3.6 (Numeric Minimally Unsatisfiable SubSet).** Given an instance $\Psi$ of a $NCSP$, a MUS $\mu$ is a set of numeric constraints s.t. $\mu \subset C^\Psi$, $\mu$ is unsatisfiable and $\forall \delta \in \mu$, $\mu \backslash \{\delta\}$ is satisfiable.

The number of constraints in a MUS is its cardinality and it is represented by $\#\mu$. Generally, we can have more than one MUS in the same $NCSP$. Some of them can overlap, in the sense that they can share some constraints, but they cannot be fully contained one in another. This concept of $MUS$ have similarities with that one of $IIS$ in the case of systems of linear inequalities.

# 4    Neighborhood-Based Structural Analysis

To construct a practical system developing a complete and efficient method for deriving numeric $MUSes$ is a key issue in real-world and industrial applications. In this paper, the option for an important reduction of the search space is based on the structural analysis. For this reason, the concept of neighbors of a given assignment of the constraints of a $NCSP$ is defined.

**Definition 4 (Assignment).** It is the tuple of values $\{0, 1\}$ assigned to each constraint of a $NCSP$ instance $\Psi$, meaning the truth value of each constraint. It is represented by $A(C^\Psi)$.

For example, in a $NCSP$ with five numeric constraints an assignment could be $(c_1, c_2, c_3, c_4, c_5) \equiv (1, 0, 0, 1, 0)$.

## 4.1    General Neighborhood

**Definition 4.1 (Neighbor Assignment).** Given an assignment $A(C^\Psi)$, a neighbor assignment is defined by a new assignment $A'(C^\Psi)$ that differs in exactly one truth value.

For a given assignment $A(C^\Psi)$, one option could be to consider all alternatives whose variable assignments differ in exactly one position; for example, the assignment $(c_1, c_2, c_3, c_4, c_5) \equiv (1, 0, 0, 1, 0)$ would be a neighbor of $(c_1, c_2, c_3, c_4, c_5) \equiv (1, 0, 0, 1, 1)$, since they both differ only on the assignment to $c_5$. However, as each $c_i$ variable may take these different values, the cardinality of the set of possible neighbors could be very high. But, it could be reduced in a significant way, taking into account the structural aspects of the constraint network of the $NCSP$. In this article, two clear options of neighborhood are used: when the variables of all the constraints of $NCSP$ are identical then we define the concept of domain-based neighborhood; in other cases we define the concept of variable-based neighborhood.

## 4.2   Variable-Based Neighborhood

An important aspect in this concept is the notion of *Non-Observable Numeric Variable* of a $NCSP$ instance. For these variables, there is not any information about their domains.

**Definition 4.2.1 (Non-Observable Numeric Variable).** It is a numeric variable of a $NCSP$, whose initial domain in the problem specification is $(-\infty, +\infty)$.

For the example in the subsection 2.2, the neighborhood is based on the common *non-observable numeric variables* between constraints.

**Definition 4.2.2 (Variable-based Neighbor Assignment of Constraints).** Given an assignment of $A(C^\Psi)$, a neighbor is defined by a new assignment $A'(C^\Psi)$ that differs in exactly one truth value of a constraint with some common non-observable variable to the constraints with truth values equals 1.

## 4.3   Domain-Based Neighborhood

Another neighborhood concept is when all numeric constraints of an overconstrained $NCSP$ instance have the same variables. In this case we could use the projection operator of a variable $x_i \in X^\Psi$ w.r.t. a constraint $c_j \in C^\Psi$ is represented as $\Pi_{x_i}(c_j)$. In the same way, the projection operator of a variable $x_i \in X^\Psi$ w.r.t a set of constraint $C^\Gamma \subset C^\Psi$ that is represented as $\Pi_{x_i}(C^\gamma)$. Then, the new concept for deriving $MUSes$ is the domain-based neighborhood. A constraint $c_i \in C^\Psi$ could be domain-based neighbor of another set of constraint $C^\gamma \subset C^\Psi | c_i \notin C^\gamma$ when the intersection of the projections for all variables of set $X^\Psi$ is not empty:

$$\forall x_k \in X^\Psi \quad \Pi_{x_k}(c_i) \cap \Pi_{x_k}(C^\gamma) \neq \emptyset$$

**Definition 4.3 Domain-based Neighbor Assignment of the Constraints** Given an assignment of $A(C^\Psi)$, a neighbor is defined by a new assignment $A'(C^\Psi)$ that differs in exactly one truth value of a constraint and all projection operations of the variables w.r.t. a set of the numeric constraints with truth value equals 1 is not empty.

With this definition we are sure of the domain-based neighborhood, but it could happen that the intersection of all the projections are not empty and the constraints are unsatisfiable. For this reason, it is necessary to solve a $NCSP$.

## 5   NMUS: Numeric MUSes Search Methods

In this section, a set of methods $NMUS$ is presented to efficiently derive all $MUSes$ using the Neighborhood-based Structural Analysis on overconstrained $NCSP$. We describe different bottom-up derivation strategies taking into account the concept of neighborhood for the different types of problems. The search methods are different depending on the structural aspects of these problems.

## 5.1  NMUS for NCSPs with the Same Variables for All Constraints

A basic algorithm would study all the $2^n - 1$ combinations of constraints in order to determine all $MUSes$ of an overconstrained $NCSP$ instance $\Psi$, where $n$ is the cardinality of the set $C^{\Psi}$. The proposed method is complete, but it is very inefficient and no practical. For this reason, this work proposes different strategies to improve this algorithm.

Let $\mathcal{MUS}$ be a data structure List of Sets where the $MUSes$ are stored and $\mathcal{Q}$ a data structure type Queue of Sets where the active constraints and its projections w.r.t the variables of the problem are stored. The function $poll()$ retrieves and removes the head of a queue or null if the queue is empty.

**First Improvement (NMUS-1): Only Inclusion in queue of satisfiable subsets.** This first improvement will include in the queue $\mathcal{Q}$ only subset of constraints that are satisfiable. Given an overconstrained $NCSP$ instance $\Psi$, the algorithm is shown in Algorithm 1.

> **Alg. NMUS-1** ($\Psi : NCSP$)
> Let $C^{\Psi} = \{c_1, \ldots, c_n\}$ be constraints of the overconstrained NCSP instance
> $\mathcal{Q} :=$ Queue with a set for each satisfiable numeric constraints belong to $C^{\Psi}$
> $\mathcal{MUS} :=$ List with the set of unsatisfiable numeric constraints belong to $C^{\Psi}$
> while ($\mathcal{Q}$ is not Empty)
>     $\{c_i \ldots c_j\} := \mathcal{Q}.poll()$
>     for ($c_k \in \{c_{j+1}$ to $c_n\}$)
>         if (NOT $\exists SubSet^{1 \ldots n-1}_{\{c_i \ldots c_j\}} \cup c_k \in \mathcal{MUS}$) // n is cardinality of $\{c_i \ldots c_j\}$
>             if ($\{c_i \ldots c_j\} \cup c_k$ is satisfiable) // a $NCSP$ must be solved
>                 $\mathcal{Q}.add(\{c_i \ldots c_j\} \cup c_k)$
>             else
>                 $\mathcal{MUS}.add(\{c_i \ldots c_j\} \cup c_k)$
>             endIf
>         endIf
>     endFor
> endWhile

**Algorithm 1.** NMUS-1 ($\Psi : NCSP$)

In this algorithm, the neighborhood concept is not taken into account and the satisfiability could be checked using $NCSP$ solvers.

**Second Improvement (NMUS-2): Using Domain-based neighborhood**
In this algorithm, two concepts are used: domain-based neighborhood and overlapping projection. The initialization procedure is the same as the previous algorithm. The new algorithm is shown in Algorithm 2.

The function **Overlap_Projection**(*Constraint c, Constraints List lc*) returns true if it exists overlapping between the projection of the constraint $c$ and the projection of $lc$ w.r.t. every variable. If this function returns false, it means that it exists a $MUS$ formed by $c$ and some constraints of $lc$, thereby $c \cup lc$ is not a $MUS$.

**Alg. NMUS-2($\Psi : NCSP$)**
.............. // Initialization
while ($Q$ no Empty)
    $\{c_i \ldots c_j\}:= Q$.poll() // a list of satisfiable constraints are obtained
    for ($c_k$ in $\{c_{j+1}$ to $c_n\}$) // it avoids to obtain redundant solutions
    if (Overlap_Projection($c_k, \{c_i \ldots c_j\}$) AND
                    NOT $\exists SubSet_{\{c_i \ldots c_j\}}^{1 \ldots n-1} \cup c_k \in \mathcal{MUS}$
        if ($\{c_i \ldots c_j\} \cup c_k$ is satisfiable) // a $NCSP$ is created
          $Q$.add($\{c_i \ldots c_j\} \cup c_k$)
        else
          $\mathcal{MUS}$.add($\{c_i \ldots c_j\} \cup c_k$)
        endIf
    else
        if($\#\{c_i \ldots c_j\}=1$)
          $\mathcal{MUS}$.add($\{c_i \ldots c_j\} \cup c_k$)
        endIf
    endIf
    endFor
endWhile

**Algorithm 2.** NMUS-2 ($\Psi : NCSP$)

**Third Improvement (NMUS-3): Sorting constraints according to the overlapped domain.** The heuristic used in this algorithm is based on the quick search of $MUSes$. First of all, the algorithm sorts the constraints depending on the number of projections that intersect with the projections of other constraints.

It is possible to check the satisfiability only analysing the minimum and maximum value of each variable in the different constraints, no being necessary to solve a $NCSP$. The previous algorithms add subsets of constraints in the queue $Q$ when a subset of constraints is satisfiable. If we analyze first the less promising subsets, there will be less possibilites yo add these constraints to $Q$.

## 5.2    NMUS for NCSPs with Some Different Variables for the Numeric Constraints

In this algorithm, we will apply a different neighborhood concept, the variable-based one. The initialization procedure is the same as in the previous algorithm, but the data structure $Q$ can be now a Queue, a Stack or another data structure depending on the different search strategy. This structure must have a new method *add* which includes a tuple $\langle C^\gamma, NOBV(C^\gamma) \rangle$, where $NOBV(C^\gamma)$ represents the set of non-observable variables of $C^\gamma$.

Depending on the type of structure $Q$, the search process will be depth-search or breadth-search, what will determine two different algorithms **NMUS-4** and **NMUS-5** respectively (Algorithm 3).

**Alg. NMUS-4-5**($\Psi : NCSP$)
.............. // Initialization
while($Q$ is not Empty)
    $\langle C^\gamma, NOBV(C^\gamma)\rangle := Q$.poll() // chose a element belong to $Q$
    neighbors := expand $(\langle C^\gamma, NOBV(C^\gamma)\rangle)$ // generate neighbours
                                    according variable-based neighborhood
    foreach $(\langle c_k, NOBV(c_k)\rangle \in$ neighbors$)$
      if$(C^\gamma \cup c_k$ is satisfiable)// a $NCSP$ is created
          $Q$.add($\langle C^\gamma, NOBV(C^\gamma)\rangle \cup \langle c_k, NOBV(c_k)\rangle$)
      else
            $MUS$.add($\langle C^\gamma, NOBV(C^\gamma)\rangle \cup \langle c_k, NOBV(c_k)\rangle$)
      endIf
    endFor
endWhile

**Algorithm 3.** NMUS-4-5($\Psi : NCSP$)

## 6     Experimental Results

NMUS is a prototype that includes all previous algorithms. This prototype is implemented in Java and runs on an AMD Athlon Dual Core 2.21 GHz with 1.78 GB Ram. The standard routine used for solving $NCSP$ belongs to $ILOG^{TM} JSolver$.

The different algorithms of this prototype improve the performance of basic algorithms for numeric domains using the structural analysis. We provide experimental results showing that the use of the different strategies proposed leads to substantially improved performance and facilitates to solve larger and more realistic problems. The following table reports the experimental results for the different examples of the Section 2 when a domain-based or a variable-based neighborhood are used. NMUS-5 is more efficient than NMUS-4 since using a breadth search approach we can detect more easily the redundant sets of constraints that are generated. The examples show also a significant improvement w.r.t. the basic algorithms. Therefore these algorithms provide a realistic method for deriving all numeric $MUSes$ of a given problem.

**Table 1.** Experimental Results for examples in Section 2

| Algorithms | Example 2.1 | | Algorithms | Example 2.2 |
|---|---|---|---|---|
| | # NCSPs | Time(ms) | | Time (ms) |
| Basic Alg. | $2^{12} - 1 = 4095$ | 40210 | Basic Alg. | 1017 |
| **NMUS-1** | 88 | 8692 | **NMUS-4** | 16,8 |
| **NMUS-2** | 58 | 7500 | **NMUS-5** | 2,0 |
| **NMUS-3** | 57 | 2340 | | |

## 7     Conclusions and Future Work

The derivation of all $MUSes$ for overconstrained $NCSP$ is a computationally hard problem and arises in a lot of industrial problems. This problem has been formally defined in this paper and different methods for deriving all $NMUSes$

are also presented here. Our experimental results show that the computation time required is significantly reduced in comparison to the basic algorithms.

Future work in this problem will include moreover enhancing more the efficiency of our algorithms, the treatment of new types of problems, for example when the constraint network has cycles or a disjunctive set of constraints. Finally, an important future goal will be to use the relaxation preferences that provides a user about how to weaken constraints to achieve feasibility.

## Acknowledgements

This work has been partially supported by the Spanish *Ministerio de Educación y Ciencia* through a coordinated research project(grant DIP2006-15476-C02-01) and Feder (ERDF).

## References

1. Bailey, J., Stuckey, P.J.: Discovery of Minimal Unsatisfiable Subsets of Constraints using Hitting set dualization. In: Hermenegildo, M.V., Cabeza, D. (eds.) Practical Aspects of Declarative Languages. LNCS, vol. 3350, pp. 174–186. Springer, Heidelberg (2005)
2. Bruni, R.: Approximating minimal unsatisfiable subformulae by means of adaptive core search. Discrete Applied Mathematics 130, 85–100 (2003)
3. Ceballos, R., Gómez-López, M.T., Gasca, M.T.R.M., del Valle, C.: Integración de técnicas basadas en modelos para la determinación de la diagnosis mínima de un sistema. Inteligencia Artificial. Revista Iberoamericana de Inteligencia Artificial No. 31, pp. 41–51 (2006)
4. Chinneck, J., Dravnieks, E.: Locating minimal infeasible constraint sets in linear programs. ORSA Journal on Computing 3, 157–168 (1991)
5. de la Banda, M.G., Stuckey, P.J., Wazny, J.: Finding all minimal unsatisfiable subsets. In: PPDP 2003. Proceedings of the 5th ACM SIGPLAN international conference on Principles and practice of declaritive programming, pp. 32–43. ACM Press, New York (2003)
6. Gómez, M.T., Ceballos, R., Gasca, R.M., Del Valle, C.: Constraint Databases Technology for Polynomial Models Diagnosis. In: Proceedings DX 2004 (2004)
7. Grégoire, É., Mazure, B., Piette, C.: Local-Search Extraction of MUSes. Constraints 12(3) (2007)
8. Junker, U.: QuickXPlain. In: Conflict Detection for Arbitatrary Constraint Propagation Algorithms Proceedings IJCAI 2001 (2001)
9. Liffiton, M., Sakallah, K.: On finding all minimally unsatisfiable subformulas. In: Bacchus, F., Walsh, T. (eds.) SAT 2005. LNCS, vol. 3569, pp. 173–186. Springer, Heidelberg (2005)
10. Mauss, J., Tatar, M.: Computing Minimal Conflicts for Rich Constraint Languages. In: ECAI, pp. 151–155 (2002)
11. Moffitt, M.D., Pollack, M.E.: Applying Local Search to Disjunctive Temporal Problems. In: Proced. IJCAI (2005)
12. Liffiton, M.H., Moffitt, M.D., Pollack, M.E., Sakallah, K.A.: Identifying Conflicts in Overconstrained Temporal Problems. In: Proceedings IJCAI 2007 (2007)
13. Oh, Y., Mneimneh, M.N., Andraus, Z.S., Sakallah, K.A., Markov, I.L.: AMUSE: A Minimally-Unsatisfiable Subformula Extractor. In: Proceedings of the Design Automation Conference (DAC 2004), ACM/IEEE, pp. 518–523 (2004)

# Interest Point Detectors for Visual SLAM

Óscar Martínez Mozos[1], Arturo Gil[2], Monica Ballesta[2], and Oscar Reinoso[2]

[1] Department of Computer Science, University of Freiburg, Germany
[2] Department of Systems Engineering, Miguel Hernández University, Spain

**Abstract.** In this paper we present several interest points detectors and we analyze their suitability when used as landmark extractors for vision-based simultaneous localization and mapping (vSLAM). For this purpose, we evaluate the detectors according to their repeatability under changes in viewpoint and scale. These are the desired requirements for visual landmarks. Several experiments were carried out using sequence of images captured with high precision. The sequences represent planar objects as well as 3D scenes.

## 1  Introduction

Acquiring maps of the environment is a fundamental task for autonomous mobile robots, since the maps are required in different higher level tasks. As a result, the problem of simultaneous localization and mapping (SLAM) has received significant attention. Typical approaches use range sensors to build maps in two and three dimensions (see, for example, [1,2,3] [4,5,6]). In recent years there is an increasing interest on using cameras as sensors. Such approach is sometimes denoted as visual SLAM (vSLAM). Cameras offer higher amount of information and are less expensive than lasers. Moreover, they can provide 3D information when stereo systems are used.

Usual approaches using vision apply a feature-based SLAM, in which visual features are used as landmarks. The main issue when using vSLAM is how select suitable features on the images to be used as reliable landmarks. When the map to construct has three dimensions, the landmarks must additionally be robust to changes in the scale and viewpoint. Different vision features has been used for mapping and localization using monocular or stereo vision, as for example, lines [7], region of interest [8]; and interest points, as SIFT [9,10,11], Harris corner detector [12,13] or SURF [14]. The interest points detectors have received most of the attention in vSLAM. The points detected are typically invariant under rotation, translation, scale and only partially invariant under changes in viewpoint. These theoretical properties made them suitable for been used as visual landmarks. In practice, however, the stability of the points is not always maintained and the matching between them becomes difficult. Some solutions have been proposed to solve this problem, as combining several methods in one detector [15] or tracking the points during several frames to keep the stability [16,10]. However, the question of which interest point detector is more suitable for vSLAM is still open.

D. Borrajo, L. Castillo, and J.M. Corchado (Eds.): CAEPIA 2007, LNAI 4788, pp. 170–179, 2007.
© Springer-Verlag Berlin Heidelberg 2007

In this paper we present several evaluations of different point detectors that are typically used in vSLAM. The extracted points used as landmarks should be robust under scale and viewpoint changes. These requirements are necessary for vSLAM, since the robot must be able to detect and associate new landmarks to previous ones. Under these conditions we analyze the repeatability of the points in consecutive images and the probability of been detected in future ones.

The rest of the paper is organized as follows. After discussing some related work in Section 2, we present different interest point detectors in Section 3. Section 4 introduces the evaluation methods used in this work. Several experiments are presented in Section 5. We finally conclude in Section 6.

## 2   Related Work

Visual SLAM has been an interesting topic in mobile robotics for the last years. Different methods has been used to extract visual landmarks. Lemaire and Lacroix [7] use segments as landmarks together with and EKF-based SLAM approach. Frintrop *et al.* [8] extract regions of interest (ROI) using the attentional system VOCUS. Other authors use SIFT features as landmarks in the 3D space [9,16]. Little *et al.* [17] and Gil et al. [10] additionally track the SIFT features to keep the most robust ones; and Valls Miro *et al.* [11] use SIFT to map large environments. Harris corner detectors has also been used as landmarks for monocular SLAM (Davison and Murray [12]) or in Autonomous Blimps (Hygounenc *et al.* [13]). Finally, Murillo *et al.* [14] present a localization method using SURF features.

In the context of matching and recognition, many authors have presented their works evaluating several interest point detectors. The work presented by Mikolajczyk and Schmid [18], uses different detectors to extract affine invariant regions, but only focuses on the comparison of different description methods. In [19], a collection of detectors is evaluated. The criteria used measures the quality of these features for tasks like image matching, object recognition and 3D reconstruction. However they do not take into account the repeatability in the successive frames of a sequence. In contrast to the previous works we evaluate the different interest point detectors under the particular conditions of vSLAM.

## 3   Interest Point Detectors

Along this paper we suppose that a mobile robot is used for constructing the map of the environment. The robot is equipped with a camera used to acquire images. Interest points are then extracted from these images and used as landmarks. We also suppose that the height of the camera on the robot is fixed as well as its orientation. This is the typical configuration in visual SLAM systems. Additionally, we assume that visual landmarks are static, i.e. they do not change their position or oriention during the experiments. According to the previous criterion, we following present five different interest point detectors used to extract visual landmarks.

## 3.1  Harris Corner Detector

The Harris Corner Detector [20] is probably the most widely interest point detector used due to its strong invariance to scale, rotation and illumination variations, as well as image noise. The detector is based on the matrix $C(x,y)$ which is computed over a $pxp$ patch for each interest point at position $(x,y)$ as:

$$C(x,y) = \begin{pmatrix} \sum I_x^2 & \sum I_x I_y \\ \sum I_x I_y & \sum I_y^2 \end{pmatrix} , \qquad (1)$$

where $I_x, I_y$ are the image gradients in horizontal and vertical direction. Let $\lambda_1$ and $\lambda_2$ be the eigenvalues of the matrix $C(x,y)$, we define the auto-correlation function $R$ as:

$$R = \lambda_1 \lambda_2 - k(\lambda_1 + \lambda_2)^2 . \qquad (2)$$

This function will be sharply peaked if both of the eigenvalues are high. This means that shifts in any direction will produce a significant increase, indicating that it is a corner. A typical value for $k$ is 0.04 [12].

## 3.2  Harris-Laplace

The interest points extracted by the Harris-Laplace detector [21] are invariant to rotation and scale. These points are detected by a scale adapted Harris function and selected in scale-space by the Laplacian operator. The selected scale determines the size of the support region.

## 3.3  SIFT

The Scale-Invariant Feature Transform (SIFT) is an algorithm that detects distinctive keypoints from images and computes a descriptor for them. This algorithm was initially presented by Lowe [22] and used in object recognition tasks. The interest points extracted are said to be invariant to image scale, rotation, and partially invariant to changes in viewpoint and illumination. SIFT features are located at maxima and minima of a difference of Gaussians (DoG) function applied in scale space. They can be computed by building an image pyramid with resampling between each level [23]. In this work, we only use the detected points and we discard the descriptors.

## 3.4  SURF

Speeded Up Robust Features (SURF) is a scale and rotation invariant detector and descriptor which was recently presented by Bay et al. [24]. This detector is based on the Hessian matrix because of its accuracy and low computational time. SURF is based on sums of 2D Haar wavelet responses and makes an efficient use of integral images. According to [24], this algorithm outperforms existing methods with respect to repeatability, robustness and distinctiveness of the descriptors. As with SIFT features, we concentrate only on the detected points and we discard the descriptors.

## 3.5   SUSAN

SUSAN (Smallest Univalue Segment Assimilating Nucleus) is an approach to low level image processing [25]. The SUSAN principle is implemented using digital approximation of circular masks. If the brightness of each pixel within a mask is compared with the brightness of that mask's nucleus, then an area of the mask can be defined which has the same brightness as the nucleus. SUSAN has been traditionally used for object recognition.

# 4   Evaluation Methods

To evaluate the previous methods we use sequences of images representing the same scene under different scales and viewpoints. In this section we explain how these sequences were evaluated. We first introduce the tracking method used to follow the interest points in each frame of the sequences. We then describe the measurements used to study the repeatability and robustness of each method under changes in scale an viewpoint. In this work we do not study the invariance under changes in illumination.

## 4.1   Tracking

For each image in a sequence, we first extract the interest points using the methods explained in Section 3. To track each point in successive images we try to match the interest points using the homography matrix for each pair of consecutive images as follows [26]. Given a point $Y$ in 3D space, we assume that this point projects at position $y_1 = P_1Y$ in image $I_1$ and at position $y_i = P_iY$ in image $I_i$, with projection matrices $P_1$ and $P_i$. If we suppose that the point $Y$ is detected in both images, then

$$y_i = H_{1i} \times y_1, \text{ with } H_{1i} = P_iP_1^{-1} \ . \tag{3}$$

The homography matrix $H_{1i}$ can be computed by selecting manually four correspondences of coplanar points between images 1 and $i$. Given a detected point in one image, we predict its position in the consecutive image using the homography matrix. If the predicted position lies at a distance below 2 pixels from an interest point detected in the second image, then we consider that the interest point is successfully tracked. If no interest point lies in the neighborhood of the predicted point, then the tracking of the point is lost. This method has been applied to sequences of images containing planar objects, since the computation of the homography matrix can only be made for coplanar points in the space. In the case of 3D images a similar method was used but with manual correction if the interest point in the second image was not found because of some occlusion.

An example of a tracking using this method is shown in Figure 1 in which the interest points were extracted with the Harris detector (white points). In this sequence, the red points in the last image indicate points that could be tracked along the whole sequence. The blue points are those ones that have been lost

0–1          1–2          2–3          3–4          4–5          5–6

**Fig. 1.** Sequence of images with persistent points (red), lost points (blue) and points detected (white)

from the previous image. A point that is lost, even only once, is rejected by our tracking algorithm since we have considered that this kind of points are not stable enough for our purpose.

### 4.2   Evaluation Measurements

As explained in Section 3, we want to evaluate the detectors according to the SLAM requirements. In this sense, we have followed a repeatability criterion which means that the detection is independent of changes in the imaging conditions, i. e. scale and viewpoint. Applying our tracking method we first define the survival ratio $S_i$ in the frame $i$ as:

$$S_i = \frac{np_i}{np_0} \cdot 100 \ , \tag{4}$$

where $np_i$ and $np_0$ are the number of points detected in the frame $i$ and the first frame respectively. A perfect detector would detect the same points in the first and the last frame, i.e. $S_i = 100\%$ for every frame. However, as we will see in the experiments, we normally observe a decreasing tendency in $S_i$, meaning that some of the points observed in the first frame are lost in subsequent frames.

When the robot explores the environment, it is desirable to extract visual landmarks that are stable and can be detected in a number of $p$ consecutive frames [17,10]. As a result, the number of landmarks in the map is reduced and also the complexity of the SLAM problem. However, setting $p$ poses a problem: if $p$ is low, a high number of spurious points will be integrated in the map. If $p$ is high, the number of landmarks in the map will be too low. For example, when the robot turns, the landmarks disappear rapidly from the camera field of view and will not be integrated in the map if $p$ is high. Taking into account this requirement we analyze for how many frames we should track a landmark before integrating it in the map. We use the following conditional probability:

$$P(t_{f_a}|t_{f_b}) = \frac{t_{f_a}}{t_{f_b}}, \tag{5}$$

where $t_{f_i}$ is the number of points tracked until frame $f_i$. This value represents the probability of an interest point to be tracked until frame $f_a$ given that it was tracked until frame $f_b$. This value ranges between 0 and 1. It is 0 when all points

**Fig. 2.** The top sequence shows images of a poster from different viewpoints. The bootom sequence shows the same poster with changes in scale.

tracked until $f_b$ are lost in frame $f_a$, and 1 if both frames $f_a$ and $f_b$ contains the same tracked points.

Expression (5) gives a prediction of the survival of an interest point in future frames if the movement of the robot maintains similar. This expression can be used to estimate the number of frames $p$ a landmark has to be tracked before it is incorporated in the map.

## 5   Experiments

In order to evaluate the different interest point detectors, we captured 12 sequences of viewpoint changing images each containing 21 images. For each image we increased the angle in 2.5 degrees. Additionally we captured 14 sequences of images with scale changes each containing 12 images. In this last case the camera moved 0.1 meters in each image. The sequences contain images of planar objects (as posters) and 3D scenes. Examples of both types of images are shown in Figure 2 and Figure 3 respectively.

All images were captured using a STH-MDCS2 stereo head from Videre Design. Only one of the stereo images was used at each time to form the sequences. The stereo head was mounted on a robotic arm to achieve constant variations of viewing angle and distance change. Finally, the images were captured at different resolutions (320x240, 640x480 and 1280x960), so that the set of images could be as much representative as possible.

In a first experiment we analyze the repeatability of the different detectors in the sequences with changes in the viewpoint. In SLAM it is important that the landmarks detected with a certain angle and distance are also detected from different ones. This comes from the fact that a mobile robot will see the same point in the scene from different poses in the environment. For this experiment

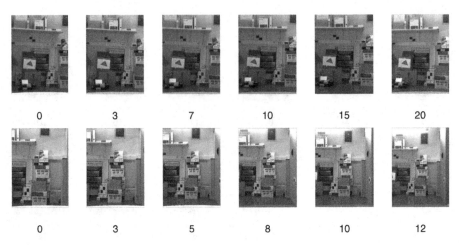

**Fig. 3.** The top sequence shows images of a 3D scene from different viewpoints. The bottom sequence shows a similar scene with changes in scale.

we use as data all the sequences simultaneously and we calculate Expression (4) using the interest points of the images in all sequences, that is, $np_i = \sum_{s=1}^{s=12} np_i^s$ for all the 12 sequences.

As the left image of Figure 4 suggests, the Harris detector seems to be the most stable, being able to maintain almost 30% of the initial points in all images of the sequences with viewpoint changes of 50 degrees. Similar results are obtained when using Harris at different scales (right image of Figure 4). The SIFT detector obtain also good results at different viewpoints, but it gets worse under changes in scale.

Figure 5 presents a different way of comparing the detectors. In this case, the plots show the probability that a point is found in the last frame given that it was tracked until the frame $i$, as shown in Expression (5). Again the Harris detector gives the best results under changes in viewpoint and scale. We can see that, for example, a Harris-point which is tracked for 10 frames will have a probability of 0.7 of being tracked until frame 20.

Although the plots of Figure 4 and Figure 5 contain similar information, the second one can be used to further discriminate between different detectors. For example, in the right image of Figure 4, the SIFT, SURF and Harris-Laplace descriptors show a similar behavior, however the right image in Figure 5 shows that the SURF descriptor is more stable. If we follow a landmark extracted with the SURF descriptor for 6 frames, it will have a probability of 0.5 of being tracked until frame 12, while this probability decreases to 0.4 when the point was extracted using SIFT or Harris-Laplace.

Table 1 presents the number of interest points detected in the first image and the number of points that were tracked until the last frame. It can be clearly seen that the number of points detected differs when using different methods. This stems from the fact that we are using an heterogeneous image database and it is not possible to adjust each of the detectors in a way that the number of detected points is the same for all the methods. For instance, the parameters for each of

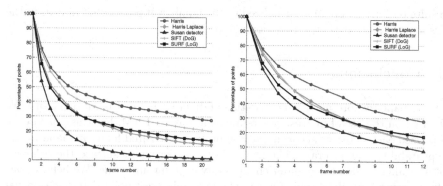

**Fig. 4.** The left plot shows the survival ratio for each of the frames in the sequences with change in viewpoint. The right plot shows the same value in the sequences with change in scale.

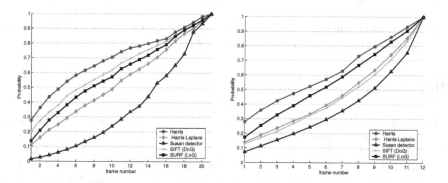

**Fig. 5.** The figures show the probability of a point being detected in the last frame given that it was detected in the frame $i$ of the sequences: left with changes in viewpoint, and right with changes in scale

**Table 1.** Number of points detected in the first and last image of each sequence

| Changes in Viewpoint | Harris | Harris Laplace | SUSAN | SIFT | SURF |
|---|---|---|---|---|---|
| Number of points detected in the first image | 2064 | 2588 | 2967 | 3808 | 10372 |
| Number of points tracked to the last image | 568 | 282 | 68 | 407 | 1415 |
| Changes in Scale | Harris | Harris Laplace | SUSAN | SIFT | SURF |
| Number of points detected in the first image | 5728 | 5685 | 6421 | 8207 | 24996 |
| Number of points tracked to the last image | 1594 | 788 | 465 | 1058 | 4295 |

the five methods can be adjusted in a way that the number of points detected in a single image would be equal. However, the same parameters applied to a different image would result in differing number of points detected. In consequence, the results presented here are normalized to the number of points that appear in the first frame, so that they can be compared.

## 6  Conclusions

In this paper we presented an evaluation of different interest point detectors. We focused on the use of interest points in visual-based SLAM. For this purpose we analyzed each detector according to the properties desired for visual landmarks: repeatability and accuracy. The results of the experiments showed the behavior of five different detectors under changes in viewpoint and scale. We believe that this information will be usefull when selecting an interest point detector as visual landmark extractor for SLAM.

## Acknowledgment

This work has been supported by the Spanish Government under the projects DPI2004-07433-C02-01 and PCT-G54016977-2005.

## References

1. Grisetti, G., Stachniss, C., Burgard, W.: Improved techniques for grid mapping with rao-blackwellized particle filters. IEEE Transactions on Robotics 23(1) (2007)
2. Hähnel, D., Burgard, W., Fox, D., Thrun, S.: An efficient FastSLAM algorithm for generating maps of large-scale cyclic environments from raw laser range measurements. In: IEEE/RSJ Int. Conf. on Intelligent Robots & Systems, Las Vegas, NV, USA (2003)
3. Leonard, J., Durrant-Whyte, H.: Mobile robot localization by tracking geometric beacons. IEEE Transactions on Robotics and Automation 7(4) (1991)
4. Biber, P., Andreasson, H., Duckett, T., Schilling, A.: 3d modelling of indoor environments by a mobile robot with a laser scanner and panoramic camera. In: IEEE/RSJ Int. Conf. on Intelligent Robots & Systems (2004)
5. Eustice, R., Singh, H., Leonard, J.: Exactly sparse delayed-state filters. In: IEEE Int. Conf. on Robotics & Automation (2005)
6. Triebel, R., Burgard, W.: Improving simultaneous mapping and localization in 3d using global constraints. In: National Conference on Artificial Intelligence (2005)
7. Lemaire, T., Lacroix, S.: Monocular-vision based SLAM using line segments. In: IEEE Int. Conf. on Robotics & Automation (2007)
8. Frintrop, S., Jensfelt, P., Christensen, H.I.: Attentional landmark selection for visual slam. In: IEEE/RSJ Int. Conf. on Intelligent Robots and Systems (2006)
9. Little, J., Se, S., Lowe, D.: Vision-based mobile robot localization and mapping using scale-invariant features. In: IEEE Int. Conf. on Robotics & Automation, IEEE Computer Society Press, Los Alamitos (2001)
10. Gil, A., Reinoso, O., Burgard, W., Stachniss, C., Martínez Mozos, O.: Improving data association in rao-blackwellized visual SLAM. In: IEEE/RSJ Int. Conf. on Intelligent Robots & Systems (2006)

11. Valls Miro, J., Zhou, W., Dissanayake, G.: Towards vision based navigation in large indoor environments. In: IEEE/RSJ Int. Conf. on Intelligent Robots & Systems (2006)
12. Davison, A.J., Murray, D.W.: Simultaneous localisation and map-building using active vision. IEEE Transactions on Pattern Analysis and Machine Intelligence (2002)
13. Hygounenc, E., Jung, I.K., Souères, P., Lacroix, S.: The autonomous blimp project of laas-cnrs: Achievements in flight control and terrain mapping. International Journal of Robotics Research 23(4–5) (2004)
14. Murillo, A.C., Guerrero, J.J., Sagüés, C.: Surf features for efficient robot localization with omnidirectional images. In: IEEE Int. Conf. on Robotics & Automation (2007)
15. Jensfelt, P., Kragic, D., Folkesson, J., Björkman, M.: A framework for vision based bearing only 3D SLAM. In: IEEE Int. Conf. on Robotics & Automation (2006)
16. Se, S., Lowe, D.G., Little, J.: Vision-based mobile robot localization and mapping using scale-invariant features. In: IEEE Int. Conf. on Robotics & Automation, IEEE Computer Society Press, Los Alamitos (2001)
17. Little, J., Se, S., Lowe, D.: Global localization using distinctive visual features. In: IEEE/RSJ Int. Conf. on Intelligent Robots & Systems (2002)
18. Mikolajczyk, K., Schmid, C.: A performance evaluation of local descriptors. IEEE Transactions on Pattern Analysis and Machine Intelligence 27(10) (2005)
19. Schmid, C., Mohr, R., Bauckhage, C.: Evaluaton of interest point detectors. International Journal of computer Vision 37(2) (2000)
20. Harris, C.G., Stephens, M.: A combined corner and edge detector. In: Alvey Vision Conference (1998)
21. Mikolajczyk, K., Schmid, C.: Indexing based on scale invariant interest points. In: Int. Conf. on Computer Vision (2001)
22. Lowe, D.: Object recognition from local scale-invariant features. In: Int. Conf. on Computer Vision (1999)
23. Lowe, D.: Distinctive image features from scale-invariant keypoints. Int. Journal of computer Vision 2(60) (2004)
24. Bay, H., Tuytelaars, T., Van Gool, L.: Object recognition from local scale-invariant features. In: European Conference on Computer Vision (2006)
25. Smith, S.: A new class of corner finder. In: British Machine Vision Conference (1992)
26. Dorkó, G., Schmid, C.: Selection of scale invariant neighborhoods for object class recognition. In: Int. Conf. on Computer Vision (2003)

# TBL Template Selection: An Evolutionary Approach

Ruy Luiz Milidiú[1], Julio Cesar Duarte[2], and Cícero Nogueira dos Santos[1]

[1] Departamento de Informática, Pontifícia Universidade Católica,
Rio de Janeiro, Brazil
{milidiu,nogueira}@inf.puc-rio.br
[2] Centro Tecnológico do Exército, Rio de Janeiro, Brazil
jduarte@ctex.eb.br

**Abstract.** Transformation Based Learning (TBL) is an intensively Machine Learning algorithm frequently used in Natural Language Processing. TBL uses rule templates to identify error-correcting patterns. A critical requirement in TBL is the availability of a problem domain expert to build these rule templates. In this work, we propose an evolutionary approach based on Genetic Algorithms to automatically implement the template selection process. We show some empirical evidence that our approach provides template sets with almost the same quality as human built templates.

## 1 Introduction

Transformation Based error-driven Learning (TBL) is a symbolic machine learning method introduced by Eric Brill [1]. The TBL technique builds an ordered set of rules that correct mistakes of a base line classifier. It has been used for several important linguistic tasks, such as part-of-speech (POS) tagging [1], parsing, prepositional phrase attachment [2] and phrase chunking [3,4], having achieved state-of-the-art performance in many of them.

Within the TBL framework, the generated rules must follow patterns called templates, which are meant to capture the relevant feature combinations. The accuracy of the TBL classifier is highly dependent on the template set used in the learning process. Unfortunately, the process of generating *good* templates is highly expensive and depends on the problem expert skills.

In this work, we address the problem of automatic TBL template selection through an evolutionary approach based on Genetic Algorithms (GAs). We show four genetic approaches, each one with a different degree of understanding of the problem. The better the understanding, the better is the accuracy of the generated classifier. Our experiments show that we can achieve the same quality as the best template set for some benchmark problems.

The remainder of this paper is organized as follows. Section 2 presents a brief overview of GAs and TBL. In Section 3, we describe our genetic approaches. Section 4 presents our experimental results. In the final section, we make some conclusions.

D. Borrajo, L. Castillo, and J.M. Corchado (Eds.): CAEPIA 2007, LNAI 4788, pp. 180–189, 2007.
© Springer-Verlag Berlin Heidelberg 2007

# 2    Techniques

## 2.1    Genetic Algorithms

Genetic Algorithms (GAs) [5] are a family of computational models inspired in the mechanisms of Evolution and Natural Selection. They model the solution of the problem into a data structure called **chromosome**, or *genotype* or *genome*, which represents the possible solutions, called **individuals**, or *creatures* or *phenotypes*. A series of genetic operators are applied to these chromosomes in order to achieve a high optimization of the problem.

Two components play an important role in the GA method: the problem codification and the evaluation function. The problem codification is the mapping that is made between the chromosomes and the individuals. Usually, the individuals are mapped into a string of 1's and 0's indicating the presence, or not, of some feature or characteristic. The evaluation function takes one individual and calculates its fitness. Usually, the fitness is a performance measure of the individual as a solution to the problem.

Normally, a genetic algorithm starts with a random population of individuals, which is influenced by the genetic operators over the generations. The main objective of a generation is to keep the *best* individuals, enhancing the overall fitness of the population, until some stopping criteria is achieved.

There are two kinds of genetic operators: selection and recombination. Selection operators use the evaluation function to decide which individuals have the highest potential. These individuals should persist in the population and be used by the other kind of operators.

The recombination operators are used to create new individuals using one or more high potential individuals. The most famous operators in this class are cross-over and mutation. The cross-over operator uses two or more fractions of high potential individuals to build a new individual which is appended to the next generation of the population. The mutation operator, on other hand, takes one high potential individual and makes a slight change in one of its components. The new individual is also appended in the next generation of the population.

## 2.2    Transformation Based Learning

Transformation Based error-driven Learning (TBL) uses a greedy error correcting strategy. Its main propose is to generate an ordered list of rules that correct classification mistakes in the training set, which have been produced by an initial classifier.

The requirements of the TBL algorithm are: a training corpus, a template set, an initial classifier and a score threshold. The learning method is a mistake-driven greedy procedure that iteratively acquires a set of transformation rules from the template set maximizing its score. The score from a rule can be defined as the number of corrections that it achieves in the training corpus in some iteration of the learning process, discounting the number of mistakes it makes in the same corpus. At each iteration, the rule with best score (better than the threshold) is chosen to be used in the generated classifier. The threshold value can be tuned to avoid overfitting to the training corpus. The classification process of a new sample can be done by simply applying the baseline classifier $BC$ and the ordered rule set $R$. The pseudo-code of the TBL algorithm is shown in Algorithm 1

---

**Algorithm 1.** The TBL Algorithm Pseudo-Code

---

**input** A training corpus $C_0$, a template set $T$, a baseline classifier $BC$ and an integer
　　threshold $\tau$
　Apply $BC$ to $C_0$ generating $C_1$
　$R \leftarrow \{\}$
　$k \leftarrow 1$
　**repeat**
　　Generate $CR_k$, instantiating all candidate rules from $T$ using $C_k$,
　　**for all** r such that $r \in CR_k$ **do**
　　　score(r) $\leftarrow$ #(good corrections of r) - #(bad corrections of r) in $C_k$
　　**end for**
　　Choose $r_M$ from $CR_k$ with highest positive score above $\tau$
　　**if** $r_M$ exists **then**
　　　Apply $r_M$ to $C_k$ generating $C_{k+1}$
　　　$R \leftarrow R + r_M$.
　　**end if**
　　$k \leftarrow k + 1$
　**until** *not* $r_M$ exists
**output** $R$

---

**TBL Templates.** A TBL template can be any sequence of patterns that generates an error correction rule. For instance, in a Part-Of-Speech(POS) tagging process, we can write a template like *word[0] word[-1] pos[0]*, which tries to make rules based on bi-grams, correcting the current POS tag based on the current and previous words.

We define a template as being a sequence of *Atomic Terms* (ATs). An AT is the smallest template unit which indicates the feature and conditions to be instantiated in a template. It is meant to identify one peace of the context that a TBL rule needs to test when applying to the target token. Some examples of ATs are:

1. **f[ds]**, which checks the feature $f$ of a token, located $ds$ tokens to the left or right (depending of the sign) of the target token. For example: word[-1];
2. **f[ds,de]**, which checks the feature $f$ in an interval of tokens positioned between $ds$ and $de$ (included), in relation to the target token. For example: word[-1,1];
3. **f[ds,de]_where(f'=v')**, which checks the feature $f$ of the token nearest to the target token, within the closed interval of $ds$ and $de$, for which the feature $f'$ equals $v'$ [6]. For example: word[-1,-5]_where(pos=VBD).

More complex atomic terms can be defined in order to create more specialized rules.

## 3   Approaches

In this section, we show the genetic coding used in our experiments. The use of genetic algorithms in conjunction with TBL has already been examined in [7], where they are used in the TBL training process to generate the instantiated rules and to provide an adaptive ranking. Nevertheless, they have not been used in the evaluation of template sets what is our proposal. In all codings, the template ordering is not taking into account, since it is the last criteria to be used when two or more rules have the same score.

### 3.1   Genetic Coding

**Fixed Context Window.** In this approach, the *chromosome* is composed by several sequences of possible atomic terms (ATs) of the simplest form $f[ds]$. The value in the *chromosome* determines the presence or absence of the corresponding AT in the template. The input for this coding is composed by the following items: the list of possible features to be used, an integer value maxOffset, the number of templates to be generated and an expected number of atomic terms in each template. The generated templates are sequences of atomic terms of the form $f[ds]$, where $ds \in \{$-maxOffset, +maxOffset$\}$. An example of this coding is given in Table 1, showing two templates with expected size 3, using 2 features, $f_1$ and $f_2$, and maxOffset equals to 1. The *chromosome* shown in the Table 1 generates the following two templates: $f_1[-1]$ $f_1[+1]$ $f_2[-1]$ $f_2[+1]$ and $f_2[-1]$ $f_2[0]$.

**Table 1.** Example of the Fixed Context Window Approach

|       | Template 1 | | | | | | Template 2 | | | | | |
|-------|----------|----------|----------|----------|----------|----------|----------|----------|----------|----------|----------|----------|
|       | $f_1[-1]$ | $f_1[0]$ | $f_1[+1]$ | $f_2[-1]$ | $f_2[0]$ | $f_2[+1]$ | $f_1[-1]$ | $f_1[0]$ | $f_1[+1]$ | $f_2[-1]$ | $f_2[0]$ | $f_2[+1]$ |
| $C_1$ | 1 | 0 | 1 | 1 | 0 | 1 | 0 | 0 | 0 | 1 | 1 | 0 |

**Fixed List of Atomic Terms.** Usually, it is easier to identify candidate atomic terms by looking at the output errors of a Machine Learning Algorithm. In Fixed List of Atomic Terms, the *chromosome* is very similar to the previous one, but it can be composed by sequences of a given set of atomic terms. The *chromosome* value also indicates the presence or the absence of the corresponding atomic term in the template. The input for this coding is the list of possible atomic terms to be used, and, as well, the number of templates to be generated and the expected number of atomic terms. An example of this coding is given in Table 2, showing two templates with expected size 3, using 6 different possible atomic terms

**Table 2.** Example of the Fixed List of Atomic Terms Approach

|       | Template 1 | | | | | | Template 2 | | | | | |
|-------|--------|--------|--------|--------|--------|--------|--------|--------|--------|--------|--------|--------|
|       | $AT_0$ | $AT_1$ | $AT_2$ | $AT_3$ | $AT_4$ | $AT_5$ | $AT_0$ | $AT_1$ | $AT_2$ | $AT_3$ | $AT_4$ | $AT_5$ |
| $C_1$ | 0 | 1 | 1 | 0 | 0 | 1 | 1 | 0 | 1 | 0 | 1 | 0 |

$f_1[-1]$, $f_1[-2]$, $f_2[0]$, $f_2[1]$, $f_1[0, 2]$ and $f_2[-2, -0]$_$where\{f_1 = v_1\}$. The *chromosome* shown in the Table 2 generates the following two templates: $f_1[-2]$ $f_2[0]$ $f_2[-2, -0]$_$where\{f_1 = v_1\}$ and $f_1[-1]$ $f_2[0]$ $f_1[0, 2]$.

**Maximum Template Size.** In this approach, the *chromosome* is quite similar to the previous one, but instead of having an expected template size we establish a maximum size for all templates. The *chromosome* value indicates the position of the corresponding atomic term in the list. A value -1 indicates the absence of an atomic term. The repetition of atomic terms in the same template is now a possibility, but they are discarded. The input for this coding is the list of possible atomic terms to be used, the number of templates to be generated and the maximum template size. An example of this coding is given in Table 3, showing three templates with maximum size 4, using the same six possible previous atomic terms. The *chromosome* shown in the Table 3 generates the following three templates: $f_1[-1]$ $f_1[-2]$ $f_2[1]$, $f_1[-2]$ $f_2[0]$ $f_2[1]$ $f_2[-2, -0]$_$where\{f_1 = v_1\}$ and $f_1[-2]$ $f_2[0]$ $f_2[1]$.

**Table 3.** Example of the Maximum Template Size Approach

|       | Template 1 | | | | Template 2 | | | | Template 3 | | | |
|-------|-----|-----|-----|-----|-----|-----|-----|-----|-----|-----|-----|-----|
|       | $AT_1$ | $AT_2$ | $AT_3$ | $AT_4$ | $AT_1$ | $AT_2$ | $AT_3$ | $AT_4$ | $AT_1$ | $AT_2$ | $AT_3$ | $AT_4$ |
| $C_1$ | 1 | 3 | -1 | 0 | 5 | 1 | 3 | 2 | 1 | 2 | 1 | 3 |

**Template List.** In this approach, the *chromosome* is composed of a sequence of predefined templates. The idea here is to find a better subset of templates than the one provided by an expert. Since TBL is a greedy algorithm, using all templates may not lead to better results than using just one of its subsets. The *chromosome* value indicates the presence or absence of the corresponding template. The input for this coding is the list of possible templates to be used and the expected number of templates to be used. An example of this coding is given in Table 4, showing templates from the fixed template list, $\{T_{00}, T_{01}, T_{02}, T_{03}, T_{04}, T_{05}, T_{06}, T_{07}, T_{08}, T_{09}, T_{10}, T_{11}\}$, with an expected number of seven templates. The *chromosome* shown in the Table 4 generates the following template set: $\{T_{00}, T_{02}, T_{05}, T_{06}, T_{08}, T_{09}, T_{10}\}$.

**Table 4.** Example of the Template List Approach

|       | $T_{00}$ | $T_{01}$ | $T_{02}$ | $T_{03}$ | $T_{04}$ | $T_{05}$ | $T_{06}$ | $T_{07}$ | $T_{08}$ | $T_{09}$ | $T_{10}$ | $T_{11}$ |
|-------|-----|-----|-----|-----|-----|-----|-----|-----|-----|-----|-----|-----|
| $C_1$ | 1 | 0 | 1 | 0 | 0 | 1 | 1 | 0 | 1 | 1 | 1 | 0 |

### 3.2 Fitness Function

Using a training set, we train a TBL classifier for each individual. The F-measure of the generated classifier for a validation set is used as the fitness value of the individual.

## 3.3   Cross-Over Operator

The cross-over operator generates a new *chromosome* by breaking apart two *chromosomes* in a random point and combining them. Table 5 shows an example of the cross-over operator for the *chromosome* described in the Fixed Context Window approach.

## 3.4   Mutation Operator

The mutation operator generates a new *chromosome* by changing the value of the atomic term in a template. Table 5 shows an example of the mutation process for the *chromosome* described in the Fixed Context Window approach.

**Table 5.** Examples of the Cross-over and Mutation operator

|  | Template 1 | | | | | | Template 2 | | | | | |
|---|---|---|---|---|---|---|---|---|---|---|---|---|
|  | $f_1[-1]$ | $f_1[0]$ | $f_1[+1]$ | $f_2[-1]$ | $f_2[0]$ | $f_2[+1]$ | $f_1[-1]$ | $f_1[0]$ | $f_1[+1]$ | $f_2[-1]$ | $f_2[0]$ | $f_2[+1]$ |
| $C_1$ | 1 | 0 | 1 | 1 | 0 | 1 | 0 | 0 | 0 | *1* | 1 | 0 |
| $C_2$ | 1 | 1 | 0 | 0 | 0 | 1 | 1 | 1 | 0 | 1 | 0 | 0 |
| $C_1 \otimes C_2$ | 1 | 0 | 1 | 1 | 0 | 1 | 0 | 1 | 0 | 1 | 0 | 0 |
| $\odot C_1$ | 1 | 0 | 1 | 1 | 0 | 1 | 0 | 0 | 0 | *0* | 1 | 0 |

For the Maximum Template Size approach, instead of changing the value from 0 to 1 and vice-versa, the value is changed to another value in the interval [-1, number of atomic terms - 1].

# 4   Experiments

We have chosen the *English Base Noun Phrase Chunking* to demonstrate the quality of our genetic approaches. Base Noun Phrase Chunking consists in recognizing non-overlapping text segments that correspond to noun phrases (NPs).

The data used in the base NP chunking is the one of Ramshaw & Marcus [3]. This corpus contains sections 15-18 and section 20 of the Penn Treebank, and is pre-divided into a 8936-sentence (211727 tokens) training set and a 2012-sentence (47377 tokens) test set. This corpus is tagged with POS tags and with base NP tags.

A small excerpt of the training corpus is used by the genetic approach. Two corpora are built: a GA-training set and a validation set. The GA-training and validation sets are used by the genetic algorithm to, respectively, train and evaluate the performance of the individuals. The *best* individual returned by the genetic algorithm is applied to the whole training corpus, generating a TBL classifier. The classifier is, then, applied to the test corpus and its performance is evaluated.

We use F-measure as our key statistics to evaluate the performance of the generated classifiers. **F-measure** is the harmonic mean between precision and recall. **Precision** informs how many good classifications the model predicted

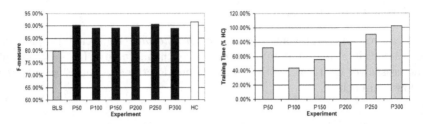

**Fig. 1.** Results for the Fixed Context Window approach

amongst all predictions made. **Recall** informs how many good classifications were predicted amongst all true classifications.

For the four genetic formulations, we report the performance of the classifier trained with the *best* template set produced by the use of different slices of the GA-training set in the genetic approach. These results are compared with the Baseline System (BLS), the same used by [3], and the handcrafted templates (HC). Although, we fixed the $\tau$ parameter used in all experiments to the same value used by the handcrafted templates, it could also be encoded and determined by the genetic algorithm without considerable loss of performance, since its set of optimal values is very limited (usually, $0 \leq \tau \leq 2$). We start with 50 sentences for the genetic training process, increasing with 50 more examples in each experiment. We also report the training time for each approach, in terms of percentage of the training time for the *handcrafted* templates. The reported training time includes both the selection of the best template set by the genetic algorithm and the training of the TBL classifier. The BLS training time is not reported since it is very small. Due to space constraints, we do not show the performance of the population in the validation set over the ten fixed generations, but it shows a consistent increase for all approaches.

The results for the Fixed Context Window (FCW) approach are reported in Figure 1. The experiment is conducted using the three possible features (word, POS and NP tag) with a window size of five ([-2, +2]). The genetic algorithm generated 20 templates with an expected atomic term size of 3. As we can see, the results are very good since we generate only 20 templates with the simplest atomic term. The loss of F-measure is smaller than 1% in the best ga-training sets. Also the genetic approaches takes less training time, since the templates are very simple.

Figure 2 shows the results for the Maximum Template Size (MTS) approach. The atomic term list used is {npt[0], npt[−1], npt[−2], npt[1], npt[2], pos[0], pos[1], pos[2], pos[−2], pos[−1], pos[−3, −1], pos[1, 3], word[0], word[1], word[2], word[−1], word[−2], word[−3, −1], word[1, 3]}. The results are almost the same. We do not use very complex atomic terms in order to maintain the simplicity of the approaches, avoiding the need of a specialist to determine the atomic term list. The genetic algorithm generated 20 templates with maximum atomic term size of 5. The overall training time is increased, since we added atomic terms that may instantiate more candidate rules.

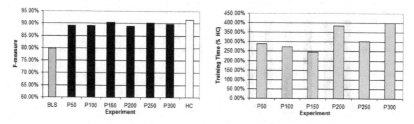

**Fig. 2.** Results for the Maximum Template Size approach

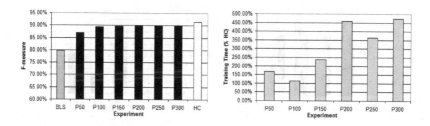

**Fig. 3.** Results for the Fixed List of Atomic Terms approach

The experiment using the Fixed List of Atomic Terms (FLAT) approach is quite similar to the previous one, with same main parameters, and is reported in Figure 3. The only difference is that we define the expected template size, which was fixed in 4. We can see that the results are very similar to the previous one, in terms of F-measure and training time, since the two approaches are quite equivalent.

The last conducted experiment uses the Template List (TL) approach. In this experiment, we try to find out a better combination of templates than the one provided by a specialist. Here, we use the template set proposed in [3]. The genetic generations are started with 80% of the templates activated. Figure 4 shows the results for this experiment. We can see that the template combination found by our approach achieve better results than the template set proposed by the specialist. However, this achievement implies in an increase of the overall training time.

We conducted other experiments with the English text chunking (CK) and Portuguese named entities (NE) tasks. The text chunking corpus is the same used in [3] and in the Base NP experiments, with the text chunking tags. The named entities corpus used is the same reported in [8]. The NE corpus was divided into a 1722-sentence (27055 tokens) training set and a 378-sentence (6084 tokens) test set. This corpus is tagged with POS tags and NE tags.

Due to space constraints, we show only the results of the best generated classifiers for each approach. The overall results in terms of F-measure and training time are similar to the ones reported for the base NP chunking. Figure 5 shows the results for the two experiments. The only aspect to except is that much more relative training time was needed in the NE problem since the TBL template designers managed to build very compact light templates with very short training

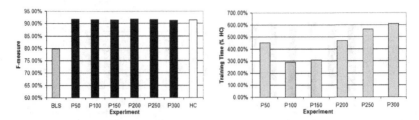

**Fig. 4.** Results for the Template List approach

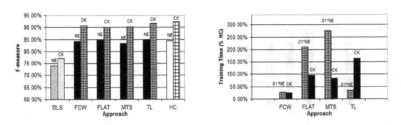

**Fig. 5.** Results for English Text Chunking and Portuguese Named Entities Extraction

times. That is why these relative training times are scaled by a factor of 1% in Figure 5.

## 5  Conclusions

TBL Template construction is a highly expensive process with strong impact in the classifier's accuracy. In this paper, we presented an evolutionary approach to help the creation of TBL templates. Our schemes use simple template design and very little training data to develop a set of templates.

We show a set of experiments that demonstrate the applicability and the effectiveness of the proposed method. The experimental results indicate that our approach achieves much better accuracy than the base line algorithm. Moreover, in many cases, our method slightly outperformed the F-measures obtained by the handcrafted templates with compatible training time since the domain expert was removed of most of the process.

## References

1. Brill, E.: Transformation-based error-driven learning and natural language processing: A case study in part-of-speech tagging. Computational Linguistics 21, 543–565 (1995)
2. Brill, E., Resnik, P.: A rule-based approach to prepositional phrase attachment disambiguation. In: Proceedings of COLING 1994, Kyoto, Japan (1994)
3. Ramshaw, L., Marcus, M.: Text chunking using transformation-based learning. In: Yarovsky, D., Church, K. (eds.) Proceedings of the Third Workshop on Very Large Corpora, New Jersey, Association for Computational Linguistics, pp. 82–94 (1995)

4. Megyesi, B.: Shallow parsing with pos taggers and linguistic features. Journal of Machine Learning Research 2, 639–668 (2002)
5. Holland, J.H.: Adaptation in Natural and Artificial Systems. University of Michigan Press, Ann Arbor (1975)
6. dos Santos, C.N., Oliveira, C.: Constrained atomic term: Widening the reach of rule templates in transformation based learning. In: Bento, C., Cardoso, A., Dias, G. (eds.) EPIA 2005. LNCS (LNAI), vol. 3808, pp. 622–633. Springer, Heidelberg (2005)
7. Wilson, G., Heywood, M.: Use of a genetic algorithm in brill's transformation-based part-of-speech tagger. In: GECCO 2005. Proceedings of the 2005 conference on Genetic and evolutionary computation, pp. 2067–2073. ACM Press, New York (2005)
8. Milidiú, R.L., Duarte, J.C., Cavalcante, R.: Machine learning algorithms for portuguese named entity recognition. In: Fourth Workshop in Information and Human Language Technology (TIL 2006), Ribeirão Preto, Brazil (2006)

# Finiteness Properties of Some Families of GP-Trees

César L. Alonso[1] and José Luis Montaña[2,*]

[1] Centro de Inteligencia Artificial, Universidad de Oviedo
Campus de Viesques, 33271 Gijón, Spain
calonso@aic.uniovi.es
[2] Departamento de Matemáticas, Estadística y Computación,
Universidad de Cantabria, 39005 Santander, Spain
montanjl@unican.es

**Abstract.** We provide upper bounds for the Vapnik-Chervonenkis dimension of classes of subsets of $\mathbb{R}^n$ that can be recognized by computer programs built from *arithmetical assignments, infinitely differentiable algebraic operations* (like $k$-root extraction and, more generally, operations defined by algebraic series of fractional powers), *conditional statements* and *while instructions*. This includes certain classes of GP-trees considered in Genetic Programming for symbolic regression and bi-classification. As a consequence we show explicit quantitative properties that can help to design the fitness function of a GP learning machine.

**Keywords:** Machine Learning, Vapnik-Chervonenkis dimension, Genetic Programming.

## 1 Introduction

In this paper, we are interested in a general class of computer programs working with real numbers that include operations like $+, -, *, /$, $\mathcal{C}^\infty$-algebraic operations, conditional statements and *while* instructions.

We propose a combinatorial model to deal with computer programs which consists of a finite directed graph whose nodes have associated either a computational instruction or a test sign condition (branch operation). This graph may contain cycles representing *while* instructions. This representation of computer programs involving real numbers is inspired in the algebraic computation tree model used by Ben-Or in ([3]) and other authors (see [1],[2],[13], [14]) to compute lower complexity bounds on certain computational problems having an algebraic flavor. Here a directed acyclic graph is used to represent computations that do not contain loops. Our computation model can also be interpreted as a finite Real Turing Machine (or BSS-machine) in the spirit of the work developed in the seminal paper by Blum, Shub and Smale, where the foundations of a computability theory and complexity over the real numbers is developed ([5]). As

---

* Partially supported by spanish grant TIN2007-67466-C02-02.

D. Borrajo, L. Castillo, and J.M. Corchado (Eds.): CAEPIA 2007, LNAI 4788, pp. 190–199, 2007.

main difference w. r. t. the BSS-model our machine incorporates infinitely differentiable algebraic operations and can be easily endowed with other operators if requested by the user. Another interpretation of our combinatorial model are the flowcharts used in programming languages to specify algorithms.

The paper is organized as follows. Section 2 describes a combinatorial model for GP-trees and contains an estimation of the number of parameters, equations and inequations necessary to specify a "generic" program. This estimation (see Theorem 8) is the main technical tool in this paper. Section 3 contains VC bounds for families of computer programs: in Theorem 11 we show that the VC dimension of programs dealing with infinitely differentiable algebraic functions of bounded degree is at most quadratic in the number of programable parameters. Combining the VC bounds given in Section 3 with classical results from Statistical Learning Theory, reviewed in Section 4, we provide, in Section 5, some general guidelines to build the fitness function of a GP learning machine. Finally, in Section 6 we point out the limitations of our results and give some pointers to related work.

## 2    A Combinatorial Machine Model for Some Computer Programs Represented by GP-Trees

Historically the first GP search space was a subset of the LISP language (see [11]). Today, GP has extended to deal with any tree structured search space. This space is usually describe from a set of leaves or terminals $T = \{x_1, x_2, ...\}$ including constants, variables and auxiliary variables and a set of nodes representing the operators with a given arity $N = \{f_{k1}, f_{k2}, ...\}$. The search space includes all well-formed expressions , recursively defined as being either a terminal or the application of a $k$-ary operator $f_k$ to a list of $k$ well formed expressions. Sometimes is convenient to interpret the search space as the set of sentences recognized by a grammar.

*Example 1. Rational functions.* A simple example of tree structured search space is that of rational functions of any degree of variables $x_1, ..., x_n$. The set of terminals includes all variables $x_i$ and a particular $\mathbb{R}$ terminal standing for any real valued constant. The set of nodes includes the binary operations $+, -, *, /$.

*Example 2. Computer programs.* Another tree-structured space is that of computer programs. The main restriction is that only functions returned a value can be represented. As in the general tree case a program or a function is recursively defined as a terminal, or as the result of a $k$-ary operator applied to $k$-functions.

(1) The terminal set includes the input variables of the program, the local variables and the constants $\mathbb{R}$.
(2) The node set includes all structured instructions and assignments:

– Branching instructions (*if - then - else, switch*) are $k$-ary operators, calling one of the 2...$k$ arguments depending on the value of the first argument.

- Loop instructions (*while - do -*) is a binary operator iteratively calling both its arguments and returning its last argument.
- Assignments: a binary operator := setting its first argument to its second argument.
- Operational instructions: a set of $k$-ary operators $f_k$, where the $f_k$ are rational functions or, more generally, $\mathcal{C}^\infty$-algebraic functions. We assume a general degree bound $d$ for all $\mathcal{C}^\infty$-algebraic functions appearing as nodes. In the case of rational functions this corresponds to the usual degree notion. In the case of a $\mathcal{C}^\infty$-algebraic function $f(x_1, ..., x_n)$ the degree is the degree of a minimal polynomial vanishing in the graph of the function $f(x_1, ..., x_n)$ (see [6] for technical details).

*Remark 3.* Examples of infinitely differentiable algebraic functions of degree bounded by $d$ are the degree $d$ polynomials, rational maps with numerator and denominator given by degree $d$ polynomials and also functions including $k$-root extraction, $k \leq d$. Other more sophisticated examples are Puiseux series, i.e. series having fractional exponents like $\sum_{i=k}^{\infty} a_i x^{\frac{i}{q}}$ with $k \in \mathbb{Z}$ , $q \in \mathbb{N}^+$ and $a_i \in \mathbb{R}$. See [6] for a definition and properties of Puiseux series.

*Remark 4.* The above tree structured space of computer programs corresponds for instance to a subset of the C (or Pascal) language. Operations like $+, -, *, /$ are included in the description of operational instructions given in Example 2 since they can be represented by degree 2 rational maps (in the case of $*$ or $/$) and by linear maps in the case of $+, -$.

Next we propose a representation of computer programs having a more combinatorial flavor. In terms of data structures this representation could be considerably shorter than a GP-tree. However we adopt here the opposite viewpoint: GP-trees are data structures representing programs.

**Definition 5.** *A program* $\mathcal{P}$ *with* $n$ *input variables, using* $m$ *variables and size* $N$ *is a finite directed connected graph with nodes numbered* $\mathcal{N} = \{1, ...N\}$. *There are four type of nodes: input, computation, branch and output. In addition the machine has three spaces: the input space* $I_\mathcal{P} = \mathbb{R}^n$, *the work space* $S_\mathcal{P} = \mathbb{R}^m$ *and the output space* $O_\mathcal{P} = \mathbb{R}$. *Associated with each node of the graph there is computational instruction and a next node.*

*(1) Associated with the input node there is a linear map* $I : I_\mathcal{P} \longrightarrow S_\mathcal{P}$ *and a unique next node that we denote by* $\eta(1)$.

*(2) Each computation node* $\nu$ *has associated a computation map* $f_\nu : S_\mathcal{P} \longrightarrow S_\mathcal{P}$ *and a unique next node* $\eta(\nu)$. *The computation map is either a rational map in the variables* $x_1, .., x_m$ *or a infinitely differentiable algebraic map belonging to a fix set* $\{h_1, ..., h_l\}$. *We assume a uniform degree bound* $d$ *for both, rational maps and the* $h_i$.

*(3)Each branch node* $\nu$ *has an associated branching function* $f_\nu$ *of the same kind as computation nodes. The next node along the* $YES$ *outgoing edge,* $\eta^+(\nu)$, *is*

associated with the condition $f_\nu \geq 0$ and the next node along the NO outgoing edge, $\eta^-(\nu)$, with $f_\nu < 0$.

*(4)each output node $\eta$ has an associated linear map that we also denote by $O_\eta$ : $S_P \longrightarrow \mathbb{R}$ and no next node.*

*Remark 6.* To a flowchart $\mathcal{P}$ represented as before one can associate a function from a subset of the input space to the output space, $O_\mathcal{P}$. Function $O_\mathcal{P}$ is defined by "following the flow".

We give next lemma without proof. Its meaning is the following: without lost of computational power we can assume that for every branching node $\nu$, $f_\nu = x_1$. The technical details are tedious but the argument is clear: just add a new computational node before each branching node keeping $f_\nu$ in the first memory register $x_1$.

**Lemma 7.** *For each program $\mathcal{P}$ with $n$ input variables, using $m$ variables and size $N$ there is a program $\mathcal{P}'$ with $n$ input variables, using $m + 1$ variables and size at most $2N$ such that:*

*(1)Every branching node $\nu$ of $\mathcal{P}'$ satisfies $f_\nu = x_1$.*

*(2)Both programs compute the same function, this is $f_\mathcal{P} = f_{\mathcal{P}'}$.*

*(3)If $D_\mathcal{P}$ is the maximum of the degrees of the rational maps $f_\nu$ then the corresponding degree $D_{\mathcal{P}'} \leq D_\mathcal{P} + 1$.*

*(4) The number of nodes traversed by input $x$ until the computation of $\mathcal{P}'$ over $x$ halts is at most the double of the number of nodes traversed by input $x$ until the computation of $\mathcal{P}$ over $x$ halts.*

We call a program as that described in Lemma 7 *normal*. From now on we deal with normal programs.

**Theorem 8.** *For any natural numbers $n, m, N \in \mathbb{N}$ (representing the dimension of the input space, the dimension of the work space and the program size, resp.), for any degree bound $d > 0$, and any set $\{h_1, ..., h_l\}$ of $\mathcal{C}^\infty$ -algebraic functions and any time bound $T > 0$ there exists a universal boolean formula $\Phi(x, z)$ such that for any program $\mathcal{P}$ having parameters $(n, m, N, d)$ and using operations in $\{h_1, ..., h_l\}$ and for any $x \in \mathbb{R}^n$ the following holds: $x$ is accepted by program $\mathcal{P}$ within time complexity $T$ if and only if there is $z \in \mathbb{R}^t$ such that $\Phi(x, z)$ is satisfied. Moreover, the formula $\Phi(x, z)$ has the following properties.*

*(1) $x = (x_1, ..., x_n)$, $z = (z_1, z_2, ..., z_t)$, and*

$$t \in O((4N + m + 2mDN)(T + 1)), \qquad (1)$$

*where $D = \binom{m + d}{d}$ is the number of monomials of a degree $d$ polynomial in $n$ variables.*

*(2) $\Phi(x, z)$ contains at most*

$$s \in O((N + m)(T + 1)) \tag{2}$$

*polynomial equations in*

$$(z_1, z_2, ..., z_t, h_j).$$

*(3) the equations have degree at most $O(Nd)$.*

**Sketch of the proof.** We use the idea of describing the computation process by a "computer endomorphism" (see [4]). Let $\mathcal{P}$ be a program. Let $\mathcal{N} = \{1, ..., N\}$ be the set of nodes of $\mathcal{P}$ with 1 the input node and $N$ the output node. We call the space of node/state pairs $\mathcal{N} \times S_{\mathcal{P}}$ the full state space of the program. Associated with $\mathcal{P}$ there is the computer endomorphism:

$$H : \mathcal{N} \times S_{\mathcal{P}} \to \mathcal{N} \times S_{\mathcal{P}} \tag{3}$$

of the full state space to itself. To describe $H$ explicitly, it is convenient to have the next node assignment and the computation maps defined for each node $\nu \in \mathcal{N}$. Thus we let

$$\eta_\nu = N \ for \ \nu = N \ and \tag{4}$$

$$f_\nu(x) = x \ for \ \nu = 1, \ N \ or \ a \ branch \ node. \tag{5}$$

Let $\mathcal{B}$ be the subset of branch nodes of $\mathcal{P}$ and let $\mathcal{C}$ be $\mathcal{N} - \mathcal{B}$. Then

$$H(\nu, x) = (\eta_\nu, f_\nu(x)) \ for \ \nu \in \mathcal{C} \tag{6}$$

and according to Lemma 7 for $\nu \in \mathcal{B}$

$$H(\nu, x) = (\eta_\nu^-, f_\nu(x)) \ if \ x_1 < 0 \tag{7}$$

$$H(\nu, x) = (\eta_\nu^+, f_\nu(x)) \ if \ x_1 > 0 \tag{8}$$

To say that $x$ can be recognized by program $\mathcal{P}$ within time $T$ is to say that there is a sequence $(z^0, z^1, ..., z^T) \in (\mathcal{N} \times S_{\mathcal{P}})^{T+1}$ satisfying the conditions:

$$z^k = H(z^{k-1}), \ 1 \le k \le T \tag{9}$$

$$z^0 = (1, I_{\mathcal{P}}(x)) \ and \ z^T = (N, u) \tag{10}$$

for some $u \in S_{\mathcal{P}}$.

Now the result follows analyzing each equation in systems 9, and 10.

To show bound in Equation 1, since there are $T + 1$ equations in system 9, 10, we can write $t \le h(T + 1)$, where $h$ is a bound on the number of variables for each equation in this system. Next we show that $h \le 4N + m + 2mND$. Note that:

- $3N$ parameters to codify the next node map $\eta$. Briefly, this is done as follows. A sequence $(i, k_i, j_i)_{1 \leq i \leq N}$ where $i \in \mathcal{N}$, $k_i = j_i = \eta(i)$ if $i$ is a computation node and $k_i = \eta^-(i)$, $j_i = \eta^+(i)$ if $i$ is a branch node.
- $N$ parameters to represent the current node. This is done as follows. Node $i \in \mathcal{N}$ is represented as an element of the vector space $\mathbb{R}^N$ by considering the injection from $\mathcal{N}$ in $\mathbb{R}^N$ given by $j \rightarrow e_j$ where $e_j$ is the $j$- canonical vector.
- $m$ parameters for the work space $\mathcal{S} = \mathbb{R}^m$.
- $mD$ parameters to codify a polynomial map $f_v : \mathbb{R}^m \rightarrow \mathbb{R}^m$ and consequently $2mD$ parameters to codify a rational map giving a total of $2mND$ parameters to codify the set of all possible computation maps, since there are at most $N$ of them.

To analyze the number of equations at each step we need a linear number of equations and inequations in $N$ to express the next node operation and a linear number of equations and inequations in $N + m$ to express the next state. Giving a total of $s \in O((N + m)(T + 1))$ number of such equations and inequations. The degree bound easily follows taking into account that we deal with degree $d$ polynomial maps of the form $\sum_{v_1, \ldots v_n} a_{v_1, \ldots v_n} x^{v_1} \ldots x^{v_n}$, and we consider coefficients $a_{v_1, \ldots v_n}$ as new variables. Since the system may contain rational maps, the operation "clearing denominators" gives the bound $O(Nd)$.

## 3   VC Dimension Bounds

The Vapnik-Chervonenkis dimension of a family of sets is defined as follows ([15]).

**Definition 9.** *Le $\mathcal{F}$ be a class of subsets of a set $X$. We say that $\mathcal{F}$ shatters a set $A \subset X$ if for every subset $E \subset A$ there exists $S \in \mathcal{F}$ such that $E = S \cap A$. The VC dimension of $\mathcal{F}$ is the cardinality of the largest set that is shattered by $\mathcal{F}$.*

In order to proof our main result it is necessary to bound the VC dimension of families of sets defined by equalities and inequalities. The following lemma is a consequence of [10] and [13]. It generalizes a previous result in [9] that deals with the easier case of polynomials.

**Lemma 10.** *Let $\Psi(x, y)$ be a boolean formula containing $s$ distinct atomic predicates where each predicate is an equality or inequality over $n + k$ variables (representing $x \in \mathbb{R}^n$, and $y \in \mathbb{R}^k$, respectively). We suppose that the terms in $\Psi$ are polynomials of degree at most $d$ in the variables in $x$, $y$ and $h_i(x, y)$, $i = 1, \ldots, q$, where the $h_i$ are infinitely differentiable algebraic functions of degree at most $d$. For any $y \in \mathbb{R}^k$, let $W_y \subset \mathbb{R}^n$ be the set of instances $x$ such that $\Psi(x, y)$ is satisfied. The family $\Omega = \{W_y\}_{y \in \mathbb{R}^k}$ verifies:*

$$VC - dim(\Omega) \leq 4(k + q + 1)^2 \log(2d) + (16 + 2 \log s)k \tag{11}$$

Next, we state our main result.

**Theorem 11.** *Let* $\mathcal{H} = H_{n,m,N,d,T}$ *be the family of subsets* $W \subset \mathbb{R}^n$ *that can accepted within time* $T$ *by some computer program of size* $N$, *with* $n$ *input variables,* $m$ *auxiliary variables, using rational maps and* $\mathcal{C}^\infty$-*algebraic functions in the set* $h_1, ..., h_l$ *of degree at most* $d$. *Let* $t$ *and* $s$ *as in Theorem 8. Then, the VC dimension of* $\mathcal{H}$ *satisfies:*

$$VC - dim(\mathcal{H}) \in O((t + l + 1)^2 log(2Nd) + (16 + 2\ log\ s)t) \tag{12}$$

*Proof.* Just plug Theorem 8 in Lemma 10.

**Interpretation.** Note that quantity $t$ in Theorem 8 represents the number of programable parameters (i.e., variables needed to parameterize a program) of the class $\mathcal{H}$. Hence, Theorem 11 provides an upper bound for the VC-dimension which is quadratic in the number of programable parameters.

## 4   Elements of Statistical Learning Theory

Along this paper we restrict ourselves to binary classification. We consider an input space $X = \mathbb{R}^n$ and an output space $Y = \{-1, 1\}$. We observe a sequence of $n$ i.i.d. pairs $(X_i, Y_i)$ sample according to an unknown probability measure $\rho$ on the product space $X \times Y$. The goal is to construct a function $f : X \longrightarrow Y$ which predicts the value $y \in Y$ from a given $x \in X$. The criterium to choose function $f$ is a low probability of error $\rho\{x \in X : f(x) \neq y\}$. The *error* of a function $f$ is defined as

$$\varepsilon(f) = \rho\{(x, y) \in X \times Y : f(x) \neq y\} \tag{13}$$

As usual, $\rho$ can be decomposed as the product given by the marginal distribution $\rho_X$ and the conditional distribution $\rho(Y|X = x)$. According to well known results from Statistical Learning Theory (c. f. [12] ), the Bayes classifier $t_\rho(x) = sgn\ f_\rho(x)$ defined by the sign of the regression function $f_\rho(x) = \int y d\rho(Y|X = x)$, achieves the minimum error over all possible measurable functions, that is:

$$\varepsilon(t_\rho) = inf_f \varepsilon(f) \tag{14}$$

We now consider the sampling. Let $Z = X \times Y$. Let $z = (x_i, y_i)_{1 \leq i \leq m} \in Z^m$ i.e. $m$ samples independently drawn according to $\rho$. Here $Z^m$ denotes the $m - fold$ Cartesian product of $Z$. The empirical error of $f$ (w.r.t. $z$) is

$$\varepsilon_z(f) = \frac{1}{m}\sharp\{i \in \{1..m\} : y_i \neq f(x_i)\} \tag{15}$$

Next, we recall a well known result from Statistical Learning Theory about structural risk minimization. A more complete statement can be found in [12].

**Theorem 12.** *Let $\{F_k\}_k$ be a family of hypothesis spaces with finite $VC$ dimensions $\{V_k\}_k$ . Let $F = \cup_{k \in \mathbb{N}} F_k$. Assume that for all probability distributions $\rho$ the error of the Bayes classifier $\varepsilon(t_\rho)$ is $L* = \inf_{f \in F} \varepsilon(f)$. Then, given $z = (x_i, y_i)_{1 \leq i \leq n} \in Z^s$ i.e. $s$ examples, consider a function $f \in F$ minimizing*

$$\varepsilon_z(f) + \sqrt{\frac{32}{s} V_k} \ (log \ e + log \ s), \tag{16}$$

*where*

$$k = min\{l \in \mathbb{N} : f \in F_l\} \tag{17}$$

*Then*

*(1) The generalization error $\varepsilon(f)$ with probability 1 converges to $L*$ when $s$ goes to infinity.*

*(2) If additionally one optimal function $f$ belongs to $F_k$ then for any $s$ and $\epsilon$ such that $V_k(log \ e + log \ s) \ \leq s \ \epsilon^2/512$, the error $\varepsilon(f) < \epsilon$ with probability at most*

$$\Delta e^{-s\epsilon^2/128} + 8 s^{V_{fP}} e^{-s\epsilon^2/512} \tag{18}$$

*Here $\Delta = \sum_{k=1}^{\infty} e^{-V_k}$ is assumed finite.*

## 5   Some Remarks About the Selection of the Fitness Function in GP

Next result is the algebraic counterpart of [8], Theorem D, for the case of concept classes represented by GP-trees including infinitely differentiable algebraic functions.

**Theorem 13.** *Consider $q_f, t_f, d_f, n_f$ and $z_f$ integer sequences, non-decreasing functions of $f \in \mathbb{N}$. Let $H_f$ be the set of GP-trees representing programs with time complexity $t_f$, with state space $\mathbb{R}^{z_f}$, size $n_f$, $q_f$ operational instructions of degree bounded by $d_f$. For each $f$ let*

$$V_f = (r_f + 1 + q_f)^2 \ log \ (2n_f d_f) + (16 + 2s_f)r_f,$$

*where $r_f$ is the number of programable parameters of $H_f$ and*

$$s_f = (n_f + z_f)(t_f + 1).$$

Let $H = \cup_{f \in \mathbb{N}} H_f$. Assume that for all probability distributions $\rho$ the error of the Bayes classifier $\varepsilon(t_\rho)$ is $L* = \inf_{f \in H}$. Then, given $z = (x_i, y_i)_{1 \leq i \leq s} \in Z^s$ i.e. $s$ examples, consider a program $\mathcal{P} \in H$ minimizing

$$\varepsilon_z(\mathcal{P}) + \sqrt{\frac{32}{s} V_{fP}} \ (log \ e + log \ s), \tag{19}$$

where

$$f_P = min\{f \in \mathbb{N} : \mathcal{P} \in H_f\} \tag{20}$$

*Then*

*(1) The generalization error $\varepsilon(P)$ converges in probability to the error of the Bayes classifier $L*$.*

*(2) If additionally one optimal program $P$ belongs to $H_{f_P}$ then for any $s$ and $\epsilon$ such that $V_{f_P}(\log e + \log s) \leq s\,\epsilon^2/512$, the error $\varepsilon(P) < \epsilon$ with probability at most*

$$\Delta e^{-s\epsilon^2/128} + 8s^{V_{f_P}} e^{-s\epsilon^2/512} \tag{21}$$

*Here $\Delta = \sum_{f=1}^{\infty} e^{-V_f}$ is assumed finite*

*Proof.* Just plug Theorem 11 in Theorem 12.

**Interpretation.** Suppose we have to design a GP algorithm to find a computer program that explains $s$ classified examples $z = (x_i, y_i) \in X \times Y$. There are two problems involved : (1) what search space should be used, and (2) how to define the fitness function. A naive approach yields to conjecture a class $H$ of computer programs after some previous experimentation have being performed and then use as fitness of a program $P \in H$ the empirical risk $\varepsilon_z(P)$, i. e. the number of examples that are misclassified by program $P$. A second approach is the following. Consider as fitness of program $P$ a compromise between empirical accuracy and regularization as suggested by Equation 19:

$$fitness(P) = \frac{1}{m}\sharp\{i \in \{1..m\} : y_i \neq O_P(x_i)\} + \sqrt{\frac{32}{s}V_{f_P}\,(\log e + \log s)} \tag{22}$$

According to Theorem 13 this yields to universal consistency plus a strong convergence rate property provided that the GP algorithm minimizes the fitness function.

## 6   Discussion and Related Work

Universal consistency, the convergence to the minimum possible error rate in learning through genetic programming, and code bloat (excessive increase of code size) are important issues in GP. A recent paper by Gelly, Teutaud and Schoenauer ([8]) proposes a theoretical analysis of universal consistency and code bloat in the framework of symbolic regression in GP from the view point of Statistical Learning Theory. They have shown that minimizing the empirical risk, that is, choosing the program that minimizes the number of misclassified examples (in bi- classification problems) is not enough for ensuring any satisfactory form of consistency while minimizing the structural risk warrants convergence and universal consistency when the search space is given by computer programs including the usual arithmetic operations and exponentials. We have stated an analogous result in the context of computer programs that include infinitely differentiable algebraic functions as described in Section 2. We have also pointed out how to use this result to define the fitness of a program in GP. The main limits of these results, in the boundary between theory and practice, is the fact that we assume that GP finds a program which is empirically the best, that is, given a set of examples and a fitness function based for instance in structural risk minimization (i.e. including some penalization) it is supposed that GP does find one program in that search space that minimizes the fitness. Of course this can fail in practice. Nevertheless, as it is pointed in [8], consistency is vital for the practitioner too: it would be totally pointless to try to approximate an empirical optimal function without any guarantee that the empirical optimum is anywhere close to the ideal optimal solution we are in fact looking for.

# References

1. Aldaz, M., Heintz, J., Matera, G., Montaña, J.L., Pardo, L.M.: Time-space trade-offs in algebraic complexity theory. Real computation and complexity (Schloss Dagstuhl, 1998). J. Complexity 16(1), 2–49 (2000)
2. Aldaz, M., Heintz, J., Matera, G., Montaña, J.L., Pardo, L.M.: Combinatorial hardness proofs for polynomial evaluation (extended abstract). In: Brim, L., Gruska, J., Zlatuška, J. (eds.) MFCS 1998. LNCS, vol. 1450, pp. 167–175. Springer, Heidelberg (1998)
3. Ben-Or, M.: Lower Bounds for Algebraic Computation Trees STOC 1983, pp. 80–86 (1981)
4. Blum, L., Cucker, F., Shub, M., Smale, S.: Complexity and real computation. Springer, New York (1997)
5. Blum, L., Shub, M., Smale, S.: On a theory of computation over the real numbers: NP completeness, recursive functions and universal machines [Bull. Amer. Math. Soc (N.S.) 21 (1989), no. 1, 1–46; MR0974426 (90a:68022)]. In: Workshop on Dynamical Systems (Trieste, 1988), pp. 23–52, Pitman Res. Notes Math. Ser. 221, Longman Sci. Tech., Harlow (1990)
6. Bochnak, J., Coste, M., Roy, M.-F.: Géométrie algébrique réelle (French) [Real algebraic geometry] Ergebnisse der Mathematik und ihrer Grenzgebiete (3) [Results in Mathematics and Related Areas (3)], vol. 12. Springer-Verlag, Berlin (1987)
7. Cucker, F., Smale, S.: On the Mathematical foundations of learning. Bulletin (New Series) Of the AMS 39(1), 1–4 (2001)
8. Gelly, S., Teytaud, O., Bredeche, N., Schoenauer, M.: Universal Consistency and Bloat in GP. Revue d'Intelligence Artificielle 20(6), 805–827 (2006)
9. Goldberg, P., Jerrum, M.: Bounding the Vapnik-Chervonenkis dimension of concept classes parametrizes by real numbers. Machine Learning 18, 131–148 (1995)
10. Karpinski, M., Macintyre, A.: Bounding VC-dimension for neural networks: progress and prospects. In: Vitányi, P.M.B. (ed.) EuroCOLT 1995. LNCS, vol. 904, pp. 337–341. Springer, Heidelberg (1995)
11. Koza, J.R.: Genetic Programming: On the Programming of Computers by Means of Natural Selection. MIT Press, Cambridge, MA, USA (1992)
12. Lugosi, G.: Pattern clasification and learning theory. In: Gyorfi, L. (ed.) Principles of nonparametric learning, pp. 5–62. Springer, Vienna (2002)
13. Montaña, J.L., Pardo, L.M., Ramanakoraisina, R.: An extension of Warren's lower bounds for approximations. J. Pure Appl. Algebra 87(3), 251–258 (1993)
14. Montaña, J.L., Pardo, L.M.: Lower bounds for arithmetic networks. Appl. Algebra Engrg. Comm. Comput. 4(1), 1–24 (1993)
15. Vapnik, V.: Statistical learning theory. John Willey & Sons, Chichester (1998)

# A Workflow for the Networked Ontologies Lifecycle:
# A Case Study in FAO of the UN

Óscar Muñoz-García[1], Asunción Gómez-Pérez[1], Marta Iglesias-Sucasas[2],
and Soonho Kim[2]

[1] Ontology Engineering Group - Universidad Politécnica de Madrid
[2] Food and Agriculture Organization of the United Nations

**Abstract.** This document shows a preliminary framework for editing *networked ontologies* in the context of the NeOn project. The goal is to manage, in a collaborative way, multiple networked ontologies for large-scale semantic applications. This paper shows the main concepts on the editorial workflow and several lifecycle use cases. The ontologies produced with this framework will be used by the Food and Agriculture Organization of the United Nations (FAO) in many different large applications such the *Fisheries Stock Depletion Assessment System*[4]. Therefore a major goal for FAO is to have a strong and reliable ontology management system for editing the networked ontologies that applications will use as a basis. This framework for editing networked ontologies is being developed in the context of the NeOn Project[1]. What we present here is a brief summary of the activities carried out in this project regarding user requirements and subsequent use case analysis.

**Keywords:** networked, ontology, workflow, fisheries, lifecycle, FAO, NeOn.

## 1   Introduction

The Food and Agriculture Organization of the United Nations (FAO) leads international effort to defeat hunger. The Organization acts as a neutral forum where all nations dialogue as equals to debate policy and negotiate agreements FAO is also a source of knowledge and information to help developing countries and countries in transition modernise and improve Agriculture, Forestry and Fisheries practices and ensure good nutrition for all.

Efficiently managing information and knowledge is extremely important to FAO and that is reflected in Article 1 of its Constitution, which reads that "The Organization must collect, analyse, interpret, and disseminate information relating to nutrition, food Agriculture and development."

In this line, in the Fisheries domain, one of the biggest challenges both at present and in the future is to manage the world's fish stocks for achieving long-term sustainable Fisheries. For this purpose, the Fisheries department of the

---

[1] For more information see: http://www.neon-project.org

D. Borrajo, L. Castillo, and J.M. Corchado (Eds.): CAEPIA 2007, LNAI 4788, pp. 200–209, 2007.
© Springer-Verlag Berlin Heidelberg 2007

FAO has several information and knowledge organization systems to facilitate and secure the long-term, sustainable development and utilisation of the world's Fisheries and Aquaculture. However, currently each system has its own community having each of them its own vocabulary, different languages, etc. This constitutes a separate knowledge collective.

Current FAO Fisheries systems manage and disseminate statistical data on fishing, GIS data, information on aquaculture, geographic entities, description of fish stocks, etc. Although much of the data are 'structured', they are not necessarily interoperable because they are expressed in different representation languages and according to different models, developed using different technologies or deployed in different platforms. These data sources could be better exploited by bringing together related and relevant information, along with the use of the Fisheries ontologies, to provide inference-based services, enabling policy makers and national governments to make informed decisions.

The current technical state does not solve the problem in applications where complex ontologies should be created and managed collaboratively and in highly dynamic, multilingual and constantly evolving environments. There are several tools such Protégé[2] for editing ontologies, $R_2O$ [6] for making mappings between ontologies and data bases, RDF-Gravity for visualising[3], the ontology alignment API and Server[4], etc. Despite there are a lot them that solve many problems such ontology learning, ontology upgrade and ontology alignment, these tools are stand alone and make the process of managing ontological information very complex basing the interoperability between them in exporting and importing processes that sometimes degrades the information. With respect to methodologies, Methontology [7] and On-To-Knowledge [5] do not define a workflow for editing ontologies taking into account the roles involved in the ontology development. Also these methodologies are defined for building ontologies from scratch not taking into account the reuse of existing ones. All the aforementioned approaches do not consider collaborative and distributed construction of ontologies when developers are geographically distributed using different languages. In fact the first method that included a proposal for collaborative construction was Co4 [2] and the first tool was Tadzebao and WebOnto[8].

To solve the above problems, the goal of the NeOn project is to create the first ever service-oriented, open infrastructure, and associated methodology to support the development lifecycle for a new generation of semantic applications being the FAO case study a complex use case that will validate the NeOn methodologies and the NeOn Toolkit (which is on development, but includes several parts partially tested). NeOn provides FAO with a great opportunity to develop an appropriate framework to manage the Fisheries ontologies and their lifecycles, as well as to implement a semantic web Fisheries Stock Depletion Assessment System that exploits those ontologies.

---

[2] For more information see: http://protege.stanford.edu
[3] See: http://semweb.salzburgresearch.at/apps/rdf-gravity/index.html
[4] For more information see: http://alignapi.gforge.inria.fr

In this context, one of the most important goals for FAO, is to develop a framework and support tools where ontologies can be modelled, populated, validated and deployed, and at the same time, mechanisms are put in place to facilitate that the existing ontological resources used by applications are maintained and kept up-to-date, and that when applying changes (to single ontologies or networks) all dependencies between systems continue to hold.

While requirements for ontology design, population and validation are common in ontology engineering environments, the FAO case study looks for a more articulated approach paying special attention to an editorial workflow, key to ensure that users can modify and update ontologies in a controlled and coherent manner, especially for those ontologies already deployed on the Internet. At the same time, this controlled environment for the editorial workflow will provide the necessary support to appropriately version ontologies deployed on the Internet, and to ensure semantic web applications reliability on the ontologies exploited.

# 2    Fisheries Ontologies Lifecycle

## 2.1    Users

The Fisheries ontologies lifecycle will be managed by a combination of two major types of users: ontology engineers and subject experts.

Ontology engineers are specialised in ontology modelling techniques and issues; have from basic to advanced knowledge of ontology engineering tools and inference engines, but may know little about the domain to be modelled. Usually, they are in charge of defining the initial skeleton of the ontology, and in so doing, they take into account the purpose of the ontology, possible interactions with legacy systems, and other relevant issues.

Ontology editors are domain experts, although they can also be information management specialists, terminologists or translators. they are in charge of the everyday editing and maintenance work of the networked multilingual ontologies and they can be in charge of developing specific fragments of ontologies, revising work done by others, and developing multilingual versions of ontologies.

## 2.2    Roles

Users participating in the Fisheries Ontologies Lifecycle will need to be authorised in the system to get access rights by the system Administrators. Authorised users will be assigned roles to various ontology modules as either Ontology engineers, Subject experts, Validators or Viewers, depending on the kind of rights they will have and the kind of tasks they will be assigned to.

Subject expert, validator and viewer correspond to the possible roles of the Ontology editors within the editorial workflow.

- Subject experts are the editors inserting or modifying ontology content.
- Validators revise, approve or reject changes made by subject experts, and they are the only ones who can copy changes into the production environment for external availability.

– Viewers are users authorised to enter in the system and consult approved information about ontologies but they cannot edit the ontologies.

## 2.3  Major Processes

As illustrated in figure 1, the Fisheries ontologies lifecycle consists of the following major processes:

**1. Ontology conceptualisation:** Ontology engineers organise and structure the domain information into meaningful models at the knowledge level. In the fishery domain, they collect the information from Fisheries databases, information system and documents, and analyse it together with Fisheries domain experts in FAO. The conceptualisation process results in an ontology model with most of the concept level entities, such as, classes, properties and restrictions.

**2. Ontology population:** Ontology engineers perform the knowledge acquisition activities with various manual or (semi)automatic methods various methods to transform unstructured, semi-structured and/or structured data sources into ontology instances. In the Fisheries domain, this process consist mainly in converting semi-structured data sources (fishery fact sheets in XML format) and structured data source (from relational databases) into corresponding instances in the conceptualised Fisheries ontology. Figure 2 shows the possible population sources.

**3. and 4. Iteration of conceptualisation and population process until getting a stable version:** Ontology engineers will iterate the conceptualisation and population processes until getting a populated ontology that satisfies all requirements and it is considered stable. Once achieved, the ontology will enter into the test and maintenance environment, implemented through the editorial workflow.

**5. Ontology validation and update through editorial workflow:** The editorial workflow will allow Ontology editors to consult, validate and modify the

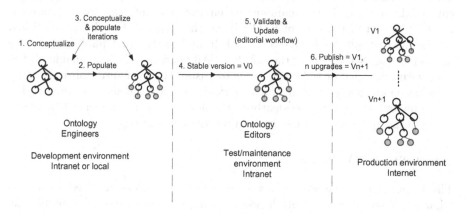

**Fig. 1.** Fisheries Ontologies Lifecycle

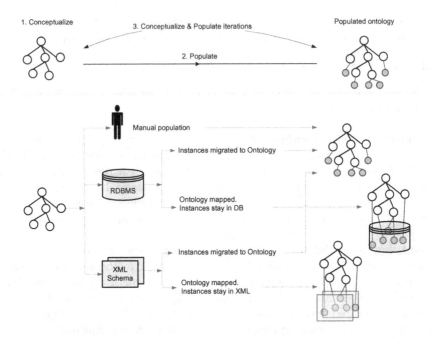

**Fig. 2.** Ontology Population

ontology keeping track of all changes in a controlled and coherent manner. Any ontology to be released on the production environment needs to pass through the editorial workflow being it the first time for version 1 or for any subsequent upgrade. The editorial workflow is explained in detail in the following section.

**6. Ontology publication:** Once ontology editors in charge of validation consider the ontology final, they are authorised to release it on the Internet and make it available to end users and systems. A release will consist in making a copy of the ontology in the maintenance environment into the production environment, which in the case of FAO will be the Internet. Ontologies published on the Internet will be always versioned, from 1 for the first published version to N+1 to the N upgrade of the ontology. All versions will be available all the time with necessary metadata in order to ensure that semantic third party semantic web applications relying on a particular version will keep working relying on a previous version independently of the new one until a decision is made to upgrade the application, if required, to use the new ontology version.

### 2.4   Editorial Workflow

The Fisheries editorial workflow will implement the necessary mechanisms to allow Ontology editors to consult and if authorised, validate and/or modify the ontology in a controlled and coherent manner, ensuring that only fully validated ontologies will be released on the Internet.

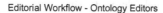

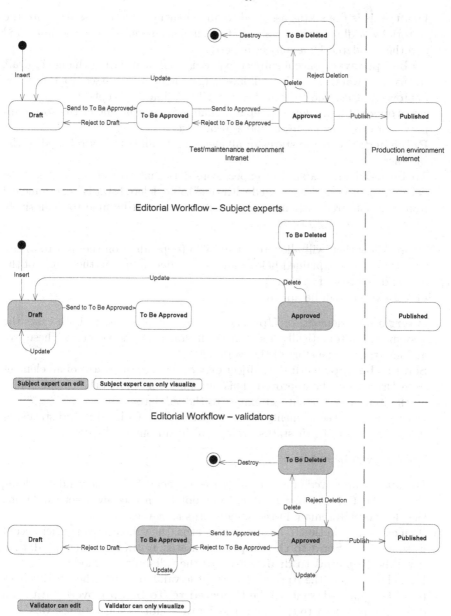

**Fig. 3.** Editorial Workflow

The workflow is based on the assignation of a status to each element of the ontology. Only if all the elements have "Approved" status, the ontology can be published or upgraded.

The possible statuses for each element are:

- **Draft:** this is the status assigned to any element when it pass first into the editorial workflow, or it is assigned to a single element when it was approved and then updated by a subject expert.
- **To be approved:** once a subject expert is confident with a change in draft status and wants it to be validated, the element is passed to the to be approved status, and remains there until a validator accepts it.
- **Approved:** if a validator accepts a change in an element in the to be approved status, this passes to the approved status.
- **Published:** this is the status of all elements in an ontology released to the Internet.
- **To be deleted:** if a subject expert considers that an element needs to be deleted, the item will be flagged with the "to be deleted status" and removed from the ontology, although only a validator would be able to definitively delete it.

The workflow then will allow to set up who (depending on the user role) can do what (actions as explained below) and when (depending on the status of the element and the role of the user).

Subject experts will be able to:

- **Insert** a new element, or **Update** an approved element. In both cases the system will automatically assign a Draft status to the element. These two actions triggers the start of the workflow.
- **Send to be approved:** the subject expert changes the status of an element from Draft to To be approved. This automatically moves the responsibility on the item from the subject expert to the validator.
- Delete an approved element, which will be sent to **To be deleted** status; or delete an item in Draft status, which will be automatically deleted.

Validators will be able to:

- **Update** an approved or a to be approved element. Being the validator doing the modification, and not needing to be double checked by other validators, the element will remain in the same status as it was.
- If an element is in the To be approved status, the validator can either accept it, so it will be **Send to the Approved** status; it can be not accepted, then it will be **Rejected to draft** status, or the validator can modify it.
- If an element is in the Approved status, the validator can either send it back to To be approved, so it will be **Rejected to To be approved** status, can delete it and send it to the bin or the **To be deleted** status or the validator can modify it.
- **Delete** an element in the Approved and **Destroy** an element in the To be deleted status.
- If the validator does not agree with an element proposed To be deleted by a subject expert, and thus in the To be deleted status, the validator can **Reject the deletion**, and pass back the element to the Approved status.

– When all the elements of the ontology are approved the validator can decide to **Publish** it. This action will copy the Approved ontology into the production environment assigning it the right version, $V_1$ for the first release and $V_{N+1}$ for N subsequent releases.

# 3   Use Cases

A model of the system's functionality and environment has been developed following the Unified Process methodology [1] coming from software engineering. This section makes a brief summary of the Use-Case Model obtained.

Next we put a description of the most relevant use cases. These use cases take the NeOn metamodel as a basis. This networked ontology model has been designed in the NeOn project and is derived from the modeling primitives offered by OWL[3].

1. **Search:** While editing an ontology, the Ontology Editor is able to perform searches across the whole ontologies being edited, independently of whether the text appears in a concept label, annotation, property name, etc.
2. **Answer Query:** While editing an ontology, the Ontology Editor is able to perform queries within the ontologies being edited. The queries could be using and standard query language (e.g. SPARQL), a natural language query or a predefined query from a template . As an example, these constraints or predefined queries could be:
   – For concepts: "having parent such that ...", "having child such that ..."
   – For instances: "being an instance of ..."
   – For properties: "attached to ...", "linking..."
3. **Manage Multilinguality:** The Ontology Editor deals with the multilingual aspect of the ontologies adding languages to the ontology; doing spell-checking, managing the multilingual labels, selecting the working language, and coping with specificities of translation (i.e., no lexicalization available for concepts, available lexicalization correspond to more than once concept or conversely, several lexicalizations are possible).
4. **Export:** exporting an ontology to other formats. In example exporting ontologies into thesaurus format, which implies conversion to: TagText, RDBMS, ISO2709, SKOS and TBX.
5. **Convert:** convert an ontology from other formats, including population from databases using $R_2O$ [6] and from existing resources with implicit schema (XML).
6. **Manage Mappings:** creation of alignments between ontologies in a manual way and an semi-automatic way. Mappings between concepts or modules in different ontologies are created. For the creation of an automatic alignment the Ontology Editor gives the System two ontologies. The System returns the Ontology Editor the candidate mappings. The Ontology Editor inspects the proposed candidates one by one selecting the appropriate candidate and confirming the proposed mapping. Finally the System creates the alignment taking into account the mappings chosen.

7. **Visualize:** visualisation of ontologies and fragments of them in different ways, depending on the task to be performed. Mappings and relations between the concepts and modules in networked ontologies are visualised. Browsing an ontology and printing the visualisation is included.

8. **Modularize:** working with ontology modules; creation of modules manually and semi-automatically and merging modules. For more information about an ontology module is please see [3].

9. **Manage Provenance and Statistics:** the System captures ontology changes. The users can see the changes history, view use statistics (provenance, which system they are used by, by whom they are edited, frequency of changes, fragment/domain of the ontology changed at fastest rate) and view ontology statistics (depth, number of child nodes, number of relations and properties, number of concepts per "branch").

10. **Populate from text:** the Ontology Editor chooses the textual corpora. The System provides Ontology Editor with a list of candidate elements of the ontology (classes, instances and relations between concepts). The System shows the documents and excerpts supporting the extracted terminology, including the document metadata such as title of the document, author, data, owner, publication date. The Ontology Editor inspects and selects the appropriate candidate, and adds the selected ones to the ontology. The System populates the ontology doing previously a consistency checking of the ontology with the newly added elements.

11. **Evaluate and Validate Ontology:** the Ontology Editor can check the quality of the development of the ontology, checking for duplicates within the ontology, making comparisons with other ontologies and evaluating structural properties of the ontology.

12. **Obtain Documentation:** automatic creation of relevant metadata concerning the ontology design, such as UML-like diagrams, and documentation concerning the relations and properties used.

## 4   Conclusions

In this paper we have described the lifecycle needed for managing the networked ontologies that are used by the Food and Agriculture Organization of the United Nations. We have focussed the description in the editorial workflow and also we have enumerated some relevant use cases that describe the features demanded by FAO in order to create and maintain the ontologies.

The current technical state is not enough to cover the needs because there is not an integrated tool that provides all the features needed. So we have introduced the NeOn Toolkit that is been developed in the context of the NeOn project where FAO takes part as a case study partner.

## Acknowledgements

This work has been supported by the NeOn project (IST-2005-027595). We are very grateful to our NeOn partners for their revisions and comments.

# References

1. Larman, C., O'Hagan, D. (eds.): Applying UML and patterns: an introduction to object-oriented analysis and design and iterative development, 3rd edn. Prentice Hall, Upper Saddle River (2005)
2. Euzenat, J.: Building Consensual Knowledge Bases: Context and Architecture. In: Mars, N. (ed.) KBKS 1995. Second International Conference on Building and Sharing of Very Large-Scale Knowledge Bases, University of Twente, Enschede, The Netherlands, pp. 143–155. IOS Press, Amsterdam (1995)
3. D1.1.1 Networked Ontology Model v1. Technical report. NeOn (2006)
4. D7.1.1 Specification of users and user requirements. Technical report. NeOn (2006)
5. Staab, S., Schnurr, H.P., Studer, R., Sure, Y.: Knowledge Processes and Ontologies. IEEE Intelligent Systems 16(1), 26–34 (2001)
6. Modelo para la definición automática de correspondencias semánticas entre ontologías y modelos relacionales, Jesús Barrasa Rodríguez. PHD Thesis (December 2006)
7. Gómez-Pérez, A., Fernández-López, M., Corcho, O.: Ontological Engineering. Springer, Heidelberg (2003)
8. Domingue, J.: Tadzebao and WebOnto: Discussing, Browsing, and Editing Ontologies on the Web. In: Gaines, B.R., Musen, M.A. (eds.) KAW 1998. 11th International Workshop on Knowledge Acquisition, Modeling and Management, Banff, Canada, vol. KM4(120) (1998)

# A Logic for Order of Magnitude Reasoning with Negligibility, Non-closeness and Distance[*]

A. Burrieza[1], E. Muñoz-Velasco[2], and M. Ojeda-Aciego[2]

[1] Dept. Filosofia. Universidad de Málaga. Spain
burrieza@uma.es
[2] Dept. Matemática Aplicada. Universidad de Málaga. Spain
{emilio,aciego}@ctima.uma.es

**Abstract.** This paper continues the research line on the multimodal logic of qualitative reasoning; specifically, it deals with the introduction of the notions non-closeness and distance. These concepts allow us to consider qualitative sum of medium and large numbers. We present a sound and complete axiomatization for this logic, together with some of its advantages by means of an example.

## 1 Introduction

Qualitative reasoning is an adequate tool for dealing with situations in which information is not sufficiently precise (e.g., exact numerical values are not available) or when numerical models are too complex. A form of qualitative reasoning is to manage numerical data in terms of orders of magnitude (see, for example, [13,17,10,11,15,20]). There are crucial problems in order of magnitude reasoning which remain to be solved: the difficulty to incorporate quantitative information when available, and the difficulty to control the inference process [10]. Two approaches to order of magnitude reasoning have been identified in [20]: Absolute Order of Magnitude, which is represented by a partition of the real line $\mathbb{R}$ where each element belongs to a qualitative class; and Relative Order of Magnitude, introducing a family of binary order of magnitude relations which establishes different comparison relations in $\mathbb{R}$ (e.g. *negligibility*, *closeness* and *distance*). In general, both models need to be combined in order to capture all the relevant information. This fact has led us to define a logic which bridges the absolute and relative order of magnitude models.

Previous works in logic to deal with qualitative reasoning, are presented in [18, 2, 3, 22, 16] for managing qualitative spatial reasoning, qualitative spatio-temporal representations, and the use of branching temporal logics to describe the possible solutions of ordinary differential equations when we have a lack of complete information about a system. However, an analogous development of order of magnitude reasoning from a logical standpoint has received little attention: to the best of our knowledge, the only logics dealing with order-of-magnitude reasoning have been developed in [6,7,8]. More recently, a relational

[*] Partially supported by projects TIN2006-15455-C03-01 and P6-FQM-02049.

D. Borrajo, L. Castillo, and J.M. Corchado (Eds.): CAEPIA 2007, LNAI 4788, pp. 210–219, 2007.
© Springer-Verlag Berlin Heidelberg 2007

theorem prover has been developed in [9] for the logic of order-of-magnitude with negligibility introduced in [7].

The present paper generalizes the line of research presented in [8], where a notion of *negligibility* relation was considered, by introducing a logic to deal with two new relations: *non-closeness* and *distance* [12, 17, 21] defined in an arbitrarily chosen strict linearly ordered set. We present a sound and complete axiomatization for this logic, together with some of its advantages, which are shown by means of an example. The non-closeness relation is introduced following the ideas of the *Near* relation in [17], that is, a real number $x$ is *Near* to $y$, when $y = x + Small$. If we work with real numbers, our definition says that $x$ is *non-close* to $y$ when either they have different *order of magnitude* or $y$ is obtained by adding a *medium* or *large* number to $x$. The same idea is introduced to define distance: a real number is *distant* from another one when it is obtained by adding a *large* number. These definitions have the additional advantage that enables us to introducing the operation of qualitative sum of medium and large numbers.

We will consider a strict linearly ordered set $(\mathbb{S}, <)$[1] divided into seven equivalence classes using five landmarks chosen depending on the context [19, 14]. The system considered corresponds to the schematic representation shown below:

| NL | NM | NS | PS | PM | PL |
|---|---|---|---|---|---|
| $c_{-2}$ | $c_{-1}$ | $c_0$ | $c_1$ | $c_2$ | |

where $c_i \in \mathbb{S}$ for $i \in \{-2, -1, 0, 1, 2\}$ such that $c_j < c_{j+1}$ for all $j \in \{-2, -1, 0, 1\}$. In this work we consider the following set of qualitative classes:

$$\text{NL} = (-\infty, c_{-2}), \quad \text{NM} = [c_{-2}, c_{-1}) \quad \text{NS} = [c_{-1}, c_0), \quad \text{C}_0 = \{c_0\}$$

$$\text{PS} = (c_0, c_1], \quad \text{PM} = (c_1, c_2], \quad \text{PL} = (c_2, +\infty)$$

As it could be expected, the labels correspond to "negative large", "negative medium", "negative small", "zero", "positive small", "positive medium" and "positive large", respectively. By convention, the constants $c_{-2}, c_2$ are considered to belong to the medium-size classes, whereas $c_{-1}, c_1$ are considered to belong to the small-size classes.

The logic introduced in this paper is a special type of hybrid logic [1] because we just use a finite number of constants (i.e. nominals) which are used not only to represent points but also to represent distances. More differences arise from the specificity of our modal connectives and the fact that we do not have a nominal for each point, this fact would allow us to work with the set of real numbers.

The paper is organized as follows: In Section 2, the concepts of negligibility, non-closeness and distance are introduced; then, syntax and semantics of the proposed logic is introduced in Section 3 and some of its advantages on the basis of an example; the axiom system for our language is presented in Section 4. Finally, some conclusions and prospects of future work are presented.

---

[1] For practical purposes, this set could be the real line.

## 2   Non-closeness, Distance and Negligibility

As stated in the introduction, we will combine absolute and relative order of magnitude models. For this purpose, regarding the underlying representation model, it seems natural to consider an absolute order of magnitude model with a small number of landmarks, so that the size of the axiom system obtained is reasonable.

The concepts of order of magnitude, non-closeness, distance and negligibility we consider in this paper introduce the 'relative part' of the approach, which builds directly on the 'absolute part' just presented.

First of all, we define the following relation to give the intuitive meaning of constant distance.

**Definition 1.** *Let $(\mathbb{S}, <)$ a strict linearly ordered set which contains the constants $c_i$ for $i \in \{-2, -1, 0, 1, 2\}$ as defined above. Given $n \in \mathbb{N}$, we define $\overrightarrow{d_\alpha}$ as a relation in $\mathbb{S}$ such that, for every $x, y, z, x', y' \in \mathbb{S}$:*

- $c_r \overrightarrow{d_\alpha} c_{r+1}$*, for $r \in \{-1, 0\}$ and $c_s \overrightarrow{d_\alpha}^n c_{s+1}$ [2]*, for $s \in \{-2, 1\}$*.
- *If $x \overrightarrow{d_\alpha} y$, then $x < y$*
- *If $x \overrightarrow{d_\alpha} y$ and $x \overrightarrow{d_\alpha} z$, then $y = z$.*
- *If $x \overrightarrow{d_\alpha} y$, $x' \overrightarrow{d_\alpha} y'$ and $x < x'$ then $y < y'$.*

*We denote by $\overleftarrow{d_\alpha}$ the inverse of relation $\overrightarrow{d_\alpha}$.*

We assume in the previous definition that both constants $c_{-1}$ and $c_1$ are at the same distance (called $\alpha$) from $c_0$. Moreover, the distances from $c_{-2}$ to $c_{-1}$ and from $c_1$ to $c_2$ are assumed to be a multiple of $\alpha$ (that is, $n$ times $\alpha$). This choice arises from the idea of taking $\alpha$ as the basic pattern for measuring. As a consequence, the distance between two consecutive constants should be measurable in terms of $\alpha$.

**Definition 2 (Order of Magnitude).** *Let $(\mathbb{S}, <)$ be defined as above. For every $x, y \in \mathbb{S}$ we say that $x\text{OM}y$ if and only if $x, y \in$ EQ, where EQ denotes a qualitative class, that is, an element in the set $\{$NL, NM, NS, $C_0$, PS, PM, PL$\}$. Analogously, we define $x\overline{\text{OM}}y$ when $x, y$ do not belong to the same class.*

**Definition 3 (Non-Closeness and Distance).** *Let $(\mathbb{S}, <)$ and $n \in \mathbb{N}$ be given as above. We define the relations $\overrightarrow{\text{NC}}$ and $\overrightarrow{\text{D}}$ in $\mathbb{S}$ as follows:*

$$x\overrightarrow{\text{NC}}y \quad \text{if and only if} \quad \text{either } x\overline{\text{OM}}y \text{ and } x < y$$
$$\text{or there exists } z \in \mathbb{S} \text{ such that } z < y \text{ and } x\overrightarrow{d_\alpha}z$$
$$x\overrightarrow{\text{D}}y \quad \text{if and only if} \quad \text{there exists } z \in \mathbb{S} \text{ such that } z < y \text{ and } x\overrightarrow{d_\alpha}^{n+1}z$$

*We denote by $\overleftarrow{\text{NC}}$ and $\overleftarrow{\text{D}}$ the inverses of relations $\overrightarrow{\text{NC}}$ and $\overrightarrow{\text{D}}$, respectively.*

---

[2] $\overrightarrow{d_\alpha}^n$ is defined by $\overrightarrow{d_\alpha}^1 = \overrightarrow{d_\alpha}$ and $\overrightarrow{d_\alpha}^n = \overrightarrow{d_\alpha} \circ \overrightarrow{d_\alpha}^{n-1}$, for $n \in \mathbb{N}, n \geq 2$, being $\circ$ the usual composition of relations.

If we assume that $\mathbb{S}$ is a set of real numbers, the intuitive interpretation of non-closeness relation is that $x$ is non-close to $y$ if, and only if, either $x$ and $y$ have not the same order of magnitude, or $y$ is obtained from $x$ by adding a medium or large number. On the other hand, $x$ is distant from $y$ if and only if $y$ is obtained from $x$ by adding large number. On the other hand, we introduce the definition of non-closeness instead of closeness directly in order to have an easier way to prove the completeness of the axiom system given later. Nevertheless, as we will see in example below, this definition gives us enough expressive power.

In order to define the negligibility relation, it seems to be reasonable that if $x \neq c_0$ is *neglibible* with respect to $y$, then $x$ is distant to $y$. With this aim, we give the following definition.

**Definition 4 (Negligibility).** *Let $(\mathbb{S}, <)$ be defined as above. If $x, y \in \mathbb{S}$, we say that $x$ is* negligible *with respect to (wrt from now on) $y$, usually denoted $x\overrightarrow{N}y$, if and only if, we have one of the following cases:*

$$(i) \quad x = c_0 \qquad (ii) \quad x \in \mathrm{NS} \cup \mathrm{PS} \text{ and, either } c_{-1}\overleftarrow{\mathrm{D}}y \text{ or } c_1\overrightarrow{\mathrm{D}}y$$

*We denote by $\overleftarrow{N}$ the inverse of relation $\overrightarrow{N}$.*

Note that item (i) above corresponds to the intuitive idea that zero is negligible wrt any real number and item (ii) corresponds to the intuitive idea that a number *sufficiently small* is negligible wrt any number *sufficiently large*, independently of the sign of these numbers. This definition ensures that if $x \neq c_0$ and $x\overrightarrow{N}y$, then either $x\overleftarrow{\mathrm{D}}y$ or $x\overrightarrow{\mathrm{D}}y$.

# 3   Syntax and Semantics of the Language $\mathcal{L}(OM)^{\mathrm{NCD}}$

The language $\mathcal{L}(OM)^{\mathrm{NCD}}$ is an extension of $\mathcal{L}(OM)$ presented in [8]. To begin with, let us define informally the meaning of the modal connectives we will consider in our language. Their intuitive meanings of some of its connectives are given below (the rest are similar), where $A$ is any formula:

- $\overrightarrow{\Box}A$ means $A$ *is true for all point greater than the current one.*
- $\Box_{\overrightarrow{d_\alpha}}A$ is read $A$ *is true for all point which is greater than the current one and its distance to this one is $\alpha$.*
- $\Box_{\overrightarrow{N}}A$ is read $A$ *is true for all point with respect to which the current one is negligible.*
- $\Box_{\overrightarrow{NC}}A$ is read $A$ *is true for all point which is non-close and greater than the current one.*
- $\Box_{\overrightarrow{D}}A$ is read $A$ *is true for all point which is distant from and greater than the current one.*

The syntax of our logic is the usual modal propositional language on the modal connectives described above and a set of specific constants to denote the landmarks. Formally, the alphabet of our language is defined by using:

- A stock of atoms or propositional variables, $\mathcal{V}$.
- The classical connectives $\neg, \wedge, \vee, \rightarrow$ and the constant symbols $\top$ and $\bot$.
- The unary modal connectives $\overrightarrow{\square}, \overleftarrow{\square}, \square_{\overrightarrow{\mathcal{R}}}, \square_{\overleftarrow{\mathcal{R}}}$ being $\mathcal{R} \in \{d_\alpha, \mathrm{NC}, \mathrm{D}, N\}$.
- The finite set of specific constants defined by $\mathcal{C} = \{\overline{c}_{-2}, \overline{c}_{-1}, \overline{c}_0, \overline{c}_1, \overline{c}_2\}$.
- The auxiliary symbols $(,)$.

Well-formed formulae of $\mathcal{L}(OM)^{\mathrm{NCD}}$ are generated from $\mathcal{V} \cup \mathcal{C}$ by the construction rules of classical propositional logic plus the following rule which introduces the modal connectives:

*If $A$ is a formula, then so are $\overrightarrow{\square}A$, $\overleftarrow{\square}A$, $\square_{\overrightarrow{\mathcal{R}}}A$ and $\square_{\overleftarrow{\mathcal{R}}}A$ being $\mathcal{R} \in \{d_\alpha, \mathrm{NC}, \mathrm{D}, N\}$*

As usual, the *mirror image* of $A$ is the result of replacing in $A$ the occurrences of $\overrightarrow{\square}, \overleftarrow{\square}, \square_{\overrightarrow{\mathcal{R}}}, \square_{\overleftarrow{\mathcal{R}}}, \overline{c}_j, \overline{c}_0$ by $\overleftarrow{\square}, \overrightarrow{\square}, \square_{\overleftarrow{\mathcal{R}}}, \square_{\overrightarrow{\mathcal{R}}}, \overline{c}_{-j}$ and $\overline{c}_0$, respectively, being $j \in \{-2, -1, 1, 2\}$.

Moreover, we use $\overrightarrow{\lozenge}, \overleftarrow{\lozenge}, \lozenge_{\overrightarrow{\mathcal{R}}}, \lozenge_{\overleftarrow{\mathcal{R}}}$ as abbreviations, respectively, of $\neg\overrightarrow{\square}\neg$, $\neg\overleftarrow{\square}\neg$, $\neg\square_{\overrightarrow{\mathcal{R}}}\neg$ and $\neg\square_{\overleftarrow{\mathcal{R}}}\neg$.

**Definition 5.** *A* qualitative frame *for $\mathcal{L}(OM)^{\mathrm{NCD}}$ or, simply a frame, is a tuple $\Sigma = (\mathbb{S}, <, \overrightarrow{\mathcal{R}}, \overleftarrow{\mathcal{R}})$, being $(\mathbb{S}, <)$ a strict linearly ordered set which contains the constants $c_i$ for $i \in \{-2, -1, 0, 1, 2\}$ as defined above, and $\mathcal{R} \in \{d_\alpha, \mathrm{NC}, \mathrm{D}, N\}$ are respectively the relations on $\mathbb{S}$ given in Definitions 1, 3 and 4.*

We can now give the definition of qualitative model. In its formulation, given $R$ any relation in a set $X$ and $x \in X$, we write $R(x)$ with the usual meaning:

$$R(x) = \{x' \in X \mid xRx'\}$$

**Definition 6.** *Let $\Sigma = (\mathbb{S}, <, \overrightarrow{\mathcal{R}}, \overleftarrow{\mathcal{R}})$ be a qualitative frame for $\mathcal{L}(OM)^{\mathrm{NCD}}$, a* qualitative model *for $\Sigma$ (or, simply $\Sigma$-model) is an ordered pair $\mathcal{M} = (\Sigma, h)$ where $h : \mathcal{V} \rightarrow 2^{\mathbb{S}}$ is a function called* interpretation. *Any interpretation can be uniquely extended to the set of all formulae in $\mathcal{L}(OM)^{\mathrm{NCD}}$ (also denoted by $h$) by means of the usual conditions for the classical boolean connectives and for $\top, \bot$, and the following conditions, being $\mathcal{R} \in \{d_\alpha, \mathrm{NC}, \mathrm{D}, N\}$, and $i \in \{-2, -1, 0, 1, 2\}$ [3]:*

$$h(\overrightarrow{\square}A) = \{x \in \mathbb{S} \mid (x, +\infty) \subseteq h(A)\} \qquad h(\overleftarrow{\square}A) = \{x \in \mathbb{S} \mid (-\infty, x) \subseteq h(A)\}$$
$$h(\square_{\overrightarrow{\mathcal{R}}}A) = \{x \in \mathbb{S} \mid \overrightarrow{\mathcal{R}}(x) \subseteq h(A)\} \qquad h(\square_{\overleftarrow{\mathcal{R}}}A) = \{x \in \mathbb{S} \mid \overleftarrow{\mathcal{R}}(x) \subseteq h(A)\}$$
$$h(\overline{c}_i) = \{c_i\}$$

*The concepts of truth and validity are defined in a standard way.*

Notice that the connectives $\square_{\overrightarrow{\mathrm{NC}}}$, $\square_{\overrightarrow{\mathrm{D}}}$ allow us to manage the concepts of non-closeness and distance defined above which were not introduced in [8]. Thus, we extend the example presented in this previous paper with some uses of these new concepts.

---

[3] Note that these algebraic conditions for modal connectives are based on the intuitive meanings presented above.

*Example 1.* Let us suppose that we want to specify the behaviour of a device to automatically control the temperature, for example, in a museum, subject to have some specific conditions.

If we have to maintain the temperature close to some limit $T$, for practical purposes any value of the interval $[T - \epsilon, T + \epsilon]$ for small $\epsilon$ is admissible. Then the extreme points of this interval can be considered as the milestones $c_{-1}$ and $c_1$, respectively.

Moreover, assume that if the temperature is out of this interval (for example, because the number of people within the museum is changing), it is necessary to put into operation some *heating* or *cooling* system. In addition, we have another interval $[T - \lambda, T + \lambda]$, such that if the temperature does not belong to this interval, we need to use an extra system of *cooling* or *heating*, because the default system is not enough. Now, the extreme points of this interval are the milestones $c_{-2}$ and $c_2$, respectively.

We also assume that, when the normal system of *cooling* or *heating* is operating, a system to maintain the humidity is needed, and when the extra system is operating, we also need an extra system of humidification.

The qualitative classes NL, NM, NS $\cup$ C$_0$ $\cup$ PS, PM and PL can be interpreted by VERY_COLD, COLD, OK, HOT and VERY_HOT, respectively. The following conditions specify the general behaviour of the system:

$$\text{OK} \rightarrow \textit{off} \qquad\qquad \text{VERY\_COLD} \rightarrow \textit{X-heating}$$

$$\text{COLD} \rightarrow \textit{heating} \qquad\qquad \text{HOT} \rightarrow \textit{cooling}$$

$$\text{VERY\_HOT} \rightarrow \textit{X-cooling} \qquad (\text{COLD} \vee \text{HOT}) \rightarrow \textit{humidifier}$$

$$(\text{VERY\_COLD} \vee \text{VERY\_HOT}) \rightarrow \textit{X-humidifier}$$

The following formulae introduce relations among actions:

$$\textit{X-heating} \rightarrow (\neg\textit{heating} \wedge \neg\textit{off} \wedge \neg\textit{cooling} \wedge \neg\textit{X-cooling} \wedge \textit{X-humidifier})$$

$$\textit{heating} \rightarrow (\textit{humidifier} \wedge \neg\textit{X-cooling} \wedge \neg\textit{cooling} \wedge \neg\textit{off})$$

$$\textit{off} \rightarrow (\neg\textit{X-cooling} \wedge \neg\textit{cooling} \wedge \neg\textit{humidifier} \wedge \neg\textit{X-humidifier})$$

$$\textit{cooling} \rightarrow (\neg\textit{X-cooling} \wedge \textit{humidifier}) \qquad \textit{X-cooling} \rightarrow \textit{X-humidifier}$$

$$\textit{humidifier} \rightarrow (\textit{cooling} \vee \textit{heating}) \qquad \textit{X-humidifier} \rightarrow \neg\textit{humidifier}$$

where *off* means that the system is *off*, *cooling* means that we use the normal system of *cooling* and *X-cooling* means that we need to use an extra cooling system. Analogously, we have the meaning of *heating*, *X-heating*, *humidifier* and *X-humidifier*.

Some consequences of the previous specification that are obtained by using the proposed axiom system are the following:

1. The conditionals in the proper axioms turn out to be bi-conditionals, that is, we also have: *off* $\rightarrow$ OK, *cooling* $\rightarrow$ HOT, etc.
2. *cooling* $\rightarrow \overrightarrow{\Box}(\neg\textit{X-cooling} \rightarrow \textit{humidifier})$

3. $(off \wedge \neg \bar{c}_0) \rightarrow \Box_{\overrightarrow{N}'} X\text{-}humidifier$
4. $(X\text{-}cooling \vee X\text{-}heating) \rightarrow \Box_{\overleftarrow{N}}(\neg humidifier \wedge \neg X\text{-}humidifier)$
5. $(\text{OK} \wedge \overleftarrow{\Diamond} \bar{c}_0) \rightarrow (\Box_{\overrightarrow{NC}}(humidifier \vee X\text{-}humidifier) \wedge \Box_{\overrightarrow{D}'} X\text{-}humidifier)$
6. $\text{HOT} \rightarrow \Box_{\overrightarrow{D}'} X\text{-}humidifier$

We give now the intuitive meanings for the previous formulae.

- Formula 2 means that if the cooling system is running and the temperature increases, while the extra cooling system were not put in operation, the humidifier system is enough to maintain the desired conditions.
- Formula 3 says that if the system is off, but the temperature is not $c_0$, for every value wrt the current one is negligible, the extra humidifier system is needed.
- Formula 4 means that if the extra cooling or extra heating system are operating, the values which are negligible wrt that ones are not using neither humidifier nor humidifier systems.
- Formula 5 can be read in this way: if the temperature is OK but greater than $\bar{c}_0$ and it is incremented by a medium or large positive value to obtain a non-close value, then we have to use the *humidifier* or *extra humidifier* system because the *cooling* or *heating* systems have been put into operation. Moreover, if this temperature is incremented by a positive large value to obtain a distant value, then we have to use the *extra humidifier* system.
- Formula 6 means that if the temperature is HOT and is incremented to obtain a distant value, then we have to use the *extra humidifier* system.

If we assume that the system is more efficient (in terms of energy saving) if the temperature is OK and close to the milestone $c_1$, that is close but no greater, the following formula must be true:

$$\bar{c}_1 \rightarrow (\Box_{\text{NC}} non\text{-}efficient \wedge \Box_{\text{D}} warning)^4$$

This formula means that for every temperature non-close (smaller or greater) to $c_1$, the system is not running efficiently and if the temperature is distant to $c_1$, the system is wasting very much energy. Notice that, as $c_1$ is a milestone, every value greater than $c_1$ is not in the same order of magnitude and, as a consequence of Definition 3, it is non-close to $c_1$.

The following section is devoted to the axiomatization of this logic. For simplicity, from now on, we will assume that $n = 1$ in Definition 1, that is, the distance between every two consecutive constants is $\alpha$. On the other hand, we will only consider modal connectives $\overrightarrow{\Box}, \overleftarrow{\Box}, \Box_{\overrightarrow{d_\alpha}}, \Box_{\overleftarrow{d_\alpha}}$, because the connectives $\Box_{\overrightarrow{N}'}, \Box_{\overrightarrow{NC}}, \Box_{\overrightarrow{D}'}$ (and its inverses) can be defined by using only the first ones. As an example, we give the definition of $\Box_{\overrightarrow{NC}}$:

---

[4] We use $\Box_{\mathcal{R}} A$ as an abbreviation of $\Box_{\overleftarrow{\mathcal{R}}} A \wedge \Box_{\overrightarrow{\mathcal{R}}} A$, for $\mathcal{R} \in \{d_\alpha, \text{NC}, \text{D}, N\}$.

$$\Box_{\overrightarrow{NC}} A \equiv \Box_{\overrightarrow{d_\alpha}} \overrightarrow{\Box} A \wedge (\bigvee_{j=0}^{2} \overline{c}_j \rightarrow \overrightarrow{\Box} A) \wedge$$

$$\wedge \bigwedge_{s=-2}^{0} (\overrightarrow{\Diamond}\,\overline{c}_s \rightarrow \overrightarrow{\Box}((\overline{c}_s \vee \overleftarrow{\Diamond}\,\overline{c}_s) \rightarrow A)) \wedge \bigwedge_{r=1}^{2} (\overleftarrow{\Diamond}\,\overline{c}_r \rightarrow \overrightarrow{\Box}(\overleftarrow{\Diamond}\,\overline{c}_r \rightarrow A))$$

## 4    Axiom System for $\mathcal{L}(OM)^{\mathrm{NCD}}$

We will denote $OM^{\mathrm{NCD}}$ the axiom system containing all the tautologies of classical propositional logic together with the following axiom schemata:

**Axiom schemata for modal connectives:**

**K1** $\overrightarrow{\Box}(A \rightarrow B) \rightarrow (\overrightarrow{\Box} A \rightarrow \overrightarrow{\Box} B)$
**K2** $A \rightarrow \overrightarrow{\Box}\overleftarrow{\Diamond} A$
**K3** $\overrightarrow{\Box} A \rightarrow \overrightarrow{\Box}\overrightarrow{\Box} A$
**K4** $(\overrightarrow{\Box}(A \vee B) \wedge \overrightarrow{\Box}(\overrightarrow{\Box} A \vee B) \wedge \overrightarrow{\Box}(A \vee \overrightarrow{\Box} B)) \rightarrow (\overrightarrow{\Box} A \vee \overrightarrow{\Box} B)$

**Axiom schemata for constants:**

**C1** $\overleftarrow{\Diamond}\,\overline{c}_i \vee \overline{c}_i \vee \overrightarrow{\Diamond}\,\overline{c}_i$, where $i \in \{-2, -1, 0, 1, 2\}$
**C2** $\overline{c}_i \rightarrow (\overleftarrow{\Box}\neg\overline{c}_i \wedge \overrightarrow{\Box}\neg\overline{c}_i)$, being $i \in \{-2, -1, 0, 1, 2\}$

**Axiom schemata for specific modal connectives:**

**d1** $\Box_{\overrightarrow{d_\alpha}}(A \rightarrow B) \rightarrow (\Box_{\overrightarrow{d_\alpha}} A \rightarrow \Box_{\overrightarrow{d_\alpha}} B)$
**d2** $A \rightarrow \Box_{\overrightarrow{d_\alpha}}\Diamond_{\overleftarrow{d_\alpha}} A.$
**d3** $\overline{c}_j \rightarrow \Diamond_{\overrightarrow{d_\alpha}}\overline{c}_{j+1}$, where $j \in \{-2, -1, 0, 1\}$ [5].
**d4** $(\Diamond_{\overrightarrow{d_\alpha}} A \wedge \overrightarrow{\Diamond}\Diamond_{\overrightarrow{d_\alpha}} B) \rightarrow \overrightarrow{\Diamond}(A \wedge \overrightarrow{\Diamond} B)$
**d5** $\Diamond_{\overrightarrow{d_\alpha}} A \rightarrow \Box_{\overrightarrow{d_\alpha}} A$
**d6** $\overrightarrow{\Box} A \rightarrow \Box_{\overrightarrow{d_\alpha}} A$

We also consider as axioms the corresponding mirror images of K1–K4 and d1–d6.

**Rules of Inference:**

**(MP)** Modus Ponens for $\rightarrow$
**(R$\overrightarrow{\Box}$)** If $\vdash A$ then $\vdash \overrightarrow{\Box} A$
**(R$\overleftarrow{\Box}$)** If $\vdash A$ then $\vdash \overleftarrow{\Box} A$

**Theorem 1 (Soundness and Completeness)**

- *Every theorem of $OM^{\mathrm{NCD}}$ is a valid formula of $\mathcal{L}(OM)^{\mathrm{NCD}}$.*
- *Every valid formula of $\mathcal{L}(OM)^{\mathrm{NCD}}$ is a theorem of $OM^{\mathrm{NCD}}$.*

---

[5] This is the unique axiom which is affected by our previous assumption that $n = 1$ in Definition 1.

The soundness of the axiom system is straightforward. Regarding completeness, a *step-by-step* proof (see, for example, [4] and [5]) can be given in the following terms: Given any consistent formula $A$ , we have to prove that $A$ is satisfiable. With this purpose, the step-by-step method defines a qualitative frame $\Sigma = (\mathbb{S}, <, \overrightarrow{\mathcal{R}}, \overleftarrow{\mathcal{R}})$ and a function $f_\Sigma$ which assigns maximal consistent sets to any element of $\mathbb{S}$, such that $A \in f_\Sigma(x)$ for some $x \in \mathbb{S}$. The process to build such a frame is recursive, and follows the ideas of [7]: firstly, a pre-frame is generated which is later completed to an initial finite frame; later, successive extensions of this initial frame are defined until $\Sigma$ is obtained. Although the method of proof is the same, the technical problems which arise from the use of this more complex language need special attention. Due to lack of space, the formal details are omitted.

## 5   Conclusions and Future Work

A multimodal logic for order of magnitude reasoning to deal with negligibility, non-closeness and distance has been introduced which enriches previous works in this line of research by introducing in some way qualitative sum of medium and large numbers. Some of the advantages of this logic have been studied on the basis of an example.

As a future work, our plans are to study the decidability and complexity of this logic. Last, but not least, we want to give a relational proof system based on dual tableaux for this extension in the line of [9].

## References

1. Areces, C., ten Cate, B.: Hybrid Logics. In: Blackburn, P., Van Benthem, J., Wolter, F. (eds.) Handbook of Modal Logic. Studies in Logic and Practical Reasoning, vol. 3, pp. 821–868. Elsevier, Amsterdam (2007)
2. Bennett, B.: Modal logics for qualitative spatial reasoning. Bull. of the IGPL 3, 1–22 (1995)
3. Bennett, B., Cohn, A.G., Wolter, F., Zakharyaschev, M.: Multi-Dimensional Modal Logic as a Framework for Spatio-Temporal Reasoning. Applied Intelligence 17(3), 239–251 (2002)
4. Blackburn, P., de Rijke, M., Venema, Y.: Modal Logic. Cambridge University Press, Cambridge (2001)
5. Burgess, J.P.: Basic tense logic. In: Gabbay, D., Guenthner, F. (eds.) Handbook of Philosophical Logic: Extensions of Classical Logic, vol. 2, pp. 89–133. Reidel, Dordrecht (1984)
6. Burrieza, A., Ojeda-Aciego, M.: A multimodal logic approach to order of magnitude qualitative reasoning. In: Conejo, R., Urretavizcaya, M., Pérez-de-la-Cruz, J.-L. (eds.) Current Topics in Artificial Intelligence. LNCS (LNAI), vol. 3040, pp. 66–75. Springer, Heidelberg (2004)
7. Burrieza, A., Ojeda-Aciego, M.: A multimodal logic approach to order of magnitude qualitative reasoning with comparability and negligibility relations. Fundamenta Informaticae 68, 21–46 (2005)

8. Burrieza, A., Muñoz, E., Ojeda-Aciego, M.: Order of magnitude reasoning with bidirectional negligibility. In: Marín, R., Onaindía, E., Bugarín, A., Santos, J. (eds.) CAEPIA 2005. LNCS (LNAI), vol. 4177, pp. 370–378. Springer, Heidelberg (2006)
9. Burrieza, A., Ojeda-Aciego, M., Orłowska, E.: Relational approach to order of magnitude reasoning. In: de Swart, H., Orłowska, E., Schmidt, G., Roubens, M. (eds.) Theory and Applications of Relational Structures as Knowledge Instruments II. LNCS (LNAI), vol. 4342, pp. 105–124. Springer, Heidelberg (2006)
10. Dague, P.: Numeric reasoning with relative orders of magnitude. In: Proc. 11th National Conference on Artificial Intelligence, pp. 541–547. The AAAI Press/The MIT Press (1993)
11. Dague, P.: Symbolic reasoning with relative orders of magnitude. In: Proc. 13th Intl. Joint Conference on Artificial Intelligence, pp. 1509–1515. Morgan Kaufmann, San Francisco (1993)
12. Dubois, D., Hadj-Ali, A., Prade, H.: Granular Computing with Closeness and Negligibility Relations. In: Data mining, rough sets and granular computing, pp. 290–307. Physica-Verlag, Heidelberg (2002)
13. Mavrovouniotis, M.L., Stephanopoulos, G.: Reasoning with orders of magnitude and approximate relations. In: Proc. 6th National Conference on Artificial Intelligence, The AAAI Press/The MIT Press (1987)
14. Missier, A., Piera, N., Travé, L.: Order of Magnitude Algebras: a Survey. Revue d'Intelligence Artificielle 3(4), 95–109 (1989)
15. Sanchez, M., Prats, F., Piera, N.: Una formalización de relaciones de comparabilidad en modelos cualitativos. Boletín de la AEPIA (Bulletin of the Spanish Association for AI) 6, 15–22 (1996)
16. Shults, B., Kuipers, B.J.: Proving properties of continuous systems: qualitative simulation and temporal logic. Artificial Intelligence 92, 91–129 (1997)
17. Raiman, O.: Order of magnitude reasoning. Artificial Intelligence 51, 11–38 (1991)
18. Randell, D., Cui, Z., Cohn, A.: A spatial logic based on regions and connections. In: KR 1992. Proc. of the 3rd Intl Conf on Principles of Knowledge Representation and Reasoning, pp. 165–176 (1992)
19. Travé-Massuyès, L., Ironi, L., Dague, P.: Mathematical foundations of qualitative reasoning. AI magazine 24(3), 91–106 (2003)
20. Travé-Massuyès, L., Prats, F., Sánchez, M., Agell, N.: Consistent relative and absolute order-of-magnitude models. In: Proc. Qualitative Reasoning 2002 Conference (2002)
21. Travé-Massuyès, L., Prats, F., Sánchez, M., Agell, N.: Relative and absolute order-of-magnitude models unified. Annals of Mathematics and Artificial Intelligence 45, 323–341 (2005)
22. Wolter, F., Zakharyaschev, M.: Qualitative spatio-temporal representation and reasoning: a computational perspective. In: Lakemeyer, G., Nebel, B. (eds.) Exploring Artificial Intelligence in the New Millenium, Morgan Kaufmann, San Francisco (2002)

# A Solution to the Rural Postman Problem Based on Artificial Ant Colonies

María Luisa Pérez-Delgado

Universidad de Salamanca, Av. Requejo, 33, C.P. 49022, Zamora, Spain
mlperez@usal.es

**Abstract.** The objective of this work is to apply artificial ant colonies to solve the Rural Postman Problem on undirected graphs. In order to do so, we will transform this problem into a Traveling Salesman Problem, applying to this new problem algorithms based on artificial ant colonies, which have been applied at great length to the same, obtaining good results.

## 1 Introduction

Systems based on artificial ants represent a heuristic technique to problems solving that emerged in the Nineties from Marco Dorigo's doctoral thesis [1], [2]. This technique tries to imitate the behavior of real ants to solve optimization problems. The first proposed algorithm, called Ant-System, was first applied to solve the Traveling Salesman Problem. The algorithm was latter applied to other optimization problems, such as the Quadratic Assignment Problem [3], [4], the Vehicle Routing Problem [5], [6], or the Graph Coloring Problem [7].

Given that the **Rural Postman Problem** (RPP) can be easily transformed into the **Traveling Salesman Problem** (TSP) [8], it appears logical to assume that the algorithm proposed by Dorigo could also be applied to this new problem.

We will begin by recalling the objective of the TSP, to then describe the RPP. In following we describe the heuristic based on ant colonies. In the next section we describe the proposed solution algorithm, based on the application of artificial ants. Finally we show the computational results obtained and present the conclusions of the paper.

## 2 The Traveling Salesman Problem

The TSP is a classic among the NP-complete problems [9], [10]. Given a set of points interconnected by weighted connections, the objective of the problem is to find the closed tour of minimum cost which visits each point once and only once.

When we consider the graph-based representation, the problem is defined by a graph $G = (V, A)$, where $V$ represents the set of cities and $A$ represents the set of connections between the same. The set $A$ will include arcs if the problem is asymmetric, such that $(i, j) \in A / i, j \in V$ represents one arc that goes from city $i$

D. Borrajo, L. Castillo, and J.M. Corchado (Eds.): CAEPIA 2007, LNAI 4788, pp. 220–228, 2007.

to city $j$. If the problem is symmetric, each element $(i, j) \in A$ represents an edge connecting cities $i$ and $j$, no matter the order of the connection. Each arc or edge on the graph has a cost equal to the distance between the cities that it connects.

If we consider a Euclidean problem, the points of the problem are represented by the $(x, y)$ coordinates on the Euclidean plane, whereas the distance associated to the connections is the Euclidean distance between the endpoints that define each connection.

This is an NP-complete problem. Its high complexity has led to attempting to solve it by applying several techniques, both exact and approximate. Moreover, the TSP is one of the typical benchmark problem used to check new algorithms. For that reason, a lot of new heuristic techniques have been applied to it. Although these techniques give less precise solutions, they require less problem solving time, what is key when trying to solve problems including a large number of cities.

## 3   The Rural Postman Problem

Let $G = (V, E)$ be an undirected graph, where $V$ represents the set of points on the graph and $E$ represents the set of connections. The elements of $E$ have a cost associated with them, defined by the cost function $c$. Let $F \subseteq E$ be a subset of $E$. This subset induces a graph $G_F = (V_F, F)$ that includes the connections of $F$ and the vertex that are endpoints of those connections. Therefore $V_F \subseteq V$. The objective of the RPP is to find a closed path of minimum length containing at least once all the connections of $F$, in the subgraph of $G$ induced by the subset of $V$ [11].

This problem appears in a number of practical situations, such as school bus routing, mail delivery, street patrolling, plotter drawings, electrical lines inspection, ... [12].

Among the exact solutions to the RPP we can highlight those proposed by Christofides et al [13], Corberán et al [14], Ghiani and Laporte [15] and Letchford [16].

Given that the problem belongs to the category of NP-complete problems, various approximate methods have been applied to attempt to solve it. Among the heuristic techniques we can highlight the solutions proposed by Fernández de Córdoba et al [17], Frederickson [12], as well as the works of Hertz [18], and Groves and van Vuuren [19], which tries to improve upon the solution proposed by Frederickson. With regards to metaheuristics, we can highlight the works of Kang et al [20], which uses Genetic Algorithms, Rodrigues et al [21], which uses Memetic Algorithms, and Baldoquín et al [22], which combines the GRASP meta-heuristic with Genetic Algorithms.

## 4   Ant-Colony Based Algorithms

Ants are animals almost blind, that communicate among themselves using a chemical substance called **pheromone**, which they deposit on the ground when they walk. On average, ants prefer moving by the paths having more pheromone, contributing in this way to the accumulation of more pheromone; thus making such paths more desirable. The pheromone evaporates over time, making those paths chosen by the least number of ants the least desirable.

In 1991 Dorigo et al. proposed the Ant System algorithm, based on the behavior of natural ants, and they applied it to the TSP [2]. Let's suppose a TSP problem including $N$ cities. To solve the problem we consider a set of $m$ ants that cooperate in the search for a solution to the TSP (a tour). A **pheromone**, $\tau_{ij}$, is associated to each connection $(i, j)$ of the TSP. To ensure that each ant visits each city once and only once, we associate a data structure called **tabu list** to each ant, which stores the cities already visited by the corresponding ant. When the ant begins a search for a new path, its tabu list is empty. Each time an ant visits a city, it is added to its tabu list. When it has completed its trajectory, all the cities will be part of said list.

Each ant generates a complete tour by starting off from a randomly selected city and selecting the next city on its trajectory by means of a probabilistic state transition rule: the probability with which ant $k$, currently located in city $i$, decides to move to city $j$ is:

$$p_{ij}^k = \frac{\tau_{ij}^\alpha \eta_{ij}^\beta}{\sum_{l \in N_i^k} \tau_{il}^\alpha \eta_{il}^\beta}. \tag{1}$$

where $\tau_{ij}$ is the pheromone associated to the connection $(i, j)$, $\eta_{ij}$ is called the **visibility** of the connection $(i, j)$ and $N_i^k$ is the **feasible neighborhood** for ant $k$. For the TSP the visibility of a connection is the inverse of the distance associated to that connection. The feasible neighborhood for ant $k$, currently located at city $i$, $N_i^k$, is the set of cities accessible from city $i$ and not yet visited by the ant. The parameters $\alpha$ and $\beta$ determine the relative influence of the pheromone and the distance, respectively.

The state transition rule 1 shows that ants prefer to move to cities closer to the current one and connected to it with arcs or edges with high amounts of pheromone.

Each ant finds a solution to the problem by applying the same method. After all ants have determined a tour, a global pheromone updating rule is applied. The process is repeated until the solution converges or the prefixed maximum number of iterations has been performed.

To update the pheromone of the connections, first a fraction of the pheromone associated to the same is evaporated, in order to prevent an unlimited increase of the same, and also to represent the phenomenon observed in natural ant colonies. Then, each ant deposits an amount of pheromone on the connections of the tour it has defined, which will be in proportion to the length of that tour. This makes it possible for the pheromone amount of the connections belonging to many solutions found by the ants to be increased as much as possible. The updating rule applied is the following:

$$\tau_{ij} = (1 - \rho)\tau_{ij} + \sum_{k=1}^{m} \Delta\tau_{ij}^k. \tag{2}$$

where

$$\Delta \tau_{ij}^k = \begin{cases} \frac{1}{L_k} & \text{if } (i,j) \text{ is part of the tour defined by ant } k \\ 0 & \text{otherwise.} \end{cases} \quad (3)$$

where $\rho$ is a parameter called **evaporation factor** of the pheromone, $0 < \rho < 1$, $L_k$ is the length of the tour defined by ant $k$ and $m$ is the number of ants.

The ant colonies algorithm that we are going to use is a variant of the described algorithm, called ACS (Ant Colony System). In such algorithm local and global updating of the pheromone is applied, as described in section 5.2.

## 5   Proposed Solution

The steps we followed to solve the RPP by applying artificial ants are:

1. The RPP is transformed into a TSP
2. An ant colony-based algorithm is applied to the resulting TSP
3. The solution obtained for the TSP in transformed into a solution for the RPP

### 5.1   Transformation of the RPP into a TSP

To transform the RPP into a TSP we take into account the description given for both problems in [8].

Let $G_F = (V_F, F)$ be the subgraph of $G$ induced by F. To each node $i \in V_F$ we associate a set $S_i = \{s_i^j | j \in N(i)\}$, where $N(i)$ represents the set of neighbors of node $i$ in $G_F$.

We construct the complete weighted graph $G' = (V', E', c')$, where

$$V' = \bigcup_{i \in V_F} S_i. \quad (4)$$

$$c'(s_i^h, s_i^k) = 0 \ \forall i \in V_F \ \text{and} \ h, k \in N(i), h \neq k. \quad (5)$$

$$c'(s_i^h, s_j^k) = \begin{cases} -M & \text{if } i = k \text{ and } j = h \ \forall i, j \in V_F, i \neq j, h \in N(i), k \in N(j) \\ d(i,j) & \text{otherwise.} \end{cases} \quad (6)$$

where $d(i,j)$ represents the length of a shortest path between nodes $i$ and $j$ in $G$, while $M$ is a large value, that we will take as the sum of the costs of all connections on the graph.

It is trivial to transform an optimal Hamiltonian cycle in $G'$ into an optimal rural postman tour in $G$.

When defining the TSP graph we apply the Floyd algorithm to determine the shortest paths among all the pairs of nodes of the graph. We store the cost of said paths as well as the information that allows for their reconstruction, which will be necessary in the final phase of our solution method.

## 5.2    Ant-Algorithm Applied to the TSP

The artificial ant algorithm selected is the so-called Ant Colony System (ACS) [23].

The algorithm uses a transition rule called **pseudo-random proportional rule**. Let $k$ be an ant located on node $i$, $q_0 \in [0,1]$ a parameter and $q$ a random value uniformly distributed in the interval $[0,1]$. The next stop of the path, $j$, is selected randomly by means of the following probability distribution:

If $q \le q_0$:

$$p_{ij}^k = \begin{cases} 1 \text{ if } j = arg \ \max_{l \in N_k^i} \left\{ \tau_{il}^\alpha \cdot \eta_{il}^\beta \right\} \\ 0 \text{ otherwise} \end{cases} . \tag{7}$$

If $q > q_0$:

$$p_{ij}^k = \begin{cases} \dfrac{\tau_{ij}^\alpha \cdot \eta_{ij}^\beta}{\sum_{l \in N_i^k} [\tau_{il}^\alpha \cdot \eta_{il}^\beta]} & \text{if } j \in N_i^k \\ 0 & \text{otherwise.} \end{cases} \tag{8}$$

When $q \le q_0$ we exploit the available knowledge, by selecting the best option with respect to the heuristic information and the pheromone trails. In other case, a controlled exploration is applied. Therefore, a commitment is established between the exploration for new connections and the exploitation of the information available at this time.

The pheromone is updated locally when each ant $h$ builds its solution. Moreover, the pheromone is updated globally upon the completion of each iteration. To perform the global update we consider the globally best ant $h_g$, that is to say, the ant that has built the best tour since the start of the algorithm.

The proposed algorithm includes a stage in which a 2-OPT exchange is applied to improve the path found by the best ant. This stage is applied prior to completing the local pheromone updating. In doing so, it will be possible to obtain a shorter path, in which some of the sections of the tour will have been modified.

In order for the ant $h$ to perform the local updating of the trail, pheromone is deposited on the connections used by this ant in the solution it has defined, $S_h$, by applying the expression:

$$\tau_{ij} = \rho_L \tau_0 + (1 - \rho_L)\tau_{ij} \ \forall (i,j) \in S_h. \tag{9}$$

where $\tau_0$ is taken as the inverse of a tour length calculated by applying the nearest neighbor heuristic, while $\rho_L$ is a value of local persistence.

When global updating of the pheromone is applied, the trail is updated on the graph connections belonging to the best global tour, $S_{h_g}$, by applying the expression:

$$\tau_{ij} = (1 - \rho)\tau_{ij} + \frac{\rho}{L_{h_g}} \ \forall (i,j) \in S_{h_b}. \tag{10}$$

where the increase is inversely proportional to the length of the solution found by the best global ant, $L_{h_g}$.

The parameter $\rho$ considered for the global update may take on different value than the one considered for the local update of the pheromone, $\rho_L$ .

## 5.3   Reconstruction of the RPP Solution

Once a tour for the TSP has been determined, a solution is determined for the associated RPP.

Let $s_a^i, s_b^j, \ldots, s_N^x$ be the sequence of N stops of the TSP solution. The first stop of the RPP path will be the one identified by the sub-index associated to the first TSP stop: $a$. Then we take pairs of consecutive TSP stops to determine a new stop or stops on the RPP path. The first time stops $s_a^i$ and $s_b^j$ are considered, whereas the last time stops $s_N^x$ and $s_a^i$ are considered.

Let $s_i^h, s_j^k$ be two consecutive stops of the TSP solution. If the sub-indexes of the two consecutive stops are the same, but the super-indexes are not ($i = j, h \neq k$), this represents a zero-cost loop in the TSP tour. In this case no stops need to be added to the RPP path. If $i = k$ and $h = j$, the connection is direct. In this case stop $i$ is added to the RPP path. If we are not in either of the two previous situations, we check if there is a direct connection in the original graph, and if that connection is shorter than any other indirect connection. If such a connection exists, the stop identified by $i$ is added to the RPP path. In other cases, either there is no direct connection or there is an indirect connection shorter than the direct one; we must add to the RPP path the stops of the shortest paths identified to pass from stop $i$ to stop $j$.

**Table 1.** Best solution for the set of sample problems by applying different methods

| PROBLEM | $|V|$ | $|E|$ | $|E_r|$ | $|E_{nr}|$ | OPT | CH. | F-C | FR. | 2OPT | 3OPT | HH | nHH |
|---------|------|------|------|------|-----|-----|-----|-----|------|------|-----|-----|
| p01 | 11 | 13 | 7 | 6 | 76 | 76 | 76 | 76 | 76 | 76 | 76 | 76 |
| p02 | 14 | 33 | 12 | 21 | 152 | 164 | 163 | 155 | 153 | 152 | 163 | 163 |
| p03 | 28 | 58 | 26 | 32 | 102 | 102 | 102 | 105 | 103 | 103 | 102 | 102 |
| p04 | 17 | 35 | 22 | 13 | 84 | 84 | 86 | 84 | 84 | 84 | 84 | 84 |
| p05 | 20 | 35 | 16 | 19 | 124 | 135 | 129 | 130 | 124 | 124 | 129 | 129 |
| p06 | 24 | 46 | 20 | 26 | 102 | 107 | 102 | 107 | 107 | 102 | 102 | 102 |
| p07 | 23 | 47 | 24 | 23 | 130 | 130 | 130 | 130 | 130 | 130 | 130 | 130 |
| p08 | 17 | 40 | 24 | 16 | 122 | 122 | 122 | 122 | 122 | 122 | 122 | 122 |
| p09 | 14 | 26 | 14 | 12 | 83 | 84 | 83 | 83 | 83 | 83 | 83 | 83 |
| p10 | 12 | 20 | 10 | 10 | 80 | 80 | 84 | 80 | 80 | 80 | 80 | 80 |
| p11 | 9 | 14 | 7 | 7 | 23 | 23 | 23 | 26 | 23 | 23 | 23 | 23 |
| p12 | 7 | 18 | 5 | 13 | 19 | 22 | 21 | 22 | 19 | 19 | 21 | 21 |
| p13 | 7 | 10 | 4 | 6 | 35 | 38 | 38 | 35 | 35 | 35 | 38 | 38 |
| p14 | 28 | 79 | 31 | 48 | 202 | 212 | 209 | 207 | 204 | 202 | 209 | 209 |
| p15 | 26 | 37 | 19 | 18 | 441 | 445 | 445 | 445 | 441 | 441 | 445 | 445 |
| p16 | 31 | 94 | 34 | 60 | 203 | 203 | 203 | 215 | 205 | 203 | 203 | 203 |
| p17 | 19 | 44 | 17 | 27 | 112 | 116 | 112 | 116 | 112 | 112 | 112 | 112 |
| p18 | 23 | 37 | 16 | 21 | 147 | 148 | 148 | | | | 148 | 148 |
| p19 | 33 | 55 | 29 | 26 | 257 | 280 | 263 | 274 | 271 | 266 | 263 | 263 |
| p20 | 50 | 98 | 63 | 35 | 398 | 400 | 399 | 402 | 400 | 400 | 398 | 398 |
| p21 | 49 | 110 | 67 | 43 | 366 | 372 | 368 | 372 | 372 | 372 | 372 | 366 |
| p22 | 50 | 184 | 74 | 110 | 621 | 632 | 621 | 633 | 622 | 622 | 636 | 621 |
| p23 | 50 | 158 | 78 | 80 | 475 | 480 | 489 | 479 | 477 | 477 | 487 | 480 |
| p24 | 41 | 125 | 55 | 70 | 405 | 411 | 405 | 411 | 405 | 405 | 405 | 405 |

## 6   Tests

The algorithm described has been coded using C language. The tests have been performed on a personal computer with a 1.5GHz Intel Centrino processor and 512M RAM, and running under the Linux operating system.

The algorithm has been applied to the sample problems defined by Christofides et al. [13]. Table 1 summarizes the results obtained for this set of problems with some of the methods described in section 3. The name of the problem is indicated, the number of nodes, $|V|$, the total number of connections, $|E|$, the number of required connections, $|E_r|$, and not required connections, $|E_{nr}|$, as well as the best known solution for each problem, OPT. The remaining columns on the table show the best solution obtained for each problem by different authors: Christofides et al (CH.), Fernández de Córdoba (F-C), Frederickson (FR.), Groves y van Vuuren (2OPT and 3OPT), and the solutions proposed by Baldoquín (HH and nHH).

Table 2 summarizes the results obtained by the method proposed in this paper. For each problem 55 tests have been made, considering the following values for the parameters: $\alpha = 1$, $\beta = 2$, $\rho = \rho_L = 0.1$, $q_0 = 0.9$. The pheromone initially associated to the graph connections takes on random values at the interval $(0, 1]$. The first column on Table 2 identifies the problem and the second one shows the best known solution for each problem. In following, we show the best solution

**Table 2.** Solution obtained by applying ants

| PROBLEM | OPT | ANTS | %OP | AV | DES | $T(sec.)$ |
|---------|-----|------|-----|-----|------|-----------|
| p01 | 76 | 76 | 0 | 76 | 0.00 | 0.35 |
| p02 | 152 | 152 | 0 | 152.56 | 0.94 | 0.64 |
| p03 | 102 | 102 | 0 | 118.53 | 6.51 | 0.80 |
| p04 | 84 | 84 | 0 | 88.78 | 2.39 | 0.65 |
| p05 | 124 | 124 | 0 | 131.29 | 2.74 | 0.64 |
| p06 | 102 | 102 | 0 | 108.11 | 2.87 | 0.51 |
| p07 | 130 | 130 | 0 | 143.95 | 6.15 | 0.93 |
| p08 | 122 | 122 | 0 | 129.13 | 3.35 | 0.65 |
| p09 | 83 | 83 | 0 | 83.65 | 0.89 | 0.35 |
| p10 | 80 | 80 | 0 | 80 | 0.00 | 0.47 |
| p11 | 23 | 23 | 0 | 23 | 0.00 | 0.18 |
| p12 | 19 | 19 | 0 | 19 | 0.00 | 0 |
| p13 | 35 | 35 | 0 | 35 | 0.00 | 0.18 |
| p14 | 202 | 202 | 0 | 226.96 | 8.67 | 1.82 |
| p15 | 441 | 441 | 0 | 452.95 | 8.77 | 0.63 |
| p16 | 203 | 203 | 0 | 229.04 | 10.13 | 2.41 |
| p17 | 112 | 112 | 0 | 113.82 | 1.42 | 0.64 |
| p18 | 147 | 146 | - | 148.09 | 1.60 | 0.35 |
| p19 | 257 | 261 | 1.5 | 289.42 | 10.61 | 0.96 |
| p20 | 398 | 424 | 4.6 | 510.67 | 21.82 | 7.12 |
| p21 | 366 | 395 | 7.3 | 470.11 | 19.21 | 8.12 |
| p22 | 621 | 658 | 5.6 | 787.67 | 26.39 | 15.8 |
| p23 | 475 | 511 | 8.1 | 579.73 | 17.62 | 10.3 |
| p24 | 405 | 415 | 2.4 | 479.75 | 22.34 | 8.4 |

reached by applying ants (ANTS), the percentage over the optimum (%OP), the average (AV) and the standard deviation (DES) for the costs of the tours obtained for each problem, and the average time in second for the calculation of the solution (T).

We must point out that for problem p18 different authors give different optimal values. In [18] value 147 is considered, whereas in [17] value 148 is considered. Our method gives a feasible solution with cost equal to 146.

We observe that on more than the 70% of the problems the best known solution is obtained. Additionally, the required computational time is reduced to a few seconds. Although the optimum is not achieved for all the test problems, the results obtained during this first approximation are encouraging. We believe that by fine-tuning the basic ant algorithm applied, better solutions could be reached.

## 7   Conclusion

With this work we have proven that artificial ant colonies can be applied to solve the Rural Postman Problem.

The solution reached is comparable to that of other methods proposed for the problem. One advantage of the proposed method is that it does not require a complex mathematical representation of the problem to be solved, we simply use the graph that represents the problem. Furthermore, the method always generates a feasible solution when applied to the sample set.

The solution obtained could be improved by applying certain modifications to the basic algorithm, such as the use of candidate lists.

## References

1. Dorigo, M., Maniezzo, V., Colorni, A.: Ant System: an Autocatalytic Optimizing Process. Tech. Rep. 91-016, Dipartamento di Electtronica e Informazione - Politecnico di Milano. Italia, pp. 1–26 (1991)
2. Dorigo, M.: Optimization, Learning and Natural Algorithms. PhD Thesis, Dip. Elettronica, Politecnico di Milano (1992)
3. Maniezzo, V., Colorni, A., Dorigo, M.: The Ant System Applied to the Quadratic Assignment Problem. Technical Report IRIDIA/94-28, Université Libre de Bruxelles, Belgium (1994)
4. Maniezzo, V.: Exact and Approximate Nondeterministic Tree-search Procedures for the Quadratic Assignment Problem. Technical Report CSR 98-1, C.L. In: Scienze dell'Informazione, Universitá di Bologna, Italy (1998)
5. Bullnheimer, B., Hartl, R.F., Strauss, C.: Applying the Ant System to the Vehicle Routing Problem. Advances and Trends in Local Search Paradigms for Optimization, pp. 285–296 (1999)
6. Gambardella, L.M., Taillard, E., Agazzi, G.: Ant Colonies for Vehicle Routing Problems. In: Corne, E.D., Dorigo, M., Glover, F. (eds.) New Ideas in Optimization, McGraw-Hill, New York (1999)
7. Costa, D., Hertz, A.: Ants Can Colour Graphs. Journal of the Operational Research Society 48, 295–305 (1997)

8. Ball, M.O., Magnanti, T.L., Monma, C.L., Nemhauser, G.L.: Network Models 7. North-Holland (1995)
9. Dantzig, G.B., Fulkerson, D.R., Johnson, S.M.: Solution of a Large-scale Traveling Salesman Problem. Operations Research 2, 393–410 (1954)
10. Reinelt, G.: The Traveling Salesman. LNCS, vol. 840. Springer, Heidelberg (1994)
11. Orloff, C.S.: A Fundamental Problem in Vehicle Routing. Networks 4, 35–64 (1974)
12. Frederickson, G.: Approximation Algorithms for Some Postman Problems. Journal of the Association for Computing Machinery 26, 538–554 (1979)
13. Christofides, N., Campos, V., Corberán, A., Mota, E.: An Algorithm for the Rural Postman Problem. Imperial College Report. London (1981)
14. Corberán, A., Sanchis, J.M.: A Polyhedral Approach to the Rural Postman Problem. European Journal of the Operational Research 79, 95–114 (1994)
15. Ghiani, G., Laporte, G.: A Branch and Cut Algorithm for the Undirected Rural Postman Problem. Mathematical Programming 87, 467–481 (2000)
16. Letchford, A.N.: Polyhedral Results for Some Constrained Arc Routing Problems. PhD Dissertation, Lancaster University, Lancaster (1996)
17. Fernández de Córdoba, P., García Raffi, L.M., Sanchis, J.M.: A Heuristic Algorithm Based on Monte Carlo Methods for the Rural Postman Problem. Computers Ops. Res. 25(12), 1097–1106 (1998)
18. Hertz, A., Laporte, G., Nanchen, P.: Improvement Procedures for the Undirected Rural Postman Problem. INFORMS J. Comput. 1, 53–62 (1999)
19. Groves, G.W., van Vuuren, J.H.: Efficient Heuristics for the Rural Postman Problem. Orion 21(1), 33–51 (2005)
20. Kang, M.-J., Han, C.-G.: Solving the Rural Postman Problem Using a Genetic Algorithm with a Graph Transformation. RR: Dept. of Computer Engineering, Kyung Hee University (1998)
21. Rodrigues, A.M., Ferreira, J.S.: Solving the Rural Postman problem by Memetic Algorithms. In: MIC 2001. 4th Metaheuristics International Conference, Porto, Portugal (2001)
22. Baldoquín, M.G., Ryan, G., Rodríguez, R., Castellini, A.: Un Enfoque Hibrido Basado en Metaheurísticas para el Problema del Cartero Rural. In: Proceedings of XI CLAIO, Concepción de Chile, Chile (2002)
23. Dorigo, M., Gambardella, L.: Ant Colony System: a Cooperative Learning Approach to the Traveling Salesman Problem. IEEE Transaction on Evolutionary Computation 1(1), 53–66 (1997)
24. Dorigo, M., Gambardella, L.M.: Ant Colonies for the Traveling Salesman Problem. Biosystems 43, 73–81 (1997)

# Olive Fly Infestation Prediction Using Machine Learning Techniques

José del Sagrado and Isabel María del Águila

Dpt. of Languages and Computation, University of Almería, 04120 Almería, Spain
{jsagrado,imaguila}@ual.es

**Abstract.** This article reports on a study on olive-fly infestation prediction using machine learning techniques. . The purpose of the work was, on the one hand, to make accurate predictions and, on the other, to verify whether the Bayesian network techniques are competitive with respect to classification trees. We have applied the techniques to a dataset and, in addition, performed a previous phase of variables selection to simplify the complexity of the classifiers. The results of the experiments show that Bayesians networks produce valid predictors, although improved definition of dependencies and refinement of the variables selection methods are required.

**Keywords:** Data mining, Bayesian Networks, Knowledge Based Systems, Integrated Production.

## 1 Motivation

Present-day industrial agriculture is to a large extent consequence of new technologies and the application of technological innovation to traditional agricultural production systems. The term 'crop' is no longer used, but rather 'agricultural production plant', which includes information systems for the management of this new industry.

The control of pests and diseases in these 'agricultural production plants' has an important weight in the economy of the sector and an important effect on the environment. That is, plant health is one of the major concerns of the agricultural industry and local and national authorities.

One of the greatest contributions to plant health control has been the definition and deployment of production standards to assure the health and quality of the products.

The regional governments of Andalusia, Murcia, Valencia, and Catalonia have developed quality standards called 'Integrated Production (IP)' for their more important crops. IP is defined at http://www.juntadeandalucia.es/agriculturaypesca as: "A set of agricultural production systems using natural production resources and mechanisms to assure long-term sustainable agriculture." In IP biological and chemical treatments are carefully selected, keeping in mind consumer demands, economical issues and environmental protection. IP includes task related with management, packing, transforming and labelling of productions.

IP application experience has shown the strong need for technical support that implicitly demands large information resources throughout all the processes implied in plant production. Integrated pest control is one of the more complex processes in

D. Borrajo, L. Castillo, and J.M. Corchado (Eds.): CAEPIA 2007, LNAI 4788, pp. 229–238, 2007.

which fast decision-making, taking diverse information and multiple criteria into account, is needed.

Information technologies, and specifically, knowledge-based technologies, applied to IP pest control can improve its management and effectiveness [1], [6], [9], [11]. A decision-support system facilitates the work of agricultural technicians and growers, and is fast becoming a basic tool in plant health. These tools also allow to increase the area (number of hectares) to be supervised by a single technician, thus spreading IP to a more fields, orchards and greenhouses.

The main purpose of this work was to study olive-fly infestation estimation using machine learning techniques based on classification trees and Bayesian networks. These techniques are applied to find predictors that indicate if a plant health treatment should be applied or not to mitigate incidence of the olive fly. The results obtained by the different predictors are contrasted against each other, using as reference the model based on classification trees. Furthermore, for Bayesian network predictors, the starting point is a Naïve Bayes method, which is affected by the hypothesis that feature variables are independent of each other, and its results are compared to those found by other models based on Bayesians networks (with increased tree structure or $k$-dependencies) that do not meet this hypothesis.

This paper is organized below in four sections. In Section 2 we describe the problem and the original data set. The techniques applied to find the predictors and the experiments designed with them are described in Section 3. In Section 4, variables are selected to simplify predictors without losing their effectiveness. Finally, in Section 5, we present the conclusions and suggest how this study could be extended in future work.

## 2    Problem Definition

The pest control problem is formulated by considering the crop as a complex system made up of the field, orchard or greenhouse, the plants, the pests and any useful fauna that can control the pests. This system is affected by external variables (climate, humidity, produce market price, etc.) and, following the IP standards, control actions that are especially respectful of the crop, useful fauna and environment should be made use of to keep them in balance.

From sowing to harvest, the tasks associated with a crop's health control are: start, monitor and end the crop. In the first task, in which the plants to be sown are described, the condition of the soil and the plants themselves are verified. Some information about the crops, such as plant density or number of rows, are collected or decided during this first task. The crop lifecycle, which is mainly evaluating the produce and making reports, is closed during the end task. Most of the workload is concentred on the monitoring task, in which the agricultural technician must sample the condition of the crop in order to estimate the risks related to different plagues. When there is an imbalance, the technician must recommend IP treatment.

Crop monitoring must be done weekly, collecting data about the condition of the crop, the state of pests or their effects and other useful information. Once the necessity for intervention has been decided, the technician also decides what control action has to be applied. It is worth mentioning that there are two clearly differentiated tasks involved in advising the grower. The decision about whether or not to act on a given crop must be taken first. Then, if affirmative, the most appropriate treatment (chemical, biological or mechanical) has to be decided.

## 2.1 Dataset

The Plant Health Information and Alert Network (RAIF) has been in operation in Andalusia since 1996. From the beginning, it was a pioneering idea in Spain, attempting to manage all the information on crop health and providing an answer to the increasing demand for information at all levels. To achieve this goal, a suitable training plan was designed for the group of specialized agricultural technicians who are in charge of watching out for the health of the main crops in Andalusia. The RAIF is also in charge of special data collection on plagues of particular concern to the sector due to the issues they raise, by making use of the network's control stations.

To meet these goals, the RAIF now has a team of specialized technicians devoted to tracking major plagues and diseases affecting citrus, cotton, grapevine and olive tree crops. In the future it is planned for the RAIF to include crops with progressively new importance for Andalusia like horticultural crops, strawberries, etc.

The RAIF has made available a vast dataset related to the development of these plagues. This dataset includes weekly samples, treatments and other actions done to the crop at Andalusian control stations defined by agricultural and geographic characteristics, i.e., 2000-hectare observation areas for olive trees, 1000-hectare areas for vineyards and 200-hectare areas for citrus trees and cotton.

Parasites associated with each plant and the ways of finding out whether they are present are completely different. We thus have a binary relationship made up of crops, set $C = \{$cotton, olive tree, vineyard, citruses$\}$, and the parasites, set $F$, pairs of which define the dataset to be sampled. Table 1 shows the relationship between these two sets. Each plague-plant pair has an associated series of non-heterogeneous observations gathered in the RAIF which enables parasite incidence to be evaluated. Furthermore, information on plant phenology, fertilization and irrigation, production and treatments is also collected during monitoring.

The starting point of this study was the weekly data collected by 2647 RAIF control stations from 1995 to 2004. The complexity of these data led us to define the olive tree as the target crop, because of its economic importance in the sector and the large number of hectares devoted to it in the Andalusian Region, which reduces the number of stations to 1355. Only the data for 2004 was used, and of them, only those from the stations subject to intensive monitoring.

## 2.2 Elemental Problem Findings

Each plague-plant pair is designated as an elemental problem. Eight elemental olive tree problems (shaded in Table 1) can be distinguished that must be reviewed and sampled during each visit. Each phytopathogen has its own sampling methodology, which focuses on three essential points dependent on the phytopathogen biology: the sampling unit, the sampling technique and the size of the sample.

Twenty five trees, randomly selected and grouped in sets of five, are examined in each visit to the control station. Phenology and phytopathogens in each of the selected trees are evaluated. Three values summarize the phenological state of the tree: the delayed phenological state (EF-), the dominant phenological state (EFD) and the most advanced phenological state (EF+). These values are chosen from a list of eleven standard olive tree possibilities.

**Table 1.** Possible harmful agents

| | 1 | 2 | 3 | 4 | 5 | 6 | 7 | 8 | 9 | 10 | 11 | 12 | 13 | 14 | 15 | 16 | 17 | 18 | 19 | 20 | 21 | 22 | 23 | 24 | 25 |
|---|---|---|---|---|---|---|---|---|---|---|---|---|---|---|---|---|---|---|---|---|---|---|---|---|---|
| Lemon tree | x | x | x | x | x | x | x | x | x | x | | | | | | | | | | | | | | | |
| Orange tree | | x | | | | x | x | | | x | | | | | | | | | | | | | | | |
| Tangerine tree | | | x | | x | | x | x | | x | | | | | | | | | | | | | | | |
| Olive tree | | | | | | | | | | x | x | x | x | x | x | x | x | | | | | | | | |
| Grapevine | | | | | | | | | | | | | | | | | | | | x | x | x | x | x | x |

| | | |
|---|---|---|
| 1 *Prays citry* | 9  *Planococcus citri* | 18, *Cicloconium* |
| 2 *Paraleyrodes minei* | 10 *Aonidiella auranti* | 19 *Capnodium* |
| 3 *Aleurothrixus floccosus* | 11 Aphid | 20 *Tetranichus* |
| 4 *Parabemisia myricae* | 12 *Euzophera* | 21 *Panonichus* |
| 5 *Tetranychus urticae* | 13 *Saissetia* | 22 *Plasmopara* |
| 6 *Phyllocnistis citrella* | 14 *Prays* | 23 *Uncinula* |
| 7 *Panonychus citri* | 15 *Phloeotribus* | 24 Rottenness |
| 8 *Apidiotus nerii* | 16 *Liothrips* | 25 *Lobesia botrana* |
| | **17 Dacus** | |

Eight buds, eight fruits and sixteen leaves are examined on each tree. In addition, two "funnel" traps (to capture *prays olae*), five chromotropic traps (for *dacus olae*) and trap bait are reviewed.

The agricultural technician estimates the level of infestation of each elemental problem by piecing together all these data. In IP, when a treatment decision is made, it must be justified by the sampling data and each phytopathogen is treated individually, that is, the elemental problems are independent

The olive fly (Dacus Oleae) is considered the worst enemy of the olive tree. In Spain it is very well known in all areas where olive trees are grown, although the damage varies in different regions, depending on the incidence.

## 3  Applied Techniques

Four different models for predicting the value of a variable indicating the need to apply an olive-fly pest control treatment were considered: one based on classification trees and three Bayesian network models.

### 3.1  Classification Trees

Classification trees (CT) are based on discretization of the feature variables domain, which is represented by a tree structure in which the inner nodes represent the variables and the branches represent an interval of their possible values. Each leaf is the particular value assumed by the class variable. The path from the root to the leaf indicates the values assumed by the feature variables when making the estimation.

## 3.2 Bayesian Networks

Bayesians networks [4] have been used successfully as models representing the uncertainty in knowledge bases in many application domains [5] [7] [8] [12]. The uncertainty is represented in terms of a probability distribution with independence relationships codified in a network structure.

Formally, a Bayesian network for a set of variables $V = \{V_1, \cdots, V_n\}$ is formed by a directed acyclic graph, the vertices of which are the variables in V, and a set of conditional probability distributions $p(v_i|pa(v_i))$ for each variable $V_i$ given its set of parents $pa(V_i)$.

A Bayesian network can be used as a predictor; just by considering one of the variables as the class and the others as feature variables (characteristics or features that describe the object that has to be classified). The prediction is found by means of probability propagation on the class variable. The posterior probability of the class is computed given the observed characteristics. The value assigned to the class is the one with the highest posterior probability.

We have considered four methods of learning the Bayesian network from the dataset:

- **Naïve-Bayes (NB):** [2] is based on the ingenuous Bayes model (or Naïve-Bayes), which assumes that all the feature variables are independent if the value of the class (or predictor) variable is known. This assumption implies that the only arcs appearing in the network are those connecting the variable class with feature variables and, therefore, there are no arcs between feature variables. The advantage of this method is that only a small number of parameters must be learned from the data, improving the precision of the estimates.
- **Naïve-Bayes with augmented tree structure (TAN):** [3] is a Naïve-Bayes model in which, in addition, each feature variable can have the variable class as parents and one other feature variable at most.
- **Naïve-Bayes with K-dependences (KNB):** [10] In this case, the Naïve-Bayes model is modified so each feature variable has at most $k$ feature variables as parents in addition to the class variable.
- **Bayesian network (BNET):** [4] This model does not start out from an assumption that the variables are independent of each other and a Bayesian network model is learned from the data

## 3.3 Experiments

In order to verify the performance of the models described above with the RAIF olive fly dataset for 2004, instead of experimenting with a fixed number of test partitions, we used 10-fold cross validation for the experiments. That is, the complete data set is divided in 10 subgroups, nine of which are used as training sets and the rest as the test set. In a first stage, the model is learned from the training set and, later, the test set is used to evaluate the predictor found. This two-stage process is repeated 10 times.

**Table 2.** Outcome with the different models

| Predictor | No. of Variables | Success Rate | Sensitivity | Specificity |
|---|---|---|---|---|
| CT | 6 | 98.08 | 96.44 | 95 |
| NB | 107 | 54.20 | 100 | 9.97 |
| TAN | 107 | 94.41 | 95.54 | 36.36 |
| KNB (K=3) | 107 | 95.45 | 95.59 | 80 |
| BNET | 107 | 95.63 | 95.60 | 100 |

The goodness of each model created is measured as the rate of success, sensitivity and specificity. These three criteria, along with model simplicity (measured as the number of variables it uses), make it possible to compare them on the basis of their predictive performance. Table 2 shows the results.

In analysing the results, it should be noted that in this knowledge domain, a decision to treat when it is unnecessary, is much worse than the reverse, since the crops are visited weekly. Therefore, our interest is in focusing on predictors with a high specificity value.

Concerning the analysis of the results, we can say that:

- The best results were for CT and BNET. In addition, if its simplicity is taken into account, the CT model, which produces similar results with just 6 variables (as opposed to 107 for the BNET) is much better than the BNET.
- Performance is improved with methods based on Naïve-Bayes as they increase the number of dependencies between predicting variables. This indicates that, in addition to the influence that the high number of variables has on the predictor, they are interdependent, as confirmed by better BNET behaviour.

## 4   Selection of Variables

In this section we do not attempt to study the problem of selecting variables used to predict the olive fly infestation level, but only locate some subgroups of variables to simplify the complexity of the Bayesian network model but maintaining a similar predictive performance. To do this, we filtered the variables, creating a filter by ranking the variables. Another filtering method consists of selecting the variables used by a predictor as the starting point for learning a different model.

### 4.1   Filtering Variables

To select a good attribute subgroup, variables must be ranked to measure the relationship between each feature variable and the class variable. A commonly used measure is *mutual information* (*MI*), which measures the interdependence between variables. The *MI* between two variables $X$ and $Y$ is defined as:

$$I(X, Y) = H(X) + H(Y) - H(X, Y), \qquad (1)$$

**Table 3.** Ranking of variables found by mutual information measurement

| Variables | Mutual Information |
|---|---|
| Moth | 0.07924 |
| EFD 6, EFD 5, EFD 8, EFD 7, EFD 2, EFD 1, EFD 4, EFD 3 | 0.05877 |
| EFD 11, EFD 12, EFD 9, EFD 10 | 0.05838 |
| EFD 13 | 0.05801 |
| EFD 22, EFD 20, EFD 21, EFD 25, EFD 23, EFD 24 | 0.05764 |
| EFD 16, EFD 14, EFD 15, EFD 19, EFD 17, EFD 18 | 0.05728 |
| EF- 6, EF- 1 | 0.05347 |
| EF- 2 | 0.05292 |
| EF- 11, EF- 16 | 0.05265 |
| EF- 12, EF- 7 | 0.05185 |
| EF- 21 | 0.05158 |
| EF- 17 | 0.05132 |
| EF- 3 | 0.05079 |
| EF- 22, EF- 8 | 0.05053 |
| EF- 15, EF- 20, EF- 13 | 0.05001 |
| EF- 24, EF- 4, EF- 18, EF- 14, EF- 25, EF- 5, EF- 23, EF- 10, EF- 9,  EF- 19 | 0.04975 |
| EF+ 9, EF + 8, EF+ 10, EF+ 4, EF+ 3, | 0.04306 |
| EF+ 15, EF+ 14, EF+ 19, EF+ 25, EF+ 20, EF+ 5 | 0.04283 |
| EF+ 24, EF+ 18, EF+ 23, EF+ 22, EF+ 2,  EF+ 21, EF+ 16, EF+ 6, EF+ 17 | 0.04259 |
| EF+ 7, EF+ 1, EF+ 12, EF+ 13 | 0.04236 |
| EF+ 11 | 0.04212 |
| Presence 7 | 0.03078 |
| Presence 13, Presence 19 | 0.01521 |
| Presence 23 | 0.0147 |
| Presence 2 | 0.01057 |
| Presence 18 | 0.01052 |
| Presence 21 | 0.00837 |
| Presence 14 | 0.00756 |

where $H(X)$ is the Shannon entropy,  defined as:

$$H(X) = - \textstyle\sum_{x \in X} p(x) \, log_2(p(x)). \tag{2}$$

The first $k$ variables are selected from the resulting ranking to form a subgroup. Table 3 shows the ranking, while $MI$ is calculated for all feature variables $V_i$ with an $MI$ greater than 0. This method of selecting the variables has (at least) two problems: the choice of $k$ (which is the number of variables to be selected) and, if they have been ranked (as in our case) by measuring the relationship between the predicting variable and the class individually, the subgroup usually contains redundant variables. Here we simply discarded all the variables with an $MI$ equal to 0.

Another way to select attributes is to apply a technique, find a predictor, and select only those attributes that appear in it as the starting point for constructing a new predictor based on a technique other than the one used to filter the variables. For example, only the variables used by the classification tree, {*Month, EF- 1, Trap 7-3, EF+ 2, EF+5, Treat*}, can be selected before applying Bayesian network techniques.

## 4.2  Experiments

This subsection deals with the influence that the selection of variables has on the performance of Bayesians network models using the 2004 RAIF olive fly dataset. The experiments were done by first selecting the variables and later constructing the different models, using 10-fold cross validation. As in Section 3.3, rate of successes, sensitivity and specificity were used to compare the predictive performance of the models.

**Table 4.** Results for the different models (selection based on *MI*)

| Predictor | No. of Variables | Success Rate | Sensitivity | Specificity |
|-----------|------------------|--------------|-------------|-------------|
| CT | 4 | 95.10 | 96.23 | 53.33 |
| NB | 85 | 51.75 | 100 | 9.51 |
| TAN | 85 | 94.41 | 95.54 | 36.36 |
| KNB (K=3) | 85 | 95.45 | 95.59 | 80 |
| BNET | 85 | 95.63 | 95.60 | 100 |

With the *MI* selection (Table 4):

- The *CT* model gets worse. This is because Variable Trap 7-3 was filtered out. This variable turned out to be crucial to prediction, since the value of specificity was drastically reduced.
- The NB success rate is reduced, due to the decrease in specificity. Filtering has left redundant variables that influence the result of the prediction, just as for the *CT*, since in this model the predictor variables are independent of each other given the class.
- TAN, KNB and BNET simplify and maintain the same performance rate as before filtering. The dependencies between predictor variables enable performance to be maintained.

**Table 5.** Results with the Bayesian network models (selection based on the *CT*)

| Predictor | No. of Variables | Success Rate | Sensitivity | Specificity |
|-----------|------------------|--------------|-------------|-------------|
| NB | 6 | 61.73 | 98.80 | 10.42 |
| TAN | 6 | 94.76 | 94.92 | 0 |
| KNB (K=3) | 6 | 94.76 | 94.92 | 0 |
| BNET | 6 | 94.93 | 94.93 | 0 |

For the selection of variables using the CT (Table 5) it may be said that:

- NB simplifies and improves the results. The variables selected by the CT have more discriminative power, which influences NB positively due to its assumptions and to the elimination of a large number of redundant variables.
- TAN, KDB and BNET are worse, due to the loss of dependency relationships between the predicting variables, that translates into overestimation.

# 5 Conclusions

Application of knowledge-based techniques to the plant-health problem of control of the olive fly has been evaluated. Such techniques have proved to be valid and effective. For the RAIF dataset employed here, classification trees and the Bayesian network predictor produced the best results. Classification trees perform better in terms of model simplicity, success rate and sensitivity, but they have a little lack of specificity. We think that this lack can be corrected applying general techniques for combining models as bagging or boosting.

The fact that the Bayesian network model is better than the rest of the Naïve-Bayes models indicates the presence of dependencies of feature variables that have to be studied and elicited with the aid of expert knowledge. As in the case of CT it would be very interesting to study if the use of boosting and bagging techniques can improve the results of the classification techniques used based on Bayesian networks.

The selection of variables has simplified the models, but with different effects on performance. Reduced complexity of selection based on MI did not impact on the prediction when the models took dependencies between variables (TAN, KBD, BNET) into consideration. Nevertheless, the attempt to reduce the complexity of the models (selection based on CT), did not produce good results due to overestimation in the models. We think that work should continue in this direction, but first the relationships between variables have to be studied. Also is left to be done a forecast based on a combination of the outputs of the best classifiers obtained with each one of the techniques applied, to see if the prediction results can be improved.

**Acknowledgements.** This work was supported by the Spanish Ministry of Educations and Science under projects TIN 2004-05694 and TIN 2004-06204-C03-01 and the *Junta de Andalucía* (Andalusian Regional Government) P06-TIC-02411.

# References

1. Águila, I.M., Cañadas, J., Bosch, A., Túnez, S., Marín, R.: Knowledge model of therapy administration task applied to an agricultural domain. In: Palade, V., Howlett, R.J., Jain, L. (eds.) KES 2003. LNCS, vol. 2774, pp. 1277–1283. Springer, Heidelberg (2003)
2. Duda, R.O., Hart, P.E.: Pattern classification. John Wiley and Sons, New York (2001)
3. Friedman, N., Geiger, D., Goldszmidt, M.: Bayesian networks classifiers. Machine Learrning 29, 131–163 (1997)
4. Jensen, F.V.: Bayesian Networks and decision graphs. Springer, Heidelberg (2001)
5. Kristensen, K., Rasmussen, I.A.: The use of a Bayesian network in the design of a decision support system for growing malting barley without use of pesticides. Computers and Electronics in Agriculture 33, 197–217 (2002)
6. Maman, B.D., Harizanis, P., Filis, I., Antonopoulou, E., Yialouris, C.P., Sideridis, A.B.: A diagnostic expert system for honeybee pests. Computers and Electronics in Agriculture 36, 17–31 (2002)
7. de Melo, A.C.V., Sanchez, A.J.: Software maintenance project delays prediction using Bayesian Networks. Expert Systems with Applications doi:10.1016/j.eswa.2006.10.040 (2007)

8. Lauría, E.J., Duchessi, P.J.: A Bayesian Belief Network for IT implementation decision support. Decision Support Systems 42, 1573–1588 (2006)
9. Perini, A., Susi, A.: Developing a decision support system for integrated production in Agriculture. Environmental Modelling & Software 19, 821–829 (2004)
10. Sahami, M.: Learning limited dependence Bayesian classifiers. In: Proceedings of Second international Conference of Knowledge Discovery and Data Mining, pp. 335–338 (2002)
11. Túnez, S., Aguila, I., Marín, M.R.: An Expertise Model for Therapy Planning Using Abductive Reasoning. Cybernetics and Systems: An international Journal 32, 829–849 (2001)
12. Zhu, J.Y., Deshmukh, A.: Application of Bayesian decision networks to life cycle engineering in Green design and manufacturing Engineering. Applications of Artificial Intelligence 16, 91–103 (2003)

# Feature Selection Based on Sensitivity Analysis*

Noelia Sánchez-Maroño and Amparo Alonso-Betanzos

University of A Coruña, 15071 A Coruña. Spain
{nsanchez,ciamparo}@udc.es
http://www.dc.fi.udc.es/lidia

**Abstract.** In this paper an incremental version of the ANOVA and Functional Networks Feature Selection (AFN-FS) method is presented. This new wrapper method (IAFN-FS) is based on an incremental functional decomposition, thus eliminating the main drawback of the basic method: the exponential complexity of the functional decomposition. This complexity limited its scope of applicability, being only applicable to datasets with a relatively small number of features. The performance of the incremental version of the method was tested against several real data sets. The results show that IAFN-FS outperforms the accuracy obtained by other standard and novel feature selection methods, using a small set of features.

## 1   Introduction

Sensitivity analysis is the study of how the variation in the output of a model (numerical or otherwise) can be apportioned, qualitatively or quantitatively, to different sources of variation, and how the given model depends upon the information fed in it. This is an important method for checking the quality of a given model, as well as a powerful tool for checking the robustness and reliability of its analysis. The topic is acknowledged as essential for good modelling practice, and is an implicit part of any modelling field [1]. On the other hand, in models such as functional and neural networks, learning can be achieved through many alternative methods and variants [2,3]. Some of them present advantages with respect to others, but all of them give as output the weights values. However, learning the weights of a functional or neural network from data is not enough. People is more and more concerned about the influence of data on the resulting model, that is on the sensitivity of these models. At this respect, it is clear that giving information about the relative influence on the resulting model, in addition to the weight values, is clearly convenient and can lead to posterior decisions that include removing some of the initial features and repeat the analysis, or leave the model as is. This process, in which the number of initial features is reduced and a subset of them that retain enough information for obtaining good, or even better, performance results is selected, is called feature selection. This is a very

---

* The authors wish to acknowledge Xunta de Galicia for partial funding under project PGIDT05TIC10502PR.

D. Borrajo, L. Castillo, and J.M. Corchado (Eds.): CAEPIA 2007, LNAI 4788, pp. 239–248, 2007.
© Springer-Verlag Berlin Heidelberg 2007

interesting aspect, for example, in medical and biological applications, in which data can be scarce or expensive to acquire. Basically, feature selection methods can be classified in wrapper and filter methods [4]. Filter methods rely on general characteristics of the training data in order to provide a complete order of the features using a relevance index, without optimizing the performance of a predictor [5]. Wrapper methods use a learning algorithm to score subsets of features according to their predictive value. Wrapper methods are usually more expensive computationally, but also result in better performance [6].

In this paper, a new version of a wrapper algorithm is presented. This method, originally described in [7], is based on functional networks and analysis of variance decomposition. The method is called AFN-FS (ANOVA and Functional Networks Feature Selection), and exhibited a good accuracy results while maintaining a reduced set of variables in several experimental results, as shown in [7]. Besides, AFN-FS presents several other advantages, such as that it allows to discard several variables in just one step, and so there is no need to check all possible subsets, as it occurs in sequential backward search. Another important advantage of the method is that it permits the user the interpretation of the results obtained, because the relevance of each feature selected or rejected is given in terms of variance. However, the method also presented a drawback: the exponential complexity of the functional decomposition. So, its application was limited to data sets with a small number of features. An incremental version of the AFN-FS method is presented in this paper with the aim of solving this limitation. The new version of the method is applied to real-world classification data sets of the UCI Learning repository, and its performance results are compared to those obtained by novel feature subset selection methods developed by other authors.

## 2 The Incremental AFN-FS Method

### 2.1 The Anova Functional Network (AFN) Learning Method

A detailed description on this method can be found in [8]. Briefly, the method is based on a combination of ANOVA (ANalysis Of VAriance) and functional networks in order to estimate a function $f$ in terms of $n$ variables $f(x_1, x_2, \ldots, x_n)$, by approximating its functional components. According to Sobol [9], any square integrable function $f(x_1, x_2, \ldots, x_n)$, can always be written as the sum of the $2^n$ orthogonal summands:

$$f(x_1, \ldots, x_n) = f_0 + \sum_{i=1}^{n} f_i(x_i) + \sum_{i=1}^{n-1} \sum_{j=i}^{n} f_{ij}(x_i, x_j) + \cdots + f_{12\ldots n}(x_1, x_2, \ldots, x_n),$$

that can be rewritten, in a simplified form, as:

$$f(x_1, \ldots, x_n) = f_0 + \sum_{\nu=1}^{2^n-1} f_\nu(\mathbf{x}_\nu), \qquad (1)$$

where $\nu$ represents each possible subset formed with the variables $\{x_1, x_2, \ldots, x_n\}$ and $f_0$ is a constant that corresponds to the function with no arguments.

Besides, if $f(x_1, x_2, \ldots, x_n)$ is square integrable, then each summand is also square integrable, so

$$\int_0^1 \int_0^1 \cdots \int_0^1 f^2(x_1, \ldots, x_n) dx_1 dx_2 \ldots dx_n - f_0^2 = \sum_{\nu=1}^{2^n-1} \int_0^1 f_\nu^2(\mathbf{x}_\nu) d\mathbf{x}_\nu.$$

Calling $D$, the variance, the left part of this equation and $D_\nu$ to each summand in the right part, it results that

$$D = \sum_{\nu=1}^{2^n-1} D_\nu,$$

so, the variance of the initial function can be obtained by summing up the variance of the components. This allows assigning global sensitivity indices to the different functional components, adding up to one, such as:

$$GSI_\nu = \frac{D_\nu}{D} \qquad \nu = 1, 2, \ldots, 2^n - 1.$$

The AFN method approximates each functional component $f_\nu(\mathbf{x}_\nu)$ in (1) as:

$$f_\nu(\mathbf{x}_\nu) = \sum_{j=1}^{k_\nu} c_{\nu j} p_{\nu j}(\mathbf{x}_\nu), \tag{2}$$

where $c_{\nu j}$ are parameters to be estimated and $p_\nu$ is a set of orthonormalized basis functions. There exists several alternatives to choose those functions [8]. One possibility consists of using one of the families of univariate orthogonal functions, for example, Legendre polynomials, forming tensor products with them and selecting a subset of them.

The $c_{\nu j}$ parameters are learnt by solving an optimization problem:

$$Minimize \quad J = \sum_{s=1}^m \epsilon_s^2 = \sum_{s=1}^m (y_s - \hat{y}_s)^2, \tag{3}$$

being $m$ the number of available samples, $y_s$ the desired output for the sample $s$ and $\hat{y}_s$ the estimated output obtained by:

$$\hat{y}_s = \hat{f}(x_{s1}, \ldots, x_{sn}) = f_0 + \sum_{\nu=1}^{2^n-1} \sum_{j=1}^{k_\nu} c_{\nu j} p_{\nu j}(\mathbf{x}_{s\nu}). \tag{4}$$

Once the $c_{\nu j}$ parameters are learnt, global sensitivity indices ($GSI$) for each functional component can be directly derived as:

$$GSI_\nu = \sum_{j=1}^{k_\nu} c_{\nu j}^2 \quad \nu = 1, 2, \ldots, 2^n - 1, \tag{5}$$

adding up the contribution of a given variable $i$ to each GSI, the total sensitivity index (TSI) for that variable is obtained:

$$TSI_i = \sum_{\nu=1}^{2^n-1} GSI_\nu \text{ such that } x_i \in \nu \quad i = 1, \ldots, n. \tag{6}$$

## 2.2   The Incremental AFN-FS Method

From the AFN method, a feature selection algorithm was proposed as described in [7]. It is a wrapper method that uses a backward selection search, discarding several features in the same step. The induction algorithm employed is the AFN method described above, while the derived GSI and TSI indices are used to guide the search process. The method developed was called AFN-FS (AFN-Feature Selection) and had several advantages, such as:

- it allows to discard several variables in just one step, and so there is no need to check all possible subsets, as it occurs in sequential backward search
- it permits the user the interpretation of the results obtained, because the relevance of each feature selected or rejected is given in terms of variance.
- in the results obtained after the application of the algorithm in [7] it can be seen that the performance of the method outperforms or equals the performance of other feature selection methods, while reducing the number of features selected.

However, the method presents one fundamental drawback: it can only be used in those data sets with a high ratio between the number of samples, $m$, and the number of features, $n$. Specifically, $m > 2^n - 1$. This requirement is accomplished in a few real-world data sets, and it was necessary to modify the method in order to increase its scope of application. So, instead of estimating the desired output using the equation in (4), an incremental approximation was designed. This modification to the basic AFN-FS leads to the incremental AFN-FS method described in this work and explained in the following paragraphs.

Moreover, the AFN was initially intended for regression problems, but as most of the feature selection studies available [4,10,11] deal with classification problems, the mean squared error was substituted by the cross-entropy as cost function in order to obtain better performance results [2]. Then, for binary classification problems, the optimization problem in (3) is changed to:

$$Minimize \quad J = -\sum_{s=1}^{m} y_s ln(\hat{y}_s) + (1 - y_s) ln(1 - \hat{y}_s). \tag{7}$$

Also, as the AFN-FS is a wrapper method, it requires an evaluation function which is in our case the mean accuracy from a five-fold cross validation as in [4]. The incremental AFN-FS method follows the steps below, that can be seen in Figure 1:

**Initial selection.** The algorithm uses a backward selection method, and so it starts with the complete set of features. The algorithm AFN is applied so as to obtain the desired output by solving (7). But, to limit the exponential complexity of the estimated output in (4), an incremental approximation was used. Then, initially the desired output is estimated excluding the interactions between the features, and including only the univariate components. The estimated output is calculated as:

$$\hat{y}_s = f_0 + \sum_{\nu=1}^{n} \sum_{j=1}^{k_\nu} c_{\nu j} p_j(\mathbf{x}_{s\nu}). \tag{8}$$

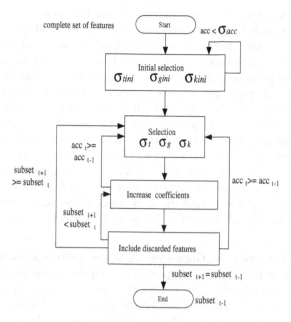

**Fig. 1.** Diagram of the IAFN-FS method, $\sigma_{gini}$, $\sigma_{tini}$,$\sigma_{kini}$, $\sigma_k$, $\sigma_t$ and $\sigma_g$ are thresholds. Stop condition: any smaller subset of features leads to worse accuracy results

where $s$ is a specific sample, $n$ the number of initial features and $k_\nu$ the set of functions used to estimate the functional component $\nu$.

As a result, a value for the evaluation function is obtained ($acc_{ini}$) and the parameters $c_{\nu j}$ in (8) are learnt. Therefore, GSI and TSI can be directly calculated by (5) and (6), respectively. Notice that the interactions between features are not considered in (8), then both sets of indices are equal in this case. Remember that the evaluation function is the mean accuracy from a five-fold cross validation, then, those features which TSI value is over an established threshold $\sigma_{tini}$ in a minimum of $\sigma_{kini}$ folds are selected. Using the selected features, the bivariate components in the functional decomposition can be considered now for the estimation of the desired output:

$$\hat{y}_s = f_0 + \sum_{i=1}^{r}\sum_{j=1}^{k_i} c_{ij}p_j(x'_{si}) + \sum_{i_1=1}^{r-1}\sum_{i_2=i_1}^{r}\sum_{j=1}^{k_{(i_1,i_2)}} c_{(i_1,i_2)j}p_j(x'_{si_1},x'_{si_2}),$$

where $\{x'_1, x'_2, \ldots, x'_r\}$ is the subset of selected features.

Again, this estimation produces a set of TSI and GSI values that would suggest a subset of features from the previous one. Each feature which TSI value is upper the established threshold ($\sigma_{tini}$) is selected. However, to determine if the feature is important by its own or by its combination with other features, the Global Sensitivity Indices (GSI) are required and another threshold needs to be established for them ($\sigma_{gini}$). Those features or combinations between features under this threshold are eliminated.

A new approximation is accomplished using this newly selected subset of features and including the trivariate components of the functional decomposition in (4). The same process continues, by means of increasing the complexity of the approximation adding new functional components. Therefore, the selection process developed for the original AFN-FS has been subdivided into several substeps that increase its complexity incrementally.

This initial selection is required to ensure the elimination of some features. But, there is no backward step to reconsider the features discarded in this step. Therefore, a wrong initial selection may lead to poor performance results. So, in order to guarantee the adequacy of this first selection, a condition was added to the algorithm that forces to repeat this step until the accuracy obtained with the subset of selected features is greater than a threshold ($\sigma_{acc}$). Notice that different approaches can be obtained for the estimation in (4), this condition is intended to select a good one from all of them.

**Cyclic selection process.** Once several features were discarded in the previous steps, the selection process is repeated iteratively. At each step $(t)$, the AFN method is applied using the features returned by the previous step $(t - 1)$. While the mean accuracy obtained at present($acc_t$) is higher or equal to the previous one $(acc_{t-1})$, the method is applied in turn. The steps of this cyclic process are detailed below,but for more detailed explanation, please see [7].

- Selecting the relevant features. Using the information provided by the TSI and GSI indices, the least relevant features are discarded such as in the initial selection step.
- Increasing the number of coefficients. Reducing the number of features means decreasing the number of coefficients. Even with an adequate set of features, a reduced number of parameters in the approximation function may not lead to a good estimation. This step increases the number of coefficients, by considering more complex functions, to avoid the degradation of the estimated output.
- Including discarded variables. Several variables are discarded in one step according to the global and total sensitivity indices. If the accuracy of the approach diminishes, this step allows to reestablish the thresholds ($\sigma_g$ and $\sigma_t$) to reconsider some of the discarded variables.

The feature selection method described is very dependent on the different thresholds employed ($\sigma_t$, $\sigma_g$ and $\sigma_{acc}$). A difficulty here is to establish an initial value for them, that were valid for any dataset. This is an important matter to fully automate the process of feature selection:

- For $\sigma_t$, its initial value was established according to different metrics obtained from the set $\{TSI_1, TSI_2, \ldots, TSI_r\}$, being $r$ the number of selected features in the different steps of the process, $r <= n$. Several attempts were carried out using different combinations with the mean and the standard deviation of this set. Finally, it was established to the value:

$$\sigma_t = \overline{TSI} - \frac{SD_{TSI}}{2}, \tag{9}$$

where $\overline{TSI}$ is the mean of the set $\{TSI_1, TSI_2, \ldots, TSI_r\}$ and SD its standard deviation.

- A similar process was carried for $\sigma_g$, but in this case the variability, depending on the specific problem, of the global sensitivity indices was very high, thus making it difficult to establish a starting value. After several trials with different data sets, it was empirically found that a value in the interval $[0.01 - 0.02]$ leads to good performance results. The meaning of this is that those features or combinations between features representing more than 1% or 2% of the total variance must be taken into account.

- Finally, $\sigma_{acc}$, was established as the value obtained after training the AFN learning method with the complete set of features.

## 3   Results

In order to evaluate the incremental AFN-FS method presented in this paper, it was applied to several real-world classification problems used in previous studies [4,10], so as to be able to establish comparisons with other feature selection methods. The selected problems are binary classification problems that can be obtained from the UCI-Irvine repository [12].

The AFN method estimates a function by approximating its functional components based on a family of basis functions that has to be orthonormalized. In a first attempt, the polynomial family was selected for the experiments carried out. The following univariate polynomial functions were selected: $\{1, x, x^2, x^3\}$ that leads to the following set of orthonormalized functions:

$$\{p_{1;1}(x), p_{1;2}(x), p_{1;3}(x)\} = \{\sqrt{3}(2x - 1), \sqrt{5}(6x^2 - 6x + 1),$$
$$\sqrt{7}(20x^3 - 30x^2 + 12x - 1)\}.$$

Tensor products with these functions were formed to obtained bivariate and trivariate functions. If we select as univariate basis functions polynomials of degree $d$, for the $n$-dimensional basis functions, the tensor product technique leads to polynomials of degree $d \times n$, which is too high.Thus, we can limit the degree of the corresponding $n$-multivariate basis to contain only polynomials of degree $d_n$ or less. This is what we have done with the datasets presented in table 1, limiting $d_n$ to 4 or 5 depending on the problem. Note that these bases are obtained independently of the data set, which means that they are valid for all the data set considered.

### 3.1   Results for the Basic AFN-FS Method

For the first approach, that is, without incremental version, the number of features of the datasets could not be very high, as the method was not able to address them. The first four rows in Table 1 describe the main characteristics of the elected datasets. The basic AFN-FS method is compared with the results shown in [4]. In this work, a broad study for feature selection mainly devoted to

**Table 1.** Dataset description. Baseline acc.: accuracy when the main class is selected.

| Dataset | Features | Number of Samples | Baseline Acc. |
|---|---|---|---|
| Breast cancer | 9 | 683 | 65.01 |
| Pima | 8 | 768 | 65.10 |
| Cleve | 13 | 303 | 54.46 |
| Crx | 15 | 699 | 55.51 |
| wdbc | 30 | 569 | 62.74 |
| wpbc | 32 | 198 | 76.26 |

wrapper methods is presented. These wrapper methods are obtained by combining different induction algorithms (Naive-Bayes, ID3 and C4.5) with standard search strategies (BFS: Best First Search and HC: Hill-Climbing). For a fair comparison, the training and testing sets were generated in the same way as in [4], then a ten-fold cross-validation was employed. Table 2 shows this comparative study. From this table, it can be seen that the method outperforms the accuracy results in three of the four datasets (breast, cleve and pima), while it gets similar results for the crx dataset. Regarding the number of elected features, the table 2 also shows that the AFN-FS method needs less features than the method that outperforms better between the others considered (*Naive Bayes-HC* for breast and *Naive Bayes-BFS back* for cleve and pima). However, it also shows that a more significant feature reduction can be achieved.

## 3.2   Results for the Incremental AFN-FS Method

The IAFN-FS is intended to overcome the main drawback of the basic AFN-FS method: its exponential complexity to the number of features. Therefore, databases with a higher number of features were required to test this quality. The databases shown on the last two rows of Table 1 were selected. Moreover, the incremental AFN-FS was also applied to the crx dataset in order to check if it outperforms the basic AFN-FS results. The last column of Table 2 presents the results obtained. Comparing them, it can be noticed that the mean accuracy slightly increases while the standard deviation decreases, and beside and more interesting, the number of features is reduced from 7.4 to 6.2. The performance of the IAFN-FS method over the first three datasets of Table 2 is the same as that of the AFN-FS, as the models already developed with the latter can be sophisticated enough so as to obtain good results. As it can be seen in Table 2, the results obtained by our method are already the best, considering together performance and number of features selected, of all the methods presented.

In Table 3, the results obtained from a very novel method for feature subset selection based on neural networks and ant colony optimization (AC-ANN) presented in [10] are shown and compared with those of the incremental method (IAFN-FS). For a fair comparison, training and testing sets were constructed as in [10], that is, a 20% of the samples were randomly selected to construct the test set, while the rest of the samples form the training set that will be used for

**Table 2.** Comparative study of the proposed method AFN-FS (basic and incremental, IAFN-FS)with the results obtained from the work of John and Kohavi [4]. They used three induction algorithms: ID3, Naive-Bayes and C4.5 with different search strategies: hill-climbing (HC), best first backward with compound operators (BSF-back) and best first forward (BFS-for. For each dataset, the mean accuracy (%) and standard deviation for the test set are shown, indicating also the mean number of features selected.

| Data | ID3 | | | Naive-Bayes | | | C4.5 | AFN-FS |
|---|---|---|---|---|---|---|---|---|
| | HC | BFS-back | BFS-for | HC | BFS-back | BFS-for | BFS-back | |
| Breast | 94.71 ± 0.5 | 93.85 ± 0.5 | 94.57 ± 0.7 | 96.57 ± 0.6 | 96.00 ± 0.6 | 96.00 ± 0.6 | 95.28 ± 0.6 | 96.19 ±2.2 |
| | 2.9 | 5.3 | 3.7 | 4.3 | 5.9 | 5.2 | 3.9 | 3.9 |
| Pima | 69.52 ± 2.2 | 67.44 ± 1.4 | 68.73 ± 2.2 | 74.34 ± 2.0 | 76.03 ± 1.6 | 75.12 ± 1.5 | 70.18 ± 1.3 | 77.75 ± 4.8 |
| | 1 | 5.7 | 2.3 | 3.8 | 4.4 | 4.0 | 4.8 | 3.7 |
| Cleve | 78.24 ± 2.0 | 75.89 ± 3.7 | 79.52 ± 2.3 | 79.56 ± 3.9 | 82.56 ± 2.5 | 80.23 ± 3.9 | 77.88 ± 2.5 | 84.78 ± 6.9 |
| | 3.1 | 4.6 | 3.4 | 3.1 | 7.9 | 5.9 | 5.3 | 3.4 |

| Crx | ID3 | | | Naive-Bayes | | | C4.5 | AFN FS | IAFN FS |
|---|---|---|---|---|---|---|---|---|---|
| | HC | BFS-back | BFS-for | HC | BFS-back | BFS-for | BFS-back | | |
| | 85.65 ± 1.6 | 83.33 ± 1.5 | 85.22 ± 1.6 | 85.36 ± 1.6 | 84.78 ± 0.8 | 86.23 ± 1.0 | 85.80 ± 0.8 | 85.07 ± 3.6 | 85.36 ± 2.1 |
| | 2.9 | 7.7 | 3.8 | 1.6 | 9.1 | 5.9 | 7.7 | 7.4 | 6.2 |

**Table 3.** Comparative results between the incremental AFN-FS method and the method based on ant colonies and artificial neural networks, AC-ANN

| Dataset | AC-ANN | | Incremental AFN-FS | |
|---|---|---|---|---|
| | Features | Test acc | Features | Test acc |
| wdbc | 12 | 95.57 | 11 | 99.00 |
| wpbc | 14 | 77.50 | 8 | 78.00 |

the feature selection process. As it can be seen, the proposed method obtains better results, both in accuracy and number of features, than this novel work.

Regarding computational time, a comparative study is not possible because of the differences of hardware and software used by the authors of each method. However, the proposed method is not very time consuming, although it requires the evaluation of different subsets of features. For example, it took around 2.5 seconds to evaluate each possible subset of the *wdbc* dataset, and required 11 different steps to reach a solution, for a total time of 11 × 2.5 seconds.

## 4   Conclusions and Future Work

As can be seen on tables 2 and 3, the IAFN-FS and AFN-FS methods obtain better (or at least equal) accuracy results than other methods, besides using a reduced number of features. The incremental version IAFN-FS allows for treating datasets with a higher number of input features, obtaining better results than other feature selection methods, including the basic AFN-FS method. However, the method tends to select a large number of features. This is due to the fact that the algorithm does not allow for a decrement in the mean accuracy obtained by the classifier, as it is stated in the cyclic selection step in section 2.2. Allowing more flexibility at this respect can possibly help to reduce the number of features selected. Besides, and as future work we are now working on two research lines: (1) developing a new version of AFN-FS that will permit to work directly with datasets that are not binary; and (2) developing a hybrid algorithm that uses a filter method before the IAFN-FS, so as to permit us to work with datasets with a high number of input features.

# References

1. Saltelli, A., Tarantola, S., Campolongo, F., Ratto, M.: Sensitivity Analysis in practice: A guide to assessing scientific models. John Wiley & Sons, Chichester (2004)
2. Bishop, C.: Neural Networks for Patter Recognition. Oxford University Press, New York (1995)
3. Castillo, E., Guijarro-Berdiñas, B., Fontenla-Romero, O., Alonso-Betanzos, A.: A very fast learning method for neural networks based on sensitivity analysis. Journal of Machine Learning Research 7, 1159–1182
4. Kohavi, R., John, G.: Wrappers for feature subset selection. Artificial Intelligence, Special issue on relevance 97(1-2), 273–324 (1997)
5. Guyon, I., Elisseeff, A.: An introduction to variable and feature selection. Journal of Machine Learning Research, Special issue on Variable and Feature Selection 3, 1157–1182 (2003)
6. Blum, A.L., Langley, P.: Selection of relevance features and examples in machine learning. Artificial Intelligence, Special issue on relevance 97(1-2), 245–271 (1997)
7. Sánchez-Maroño, N., Caamaño-Fernández, M., Castillo, E., Alonso-Betanzos, A.: Functional networks and analysis of variance for feature selection. In: Corchado, E., Yin, H., Botti, V., Fyfe, C. (eds.) IDEAL 2006. LNCS, vol. 4224, pp. 1031–1038. Springer, Heidelberg (2006)
8. Castillo, E., Sánchez-Maroño, N., Alonso-Betanzos, A., Castillo, M.: Functional network topology learning and sensitivity analysis based on anova decomposition. Neural Computation 19(1) (2007)
9. Sobol, I.M.: Global sensitivity indices for nonlinear mathematical models and their Monte Carlo estimates. Mathematics and Computers in Simulation 55, 271–280 (2001)
10. Sivagaminathan, R.K., Ramakrisham, S.: A hybrid approach for feature subset selection using neural networks and ant colony optimization. Experts systems with applications 33, 49–60 (2007)
11. Guyon, I., Gunn, S., Nikravesh, M., Zadeh, L.: Feature extraction. Foundations and applications (2006)
12. Blake, C., Merz, C.: UCI repository of machine learning databases (1998) http://www.ics.uci.edu/mlearn/MLRepository.html

# Fitness Function Comparison for GA-Based Feature Construction

Leila S. Shafti and Eduardo Pérez

Escuela Plitécnica Superior,
Universidad Autónoma de Madrid, E-28049, Spain
{leila.shafti,eduardo.perez}@uam.es
http://www.eps.uam.es

**Abstract.** When primitive data representation yields attribute interactions, learning requires feature construction. MFE2/GA, a GA-based feature construction has been shown to learn more accurately than others when there exist several complex attribute interactions. A new fitness function, based on the principle of Minimum Description Length (MDL), is proposed and implemented as part of the MFE3/GA system. Since the individuals of the GA population are collections of new features constructed to change the representation of data, an MDL-based fitness considers not only the part of data left unexplained by the constructed features (errors), but also the complexity of the constructed features as a new representation (theory). An empirical study shows the advantage of the new fitness over other fitness not based on MDL, and both are compared to the performance baselines provided by relevant systems.

**Keywords:** Machine learning, attribute interaction, feature construction, feature selection, genetic algorithms, MDL principle, Entropy.

## 1 Introduction

When data is represented by primitive attributes, Feature Construction (FC) has an outstanding impact on Data Mining results [1]. Many feature construction techniques face serious difficulties to succeed when confronted with complex attribute interactions. *Interaction* exists among attributes when the relation between one attribute and the target concept is not constant for all values of the other attributes [2,3,4]. Interactions become *complex* when changing the value of one attribute does not only change the relation between another attribute and the target concept, but it yields an opposite relation.

Most FC methods perform a local search to find interacting attributes one by one. So, they face difficulties when confronted with complex high-order interaction [2]. Due to complex interaction, it is necessary to search the space of subsets of attributes. Since the search space of attribute subsets grows exponentially with the number of attributes and has high variation, a global search such as Genetic Algorithm (GA) [5] is preferred for a FC method. Recent works [6,7,8,9,10] show that a genetic-based FC is more likely to be successful in searching through intractable and complicated search space of interacting attributes.

D. Borrajo, L. Castillo, and J.M. Corchado (Eds.): CAEPIA 2007, LNAI 4788, pp. 249–258, 2007.

There are several factors that are important in guiding a genetic-based search to converge to the optimal solution. Among them the fitness function has a major role. The fitness function intends to guide the GA toward its goal and accelerate its convergence by providing a good estimate of the quality of each individual in the population. When a GA is applied to perform FC, the goal is to generate new features that facilitate more accurate learning when they are used to change the representation of training data. Thus, the fitness function should estimate the quality of the constructed features.

Constructed features may be evaluated in different ways. Three common forms of evaluating features are MDL-based measure, Entropy-based measure, and classifier error rate measure. MDL fitness function measures the inconsistency and complexity of constructed features based on MDL (Minimum Description Length) principle [11,12]. Entropy-based fitness measures amount of uncertainty produced using new features. The third fitness first redescribes data using constructed features and then applies a learner to classify data and measure its error rate. In this paper we concentrate on the first two forms of fitness measure. The third one is not appropriate for genetic-based search since it is computationally expensive. The fitness is evaluated for each individual in each generation; thus, a fitness function with less computational time is preferable.

Considering the importance of fitness function in GA, we modified the fitness function of MFE2/GA (a multi-feature extraction using GA) [10] to conform to MDL principle and called the new system MFE3/GA. The new fitness function is empirically compared to an Entropy-based fitness function. Also the new system is compared to the performance baselines provided by relevant systems.

## 2    MDL-Based Fitness in MFE3/GA

MDL has been successfully integrated into several learning methods. The MDL principle was originally described in terms of optimizing a communication problem. In order to apply it to learning, the learning task has to be described as a communication problem. The learner has a table of pre-classified training data that needs to be sent to the receiver. As an alternative to sending the whole table, the learner can compress data into a "theory" (i.e., a decision tree, a set of rules or any other form of classifier) and send it to the receiver. Such theory may not be perfect, and hence make "errors" when classifying some of the training data. So, to make the communication correct, the errors should also be sent to the receiver along with the theory. This introduces a trade-off between a very simple theory that produces many errors and a more complex one that accounts for almost all data and makes only a few errors. The MDL principle establishes that the optimum solution is a theory that minimizes the sum of the code lengths corresponding to theory and errors. This criterion has been used, for instance, to control the growth of decision trees [13].

The integration of the MDL principle into the evolutionary approach is not as frequent as it is in other machine learning systems. Most GAs have focused on optimizing a fitness based on classification errors. When GA is used for FC and so individuals represent new constructed features, MDL may become necessary. The proposed features correspond to a theory that can grow too large and complex to produce no errors in the training data, and that we may prefer to keep simpler as long as it does not produce too many errors. In spite of this, none of the genetic-based FC systems integrates MDL into their fitness function.

A partial exception is MFE2/GA. This method is a preprocessing method that receives original attributes and data, and uses GA to search the space of different sets of attribute subsets and functions defined over them. Its fitness function measures both the complexity of constructed features and their inconsistency with training data; however, it was not explicitly designed as approximation to the MDL principle. This section briefly describes MFE2/GA and introduces a modification to its fitness function to conform to MDL principle.

Each individual in MFE2/GA is designed to represent a set of attribute subsets. Each subset is represented by a bit-string of length $N$, where $N$ is the number of original attributes; each bit showing the presence or absence of the attribute in the subset. Thus, each individual of $k$ subsets is a bit-string of length $k.N$ ($k > 0$). Since each individual has different number of subsets, the length of individuals is variable. To avoid unnecessary growth of individuals, the number of subsets in each individual is limited to the up bound $K = 5$ by default.

Each attribute subset in individual is associated with a function defined over it and extracted from the data. Functions are represented by non-algebraic form [10]. For any given subset the corresponding function is defined by assigning Boolean class labels extracted from data, to all the tuples in the Cartesian product of attributes in the subset. Changing subsets in an individual implies changing the corresponding functions. GA aims to converge the population members toward the set of attribute subsets and their corresponding functions that best represent attribute interactions. When GA is terminated the constructed functions are added to the original attribute set and the new representation of data is given to a standard learner such as C4.5 [14] to proceed learning.

Before describing how the new fitness in MFE3/GA is computed, we shall introduce the notion of function length. Each function $F_i$, defined over subset $S_i$, is represented by Binary labels of tuples in Cartesian product of attributes in $S_i$. Thus, each $F_i$ can be represented by $\prod_{j=1}^{m} |X_{i_j}|$ bits, which we refer to as *the length* of function, $len(F_i)$, where $m$ is the number of attributes in $S_i$, and $|X_{i_j}|$ is the number of values that attribute $X_{i_j}$ can take. Since all constructed functions are defined over proper subsets of $S$, the longest function $F_l$ is one defined over $S_l = S - \{X_s\}$ where $X_s$ is the attribute that can take fewest values. The length of $F_l$ is $\prod_{i=1, i \neq s}^{N} |X_i|$. To reduce the complexity of constructing functions, the length of each function is limited by a parameter of the system, $B$. By default the limit is set to $2^B$, $B = 16$, that is, 64 Kbits. In case of Binary attributes this is equivalent to a function defined over 16 attributes. So the longest function is of length $MAXLEN = min(\prod_{i=1, i \neq s}^{N} |X_i|, 2^B)$.

The fitness of each individual $Ind = \langle S_1, \ldots, S_k \rangle$ is determined by evaluating the set of corresponding functions $\{F_1, \ldots, F_k\}$ and measuring two factors: the inconsistency of the set with the training data and its complexity.

The inconsistency measure drives GA to generate more accurate functions. For measuring the inconsistency of the set of functions with training data, training data are projected onto the set of constructed features $\{F_1, \ldots, F_k\}$. Then, each tuple in the projection that matches with both positive and negative samples in data is considered as an inconsistent tuple. The inconsistency of the set of functions, $\|E\|$, is measured by the total number of samples that match with inconsistent tuples in the projection. To normalize this value we divide it by the maximum inconsistency, that is, the total number of samples in the training data, $M$.

The consistency of the individual is not the only factor to drive GA towards its goal. Recall the goal is to ease the complex relation among interacting attributes by constructing several functions each representing one complex interaction in the concept. To achieve this goal, the fitness function prefers a consistent individual with several small functions to a consistent individual with few large functions by measuring their complexities. The complexity of each individual is determined by the sum of length of functions defined over subsets in the individual. We normalize the complexity factor by dividing it by its maximum value that is $K \times MAXLEN$.

Then, the fitness of the individual is evaluated by the following formula and GA aims to minimize this value:

$$Fitness(Ind) = \frac{\|E\|}{M} + \frac{\sum_{i=1}^{k} len(F_i)}{K \times MAXLEN} \ . \tag{1}$$

Therefore, given two individuals equally consistent with the training data, the fitness function prefers the one with several functions defined over smaller subsets of attributes, rather than the one with few function defined over larger subsets. Note that the complexity evaluation corresponds to measure the length of functions and not length of individuals.

To compare this fitness function with other fitness functions, we also modified MFE2/GA to apply an Entropy-based fitness function and called it MFE2/GA$_E$. For each individual, the fitness is measured by calculating the Entropy of the concept given the values of new features [14,15]. More precisely it is calculated as follows:

$$Fitness(Ind) = \sum_{i=1}^{2^k} \frac{|T_i|}{|T|} Entropy(T_i), \tag{2}$$

where $T_i$ is set of training samples whose values for new attributes $F_1$ to $F_k$ are equal to the $i^{th}$ tuple in the Cartesian product $F_1 \times \ldots \times F_k$. To reduce overfitting, part of training data are used for constructing functions and all training data are used for Entropy-based fitness evaluation. Keeping part of data for fitness evaluation helps GA to construct individuals with smaller functions.

## 3   Experimental Results

This section empirically compares results obtained by two systems that use two different fitness functions: MFE3/GA with MDL-based fitness, and MFE2/GA$_E$

with Entropy-based fitness. We also compare them with two learners: the standard learner C4.5 (trees and rules), and HINT [16], a greedy-based feature construction method that similarly to MFE3/GA uses non-algebraic representation for constructed features. Part of these experiments uses synthetic concepts designed to focus the empirical study on situations were multiple complex attribute interactions make feature construction necessary for learning and difficult to achieve. We also report on similar experiments using real-world data from the Braille code domain.

## 3.1   Experiments with Synthetic Concepts

The synthetic concepts used as a benchmark for these experiments are composed by several complex interactions. For all concepts, attributes are Boolean except in the last 3 concepts, where there are 3-valued attributes. Table 1 gives a summary of these concepts. Columns 2 and 3 show the number of relevant and irrelevant attributes for each concept. The majority class percentage of each concept is shown in column 4. Note that for some concepts there are attributes participating in more than one underlying interaction (shared attributes). For example, in $\wedge(P_{1,4}, P_{3,6})$, $x_3$ and $x_4$ are shared by $P_{1,4}$ and $P_{3,6}$. See Appendix for a detailed definition of concepts, including a description of the complex interactions underlying these concepts.

All experiments were run 20 times independently, each using 5% of all possible instances as training data and the rest as test data. For MFE2/GA$_E$, we used only part of the 5% training data for constructing features and all training data for fitness evaluation using Entropy. Our previous experimental evaluation showed that on average, MFE2/GA$_E$ achieves higher accuracy when 30% of training data are used for feature construction. So we used 30% of training data for feature construction and all 5% training data for feature evaluation. Note that by doing this we tried to benefit MFE2/GA$_E$ and yet we believed the MDL-based MFE3/GA could out perform it.

Table 1 illustrates a summary of the empirical study. The higher of the two average accuracies obtained by C4.5 and C4.5-Rules is reported in column 5. This result is marked by $c$ if obtained by C4.5, or by $r$ if obtained by C4.5-Rules. The average accuracies of HINT, MFE2/GA$_E$, and MFE3/GA are reported in columns 6 to 8 respectively. Columns 9 and 10 show the average number of GA's generations for each genetic-based method. Numbers between parentheses indicate standard deviation. The highest average accuracy is marked by ◁, but if it is not lower than the majority class percentage. The accuracy of MFE2/GA$_E$ is marked by † when it is significantly better than the accuracy of HINT. MFE3/GA's result is significantly better than those in bold and significantly worse than those in italic ($t$-distribution test with $\alpha = 0.02$).

As it can be seen from Table 1, the MDL-based fitness function of MFE3/GA guides this method towards better solutions as expected; and therefore, it significantly outperforms MFE2/GA$_E$ for most concepts. MFE2/GA$_E$ in most cases overfits data. It constructs set of features with very small Entropy (most of the time with zero Entropy) which means the set of features classify 5% training

**Table 1.** Average accuracy and number of generations for synthetic concepts

| Concept | R | I | M % | Average accuracies | | | | Avrg. No generations | |
|---|---|---|---|---|---|---|---|---|---|
| | | | | C4.5/R | HINT | MFE2/GA$_E$ | MFE3/GA | MFE2/GA$_E$ | MFE3/GA |
| $\wedge(P_{1,4}, P_{3,6})$ | 6 | 6 | 75 | c72.5(3.2) | 100(0.0)◁ | 98.3(2.1) | 99.8(0.5) | 137(35.7) | 125(18.4) |
| $\wedge(P_{1,6}, P_{3,8})$ | 8 | 4 | 75 | c73.4(2.7) | *98.6(6.3)*◁ | 91.8(6.5) | 94.1(2.8) | **219(47.0)** | 131(18.1) |
| $\wedge(P_{1,6}, P_{7,12})$ | 12 | 0 | 75 | c72.6(3.9) | 82.5(16.5) | **77.1(6.0)** | 89.8(6.8)◁ | 230(82.4) | 144(16.0) |
| $\wedge(P_{1,3}, P_{3,5}, P_{4,6})$ | 6 | 6 | 88 | c87.6(1.2) | 94.1(9.6) | 96.7(4.9) | 99.8(0.7)◁ | 130(24.0) | 141(27.6) |
| $\wedge(P_{1,4}, P_{2,5}, P_{3,6})$ | 6 | 6 | 88 | c87.5(0.3) | 97.1(7.2) | 96.5(4.6) | 99.6(0.7)◁ | 153(46.9) | 130(29.6) |
| $\wedge(P_{1,4}, P_{3,6}, P_{5,8})$ | 8 | 4 | 88 | c87.5(0.1) | 90.3(11.0) | 91.7(5.4) | 98.6(1.7)◁ | 207(54.0) | 173(43.7) |
| $\wedge(P_{1,4}, P_{5,8}, P_{9,12})$ | 12 | 0 | 88 | c87.5(0.1) | 78.4(4.1) | 86.4(4.4)† | 92.4(7.2)◁ | 212(63.0) | 199(53.9) |
| $\wedge(P_{1,6}, P_{2,7}, P_{3,8})$ | 8 | 4 | 88 | c86.6(1.8) | 92.3(10.0) | 86.7(4.1) | 93.8(2.4)◁ | 174(43.4) | 169(40.9) |
| $\wedge(WL3_{1,5}, WL3_{3,7})$ | 7 | 5 | 64 | r90.1(3.0) | 91.2(11.6) | 90.9(3.8) | 93.1(5.9)◁ | 201(65.7) | 132(28.8) |
| $\wedge(WL3_{1,5}, WL3_{4,8})$ | 8 | 4 | 68 | r86.7(2.0) | 88.8(8.9) | 89.2(6.1) | 89.9(9.6)◁ | 230(72.9) | 156(51.8) |
| $\wedge(WL3_{1,5}, WL3_{5,9})$ | 9 | 3 | 72 | r84.9(2.6) | 87.9(10.1) | 88.5(6.2) | 93.5(7.0)◁ | 213(55.4) | 154(37.6) |
| $\wedge(WL3_{1,5}, WL3_{6,10})$ | 10 | 2 | 75 | r82.2(2.1) | 78.6(5.2) | 83.3(3.5)† | 88.1(8.4)◁ | 233(80.5) | 167(43.4) |
| $\wedge(WL3_{1,4}, WL3_{3,6}, WL3_{5,8})$ | 8 | 4 | 58 | r89.2(4.1) | 89.3(12.0) | **92.9(5.7)** | 97.5(2.2)◁ | 208(60.2) | 162(50.2) |
| $\wedge(WL3_{1,4}, WL3_{5,8}, WL3_{9,12})$ | 12 | 0 | 68 | r79.5(3.2) | 71.8(4.5) | 81.1(6.5)† | 92.3(10.5)◁ | 239(60.9) | 177(49.1) |
| $\wedge(W23_{1,6}, W23_{7,12})$ | 12 | 0 | 71 | r68.2(2.3) | 65.9(3.3) | 72.8(3.1)† | 83.4(9.3)◁ | 215(65.5) | 159(40.1) |
| $\wedge(W23_{1,4}, W23_{5,8}, W23_{9,12})$ | 12 | 0 | 76 | r74.7(1.9) | 69.7(3.0) | 80.4(4.3)† | 94.1(9.4)◁ | 250(75.0) | 207(67.3) |
| $\wedge(W23_{1,5}, W23_{6,10}, W23_{11,15})$ | 15 | 0 | 76 | r88.5(3.1) | 98.9(2.8) | 98.5(2.5) | 100(0.0)◁ | 228(66.6) | 187(24.2) |
| $\wedge(W23_{1,6}, W23_{7,12}, W23_{13,18})$ | 18 | 0 | 84 | r98.1(0.9) | 100(0.0)◁ | 99.5(0.5) | 100(0.0)◁ | 215(57.0) | 200(24.9) |
| $\wedge(A_{1,4}, A_{5,8}, A_{9,12})$ | 12 | 0 | 82 | r89.8(5.0) | 79.7(3.1) | 89.1(4.0)† | 97.8(4.3)◁ | 243(77.0) | 225(69.1) |
| $\wedge(B_{1,4}, B_{5,8}, B_{9,12})$ | 12 | 0 | 88 | c86.9(1.3) | 81.1(2.1) | 88.0(1.3)† | 89.6(4.0)◁ | 231(68.9) | 190(70.3) |
| $\wedge(C_{1,4}, C_{5,8}, C_{9,12})$ | 12 | 0 | 58 | r66.2(3.8) | 64.6(7.8) | 84.6(16.0)† | 98.5(6.9)◁ | 254(75.4) | 170(24.0) |
| $\wedge(D_{1,4}, D_{5,8}, D_{9,12})$ | 12 | 0 | 88 | r90.6(2.8) | 83.7(1.9) | 89.7(1.4)† | 92.3(3.4)◁ | 217(77.6) | 194(45.2) |
| $\wedge(E_{1,4}, E_{5,8}, E_{9,12})$ | 12 | 0 | 76 | r77.0(3.0) | 72.2(4.8) | 81.4(6.8)† | 93.0(10.5)◁ | 232(62.1) | 200(65.7) |
| $\wedge(A_{1,4}, C_{5,8}, E_{9,12})$ | 12 | 0 | 74 | r82.2(3.4) | 73.7(5.6) | 84.2(7.4)† | 97.5(6.1)◁ | 232(77.6) | 197(50.8) |
| $\wedge(A_{1,4}, B_{5,8}, D_{9,12})$ | 12 | 0 | 86 | r87.6(3.6) | 81.5(3.4) | 88.7(2.7)† | 92.0(4.7)◁ | 209(65.2) | 206(54.3) |
| $\wedge(A_{1,4}, B_{5,8}, C_{9,12})$ | 12 | 0 | 79 | r86.3(3.5) | 75.8(4.3) | 87.2(4.2)† | 94.6(7.2)◁ | 248(57.1) | 209(71.8) |
| $\wedge(B_{1,4}, C_{3,6}, A_{7,10}, D_{9,12})$ | 12 | 0 | 87 | r88.5(2.0) | 83.2(2.8) | 88.6(1.3)† | 90.8(3.6)◁ | 195(41.7) | 199(48.5) |
| $\wedge(A_{1,4}, B_{5,8}, C_{9,12}, E_{13,16})$ | 16 | 0 | 87 | r94.8(2.1) | 99.8(1.0) | 99.2(1.2) | 100(0.0)◁ | 214(64.7) | 235(35.1) |
| $\wedge(C_{1,4}, WL3_{5,8}, W23_{9,12})$ | 12 | 0 | 68 | r74.2(3.1) | 70.6(7.2) | 80.7(7.3)† | 93.7(11.1)◁ | 231(68.2) | 178(47.4) |
| $\wedge(W23_{1,5}, C_{5,8}, WL3_{8,12})$ | 12 | 0 | 77 | c76.4(1.2) | 71.2(2.4) | 78.1(2.6)† | 84.0(8.7)◁ | 219(71.8) | 169(43.1) |
| $\wedge(W23_{1,5}, C_{4,7}, WL3_{6,10})$ | 10 | 2 | 77 | r77.4(2.8) | 75.9(6.6) | 80.5(3.4)† | 88.7(8.9)◁ | 232(53.1) | 193(55.0) |
| $\vee(pal_{1,4}, pal_{3,6}, pal_{5,8})$ | 8 | 0 | 70 | r71.2(2.6) | 63.8(4.1) | 70.0(3.6)† | 71.4(1.7)◁ | 213(55.2) | 138(28.1) |
| $\vee(pal_{1,4}, pal_{4,7}, pal_{7,10})$ | 10 | 0 | 70 | r97.5(2.3) | 100(0.0)◁ | 95.7(5.4) | 100(0.0)◁ | 228(70.1) | 149(13.0) |
| palindrome$_6$ + 2 | 6 | 2 | 96 | c96.3(0.1) | 93.2(2.0) | 97.6(1.8)† | 99.6(0.7)◁ | 162(60.7) | 133(19.4) |
| AVERAGE | | | | r82.7 | 83.7 | 87.8 | 93.6◁ | 213.3 | 173.3 |

data perfectly. But when they are evaluated on test data, they produce errors. This is because Entropy does not consider the complexity of the theory proposed by the constructed features. It constructs large functions that perfectly match training data and produce overfitting.

Also comparing the average number of generations of both GA methods illustrates that MDL-based fitness function helps GA to converge to optimal solution faster than the Entropy-based method.

Comparing the results of MFE2/GA$_E$ and HINT indicates that, although Entropy-based FC achieves lower accuracy than MDL-based FC, its overall average accuracy is still better than HINT. This shows the advantage of using GA for FC when concepts are composed by several complex interactions and few training data are available. Even a genetic-based FC method with not the best fitness function outperforms the greedy-based FC. Note that the overall average

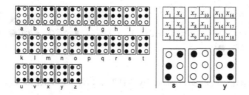

**Fig. 1.** Braille code representation and a sample of valid code

accuracy of HINT is only slightly higher than the standard learner C4.5/Rules for this type of concepts.

### 3.2 Experiments with Real-World Data

This section reports on a similar empirical comparison, but this time based on a task defined over a real-world domain. A Braille code is a $3 \times 2$ matrix of raised/unraised dots. The target concept is to distinguish Braille-coded text from randomly generated codes, using a windowing of 3 codes. Each sample consists of 3 codes, and each code is represented by 6 binary attributes, giving a total of 18 attributes. If all 3 codes are Braille, the sample is classified as true, and otherwise, it is classified as false. Figure 1 shows the Braille code as it was originally invented for French alphabet (which did not include the $w$), where raised and unraised dots are shown by black and white circles respectively.

A total of 20 data sets of 31250 samples were generated with majority class of 50%. Experimental results showed that the tree generated by C4.5 using features constructed by MFE3/GA has these features near the root, but still uses many primitive attributes at deeper levels. This indicates that the features generated were not enough for abstracting all interactions. So we increased the parameter $K$ (see Section 2) from 5 to 9, allowing MFE3/GA to generate more features. This requires more CPU time, but a single learning trial still takes only a few minutes (for 5% data about 2 min. on a Pentium 4).

Experiments were performed increasing training data from 1% to 20% to see how data size affects methods. Table 2 shows accuracies of C4.5, C4.5Rules, HINT, MFE2/GA$_E$, and MFE3/GA. MFE3/GA's accuracy is significantly better than those in bold and worse than those in italic ($t$ test, $\alpha = 0.02$).

Consider the results corresponding to 1% data in Table 2. For this size of training data, all FC methods achieve lower accuracies than C4.5 and C4.5Rules.

**Table 2.** Average accuracy over 20 runs for Braille-validation problem

| Data Size | C4.5 | C4.5 Rules | HINT | MFE2/ GA$_E$ | MFE3/ GA |
|---|---|---|---|---|---|
| 1% | *90.7(1.9)* | *94.8(2.2)*◁ | **75.9(4.1)** | 63.6(7.4) | 85.3(6.4) |
| 5% | **97.6(0.4)** | **99.6(0.3)** | **90.2(3.4)** | 96.5(5.0) | 99.8(0.3)◁ |
| 10% | **98.6(0.3)** | **99.9(0.2)** | **95.9(3.4)** | 98.2(3.0) | 100.0(0.1)◁ |
| 15% | **99.0(0.1)** | **99.9(0.1)** | **99.0(0.8)** | 97.1(4.9) | 100.0(0.0)◁ |
| 20% | **99.4(0.1)** | 100.0(0.0) | **99.4(0.6)** | 99.4(1.4) | 100.0(0.0)◁ |

**Fig. 2.** Features constructed by MFE3/GA for Braille code concept

MFE2/GA$_E$ gets the lowest accuracy comparing to other FC methods because this method uses only 30% of 1% training data for function generation and overfits data. MFE3/GA overfits data less than other FC methods due to its MDL-based fitness function.

Table 2 shows that when the number of training data increases all FC methods take the advantage of training data size and improve their accuracies. However, MFE3/GA is the only FC method in the table that gets higher accuracy than C4.5 and C4.5Rules. It significantly outperforms all other methods except for 20% data when both MFE3/GA and C4.5Rules get 100 percent accuracy. The results of MFE2/GA$_E$ with 15% and 20% training data size show that when more data are provided, this method overfits data and achieves lower accuracy.

Note that C4.5-Rules generates a large number of rules (often more than 35 for 5% data) that are difficult to interpret. Features generated by MFE3/GA can be easily interpreted. For all experiments, MFE3/GA successfully discovers that there are three relations of 6 attributes each in the training data, and constructs functions to highlight these three relations. Each relation corresponds to one position in the 3-code window. MFE3/GA usually constructs two functions for each relation of 6 attributes, representing the definition of a Braille code, in total six functions for a sequence of three Braille codes. Figure 2 shows the two functions that are usually constructed to define the valid codes represented by the first 6 attributes. Similar functions are found for the other groups of six attributes. The solid line in the figure shows the domain of each function. A black circle indicates the attribute value is '1' (raised dot), a white circle means the attribute value is '0' (unraised dot), and a '#' means "don't care" (i.e., it can be either '0' or '1'). The first function, $F_1$, highlights all codes with unraised dot 3 and raised dot 6, as invalid codes, which need to be excluded from the target. The second function, $F_2$, is a disjunction of four rules to define all Braille letters ignoring dot 3. The conjunction, $\overline{F_1} \wedge F_2$, classifies all Braille codes. When more data is available, MFE3/GA encapsulates the relation among 6 attributes and represents it by a single function. Thus, it constructs a total of just three functions, one function for each subset of 6 attributes, to represent a sequence of three Braille codes.

Also note that, in spite of using non-algebraic representation similarly to MFE3/GA, HINT needs more data to uncover the underlying concept structure and improve accuracy. This is probably due to MFE3/GA's use of GA-based search and evaluation of multiple candidate features simultaneously. Several interactions exist among 18 attributes in this concept. HINT needs to construct a complex hierarchy of functions representing interactions, which is a difficult task for its greedy procedure.

# 4    Conclusion

The accuracy advantage of the MFE2/GA approach was related to the structure of the individuals in the GA population. Each individual provides a collection of new features intended to change the representation of data, in a way that highlights underlying complex attribute interactions and, hence, simplifies learning. Due to this meaning of the genetically evolved individuals, we proposed the use of the MDL principle for evaluating the fitness of each individual. The new MDL-based fitness implemented in the MFE3/GA method includes two terms: one that approximates the complexity of the collection of new features (theory), and a second one that accounts for the misclassifications produced by those features (errors). To assess the advantage introduced by this new fitness, we performed an empirical study using a benchmark of synthetic concepts designed to involve several combinations of complex attribute interactions.

The study shows that the proposed MDL-based fitness yields significantly better predictive learning accuracy than other fitness solely based on Entropy. In addition, our empirical results show that even without the improvement of an MDL-based fitness, the MFE2/GA$_E$ approach with an Entropy-based fitness measure retains most of its accuracy advantage over two relevant learners: a standard learner as C4.5 (trees and rules), and HINT, a non-GA feature construction methods that, like MFE3/GA, uses non-algebraic representation for constructed features. Finally, similar empirical results were found using real-world data from the Braille Code domain.

**Acknowledgment.** Work has been partially supported by the Spanish Ministry of Science and Technology, under Grant number TSI2005-08225-C07-06.

# References

1. Liu, H., Motoda, H.: Feature Extraction, Construction and Selection: A Data Mining Perspective. The International Series in Engineering and Computer Science, vol. 453. Kluwer Academic Publishers, Norwell (1998)
2. Freitas, A.A.: Understanding the crucial role of attribute interaction in data mining. AI Review 16(3), 177–199 (2001)
3. Jakulin, A., Bratko, I.: Testing the significance of attribute interactions. In: Brodley, C.E. (ed.) Proc. of the Twenty-first International Conference on Machine Learning, pp. 409–416. ACM Press, New York (2004)
4. Pérez, E., Rendell, L.A.: Using multidimensional projection to find relations. In: Proc. of the Twelfth International Conference on Machine Learning, Tahoe City, California, pp. 447–455. Morgan Kaufmann, San Francisco (1995)
5. Michalewicz, Z.: Genetic Algorithms + Data Structures = Evolution Programs. Springer, New York (1999)
6. Larsen, O., Freitas, A.A., Nievola, J.C.: Constructing X-of-N attributes with a genetic algorithm. In: Proc. of the GECCO, p. 1268. Morgan Kaufmann, San Francisco (2002)
7. Muharram, M., Smith, G.D.: Evolutionary constructive induction. IEEE Transactions on Knowledge and Data Engineering 17(11), 1518–1528 (2005)
8. Otero, F., Silva, M., Freitas, A., Nievola, J.: Genetic programming for attribute construction in data mining. In: Ryan, C., Soule, T., Keijzer, M., Tsang, E.P.K., Poli, R., Costa, E. (eds.) EuroGP 2003. LNCS, vol. 2610, pp. 384–393. Springer, Heidelberg (2003)

9. Ritthoff, O., Klinkenberg, R., Fischer, S., Mierswa, I.: A hybrid approach to feature selection and generation using an evolutionary algorithm. In: UK Workshop on Computational Intelligence (September 2002)
10. Shafti, L.S., Pérez, E.: Reducing complex attribute interaction through non-algebraic feature construction. In: Proc. of the IASTED International Conference on AIA, Innsbruck, Austria, pp. 359–365. Acta Press (February 2007)
11. Grunwald, P.D.: The Minimum Description Length Principle. MIT Press, Cambridge (2007)
12. Rissanen, J.: A universal prior for integers and estimation by minimum description length. The Annals of Statistics 11(2), 416–431 (1983)
13. Quinlan, J.R., Rivest, R.L.: Inferring decision trees using the minimum description length principle. Inf. Comput. 80(3), 227–248 (1989)
14. Quinlan, R.J.: C4.5: Programs for Machine Learning. Morgan Kaufmann, San Mateo, California (1993)
15. Shannon, C.E.: A mathematical theory of communication. Bell System Tech. Journal 27, 379–423 and 623–656 (1948)
16. Zupan, B., Bohanec, M., Bratko, I., Demsar, J.: Learning by discovering concept hierarchies. Artificial Intelligence 109(1-2), 211–242 (1999)

# Appendix: Concept Definitions

All concepts in Section 3.1 are defined over Boolean attributes except the last 3 concepts in Table 1, where attributes are 3-valued. The concept $palindrome_6+2$ is palindrome of 6 attributes with 2 additional irrelevant attributes. The other concepts are defined as conjunctions $\land(f_1, \ldots, f_n)$ or disjunctions $\lor(f_1, \ldots, f_n)$. Let $w(x_{i..j}) \overset{\text{def}}{=}$ *weight of attributes* $x_i$ *to* $x_j$. Then $f_m$ is one of the followings:

- $P_{i,j} \overset{\text{def}}{=} parity(x_i, \ldots, x_j)$
- $WL3_{i,j} \overset{\text{def}}{=} w(x_{i..j}) < 3$
- $W23_{i,j} \overset{\text{def}}{=} w(x_{i..j}) \in \{2, 3\}$
- $pal_{i,j} \overset{\text{def}}{=}$ palindrome of $x_i$ to $x_j$
- Any of functions $A_{i,j}$ $B_{i,j}$, $C_{i,j}$, $D_{i,j}$, and $E_{i,j}$, defined over 4 Boolean attributes $x_i$ to $x_j$ as explained below

Functions A, B and E consider their 4 attributes as a 2-by-2 bitmap and are true if and only if the bitmap contains the following patterns: function A detects if any two (vertically or horizontally) adjacent bits are set to 1; function B is as A but excluding the case of all bits set to 1; and function E is as A but including the case of all bits set to 0. Functions C and D consider their 4 attributes as a 4-by-1 bitmap (or just a sequence) and are true if and only if the bitmap contains the following patterns: function C detects if any two adjacent bits are set to identical values but not all bits have the same value; and function D detects if there are any two adjacent bits set to 1.

To illustrate the complexity of concepts used, note for instance that the DNF of function $A_{1,4}$ is $x_1x_2 + x_2x_3 + x_3x_4 + x_4x_1$, and some concepts of Table 1 are conjunction of $A_{1,4}$, $A_{5,8}$ and, $A_{9,12}$, or other three such concepts from the above functions.

# Generation of OWL Ontologies from Concept Maps in Shallow Domains

Alfredo Simón[1], Luigi Ceccaroni[2], and Alejandro Rosete[1]

[1] Technical Institute "José Antonio Echevarría", La Habana (Cuba)
[2] Technical University of Catalonia, Software department, Barcelona (Spain)
asimon@ceis.cujae.edu.cu, luigi@lsi.upc.edu, rosete@ceis.cujae.edu.cu

**Abstract.** A proposal is presented for integration between a graphical model, such as conceptual maps, and ontologies codified in the OWL language. Conceptual maps are a flexible form of knowledge representation, very useful in education-related collaborative environments; OWL is a language of knowledge representation oriented to semantic analysis and processing carried out by machines. Integration consists of a set of formal transformation applied to conceptual maps and the semantic analysis of the relations linking concepts. The proposed method is based on a concept sense-disambiguation procedure, also defined by the authors, and in the WordNet lexical database. It applies to conceptual maps of shallow domains with labels in the Spanish language.

## 1 Introduction

In the knowledge representation oriented to the semantic analysis and processing by machines, a context in which a certain degree of formalization is required, the development and use of ontologies is increasingly common. However, the processes for the design and creation of ontologies, the tools available, such as Protégé [11], and the specification languages are still complex for non-experts in this subject. This complexity represents a difficulty in environments requiring the collaboration of humans for the development and processing of ontologies.

All the above suggests the use of a form of representation that can be used naturally by humans and integrated with ontologies in such a way that the latter can be obtained automatically. *Conceptual maps* (CMs) are proposed here as this human-friendly knowledge-representation system. CMs are a tool especially defined for application in the learning process; they are easy to be created, flexible and intuitive for people. Taking into accounts these aspects and CMs' low level of formalization, integration between CMs and ontologies is studied, specifically in the case of OWL (*Web ontology language*) ontologies.

OWL is a formal markup language to share knowledge on the Internet using ontologies. The integration between CMs and ontologies, and the OWL code generation are pursued through the incorporation of more formalization in CMs and through the semantic analysis of the relations among concepts. The proposed method is partially based on a procedure of concept disambiguation, previously defined by the authors, and on WordNet [6]. Taking into account that the knowledge in WordNet is about general terminology, the method is only applicable to shallow domains.

D. Borrajo, L. Castillo, and J.M. Corchado (Eds.): CAEPIA 2007, LNAI 4788, pp. 259–267, 2007.

This paper deals with the generation of ontologies, and the corresponding OWL code, from CMs. The inverse process of the integration (obtaining CMs from OWL ontologies) has been studied by the authors before [13] and is, in comparison, a simpler problem.

## 1.1   Conceptual Maps

*Conceptual maps* (CMs) are a type of knowledge representation that emerges within the pedagogical sciences at the end of the 1970s. They were proposed by Novak, who defines them as a *"technique that simultaneously represents a strategy of learning, a method to grasp the most significant aspect of a topic and a schematic resource included in one structure of propositions"* [10]. A CM is a kind of semantic network [15] that is more flexible and oriented to be used and interpreted by humans. In a CM, propositions are the smallest semantic structure with proper sense.

## 1.2   Ontologies and Their Languages

In artificial intelligence, ontologies were introduced to share and reuse knowledge. They provide the reference for the communication languages in distributed environments (such as multi-agent systems or the semantic Web) and a semantically formal description for automatic knowledge processing. An ontology can be defined as *a formal and explicit specification of a shared conceptualization, which is readable by a computer* [3]. Ontologies are the basis of semantic processing; they include a network of concepts, relationships and axioms to represent, organize and understand a domain of knowledge; and they provide a common reference frame for all applications in certain environment.

Knowledge is modeled in the ontologies with a logic based on *frame representation systems* (FRSs) [9] [16] and several languages have been defined to implement it, e.g. DAML+OIL [5] and OWL [12]. OWL is the latest, standardized ontology language and is based on XML, the *resource description framework* (RDF) and the *resource description framework schema* (RDFS). It includes three specifications, with different expressiveness levels: OWL Lite, OWL DL and OWL Full [12]. The code obtained by the method proposed here is a reduced set of OWL Lite (not including cardinality constraints) with additional elements from OWL DL (such as the union between classes).

# 2   Integration of Conceptual Maps and Ontologies

Important similarities exist between CMs and ontologies; especially the ontologies coded in RDF, given that the RDF language is formalized through triples (*subject, predicate, object*) and CMs use the proposition structure (*concept, link-word, concept*). Considering that the OWL language is an extension of RDF, the integration between CMs and OWL ontologies can be put forward. However, knowledge in OWL is expressed as *classes, subclasses, properties, relations, instances* and *axioms* [12] while in the CMs this formal and explicit specification does not exist and it has to be inferred.

In Simón et al. (2006) [13] it was concluded that a direct correspondence between CMs and OWL ontologies could be established. This comes from the analysis that FRSs are an extension of semantic networks (SNs) [9] and that there exists a structural correlation between the two representations: between a *frame* and a *node*, and between *slots* and *relations*. This also helps to explain the integration between CMs and OWL ontologies, given that OWL structure is based on frames and that CMs are a kind of SN.

Two basic criteria have been followed for the semantic interpretation needed for the OWL coding of CMs' knowledge:

1. **To increase the formalization levels of the *link-words* (l-w) in the CM**, on the basis of the experience in SNs. Five categories were define and combined with the different syntaxes formulated in the *propositions*. The l-w *es_un* (*is_a*, in English) and *instancia_de* (*instance_of*), frequently used in SNs, have been indirectly included through their inverses. The l-w showed in Table 1 for the Spanish language are not the only ones that can be used; it is just a selection for the demonstration of the suggested procedure. These *l-w* can be enriched according to the different contexts in which the method is used.

**Table 1.** Categories of link-words and their correspondence with the semantic relations in WordNet

| Category | Link-words | Relations in WordNet |
|---|---|---|
| Subclassification (CSC) | es_un$^{-1}$, tiene_por_subclase, tiene_parte_a, tiene_dependencia, incluye, agrupa, se_compone_de, comprende_a, puede_ser | *Hypernym/ hyponym* |
| Instantiation (CI) | tiene_por_instancia, tiene_instancia_a, instancía_como, tiene_ejemplo, instancia_de$^{-1}$ | *Hypernym/ hyponym* |
| Property (CP) | tiene, posee, tiene_propiedad, toma_valor, tiene_valor, se_compone_de | *Meronym/ holonym* |
| Direct-Property-Value (CPVD) | *Nouns*, such as: tipo, pared, rueda | --------- |
| Indirect-Property-Value (CPVI) | *Verbal forms*, such as the ones derived of: contener (contenido, contiene), ejercer (ejerce), representar (representa) | ---------- |

2. **To analyze the CM as a structured text**, assuming that each *proposition* is a sentence in natural language. The *proposition* is the smallest semantic unit of the CM with its own sense [10]. A concept sense-disambiguation algorithm, described in Simón et al. (2006) [13], is used to identify the correct sense (in terms of WordNet's *synset*) of each concept. Once identified the *synsets* of a pair of related concepts, the semantics of the relation between them is inferred, independently of the l-w used in the CM.

The *Hypernym* relations represent the inclusion among lexical units, from more general to more specific (subclassification), while *hyponym* relations are the opposite. *Meronym* relations correspond to "part of" or "is member of" (property), while holonym relations are the opposite. In WordNet, there exist several kinds of relations [6], but only the *hypernym-hyponym, meronym-holonym* ones have been considered here.

## 3  Obtaining OWL Ontologies

To explain the process of obtaining OWL ontologies, the two examples of CMs with labels in the Spanish language, shown in Fig. 1, are used. This procedure is composed of five phases.

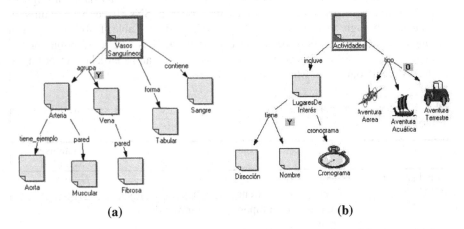

(a)                                          (b)

**Fig. 1.** Examples of concept maps: (a) representation of *vasos sanguíneos* (blood vessels) from the anatomy domain, (b) representation of *actividades* (*activities*) from the @LIS TechNET project [4]

*Phase 1. Concept sense disambiguation.* The identification of *synsets* for all concepts of the CM found in WordNet is carried out, using the disambiguation method described in Simón et al. (2006) [13]. The *synsets* and WordNet are used for inferring the semantics of the relation between two concepts, when the *l-w* does not appear in any category. The phase finishes with the creation of the *LP* list, which includes all propositions in the CM, with each concept associated to its *synset*.

*Phase 2. Initial coding of OWL classes.* All concepts are encoded as classes (*owl:Class*). Using concepts from Fig. 1 (b) as an example, the coding for concepts *activities*, *address* and *name* is:

```
<owl:Class rdf:ID = "Actividades" />
<owl:Class rdf:ID = "Dirección" />
<owl:Class rdf:ID = "Nombre" />
...
```

*Phase 3. Identification of subclass relations.* For each *proposition p* $\in$ *LP* with syntax $(c_1, l\text{-}w, c_2)$:

1.  If *l-w* $\in$ *CSC*, $c_1$ is encoded as a *class* and $c_2$ as a *subclass* in OWL. Applying this to concepts *vein* and *blood vessel* of the CM of Fig. 1 (a), the result is:

```
<owl:Class rdf:ID = "Vena" >
  <rdfs:subClassOf rdf:resource="Vasos Sanguíneos" />
...
<owl:Class/>
```

2.  If *l-w* $\notin$ *CSC*, WordNet is used for deducing the semantics of the relation. Be $s_1$ and $s_2$ synsets of $c_1$ y $c_2$ respectively, and $a(s_i, s_j)$ a path between $s_i$ and $s_j$:

    If $\exists$ $a(s_2, s_1)$ formed by *hypernymy* relations or $\exists$ $a(s_1, s_2)$ formed by *hyponymy* relations, it can be inferred that $c_2$ is a *subclass* of $c_1$. Analyzing the proposition *(Vasos Sanguíneos, agrupa, Arteria)* in Fig. 1 (a), a *hyponym* path from the *Arteria*'s synset to *Vasos Sanguíneos*'s synset is found. Therefore "*Arteria*" (artery) is a *subclass* of "*Vasos Sanguíneos*". The OWL generated code is equivalent to the one above for *vein*.

*Phase 4. Identification of instance relations.* For each *proposition p* $\in$ *LP* with syntax $(c_1, l\text{-}w, c_2)$, if *l-w* $\in$ *CI* and $c_2$ is a leaf node, it is inferred that $c_2$ is an instance of $c_1$. Applied to proposition *(Arteria, tiene_ejemplo, Aorta)* of the Fig. 1 (a), the result is:

```
<Arteria rdf:ID = "Aorta" />
```

*Phase 5. Identification of property relations.* This process is the one with greatest uncertainty and complexity within the procedure of OWL encoding, due to the number of diverse situations to analyze. For each *p* $\in$ *LP* with syntax $(c_1, l\text{-}w, c_2)$:

1.  If *l-w* $\in$ *CP*, the syntax is assumed to be *(class, l-w, property)* and it is inferred that $c_2$ is a *property* of $c_1$. Applied to the *proposition (LugaresDeInterés, tiene, Nombre)* in Fig. 1 (b), the result is:

```
<owl:ObjectProperty rdf:about="#nombre">
  <rdf:type rdf:resource="&owl; FunctionalProperty" />
  <rdfs:domain rdf:resource="#LugaresDeInterés" />
  <rdfs:range rdf:resource="#Nombre" />
</owl:ObjectProperty>
```

2.  If *l-w* $\in$ *CPVD*, the syntax is assumed to be *(class, property, value)* and it is inferred that *l-w* is the name of a *property* of $c_1$, and that $c_2$ is the value of this property. Applied to the proposition *(LugaresDeInterés, cronograma, Cronograma)* in *Fig. 1(b)*, the result is:

```
<owl:ObjectProperty rdf:about="#cronograma">
  <rdf:type rdf:resource="&owl; FunctionalProperty"/>
  <rdfs:domain rdf:resource="#LugaresDeInterés"/>
  <rdfs:range rdf:resource="#Cronograma"/>
</owl:ObjectProperty>
```

If $l$-$w \notin CPVD$, the FreeLing tool [1] is used for determining if it is a noun. If it is, the course of action is the same as above ($p$-$e \in CPVD$). If the $l$-$w$ is shared among more than one *proposition*, as in the case of *pared* (*wall*) in the Fig. 1 (a), the coding includes the tags *<owl:unionOf...>* and *<owl:unionOf rdf:parseType= "Collection"/>*:

```
<owl:ObjectProperty rdf:ID = "Pared" >
 <rdfs:domain>
  <owl:Class>
    <owl:unionOf rdf:parseType="Collection" />
      <owl:Class rdf:about="#Arteria" />
      <owl:Class rdf:about="#Vena" />
    </owl:unionOf>
  </owl:Class>
</rdfs:domain>
<rdfs:range>
  <owl:Class>
    <owl:unionOf rdf:parseType="Collection"/>
      <owl:Class rdf:about="#Muscular"/>
      <owl:Class rdf:about ="#Fibrosa"/>
    </owl:unionOf>
  </owl:Class>
 </rdfs:range>
</owl:ObjectProperty>
```

In the case the proposition of the l-w is not binary, that is, the same origin concept is related to more than one destination concept, as in *kind of activities* (*tipo de actividades*) of Fig. 1(b), it is inferred that the property identified by the l-w can take values from the various ranges corresponding to the destination concepts, with the following code:

```
<owl:Class rdf:ID = "Actividades">
    <rdfs:subClassOf>
    <owl:Restriction>
    <owl:onProperty rdf:resource = "#tipo">
    <owl:someValueFrom rdf:resource = "#Aventura_Aerea"/>
    <owl:someValueFrom rdf:resource="#Aventura_Terrestre"
/>
    <owl:someValueFrom rdf:resource="#Aventura_Acuática"
/>
    </owl:Restriction>
    </rdfs:subClassOf>
</owl:Class>
```

3.  If $l$-$w \in CPVI$, the syntax is assumed to be (*class, indirect property, value*), and it is inferred that $c_2$ is the value of the property of $c_1$ obtained from the $l$-$w$. Applied to the proposition (*Vasos Sanguíneos, contiene, Sangre*) in Fig. 1 (a), the result is:

```
<owl:ObjectProperty rdf:ID = "contenido">
   <rdfs:domain rdf:resource = "#Vasos Sanguíneos" />
   <rdfs:range rdf:resource = "#Sangre" />
</owl:ObjectProperty>
```

4.  If $l$-$w \notin \{CP, CPVD, CPVI\}$ and it is not a noun, WordNet is consulted. Be $s_1$ and $s_2$ the *synsets* of $c_1$ y $c_2$ respectively and $a(s_i, s_j)$ a path between $s_i$ and $s_j$:

    If $\exists$ $a(s_2, s_1)$ formed by *holonymy* relations or $\exists$ $a(s_1, s_2)$ formed by *meronymy* relations, it can be inferred that $c_2$ is a property of $c_1$ whose name is $l$-$w$. The OWL code generated is the same as above in point 2 ($l$-$w \in CPVD$).

# 4  Implementation

In the implementation, the coding process begins with a CM expressed in the XML language, in a format generated by MACOSOFT, a tool for the creation of CMs [14]. After having obtained LP as a result of Phase 1, the process of creation of the OWL-file starts, with the expression of each concept of the CM as a class (Phase 2). This file is in turn modified, incorporating more specifications. For example: to the code of a class, the specification of the super-class to which it belongs is incorporated (Phase 3), a concept that is initially coded as class can become an instance (Phase 4) or a property (Phase 5). A Spanish version of WordNet, developed by the Natural Language Processing Group (NLPG), of the Software Department (LSI) of the Technical University of Catalonia (UPC) has been used to test the system.

# 5  Related Work

A transformation mechanism from a CM to the OWL language has been included in Gómez et al. (2004) [7]. The transformation begins with a CM that is coded in XTM, an extension of XML and the standard specification of the topic maps [2], and, on top of this codification, a set of rules for obtaining OWL code are applied. In XTM, concepts and $l$-$w$ are expressed with the tag *topic* and the relationships among the concepts with the tag *association*, specifying the *origin-concept* and the *destination-concept* of the proposition. For the coding from XTM to OWL all the topics associated to concepts are coded as *owl:Class*, those associated to $l$-$w$ are coded as *owl:ObjectProperty* and the associations are coded as sub-classification relations (*rdfs:subClassOf*) between the classes associated to the concepts that intervene in the association. Contrary to the proposal that is being presented in this paper, not all the semantic interpretations that the relations among the concepts in a CM can have been considered, for example: not all the associations in XTM (relations in the CM) always indicate a sub-classification relation in OWL, and not all $l$-$w$ can be interpreted as properties in OWL. This happens because a direct syntactic entailment is made between XTM and OWL, without considering the whole semantics that can be associated with the knowledge that is being codified. It is not taken into account that

XTM is a language lacking explicit semantics and that this needs to be inferred from the context in which the content is represented.

Another related work is the one described in Hayes et al. (2004) [8], where an environment for collaborative development of ontologies based on CM is presented. The paper claims the implementation of the transformation from CMs to OWL and vice versa, although only the second mechanism is fully described; therefore the authors of this paper do not have enough elements to make a detailed comparison between this new proposal and that work. However, the syntactic formalizations that are proposed in it are of interest and should be certainly taken into account in the construction of CMs.

## 6 Conclusions and Future Work

In this paper, the following conclusions have been obtained: (1) it has been shown that a tight relationship exists between conceptual maps and ontologies; (2) the interpretation of conceptual maps as structured text allows the semantic inference needed for their coding in OWL, without losing flexibility; (3) the defined procedures generate OWL ontologies from conceptual maps in shallow knowledge domains. The proposed integration creates the bases for generalization to other domains and for the collaborative development of ontologies.

The paper represent an early stage of research and work is currently being carried out for the solution of the cases in which the link words are not included in any category or the concepts are not found in WordNet, which happens, in general, in very specific domains. These are today's limitations of the coding procedure presented and the main reason for which this proposal is fundamentally directed to shallow knowledge domains. As solutions, work is being done about a mechanism of machine learning for enriching the repository of link words in all categories, and about the integration and use of other knowledge bases and ontologies.

## References

[1] Atserias, J., Casas, B., Comelles, E., González, M., Padró, L., Padró, M.: FreeLing 1.3: Syntactic and semantic services in an open-source NLP library. In: 5th International Conference on Language Resources and Evaluation, ELRA, Genoa, Italy (2006)

[2] Biezunski, M., Newcomb, S., Bryan, M.: Guide to the topic map standards. ISO/IEC 13250 Projects (2002)

[3] Ceccaroni, L.: ONTOWEDSS - An Ontology-Based Environmental Decision-Support Systems for the Management of Wastewater Treatment Plants. Ph.D. thesis, Technical University of Catalonia, Barcelona, Spain (2001)

[4] Ceccaroni, L., Willmott, S., Cortés García, U., y Barbera-Medina, W.: @LIS TechNET: Hacia la enseñanza práctica de las tecnologías de Internet de la próxima generación. In: 5ta Conferencia Internacional de la Educación y la Formación basada en las Tecnologías, Madrid, Spain, pp. 139–142 (2005)

[5] DARPA.: DAML+OIL ontology Markup Language. Defense Advanced Research Projects Agency (2001)

[6] Fellbaum, Ch.: WordNet: An Electronic Lexical Database. The MIT Press, University of Cambridge (1998)

[7] Gómez, H., Díaz, B., González, A.: Two layered approach to knowledge representation using conceptual maps description logic. In: 1st International Conference on Concept Mapping, Spain (2004)

[8] Hayes, P., Eskrindge, T., Reichherzer, T., Saavedra, R.: A Framework for Constructing Web Ontologies using concept Maps. In: Proc. DALM Meeting (2004)

[9] Minsky, M.: A Framework for Representing Knowledge. The Psychology of Computer Vision, pp. 211–277. McGraw-Hill, New York (1975)

[10] Novak, J.D., Gowin, D.B.: Learning how to learn. Cambridge Press, New York (1984)

[11] Noy, N.F., Fergerson, R.W., Musen, M.A.: The knowledge model of protege-2000: Combining interoperability and flexibility. In: Dieng, R., Corby, O. (eds.) EKAW 2000. LNCS (LNAI), vol. 1937, Springer, Heidelberg (2000)

[12] Smith, M., Welty, Ch., McGuinness, D.: OWL Web Ontology Language Guide. W3C (2004)

[13] Simón, A., Ceccaroni, L., Willmott, S., Rosete, A.: Unificación de la representación de conocimiento en mapas conceptuales y ontologías para dominios poco profundos. XI Taller Internacional de Software Educativo. Universidad de Chile. Chile, pp. 72–79 (2006)

[14] Simón, A., Estrada, V., Rosete, A., Lara, V.: GECOSOFT: Un Entrono Colaborativo para la Gestión del Conocimiento con Mapas Conceptuales. In: 2nd International Conference on Concept Mapping. Costa Rica, vol. 2, pp. 114–118 (2006)

[15] Sowa, J. (ed.): Principles of semantic networks: explorations in the representation of knowledge. Morgan Kaufmann, San Francisco (1991)

[16] Lassila, O., McGuinness, D.: The Role of Frame-Based Representation on the Semantic Web (2001)

# Effectiveness Study of Lexically Mapping Two Thesauri

M. Taboada[1], R. Lalín[1], D. Martínez[2], and S. Tellado[2]

[1] Dpto. de Electrónica e Computación, Universidad de Santiago de Compostela
15782 Santiago de Compostela, Spain
chus@dec.usc.es, charo_lalin@hotmail.com
[2] Dpto. de Física Aplicada, Universidad de Santiago de Compostela
27002 Lugo, Spain
fadiego@usc.es, tellado@lugo.usc.es

**Abstract.** Mapping thesauri is the task of identifying correspondences between entities in different thesauri. Discovering these matches is intrinsically problematic to automate. Earlier research has proposed solutions based on using lexical matching techniques and then, manually revising the resulting lexical mappings with the help of graphical user interfaces. Nevertheless, these solutions cannot guarantee the validity, accuracy and quality of the vocabulary mappings, as human capacity is limited. In this paper, we propose a method to automatically evaluate the quality of the results of a lexical technique. Our method combines structural constraints and annotations with part-of-speech tags to identifying error patterns from the results of lexical matches, differentiating between those leading to fall in precision and those producing decrease in recall.

**Keywords:** thesauri iteroperability, thesauri mapping, the Unified Medical Language System (UMLS).

## 1 Introduction

Thesauri have become interesting tools for information retrieval. They improve text-driven access by supplying a standard vocabulary for indexing information and by relating relevant terms in a specific domain. The use of thesauri has been successfully proved with repositories like EMBASE[1] or PubMed[2] and nowadays we can find several of them designed in similar domains for different repositories. MeSH[3] and EMTREE[4] are only two examples of thesauri used to index repositories in the biomedical domain. With the thesauri-driven information access of today, users are obliged to search information collections separately, using the vocabulary scheme specific to each collection. If the required information is not contained within a single collection, then the user must switch over to different

---

[1] http://embase.com/
[2] http://pubmed.org
[3] http://www.nlm.nih.gov/mesh/meshhome.html
[4] http://www.elsevier.com/homepage/sah/spd/site/

D. Borrajo, L. Castillo, and J.M. Corchado (Eds.): CAEPIA 2007, LNAI 4788, pp. 268–277, 2007.
© Springer-Verlag Berlin Heidelberg 2007

collections and so, over the different thesauri indexing each collection. However, thesauri are usually designed on the general compromise of containing standard terms and definitions [4]. At least in theory, users searching collections in the same domain should be able to access all these collections using only the most familiar vocabulary. This way of accessing would remove the need of learning each vocabulary scheme and enrich the vocabulary used to access document repositories. The fact of the matter is that, even in the same domain, different thesauri display significant differences, due to the scope, level of abstraction and level of granularity what they were built for. As a result, information processing across several collections is not possible without resolving the incompatibility among the thesauri indexing collections [3,7,10].

At least, two problems hamper thesauri inter-operability: the presence of inconsistent and ambiguous definitions in thesauri [9] and the insufficiency of automatic methods simplifying the mapping process [2]. Early research has proposed methods based on lexical matching techniques, which produces high-quality mappings [7]. However, the huge volume of data in vocabularies hinders the manual revision of lexical mappings. So, a relevant human effort is needed to suitably interpret them and guarantee the validity of the resulting lexical mappings [11]. In short, the problem to solve is to provide methods to automatically interpret and evaluate the resulting lexical mappings in a most effective way than manual revision. In the present study, we propose a method to automatically evaluate the quality of the results of a lexical technique provided by the National Library of Medicine (NLM). In particular, this technique maps terms from one terminology (EMTREE) to the UMLS Metathesaurus[1,5]. The aim of our study is to supply a qualitative measure of the successfulness of a tried and tested lexical technique. Therefore, our work complements other quantitative measures on the efficacy of lexical techniques [8].

## 2   Materials

### 2.1   The Thesaurus EMTREE

EMTREE is a thesaurus developed by Elsevier to index EMBASE, an on-line database for life science researchers. The version of EMTREE used in our experiments contains 46,427 concepts distributed into 15 main categories. EMTREE supports multiple terms for every concept, where one term is choosen as the Preferred Term (PT) and the rest of the terms are the Set of Synonyms (Synset). The used version of EMTREE contains more than 200,000 terms (including PT plus Synset). Each main category is represented by a taxonomy containing concepts related to each other by *broader* and *related* relationships. Examples of main categories are *'Chemicals and drugs'*, *'Anatomical concepts'* or *'Organisms'*. In this paper, we will use examples of the *Anatomical concepts* to show our results.

### 2.2   The Unified Medical Language System

The UMLS consists of several knowledge sources providing terminological information. The largest knowledge source is the Metathesaurus, which contains information about medical concepts, terms, string-names and the relationships between them. All this information is drawn from over 130 controlled vocabularies, such as SNOMED or MeSH. The Metathesaurus also supports multiple terms for every concept, and concepts are related to each other by *broader* and *narrower* relationships, among others. The used version of UMLS contains around 1,3 millions of concepts.

*Semantic Types* (STs) are a set of basic semantic categories used to classify the concepts in the Metathesaurus. Examples of semantic types are *Chemical, Anatomical Structure* or *Organism*. Fifteen top-level categories, named *Semantic Groups (SGs)*, in turn are used to classify the STs [6]. Examples of them are *Anatomy* or *Living Beings*. One general principle of SGs is *exclusivity*, which set that each concept must belong to only one SG. So, SGs are disjoint as they have no Metathesaurus concept in common.

### 2.3    Applications

The Metathesaurus is a UMLS resource that provides detailed information on concepts and terms across multiple vocabularies. There are three ways of accessing the UMLS[5] information: via a web interface, through an Application Programmer Interface (API) that connects user programs to the UMLS Knowledge Source Server (UMLSKS) and via a TCP/IP socket interface for non-Java programs. To map 200,000 terms, the use of a web client is not viable and to program a socket client does not seem necessary when a public API is available. So, for our particular case, the most reasonable option was the RMI/XML communication with the UMLS. Therefore, all the applications required for this study were programmed in Java and they were run on a Personal Computer over Linux, in some occasions, and Microsoft Windows XP, in other occasions. We used an XML representation from both EMTREE and the UMLS.

## 3    Methods

### 3.1    Approaches to Map Terminologies

To use the UMLSKS API, the user program sends a request for one or several input terms, which are searched into the UMLS database, and a result is returned for each input term. The UMLSKS API provides six web services to perform a search in the database, each of them following different criteria: *ApproxMatch, ExactMatch, NormalizeString, NormalizeWord, Word, TruncateLeft* and *TruncateRight*. The two later are not very suitable to map terms in general. *Word, ApproxMatch* and *NormalizeWord* require an excessive time to recover UMLS concepts and the number of non-relevant retrieved concepts is very large. *ExactMatch* is the provided simplest method, which recovers those UMLS concepts containing a term (the PT or a Syn) exactly matching the input terms. *NormalizeString* normalizes the input terms before matching them. The normalization process removes lexical differences between strings, such as alphabetic

---

[5] http://umlsks.nlm.nih.gov

case, inflection, spelling variants or punctuation. From the quantitative study carried out by Sarkar et al. [8], *ExactMatch* has a higher level of precision, but it finds a smaller number of relevant UMLS concepts than *NormalizeString*. So, we decided to evaluate *NormalizeString*.

## 3.2   Implementation and Evaluation

We analyzed the results of the *NormalizeString* qualitatively, by identifying patterns of inaccuracy in the following manner. As we do not have available a gold standard nor enough resources to create it, we applied our method to the results of NormalizeString and then, we manually evaluated a subset of them. In practice, our evaluation procedure was the following.

**Step 1: Acquiring concept anchors lexically.** The *NormalizeString* technique was used to map the complete set of EMTREE terms to the entire UMLS. We used the *NormalizeString* to search the Metathesaurus for the 200,000 EMTREE terms. The UMLSKS returned zero, one or several UMLS concepts lexically equivalent to each requested EMTREE term. Examples of pairs of EMTREE-UMLS terms exhibiting lexical similarity (Fig. 1) are *disease* ↔ *Disease*, *sickness* ↔ *Sickness* and *illness* ↔ *Illness (finding)*. These pairs of terms are considered anchors, as they are going to be used as reference in the concept mapping. We call it *term anchors*.

Since we were concerned with mapping concepts, we grouped all UMLS concepts returned for the whole set of terms describing an EMTREE concept. As a result, pairs of EMTREE-UMLS concepts were achieved. These pairs of concepts are also considered anchors, and we call it *concept anchors* to distinguish them from *term anchors*. Examples of concept anchors, shown in Figure 1, include the concept *general aspects of disease* in EMTREE and *Disease* in UMLS, and the concept *general aspects of disease* in EMTREE and *Illness (finding)* in UMLS.

**Step 2: Acquiring structural similarity between top-level categories.** From the set of concept anchors, we obtained the structural similarity between the EMTREE and UMLS top-level categories. Two top-level categories across the terminologies are *structurally similar* if they have a high number of anchors in common (for example, 60-70%). A representative case is *anatomical concepts* in EMTREE and *Anatomy* in UMLS, as the first one has 83% of the anchors in common with the second one. In total, 6 top-level categories across the two terminologies have structural similarity, corresponding to the 65,29% of the EMTREE concepts. On the other hand, two top-level categories across terminologies are *disjoint* if they have no anchors in common and *almost disjoint* if they have a small number of anchors in common (around 10-20%). For example, *anatomical concepts* in EMTREE is *disjoint* with 2 and *almost disjoint* with 12 top-level categories in UMLS.

**Step 3: Identifying patterns of inaccuracy producing the decrease in recall.** First, we compared the results from only matching the PTs of concepts

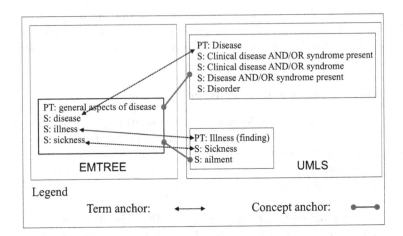

**Fig. 1.** Example data of two concept anchors between EMTREE and UMLS directly derived from three term anchors

and from matching the complete set of PTs plus synonyms. Then, we analyzed the set of EMTREE concepts that were not present in any anchor, by annotating their terms with part-of-speech tags (using the OpenNLP[6]) and classifying them as indivisible, single Noun Phrase (NP) and complex NP (that is, more than one NP connected by a conjunction). Subsequently, we requested the constituent parts of the terms to the UMLS Metathesaurus. From these results, we automatically detected different causes of mismatch producing the decrease in recall[7] of the *NormalizeString*.

**Step 4: Identifying patterns of inaccuracy leading to fall in precision,** by detecting structural similarity between concepts. Two concepts in an anchor have a *high structural similarity* if they belong to two top-level categories having structural similarity. In this case, we classify the anchor as *relevant*. For example, in Fig. 2, five concept anchors were acquired for the EMTREE concept *abdomen*. Only three of them were classified as *relevant*, those that are in structurally similar categories.

We consider that two concepts are *homonyms* if the terms describing them match lexically and they have a completely different meaning. For example, *iris blood vessel* is an *anatomy concept* in EMTREE whereas the lexical matching in UMLS *Blood vessels in iris* is a disorder. Two *homonyms* in a concept anchor always are in *disjoint* or *almost disjoint* top-level categories, so the anchor can be classified as *non-relevant*. In Fig. 2, two anchors are classified as *non-relevant*. However, the whole set of anchors belonging to *disjoint* or *almost disjoint* top-level categories are not all *homonyms*. For example, in Fig. 3 the anchor (*body*

---

[6] http://opennlp.sourceforge.net/

[7] In this context, the *recall* can be defined as the fraction between the set of the discovered relevant anchors and the set of relevant anchors.

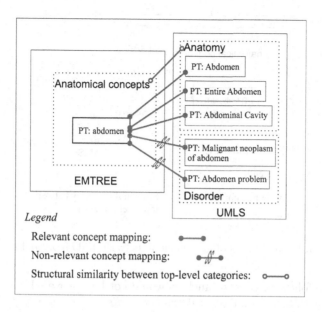

**Fig. 2.** Example data of different coverage between EMTREE and UMLS

*surface, Body surface*) belongs to *almost disjoint* categories across the terminologies. In addition, *Anatomy* and *Physiology* in UMLS are disjoint, as they have no concepts in common. However, the UMLS concept *Body surface* is a narrower concept of *Anatomical surface*, which is in the top-level category *Anatomy*. As a result, *Body surface* merges characteristics from *Anatomy* and *Physiology*. So, the anchor (*body surface,Body surface*) have some structural similarity, so it is still *relevant*.

We applied three structural constraints in order to identify anchors with a high structural similarity (those belonging to structurally similar top-level categories), anchors with some structural similarity (those belonging to disjoint or almost disjoint categories, but with some structural similarity from the intermediate categories) and homonyms (those with no structural similarity).

## 4   Results and Discussion

### 4.1   Patterns of Inaccuracy Producing the Decrease in Recall

The most straightforward method to reconcile thesauri is to lexically match only the PTs of the concepts and to generate concept anchors directly from PT anchors. But, in many domains, like biomedicine, it is very often to use several synonyms to describe a concept, and although thesauri had been designed for the same domain, they may use different PTs in a high percentage. So, this method would fail to discover relevant concept anchors. For example, the three term anchors in Fig. 1 would be never discovered, if only PTs were mapped. As

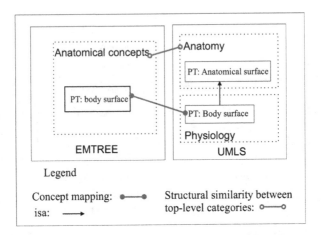

**Fig. 3.** Example data of an homonym between EMTREE and UMLS

a result, the following concept anchors would not be discovered: *general aspects of diseases* ↔ *Disease* and *general aspects of diseases* ↔ *Illness finding*. However, both concept anchors are relevant. That is, mapping PTs plus S increases the *recall* of the lexical techniques (Table 1). Additionally, a smaller number of synonyms, a lower recall. In particular, when we requested the set of EMTREE PTs plus Synset to the UMLSKS, the set of concept anchors increased more than 12%, compared with when we only requested the set of EMTREE PTs. In total, 36,539 EMTREE-UMLS concept anchors were identified lexically, accounting for about 80% of the EMTREE concepts.

Other cause decreasing recall is the use of pre-coordinated terms in a thesaurus (identified as a complex NP in the step 3), whereas the same terms are post-coordinated in the other thesaurus. For example, the *NormalizeString* does not recover any UMLS concept for the request *face, nose and sinuses*. However, this pre-coordinated term in EMTREE should match the post-coordinated concept *Face + Nose + Sinus* in UMLS.

The use of too general terms (indivisible terms) is other frequent cause of a fall in recall. For example, the term *antenna*, classified as a part of the *head* in EMTREE, is a so general term that the *NormalizeString* returns no UMLS concept.

In some ocassions, a term in a thesaurus may be present in the other thesaurus, but as a broader term. For example, the *NormalizeString* recover no UMLS concept for the EMTREE term *craniofacial morphology* (a single NP). However, the term *craniofacial* exists in UMLS. This is a broader term in UMLS as it only describes a part of the body (as a narrower of the concept *skeletal bone*), while in EMTREE describes the morphology of that part of the body, that is, it has two broaders: *head* and *morphology*.

Other cause of fall in recall is the presence of terms in a thesaurus that are too specific for the other thesaurus. For example, the EMTREE concepts *arm blood vessel* and *leg blood vessel* were not recovered from the UMLS database. However, it contains a more general concept, *peripherical blood vessels*.

Table 1. Some patterns of inaccuracy that explain the fall in recall

| Patterns of inaccuracy | EMTREE | UMLS |
|---|---|---|
| Matching only PTs | *general aspects of diseases* | *Disease* |
| Use of a small set of synonyms | *general aspects of diseases* *disease* *illness* *sickness* | *Illness (finding)* *Sickness* *ailment* |
| Pre-coordinated and Post-coordinated terms | *face, nose and sinuses* | Face + Nose + Sinus |
| Use of too general terms in a thesaurus | *antenna* | — |
| Presence of broader terms in a thesaurus | *craniofacial morphology* | *craniofacial* |
| Too specific terms in a thesaurus | *arm blood vessel* *leg blood vessel* | *peripherical blood vessels* |

## 4.2  Patterns of Inaccuracy Leading to Fall in Precision

Contrary to the recall, if the complete set of synonyms is mapped, the *precision* of lexical techniques decreases. There are patterns that may explain the fall in precision. First, one thesaurus may have a more ambiguous representation of some terms than another. A cause of ambiguity is a wider coverage of concepts in a thesaurus (Table 2). An example is the UMLS term *Abdomen*, which is used to describe a portion of the body (anatomy), a disordered process (disorder) and a finding in this portion of the body (Fig. 2). However, the EMTREE term *abdomen* is only used to designate an anatomy concept. As a result, the following discovered lexical anchors are non-relevant: *abdomen* ↔ *Abdomen problem* and *abdomen* ↔ *Malignant neoplasm of abdomen*.

A second case of ambiguity is presented when a term is used to represent both a concept and a category. For example, the term *virus* is the PT of a UMLS concept and the name of an intermediate category, whereas it only represents a concept in EMTREE.

A third case of ambiguity is the use of very general terms in a thesaurus. For example, EMTREE uses the term *axis* to represent an anatomy concept. However, this is a general purpose term and it does not identify a concept clearly. On the contrary, UMLS uses more specific terms (with separate keywords) to disambiguate the concepts identified by the term *axis*: *Axis vertebra*, *Electrocardiographic axis*, *Genus Axis* and *Entire axis vertebra*.

A different granularity in thesauri is also a frequent cause of a fall in precision. A thesaurus may use different PTs (with separate words) to distinguish a concept, whereas the other thesaurus may include only one concept. For example, the UMLS distinguishes among *Abdomen*, *Entire abdomen* and *Abdominal cavity* whereas EMTREE only includes the concept *abdomen*.

**Table 2.** Patterns of inaccuracy leading to fall in precision

| Patterns of inaccuracy | EMTREE | UMLS |
|---|---|---|
| **Ambiguous use of terms by a higher coverage of concepts** | *abdomen* used for an anatomy concept | *abdomen* used for anatomy and disorder concepts |
| **Ambiguous use of terms for both concepts and categories** | *virus* used for a concept | *virus* used for both a concept and a facet |
| **Ambiguous use of very general terms** | *axis* | *Axis vertebra* *Electrocardiographic axis* *Genus Axis* |
| **Different granularity** | *abdomen* | *Abdomen* *Entire abdomen* *Abdominal cavity* |
| **Homonyms** | *iris blood vessel* used for an anatomy concept | *Blood vessels in iris* used for a disorder |

The presence of homonyms also decreases the precision. For example, *iris blood vessel* is an anatomy concept in EMTREE whereas its lexical matching in UMLS *Blood vessels in iris* is a disorder.

## 5   Conclusions and Future Work

In this paper, we propose a method to automatically evaluate the quality of a lexical mapping technique in a most effective way than manual revision. Sharkar et al. [8] already examined and compared several lexical techniques to map a vocabulary to the UMLS Metathesaurus, by quantitatively measuring the efficacy in terms of precision and recall. Our qualitative study contribute to have more knowledge about how interpret and evaluate lexical mappings, with the aim of improving them.

The work outlined here shows up a main problem that comes to light when lexically mapping a terminology to the UMLS Metathesaurus: the ambiguous representation of a large number of terms. For more than 50% of the EMTREE concepts, UMLSKS returned two or more UMLS concepts. Obviously, this is a consequence of integrating a large number of vocabularies, which increases the coverage of returned concepts. But, it requires an extra effort to disambiguate and to detect redundancies and incompatibilities. In this work, we identified homonyms by checking the consistency between main categories through applying structural constraints. In a future, we plan to disambiguate anchors using new structural similarity constraints.

**Acknowledgements.** This work has been funded by the *Secretaría General de Política Científica y Tecnológica del Ministerio de Educación y Ciencia*, through the research project TIN2006-15453-C04-02.

# References

1. Bodenreider, O.: The Unified Medical Language System(UMLS): integrating biomedical terminology. Nucleic Acids Research 32, Database issue D267-D270 (2004)
2. Doan, A., Noy, N., Halevy, A.: Introduction to the Special Issue on Semantic Integration. SIGMOD Record 33 (4), 11–13 (2004)
3. Doerr, M.: Semantic problems of thesaurus mapping. Journal of Digital Information 1(8) (2001)
4. ISO 2788. Guidelines for the establishment and development of monolingual thesauri. International Organization for Standarization (1986)
5. Lindberg, D., Humphreys, B., Mc Cray, A.: The Unified Medical Language System. Methods of Information in Medicine 32, 281–291 (1993)
6. McCray, A.T., Burgun, A., Bodenreider, O.: Aggregating UMLS semantic types for reducing conceptual complexity. Medinfo. 10, 216–220 (2001)
7. Vizine-Goetz, D., Hickey, C., Houghton, A., Thompson, R.: Vocabulary Mapping for Terminology Services. Journal of Digital Information 4(4) (2004)
8. Sarkar, I.N., Cantor, M.N., Gelman, R., Hartel, F., Lussier, Y.A.: Linking biomedical language Information and knowledge resources in the 21st Century: GO and UMLS. In: Pacific Symposium on Biocomputing, vol. 8, pp. 439–450 (2003)
9. Smith, B., Ceusters, W., Klagges, B., Köhler, J., Kumar, A., Lomax, J., Mungall, C., Neuhaus, F., Rector, A., Rosse, C.: Relations in biomedical ontologies. Genome Biology 6(R46) (2005)
10. Yu, A.C.: Methods in biomedical ontology. Journal of Biomedical Informatics 39(3), 252–266 (2006)
11. Zeng, M.L., Chang, L.M.: Trends and issues in establishing interoperability among knowledge organization systems. Journal of the American Society for Information Science and Technology 55 (5), 377–395 (2004)
12. Zhang, S., Bodenreider, O.: Aligning representations of Anatomy using lexical and structural methods. In: Proc. of AMIA Symposium, Washington, DC, pp. 753–757 (2003)

# Author Index

# Lecture Notes in Artificial Intelligence (LNAI)

Vol. 4795: F. Schilder, G. Katz, J. Pustejovsky (Eds.), Annotating, Extracting and Reasoning about Time and Events. VII, 141 pages. 2007.

Vol. 4790: N. Dershowitz, A. Voronkov (Eds.), Logic for Programming, Artificial Intelligence, and Reasoning. XIII, 562 pages. 2007.

Vol. 4788: D. Borrajo, L. Castillo, J.M. Corchado (Eds.), Current Topics in Artificial Intelligence. XI, 280 pages. 2007.

Vol. 4772: H. Prade, V.S. Subrahmanian (Eds.), Scalable Uncertainty Management. X, 277 pages. 2007.

Vol. 4766: N. Maudet, S. Parsons, I. Rahwan (Eds.), Argumentation in Multi-Agent Systems. XII, 211 pages. 2007.

Vol. 4755: V. Corruble, M. Takeda, E. Suzuki (Eds.), Discovery Science. XI, 298 pages. 2007.

Vol. 4754: M. Hutter, R.A. Servedio, E. Takimoto (Eds.), Algorithmic Learning Theory. XI, 403 pages. 2007.

Vol. 4737: B. Berendt, A. Hotho, D. Mladenic, G. Semeraro (Eds.), From Web to Social Web: Discovering and Deploying User and Content Profiles. XI, 161 pages. 2007.

Vol. 4733: R. Basili, M.T. Pazienza (Eds.), AI*IA 2007: Artificial Intelligence and Human-Oriented Computing. XVII, 858 pages. 2007.

Vol. 4724: K. Mellouli (Ed.), Symbolic and Quantitative Approaches to Reasoning with Uncertainty. XV, 914 pages. 2007.

Vol. 4722: C. Pelachaud, J.-C. Martin, E. André, G. Chollet, K. Karpouzis, D. Pelé (Eds.), Intelligent Virtual Agents. XV, 425 pages. 2007.

Vol. 4720: B. Konev, F. Wolter (Eds.), Frontiers of Combining Systems. X, 283 pages. 2007.

Vol. 4702: J.N. Kok, J. Koronacki, R. Lopez de Mantaras, S. Matwin, D. Mladenič, A. Skowron (Eds.), Knowledge Discovery in Databases: PKDD 2007. XXIV, 640 pages. 2007.

Vol. 4701: J.N. Kok, J. Koronacki, R. Lopez de Mantaras, S. Matwin, D. Mladenič, A. Skowron (Eds.), Machine Learning: ECML 2007. XXII, 809 pages. 2007.

Vol. 4696: H.-D. Burkhard, G. Lindemann, R. Verbrugge, L.Z. Varga (Eds.), Multi-Agent Systems and Applications V. XIII, 350 pages. 2007.

Vol. 4694: B. Apolloni, R.J. Howlett, L. Jain (Eds.), Knowledge-Based Intelligent Information and Engineering Systems, Part III. XXIX, 1126 pages. 2007.

Vol. 4693: B. Apolloni, R.J. Howlett, L. Jain (Eds.), Knowledge-Based Intelligent Information and Engineering Systems, Part II. XXXII, 1380 pages. 2007.

Vol. 4692: B. Apolloni, R.J. Howlett, L. Jain (Eds.), Knowledge-Based Intelligent Information and Engineering Systems, Part I. LV, 882 pages. 2007.

Vol. 4687: P. Petta, J.P. Müller, M. Klusch, M. Georgeff (Eds.), Multiagent System Technologies. X, 207 pages. 2007.

Vol. 4682: D.-S. Huang, L. Heutte, M. Loog (Eds.), Advanced Intelligent Computing Theories and Applications. XXVII, 1373 pages. 2007.

Vol. 4676: M. Klusch, K.V. Hindriks, M.P. Papazoglou, L. Sterling (Eds.), Cooperative Information Agents XI. XI, 361 pages. 2007.

Vol. 4667: J. Hertzberg, M. Beetz, R. Englert (Eds.), KI 2007: Advances in Artificial Intelligence. IX, 516 pages. 2007.

Vol. 4660: S. Džeroski, L. Todorovski (Eds.), Computational Discovery of Scientific Knowledge. X, 327 pages. 2007.

Vol. 4659: V. Mařík, V. Vyatkin, A.W. Colombo (Eds.), Holonic and Multi-Agent Systems for Manufacturing. VIII, 456 pages. 2007.

Vol. 4651: F. Azevedo, P. Barahona, F. Fages, F. Rossi (Eds.), Recent Advances in Constraints. VIII, 185 pages. 2007.

Vol. 4648: F. Almeida e Costa, L.M. Rocha, E. Costa, I. Harvey, A. Coutinho (Eds.), Advances in Artificial Life. XVIII, 1215 pages. 2007.

Vol. 4635: B. Kokinov, D.C. Richardson, T.R. Roth-Berghofer, L. Vieu (Eds.), Modeling and Using Context. XIV, 574 pages. 2007.

Vol. 4632: R. Alhajj, H. Gao, X. Li, J. Li, O.R. Zaïane (Eds.), Advanced Data Mining and Applications. XV, 634 pages. 2007.

Vol. 4629: V. Matoušek, P. Mautner (Eds.), Text, Speech and Dialogue. XVII, 663 pages. 2007.

Vol. 4626: R.O. Weber, M.M. Richter (Eds.), Case-Based Reasoning Research and Development. XIII, 534 pages. 2007.

Vol. 4617: V. Torra, Y. Narukawa, Y. Yoshida (Eds.), Modeling Decisions for Artificial Intelligence. XII, 502 pages. 2007.

Vol. 4612: I. Miguel, W. Ruml (Eds.), Abstraction, Reformulation, and Approximation. XI, 418 pages. 2007.

Vol. 4604: U. Priss, S. Polovina, R. Hill (Eds.), Conceptual Structures: Knowledge Architectures for Smart Applications. XII, 514 pages. 2007.

Vol. 4603: F. Pfenning (Ed.), Automated Deduction – CADE-21. XII, 522 pages. 2007.

Vol. 4597: P. Perner (Ed.), Advances in Data Mining. XI, 353 pages. 2007.

Vol. 4594: R. Bellazzi, A. Abu-Hanna, J. Hunter (Eds.), Artificial Intelligence in Medicine. XVI, 509 pages. 2007.

Vol. 4585: M. Kryszkiewicz, J.F. Peters, H. Rybinski, A. Skowron (Eds.), Rough Sets and Intelligent Systems Paradigms. XIX, 836 pages. 2007.

Vol. 4578: F. Masulli, S. Mitra, G. Pasi (Eds.), Applications of Fuzzy Sets Theory. XVIII, 693 pages. 2007.

Vol. 4573: M. Kauers, M. Kerber, R. Miner, W. Windsteiger (Eds.), Towards Mechanized Mathematical Assistants. XIII, 407 pages. 2007.

Vol. 4571: P. Perner (Ed.), Machine Learning and Data Mining in Pattern Recognition. XIV, 913 pages. 2007.

Vol. 4570: H.G. Okuno, M. Ali (Eds.), New Trends in Applied Artificial Intelligence. XXI, 1194 pages. 2007.

Vol. 4565: D.D. Schmorrow, L.M. Reeves (Eds.), Foundations of Augmented Cognition. XIX, 450 pages. 2007.

Vol. 4562: D. Harris (Ed.), Engineering Psychology and Cognitive Ergonomics. XXIII, 879 pages. 2007.

Vol. 4548: N. Olivetti (Ed.), Automated Reasoning with Analytic Tableaux and Related Methods. X, 245 pages. 2007.

Vol. 4539: N.H. Bshouty, C. Gentile (Eds.), Learning Theory. XII, 634 pages. 2007.

Vol. 4529: P. Melin, O. Castillo, L.T. Aguilar, J. Kacprzyk, W. Pedrycz (Eds.), Foundations of Fuzzy Logic and Soft Computing. XIX, 830 pages. 2007.

Vol. 4520: M.V. Butz, O. Sigaud, G. Pezzulo, G. Baldassarre (Eds.), Anticipatory Behavior in Adaptive Learning Systems. X, 379 pages. 2007.

Vol. 4511: C. Conati, K. McCoy, G. Paliouras (Eds.), User Modeling 2007. XVI, 487 pages. 2007.

Vol. 4509: Z. Kobti, D. Wu (Eds.), Advances in Artificial Intelligence. XII, 552 pages. 2007.

Vol. 4496: N.T. Nguyen, A. Grzech, R.J. Howlett, L.C. Jain (Eds.), Agent and Multi-Agent Systems: Technologies and Applications. XXI, 1046 pages. 2007.

Vol. 4483: C. Baral, G. Brewka, J. Schlipf (Eds.), Logic Programming and Nonmonotonic Reasoning. IX, 327 pages. 2007.

Vol. 4482: A. An, J. Stefanowski, S. Ramanna, C.J. Butz, W. Pedrycz, G. Wang (Eds.), Rough Sets, Fuzzy Sets, Data Mining and Granular Computing. XIV, 585 pages. 2007.

Vol. 4481: J. Yao, P. Lingras, W.-Z. Wu, M. Szczuka, N.J. Cercone, D. Ślęzak (Eds.), Rough Sets and Knowledge Technology. XIV, 576 pages. 2007.

Vol. 4476: V. Gorodetsky, C. Zhang, V.A. Skormin, L. Cao (Eds.), Autonomous Intelligent Systems: Multi-Agents and Data Mining. XIII, 323 pages. 2007.

Vol. 4460: S. Aguzzoli, A. Ciabattoni, B. Gerla, C. Manara, V. Marra (Eds.), Algebraic and Proof-theoretic Aspects of Non-classical Logics. VIII, 309 pages. 2007.

Vol. 4457: G.M.P. O'Hare, A. Ricci, M.J. O'Grady, O. Dikenelli (Eds.), Engineering Societies in the Agents World VII. XI, 401 pages. 2007.

Vol. 4456: Y. Wang, Y.-m. Cheung, H. Liu (Eds.), Computational Intelligence and Security. XXIII, 1118 pages. 2007.

Vol. 4455: S. Muggleton, R. Otero, A. Tamaddoni-Nezhad (Eds.), Inductive Logic Programming. XII, 456 pages. 2007.

Vol. 4452: M. Fasli, O. Shehory (Eds.), Agent-Mediated Electronic Commerce. VIII, 249 pages. 2007.

Vol. 4451: T.S. Huang, A. Nijholt, M. Pantic, A. Pentland (Eds.), Artifical Intelligence for Human Computing. XVI, 359 pages. 2007.

Vol. 4441: C. Müller (Ed.), Speaker Classification II. X, 309 pages. 2007.

Vol. 4438: L. Maicher, A. Sigel, L.M. Garshol (Eds.), Leveraging the Semantics of Topic Maps. X, 257 pages. 2007.

Vol. 4434: G. Lakemeyer, E. Sklar, D.G. Sorrenti, T. Takahashi (Eds.), RoboCup 2006: Robot Soccer World Cup X. XIII, 566 pages. 2007.

Vol. 4429: R. Lu, J.H. Siekmann, C. Ullrich (Eds.), Cognitive Systems. X, 161 pages. 2007.

Vol. 4428: S. Edelkamp, A. Lomuscio (Eds.), Model Checking and Artificial Intelligence. IX, 185 pages. 2007.

Vol. 4426: Z.-H. Zhou, H. Li, Q. Yang (Eds.), Advances in Knowledge Discovery and Data Mining. XXV, 1161 pages. 2007.

Vol. 4411: R.H. Bordini, M. Dastani, J. Dix, A.E.F. Seghrouchni (Eds.), Programming Multi-Agent Systems. XIV, 249 pages. 2007.

Vol. 4410: A. Branco (Ed.), Anaphora: Analysis, Algorithms and Applications. X, 191 pages. 2007.

Vol. 4399: T. Kovacs, X. Llorà, K. Takadama, P.L. Lanzi, W. Stolzmann, S.W. Wilson (Eds.), Learning Classifier Systems. XII, 345 pages. 2007.

Vol. 4390: S.O. Kuznetsov, S. Schmidt (Eds.), Formal Concept Analysis. X, 329 pages. 2007.

Vol. 4389: D. Weyns, H. Van Dyke Parunak, F. Michel (Eds.), Environments for Multi-Agent Systems III. X, 273 pages. 2007.

Vol. 4386: P. Noriega, J. Vázquez-Salceda, G. Boella, O. Boissier, V. Dignum, N. Fornara, E. Matson (Eds.), Coordination, Organizations, Institutions, and Norms in Agent Systems II. XI, 373 pages. 2007.

Vol. 4384: T. Washio, K. Satoh, H. Takeda, A. Inokuchi (Eds.), New Frontiers in Artificial Intelligence. IX, 401 pages. 2007.

Vol. 4371: K. Inoue, K. Satoh, F. Toni (Eds.), Computational Logic in Multi-Agent Systems. X, 315 pages. 2007.

Vol. 4369: M. Umeda, A. Wolf, O. Bartenstein, U. Geske, D. Seipel, O. Takata (Eds.), Declarative Programming for Knowledge Management. X, 229 pages. 2006.

Vol. 4363: B.D. ten Cate, H.W. Zeevat (Eds.), Logic, Language, and Computation. XII, 281 pages. 2007.

Vol. 4343: C. Müller (Ed.), Speaker Classification I. X, 355 pages. 2007.